SCOTTISH VERNACULAR LITERATURE

PRESS NOTICES OF FIRST EDITION

SCOTTISH VERNACULAR LITERATURE

LITERATURE

A SUCCINCT HISTORY

BY

T. F. HENDERSON

SECOND REVISED EDITION

LONDON

PUBLISHED BY DAVID NUTT

57-59 LONG ACRE

1900

Edinburgh : T. and A. Constable, Printers to Her Majesty

PREFACE TO THE FIRST EDITION

In his Preface to *The Evergreen*, Allan Ramsay explains that he had intended to have given 'an account of the Authors of the following Collection,' but had 'delayed the Design' for the sufficient reason that he had not been 'furnished with such distinct Information as could be wished for that End at present'; and he virtually had to content himself with 'marking the Names of the Authors before and after their poems.'

Such was the total oblivion which, in the course of a few short generations, had engulfed the old 'makaris' and all their works! Already had they become

> 'subjects all
> To envious and calumniating time.'

But many things have happened since the days of Ramsay, among them the birth of Robert Burns, whose striking poetic success, very much on the lines of the old vernacular 'makaris,' inevitably tended to strengthen the reviving interest in those forgotten masters of the fifteenth and sixteenth centuries. Within the present century those old 'makaris' ceased among the educated Scots to be merely 'names,' and again became poetic personalities; and within the last few years the studious attention directed to this old vernacular poetry has been rapidly widening even on the Continent and in the United States, where many professors of English Literature have set an example to those in Great Britain by systematically including the subject in the English Literature course.

In such auspicious circumstances a succinct handbook of the whole subject—a handbook which should summarise the main features of this in many ways admirable literature, should trace its interdependence, even in prosody, from its earliest beginnings down to Burns and his immediate successors, and should serve as, at least, an introduction and guide to its more general and systematic study—is surely an almost imperative desideratum. No such handbook has up to the present been attempted, nor does any History of Scottish Literature exist that can be regarded as a substitute for it, the few Histories that have from time to time appeared, embracing only special aspects or special periods of general Scottish literature, while in none has the vernacular literature been dealt with as a separate entity.

It is only within recent years that such a hand-

book as that attempted in the following pages
has become possible. It in a sense represents and
summarises the labours of many preceding editors—
labours whose results are here thankfully acknowledged—from Pinkerton, Laing, Irving, and other
pioneers, to those of the Early English and Scottish
Texts. Those Text Societies are, it may be, devoted
more to the philological and antiquarian than the
strictly literary aspects of the subject, but it is
owing mainly to them and other learned Clubs—as
the Bannatyne, the Maitland, the Roxburgh, the
Hunterian—that Scottish Vernacular Literature has
begun to assert its title to full literary recognition.

The older vernacular literature being comparatively
unknown, more quotation has been deemed advisable
than is usual in literary histories. In the quotations no attempt has been made to modernise the
spelling, because (1) the special pronunciation is an
essential part of the poetical effect, and (2) a proper
knowledge of Scottish vernacular or any other literature is not obtainable by means of short cuts. It is
hoped, however, that the side glossary will not only
sufficiently guide the 'general reader' to an intelligent
appreciation of the quotations, but tend to quicken
an interest in one of the most graphic of literary
dialects—a dialect which perhaps even yet has not
wholly lost its efficacy to enrich modern English

To various peculiarities in spelling, as 'quh' for 'wh,' 'u' for 'v,' 'v' for 'u,' 'z' for 'y,' 'a' for 'o' (*e.g.* 'ane' for 'one'), and the dropping of the consonants at the end of words (*e.g.* 'fu'' for 'full'), the reader will gradually become reconciled by practice.

T. F. HENDERSON.

October 10, 1898.

CONTENTS

THE SCOTTISH VERNACULAR

THE Scottish vernacular is mainly a development of the Teutonic dialect of that Northumbria which embraced the more eastern portion of Scotland and Britain from the Humber to the Frith Northumbria. of Forth. Here the Saxons obtained a firm footing early in the sixth century, the Cymri being, after a series of desperate struggles, either conquered or forced gradually westwards until they concentred in Cumbria or Strathclyde, between the Mersey and the Clyde, where for some centuries they maintained a fragile independence. But the Saxons never wholly suspended their westward incursions; while the Scots or Gaels of the western regions beyond the Clyde indulged in attacks, of ever-augmenting severity, on their Cymric kinsmen from the north. During the next century the Northumbrian Saxons began also to push their conquests northwards over the Picts beyond the Forth, and succeeded in mastering certain districts south of the Tay; but after the great Pictish victory of Dunnichen in 685, the Saxon settlers in Pictland were either conquered or expelled; and although the Northumbrians renewed the struggle,

A

they failed to obtain permanent dominion beyond the Pentlands and the Forth. Their lack of success was due partly to internal contests, but chiefly to the creation of a new political influence through the union of the Picts and Scots under Kenneth M'Alpine some time before 843. If this federation was at first imperfect, and on the part of the Picts a matter rather of necessity than choice, it nevertheless created the germs of a northern potency, not only qualified to hold Northumbrian aggression in check, but destined to extend its influence southwards, until it embraced Northumbria north of the Tweed, and Cumbria north of the Solway.

The southern expansion of this northern state—this strange amalgamation of diverse races and principalities which became fused into the political entity known as Scotland—was powerfully aided by the effects of the great Danish immigrations of the ninth and tenth centuries, and the struggles between northern and southern England. Amid much that is uncertain as to the relations of the Scottish kings to these struggles, this much is clear, that, though they at first combined with the Danes of Northumbria and the Cymri of Cumbria in resisting the northward swoops of the west Saxons, they finally—from compulsion or self-interest—came to an understanding with the southern kings. Whether, or how far, they admitted the overlordship of these kings—Saxon or Danish—is of minor moment, since in the long-run

The Danish immigrations, and the southward expansion of Scotland.

they were able to disregard it.   Partly by right of
conquest, partly by promises to assist the southern
kings, the Scottish kings (1) were given in 945 a
kind of deputed authority over Cumbria, which they
ultimately succeeded in retaining in their full possession as far south as the Solway; and (2) between
970 and 975 obtained hold—whether in trust or not
—of Northumbria north of the Tweed, which was
also formally conceded to King Malcolm of Scotland
in 1018.

But while the dominion of the Scottish kings
was being thus consolidated in the south, it was
threatened with dire peril through the
remarkable and strenuous career of
Macbeth, Maarmor of Moray.   Though
regarded by some as mainly the cham-
pion of the conquered Picts, Macbeth seems to have
succeeded at last in enlisting the aid of the whole of
northern Scotland.   But whatever the exact blazon
on his standard—whatever the special cause, political,
racial, or dynastic, which he professed to champion
—the movement he inaugurated virtually perished
with his defeat and death in 1057.   Subsequent
Maarmors gave the Scottish kings occasional trouble,
but among none of the leaders of northern or
north-western insurrections did there arise a second
Macbeth.   If his adventurous purpose was in any
sense fruitful of political consequences, it was in a
direction entirely opposite to that intended by him—
towards weakening rather than strengthening the

The rebellion
of Macbeth,
and the Saxon-
ising of Scot-
land.

northern influences, whether Pictish, Scotic, or Norse. On the full rehabilitation of the old rule, mainly by southern aid, the southern civilisation gradually became dominant; nor was its dominance affected by subsequent temporary partitions of the kingdom. Through the marriage of Malcolm Canmohr—conqueror of Macbeth—with Margaret, sister of Edgar the Atheling, the old Scoto-Pictish dynasty became virtually Saxonised; and the triumph of the Saxon element was finally assured by the great influx of Saxons during the period of the Norman Conquest. Already much of the seaboard of Scotland north of the Forth had been overrun by the Scandinavian Vikings; and with the advent of the fugitive Northumbrians, the Teutonic speech and civilisation gradually penetrated into every district of the Scottish lowlands.

The direct effects of the Norman Conquest were late in reaching Scotland, nor when they appeared were they so potent as in the south. Though there was war with the Norman kings, there was no Norman Conquest of Scotland. The migration of Norman nobles thither was gradual and peaceful. They were patronised and favoured by the Scottish kings from the time of the marriage in 1100 of Matilda, sister of Edgar of Scotland, to Henry of England. Many of them accompanied David I., Matilda's brother, when from the Norman court of England, where he had spent his youth, he arrived

Norman influence considerable, but no Norman literature, and only slight fragments of Anglo-Saxon, preserved in Scotland.

in Scotland in 1107 to succeed to the throne of southern Scotland. Both in this southern Scotland and in northern Scotland, or Alban, to which he succeeded in 1124 — the kingdom being reunited under his rule—he introduced a feudal system of government, modelled after that of Norman England. Thus, though the Normans never effected any formal conquest of Scotland, they left indelible marks on its political and social system; and though their speech —adopted at court—did not so strongly colour the final vocabulary as in the south, yet, as in England, so in Scotland, it lent its aid in effecting that radical change in the form of the language by which, from being inflectional and synthetic, it became non-inflectional and analytic. Materials illustrative of the process of transformation are, however, in all respects, much scantier in Scotland than in England, and in truth can scarce be said to exist. Of the earlier Anglo-Saxon or Scandinavian, there survive only fragmentary remains on stone and monumental crosses, and a few Saxon words interwoven in charters and other Latin documents. Even of the minstrelsy or romances of the Normans—at least one of the fountainheads of Scottish poetry—not a verse has in Scotland been preserved; and only after the stage of transmutation is over, and the language has developed into a form of Early English, do proper data exist for determining its character.

When it first emerges from obscurity towards the close of the fourteenth century, the literary language of the Scottish lowlands is found to be practically identical with that of England north of the Humber:

The Scottish vernacular, originally identical with the Northern dialect of Early English, gradually became modified by contact with foreign tongues.

it belongs to the Northern dialect of Early English.[1] Compared with the Midland and Southern dialects, the Early Northern English, or Lowland Scottish, shows more traces of Scandinavian and Frisian, and less of Norman influences. But in Scotland this Northern dialect necessarily underwent a process of gradual change other than that merely of natural development. It was placed in a new environment which exposed it on all sides to infection from foreign tongues. For the most part, also, the process of change affected the oral speech before it manifested its presence in the literary language. The literary language tended at first to become stereotyped—to remain assimilated to the language of Northumbria south of the Tweed; and latterly, it was in some degree biassed by the ascendency of Chaucer and other southern writers; but the spoken dialect was being brought into contact with an immense variety of subtle linguistic forces—Cymric, Pictish, Gaelic, Norse, French — which, while they in many ways modified its pronunciation and altered its idioms, also enormously enriched its expressiveness.

The causes that co-operated to refashion the three

---

[1] It is almost unnecessary to mention the invaluable aid to the study of Early English which has been rendered by such pioneers as Dr. J. A. H. Murray, Richard Morris, and Professor Skeat.

dialects of Early English — Northern, Midland, and Southern — into two allied, but in many respects dissimilar, languages — English and Scottish — were mainly twofold : (1) the Midland dialect — for reasons that lie outside the present theme — gradually became the sole literary language of

Severance of Scotland from English influences, and its alliance with France — results on the vernacular.

England, the Northern and Southern dialects not being absorbed in it, but vanishing almost entirely from English literature ; and (2) Scotland — where the Northern dialect obtained supremacy — became, after Bannockburn, more and more severed from English influences, and, besides accomplishing its civilisation through the commingling of the diverse races within its own territory, entered into intimate relations with France. Scotsmen began to flock to France rather than to England to complete their education ; in large numbers they also entered the French service, and many of them winning high renown under French banners were made naturalised citizens of France ; Paris became a great Scottish resort ; the Frenchman and the Scot associated as sworn comrades against a common foe ; the royal houses of the two countries got to be strongly knit together by marriage ties, and the Scottish court formed a special centre of French customs and gaiety and culture, which began to give a certain veneer of refinement and civility to the rude and sombre Scottish manners ; every variety of commercial interchange rapidly expanded ; among the educated classes there was a flourishing appreciation of French literature, and the French language was more and more taught and spoken.

Thus it comes about that while the Early Scottish —the Scottish of Barbour and Wyntoun—differs but slightly, if at all, from Northern English, the Scottish of later writers—as, for example, Dunbar and Douglas and Sir David Lyndsay of the Mount — is a composite language, which, however the vocabulary of one writer may differ in many particulars from that of another, is characterised universally by a great, and in some respects barbarous, wealth of diction—a diction which, though it does not scruple to borrow from Chaucer and other English poets,[1] is derived largely from other sources than either the new English or the Northern dialect, and is coloured much more strongly than any of the old dialects with a French element—an element not wholly naturalised.

The vernacular of early and later writers.

Yet if the writers of this later period over-represent the French element in the oral speech of Scotland, the number both of French words and idioms which had already passed into the texture of the language is very great;[2] nor can it be doubted that had the old

[1] The old Scottish 'makaris' regarded their language—the language of lowland Scotland—as English. Thus Dunbar refers to Chaucer as 'of our Inglisch all the lycht.' Douglas distinguishes between Scottis and Inglis, and proposes to use mainly 'our own language,' though he does not disdain the occasional use of 'sudrone' speech; but Lyndsay actually refers to Douglas as 'in our Inglis rethorick the rose.'

[2] See specially on this subject Francisque-Michel's *Critical Inquiry into the Scottish Language*, 1882.

external conditions not sustained a sudden wrench, and had the Scottish vernacular literature been permitted a longer lease of full and vigorous activity so as to have afforded time for shedding of immaturities and accidental accretions, and for a more complete assimilation of French and other elements, *Enrichment of the vernacular not fully realised, and the literature checked before reaching full maturity.*

a literary language would have obtained of a more perfected individuality, of still greater variety, picturesqueness, and power, and perhaps more than rivalling literary English in fertility of idioms, and in wealth, beauty, and efficacy of diction. Is it presumptuous to even express regret that these two streams, issuing originally from a common fountainhead, had not, after each gathering volume from its own special rivulets, been permitted more fully to commingle, so that the final literature of the two reunited peoples should have represented even in its grammar and vocabulary something more of the northern genius, temperament, racial characteristics, and nationality ? But instead of contributing to any such consummation, the northern stream presently became dammed up and sank into the earth; and if at last it partially reappeared, it was in sadly diminished volume, and never again as the complete medium of the nation's literary expression. Before the influences which were fertilising and perfecting the language had time to become properly absorbed, circumstances arose which meanwhile effectually hindered any further literary advance. In truth, Scottish vernacular literature as a distinc-

tively national possession had scarce begun to exist ere
it had ceased to be; and in its original and unrevived
form may be said to have attained all the maturity
it was fated to reach some half-century before the
arrival of Shakespeare.

The Scottish Reformation, which the vernacular
literature in some sense heralded, and in many ways
assisted to bring about, in the end effectually smothered that literature. In
Scotland the Reformation assumed a
complexion exceptionally stern and rigid:
a complexion not merely sentimentally, but Calvinistically and logically Puritan. It was particularly
inimical to art, as in part a specious variety of
idolatry, in part an insidious conspiracy to drape
Satan as an angel of light. Secular poetry thus came
under its peculiar ban, and indeed almost every
form of secular literature—literature underived from
or uninterlarded with Scripture—as essentially mundane and frivolous, and therefore sinful. Its democratic spirit precluded such an illogical compromise
with the world as more or less obtained in England.
The sudden, full, and immediate contact of the rude
intelligence of the masses with a book, every word of
which was supposed to have been directly dictated
by God, upset—as it was bound to do—the nation's
mental and moral balance. Superstition, whose grip
the Renaissance and other influences had begun to
loosen, acquired a new authority, and laid hold of the
nation with a still firmer because more logical clutch—

*Scottish
literature
smothered by
the Reformation.*

a clutch which for the time being effectually strangled the national literature. By the impulse and with the guidance of this renovated superstition, an organisation was gradually perfected which endeavoured to comprehend within itself, and to utilise for its own ends, all the nation's energies, and to subject not merely what are usually termed the morals, but everything else besides, of each individual, high or low, rich or poor, cultivated and clever or illiterate and foolish, to its inspection and control. Thus, notwithstanding the impulse of a true poetic tradition, and the fostering influence of James VI., the vocation of art or literature in Scotland became gradually impossible. All this is undeniable fact, only more patently manifested by pretentious attempts to gloss it over. It must be accepted in its unvarnished drab reality, and either with condemnation or approval, or such a blending of the two as the special circumstances demand. And at least it would be churlish to withhold a certain meed of admiration from such honesty of conviction, and such a sterling—however in the long-run impossible—effort to square practice with theory. The bulk of the nation then believed what it professed to believe. In the Biblical idolatry of Scotland there was also this compensating benefit, that the Bible—general familiarity with which was so strenuously promoted, and even enforced—contains much admirable literature, and that at last it circulated in Scotland, as in England, in the marvellous English prose version whose charm is still as fresh as it was nearly three centuries ago. Its general perusal was bound in some degree to cultivate and purify the nation's literary taste, and to foster a latent capacity to appreciate good secular literature, as soon as circumstances removed the embargo from it.

But besides practically suppressing the vernacular literature, and filching from life the zest without which no healthy literature can flourish, the Scottish Reformation called into operation activities which made inevitably for the disintegration of the vernacular language: which slowly robbed the language of its characteristically northern features, and gradually but surely transformed its most picturesque peculiarities into sober and estimable English. Direct consequences of the Reformation were the severance of the old relations with France, and the resumption of a perpetual alliance with the 'auld enemy,' England. This led first to the union of the crowns, and finally to the union of the kingdoms. After these unions the vernacular could not, under any conditions, have long retained its pristine purity; but had circumstances before the union of the crowns been different, the process of disintegration, though inevitable, would also have been different. It would have been less rapid, and in the end less complete and fatal, had Scotland all along been in possession of a vigorous national literature. Sooner or later the lesser was bound to become merged in the greater literature; but it was by no means necessary that the bulk of the special vocabulary and idioms of the north should in the process utterly perish. From them English literature might have acquired still greater opulence of expression, and especially an added piquancy and vigour. But alas! the vernacular had almost ceased to be wedded to a living literature before even the union of the crowns; and the vernacular language itself had already become smitten with symptoms of decay. The universal circulation of the Bible in English gradually introduced a new fashion of expression. While the broad Scottish pronunciation of necessity retained its currency even among the educated and upper classes, many of the old Scottish words and idioms began to drop out of the oral speech, and after the creation of a kind of amorphous dialect—quaintly compounded in irregular and lawless proportions of Scottish and English—English went on conquering and to conquer. Even the common speech of the peasant in the remoter regions began to suffer from the weekly deluges of Scoto-English, and the daily enforced perusal of the English Scriptures; and so the vernacular of each succeeding generation became less purely Scottish than that of its predecessor.

It thus follows (1) that much of the vernacular Scottish—vernacular that had no place in the only partially developed and prematurely blasted literature—has hopelessly perished; (2) that some of the literary

The old and the revived vernacular.

vernacular cannot now be certainly interpreted; and
(3) that the revived vernacular from Sempill to
Burns is more or less Anglified Scottish: not, for
example, the Scottish of Dunbar and Lyndsay and
their contemporaries, but partly imitated from these
older writers, partly a dialect more or less local, and
partly English with a Scottish accent. Old ballads
entirely pagan in sentiment, and old songs of a
gaiety and frankness and ingenuous indecency which
bespeak relation with an age of primitive simplicity,
survived in the oral traditions of the people, the
anathemas of the Kirk notwithstanding; but in the
process of transmission from one generation to another, their form and cast of language—though not
of essential utterance—underwent inevitable changes.
Many of them also have come down to us only in
broken snatches and isolated refrains. As for the
literature of the revival, it was in a sense a mere
exotic—largely an imitation of a literature that had
been partly moribund for some centuries. The
literary tradition was almost hopelessly dissevered.
The gap between the present and the past became
too wide to permit of proper re-connection. At the
Reformation Scottish vernacular literature had 'a
great fall,' and by no manner of means could be
'set up again' as an adequate national symbol. In
the case of Sempill and other older poets of the
revival—many of them innominate—the antique
flavour is strong and genuine; in the case of Ramsay
and his contemporaries it is a variable quantity,

partly artificial, and too often streaked with mere vulgarity and commonplace squalor. Several poets of later date than Ramsay have achieved a certain success in isolated vernacular songs. Fergusson made not inconsiderable efforts to galvanise the dead corpse of vernacular literature into a semblance of real vitality; but Fergusson's career was too short to enable him to master more than the rudiments of his art, and it was reserved for Burns, by virtue both of unique endowments and special circumstances— his lowly birth, his peasant experiences, his deep and full humanity, his peculiarly impressionable genius, his mastery of the old national poetry in its spirit and essence, and his rare artistic sorcery—in a sense to re-create for us the old Scottish world, to breathe into the dry bones of the past the breath of life, and to fashion a form of vernacular poetry in which old and new elements are cunningly blended to the production of artistic effects unsurpassed, if not unequalled, by any vernacular predecessor. Burns had, and has, many imitators, but by the very nature of the case he could have no successors or disciples quite worthy to prolong his tradition. Necessarily he influenced, and does still influence, the poetic art of the nineteenth century, for no great poetic artist ever lived to himself alone; but while his spirit survives, his method may be said to have in great part perished with him.

II

MINSTRELSY AND ROMANCE

EARLY FRAGMENTS OF PATRIOTIC MINSTRELSY—'THOMAS
OF ERCELDOUNE' AND 'SIR TRISTREM'—HUCHOWN
OF THE AWLE RYALE, AND OTHER WRITERS OF
ALLITERATIVE ROMANCES.

THAT minstrelsy was in high repute in the Saxonised
and latterly Normanised Picto-Celtic Scotland might
have been assumed as certain, even had
there not been the many proofs there are
of early proficiency in music and song;
for the nation was a blend of peoples among whom
the vocation of the bard was ever held in high
esteem. Yet of the earlier songs all that have
reached us are a few paltry fragments, and even
these we do not possess in quite their original
dialect. Wyntoun (*c.* 1420) has preserved a 'Cantus'
of eight lines forming the whole or part of what
may be termed a national prayer for succour evoked
by the parlous state of the country through the
intestine troubles and devastating raids that followed
the death of Alexander III. :—

Early Cantus
preserved by
Wyntoun.

'Quhen Alysandyr oure kyng was dede
That Scotland led in luüe and lé

love and
law

> Away wes sons off ale and brede,   plenty
>   Off wyne and wax, off gamyn and glé :
> Oure gold wes changyd into lede.
>   Cryst borne into Vyrgynyté
> Succoure Scotland and remede
>   That stad [is in] perplexyté.'   fixed

The spelling and dialect is, of course, that of
Wyntoun; but if destitute of any special linguistic
value, the Cantus is metrically of interest as perhaps
the earliest extant example of the interwoven octave
formed of lines of four accents rhyming alternately.

Another fragment dating from the same troubled
years is that of the 'mokkyshe ryme'   The 'mok-
                                        kyshe ryme'
made by the Scots in derision of the   on the siege
                                        of Berwick,
English after they had driven them back 1296.
and burnt some of their ships during the siege of
Berwick by Edward in 1296 :—

> 'What wenys Kynge Edwarde with longe shankys   Why
>   To have wonne Berwyk all our onthankys ?   imagineth
>   Gaas pykes him.   Let us
>   And when he hath it
>   Gaas dykeis him.' [1]

It is a rude production enough; but scornful hate is
worked into the chorus with a certain realistic emphasis.

The next of our fragments is the triumphant
dance - song of the Scottish maidens   Song of the
                                        Scottish
after Bannockburn (1314): a naively   Maidens after
                                        Bannockburn,
exultant bantering of the forlorn plight 1314.
of their bereaved English sisters :—

---

[1] So in Fabyan's *Chronicle*; but in *Chron. Monast. S. Albani*
(ed. Riley, 1865) there is a simpler version : 'Kyng Edward, wanne
thu havest Berwic pike the, wanne thu havest geten, dike the.'
To dike = to fence round, to enclose so as to make escape impossible.

'Maydens of Englonde, sore may ye morne
For your lemmans ye have loste at Bannockisborne !
With heue a lowe.
What wenyth the Kynge of Englonde
So soone to haue wonne Scotlande ?
With rumbylowe.'

darlings

Why
imagineth

'This songe,' says Fabyan,[1] 'was after many dayes
sungyn in daunces, in carolles of ye maydens and
mynstrellys of Scotlande, to the reproofe and dysdane
of Englyshmen, *wt dyverse other which* I ouer passe.'

The phrases 'With heue a lowe' and 'With rumbylowe' are found both in later Scottish and English
poetry. They here probably indicate the occurrence
of a dance movement emphasised by special gestures
or the beating of musical instruments.

Our last example is a pithy but halting quatrain
made by the Scots after the marriage of David II.,
son of Robert the Bruce, to Jane or
Joanna, sister of Edward III., whom, says
Fabyan,[2] 'they, in despite of the English, call "Jane Make Peace."' The quatrain, he
further tells us, was but one of diverse 'truffys,
roundycs, and songyes' made by the Scots to the
Englishmen's 'more deryson' :—

Quatrain after
the marriage
of David II.
in 1328.

'Long berdys, hartles
Paynted hoodyes, witles
Gay cotis, graceless
Maketh England thryftles.'

Altogether these fragments form but a sorry
wreckage from devouring Time; but, such as they

[1] *Chronicle*, ed. Ellis, p. 420.   [2] *Ib.* p. 440.

are, they do more to bring us into contact with the heart of the nation, in those wild and ingenuous ages, than do the bulk of the serious political documents of the period. In those early times the carols, and rounds, and rude rhymes were almost the only means of voicing the nation's sentiments, and formed a sort of presage of our present daily press. On the other hand, the more elaborate poems scarcely touched the present at all. In these long Romances we have passing glimpses of ancient manners and customs, but they make known little or nothing of the main concerns of the nation; they are mainly translations or paraphrases of translations, and deal with times already remote from those of the narrator, and with adventures in love and war of heroes and heroines belonging to a partly mythical antiquity.

Minstrelsy is of more historic interest than Romance.

The earliest name associated with Scottish poetry is that of the mysterious soothsayer Thomas of Erceldoune, usually called Thomas the Rhymour. A certain 'Thomas Rimour de Erceldoune' is witness to a deed of the Abbey of Melrose [1] which is undated, but, from certain other signatures attached to it, may be pretty certainly assigned to the latter half of the thirteenth century. That the Thomas Rimour who signed that deed either died or was executed or murdered, or went into monastic retirement or was kidnapped—whether by mortals or fairies—sometime before 2nd November

Thomas of Erceldoune —when did he flourish?

[1] *Liber de Melros*, p. 269.

1294, may further be inferred from the fact that by deed of that date 'Thomas de Erceldoune, filius et heres Thome Rymour de Erceldoune,' conveyed all his lands held by inheritance in Erceldoune to the Trinity house of Soltra.[1]   Whether Rimour was the family name of Thomas or his professional title is matter of dispute; and the question is of some importance, since if it was the family name, the mere occurrence of it coupled with Thomas in the documents settles nothing as to the period when 'true Thomas' flourished.   Hector Boece (1527) is the first writer to call him Leirmont; but in the absence of this name from the early documents, Boece's authority must be regarded as worth little, though there is the possibility either that Leirmont was a title, or that a new family of the name of Leirmont came later into the possession of Erceldoune.   Erceldoune was a castle and village in Berwickshire—on the site of the present Earlston—belonging to the Earl of Dunbar and March, but Thomas Rimour is supposed to have inhabited a 'tower' of his own, the so-called ruins of which are still pointed out; and it is, of course, certain from the deed executed by Thomas Rimour's son that the family held their lands independent of the Earl.   The main evidence associating Thomas of the documents with Thomas of the prophecies is the statement of Bower in the continuation (c. 1430) of Fordun that the Rhymer, on the day before the death of Alexander III. (1286), pre-

---

[1] MS. Chartulary in the Advocates' Library, Edinburgh.

dicted the occurrence on the morrow of a mysterious and destructive blast; but although antiquaries have accepted the anecdote as fact, and even Sir Walter has gravely surmised that the death of Alexander accidentally saved the reputation of Thomas as a weather prophet, the mere testimony of Bower, writing a hundred and fifty years afterwards, cannot be regarded as a sufficient authentication. Blind Harry must needs of course employ the intervention of Thomas in glorification of the national hero Wallace, and for this purpose introduces him as an inmate of the Abbey of Faile, near Ayr, at the time of Wallace's captivity there in 1296, and as predicting future victories for him after he was given up for dead; but it is surely folly to attach much importance to the poetical devices of Blind Harry, unless otherwise corroborated. As to Thomas's prophecy of the succession of Robert the Bruce to the Scottish throne, referred to by Barbour,[1] Barbour's statement is too vague to warrant the conclusion that the prophecy was necessarily made after the death of Alexander; and Barbour affirms nothing as to the period when the Rhymer flourished. A like remark applies to the 'derne' saying mentioned by Wyntoun[2] as prophetic of the battle of Kilblane; but if a certain forged prophecy, written before 1320,[3] refer to the battle of Bannockburn, Thomas of Erceldoune, to

---

[1] *The Bruce*, Bk. II. v. 85-87.
[2] *Chronicle*, Bk. VIII. xxxi. 114.
[3] MS. Harleian, 2253, l. 127.

whom it is assigned, must have been alive as late as 1293.

Thus, though taken singly each item of evidence as to the date of Thomas is of somewhat uncertain significance, yet collectively its general drift is towards the identification of Thomas the Rhymer with Thomas Rimour of the documents. Nor is it difficult to understand what exceptional opportunity the troubled years following the death of Alexander III. afforded to one reputed to possess the awesome gift of speaking in 'derne.' Since also Thomas rhymed on the eve of the great struggle with Edward I., it was inevitable that after his death his sayings should acquire a factitious importance, that his fame should deepen and expand with each supposed fulfilment of his prophecies, and his rhymes be distorted or mutilated to fit particular emergencies, and at last be gradually submerged by a countless variety of forgeries. Having died, moreover, before war with England had begun, he was not originally regarded as specially a Scottish partisan, and therefore his repute seems to have been, at first, quite as great in England as it was in Scotland. But being a Scot, it was inevitable that he should in the end be appropriated as the one great Scottish prophet —with gifts outrivalling even those of the more ancient but un-Scottish Merlin—who had special intimations of all the main events of Scottish history down to a period of indefinite futurity; and it was equally inevitable that his character as 'true Thomas'

His fame as a prophet.

should be assiduously preserved by apparently whole hosts of forgeries composed after the occurrence of the events foretold. Thus, notwithstanding the Rhymer's fame, or rather perhaps because of it, no rhyming prophecy exists that can be certainly authenticated as his. Neither Barbour, nor Wyntoun, nor Blind Harry has professed to quote verbatim any of his prophetic rhymes; and it is vain, from among the many forgeries that have passed current as sayings of his, to attempt to select a single specimen that actually represents his opinions or forecasts, far less enables us to form any judgment as to his literary or poetic gifts.

As for the old romance of *Thomas of Erceldoune* in three fyttes,[1] detailing the confabulations of Thomas with the Elf Queen, it is plainly, in great part, the work of an Englishman, who could not have written or refurbished it earlier than 1400; and even if he made use of an old romance of which some Scotsman was the author, that romance was indubitably derived from the older one *Ogier le Danois*. The prophecies of the third fytte Dr. Murray regards as refurbished prophecies, originally of very ancient date; and of course it is just possible that Thomas was himself a refurbisher of ancient prophecies, which were again refurbished by the author of the fytte. Nor is more

The old romance of 'Thomas of Erceldoune.'

---

[1] Published complete, so far as the several MSS. permit, by the Early English Text Society, ed. Dr. J. A. H. Murray, 1875 ; and by A. Brandl, Berlin, 1880.

light, but rather darkness visible, to be got from the
consultation of the *Whole Prophecie of Scotland,
England*, etc.,[1] even after comparison with certain
Scottish Prophecies, printed by J. R. Lumby, from
a manuscript of the fifteenth century.[2]

We come then, last, to the traditional rhymes collected by Scott,[3] Robert Chambers,[4] and Henderson;[5]
Traditional rhymes attributed to Thomas. but how interesting soever these may be
as specimens of folk inventiveness and
credulity, it would be vain to pretend that
they are in the remotest degree representative either
of the prophetic or poetic gifts of 'true Thomas.' Here,
however, is one of them. It is not known to have
been as yet fulfilled, but its ' derne ' gruesomeness is
almost enough in itself to account for the mysterious
awe attaching to the name of Thomas—whether he
really uttered it or not :—

> ' At three-burn Grange in after day
> There shall be a lang and bloody fray ;
> When a three-thumbed wight by the reins shall hald
> Three kings' horses baith stout and bauld ;
> And the three Burns three days will rin
> Wi' the blude o' the slain that fa' therein.'

fellow
bold

In addition to his prophecies, true Thomas is
' The Horn Child.' credited by Sir Walter Scott with the
authorship of two romances—*The Horn
Child, or the Gest of King Horn*,[6] and *Sir Tristrem.*

---

[1] 1603, and in the Bannatyne Club, 1833.
[2] Early English Text Society, 1870.
[3] *Minstrelsy of the Scottish Border.*
[4] *Popular Rhymes of Scotland.*
[5] *Popular Rhymes of Berwickshire.*
[6] Published by the Early English Text Society, ed. Lumby, 1866.

Sir Walter thought the French romance of *King Horn* might be a version from the English one, and that the Thomas therein mentioned might be he of Erceldoune; but this Anglo-Norman version is of older date than the English one, being written about 1170; and besides, the English version of *King Horn* is not the work of a northern poet.

The claims of Thomas to some sort of authorship of *Sir Tristrem* deserve more serious consideration; and the question is besides of greater literary moment. Since Sir Walter's time the balance of learned opinion has turned very much against the claims of Thomas; but Mr. G. P. M'Neill, the latest editor, 'is unable to concur in regarding *Sir Tristrem* as the work of an unknown author other than Thomas of Erceldoune.' The main authority on the subject is the *Chronicle* of Robert Mannyng, or De Brunne; and the most probable—if not the only—interpretation of Mannyng's words is that he believed, rightly or wrongly, that *Tristrem* was written by Erceldoune. In explaining why he had written his own *Chronicle* in the octo-syllabic couplet, and not in one of the more complicated staves then so much in fashion— as *ryme couée*, or *étrangère*, or *enterlace*—Mannyng goes on to remark:—

'Sir Tristrem'
—was it written
by Thomas of
Erceldoune?
Evidence of
Mannyng.

> 'I see in song in sedgeyng tale
> Of Erceldoun and of Kendale,
> Non tham says as thai tham wroght
> And in ther saying it semes noght :

> That may thou here in Sir Tristrem,
> Ouer gestes it has the esteem,
> Ouer all that is or was,
> If men it sayd as made Thomas.
> But I here it no man so say
> That of som copple som is away.
> So thare fayre sayng her beforne
> Is thare travayle nere forlorne.'

These lines as they stand might be interpreted to mean that Mannyng attributes *Tristrem* either to Thomas of Kendale or to Thomas of Erceldoune, or to a third Thomas. But there is even a fourth theory very much in favour with ingenious antiquaries. Since the author of the only copy of *Tristrem* known to exist[1] begins his tale thus—

The four theories.

> 'I was a[t Erceldoun]
>   With tomas spak y thare ;
>   Ther herd y rede in roune
>   Who tristrem gat and bare '—

rhyme

it has been argued that Mannyng meant to indicate a joint authorship; or more precisely, referred to *Tristrem* as a vamp by Kendale of an earlier romance by Erceldoune. But is it likely that Kendale could have the effrontery to attempt the refurbishing of a poem by such a famous contemporary? Of course Mannyng —if misled by these introductory lines—might have made this (very foolish) supposition; but Mannyng

---

[1] Auchinleck MS. in the Advocates' Library, Edinburgh, by a southern fourteenth-century transcriber of some northern copy of much earlier date. Published by Sir Walter Scott, 1804; by Kölbing at Heilbronn, 1882; and by the Scottish Text Society, ed. G. P. M'Neill, 1886.

was himself approaching manhood before Erceldoune died, and as he also professes to be thoroughly versed in the history of the tale, we may assume that he knew the facts at first hand. Besides, he plainly refers to the romance as it was first written, not as altered by a later author, however skilled: ' as made Thomas,' he writes—not ' as made Thomas the first and vamped Thomas the second.' Further, Mannyng elsewhere in his *Chronicle* mentions definitely the tale of Kendale as a chronicle of north of England events; and we must therefore infer that unless Mannyng meant to attribute the authorship of *Tristrem* to another Thomas than either he of Kendale or he of Erceldoune, he meant to attribute it to the last. True, a tale of *Tristrem*—of which the writer of this later *Tristrem* must undoubtedly have made use—was written about 1170 by an Anglo-Norman Thomas, but it was written in French, and written in couplets.[1] We have thus no other Thomas to whom to ascribe *Sir Tristrem* except he of Erceldoune; and whether he wrote it or not, if once the claims of Thomas of Kendale be excluded, no reason is left for assigning its authorship to one on the English rather than on the Scottish side of the Border. Nor can it be said that the references in the poem to Thomas of Erceldoune are inconsistent with his own authorship of it. On the contrary, may not the introductory lines be interpreted to mean that the scribe wrote the poem

[1] Published in Francisque-Michel's *Poetical Romances of Tristan in French, in Anglo-Norman, and in Greek*; London, 1835-39.

from the dictation of Thomas? But whether this be
so or not, the version that has reached us is in substance—as well as in metre—clearly that of the
author whom Mannyng believed to be Erceldoune.

If there be exaggeration in Mannyng's praise of
Sir Tristrem as the best of all the 'gestes' that 'ever
is or was,' it is at least the most elaborate
*Literary merit
of 'Sir Tristrem.'* and perfect of the early romances dealing
with the story of Tristan and Ysonde: a story which,
after passing through many prose versions—in French,
German, Danish, Spanish, Italian, and English,—has
in modern times furnished a theme for varied imaginative treatment, has inspired Wagner with one of his
greatest achievements in music, and has mirrored the
several idealisms of Arnold, Tennyson, and Swinburne.
The *Sir Tristrem* of Erceldoune is hardly poetical. It
is only a rhymed story, told in the simple, naïve, and
spirited style which would best impress the wonder-
ing and childlike audiences of the Middle Ages: it
relates in a manner well fitted to captivate their
unsophisticated hearts the marvellous adventures in
love and war of Tristan. The hero and the other
personages of the story are not undeftly drawn, but
their motives are elementally simple, direct, and
unconventional; and whenever the narrator is in
difficulties, the miraculous is ever at hand to supply
the needed solution. Yet is the narrative far from
being prolix; on the contrary, it is crowded with
incident, and abounds in graphic natural touches;
and when it is added that metrically the work is

one of high accomplishment, it is not difficult to
account for the praise bestowed on it by Mannyng,
nor to understand that, recited by a minstrel
thoroughly versed in all the methods of giving
emphasis and effect to the story, it must have made
a quite exceptional impression. The romance has
also a certain perennial interest for its pictures of
ancient observances, but regarded as literature it is
its stave that is chiefly worthy of note. Here is an
example:—

> 'To prison thai gun take
>   Erl baroun and knight.
> For Douke Morgan sake
>   Mani on dyd dounright.
> Schaftes thai gun shake
>   And riuen scheldes bright ;
> Crounes thai gun crake
>   Mani, ich wene, aplight.
>   Saunfayl,
> Betvene the none and the night
>   Last the batayle.'

outright
without
pause

The stave of *Sir Tristrem* is an admirable example
of interwoven rhyme in short lines, combined with
alliteration. No earlier instance of this The stave of
rhymed stave is known to exist in any of 'Sir Tristrem.'
the old English dialects, although it is employed by
Lawrence Minot in one of his songs on Edward III.[1]
It consists of eight lines each of three accents, with
alternate rhymes, and to this is added a bobwheel,[2]

[1] Wright's *Political Poems*, i. 74.
[2] The wheel is the return of a peculiar rhythm at the end of each
stanza. In its simplest form it consists of two short lines rhyming
with each other. The bobwheel is a wheel beginning with a short
abrupt line or bob (*i.e.* small wheel), as 'Saunfayl' in the example
now given.

consisting of a bob of one accent introducing a new rhyme, and followed by two lines generally of three accents—but occasionally, as in the stanza quoted above, of only two,—the former of which lines rhymes with the line preceding the bob, and the latter with the bob.   There are early monkish Latin examples of the interwoven octave in lines of three accents, and the bob itself probably derives from the Latin staves.   The simplest form of the bobwheel consists of the bob and a single line rhyming with the bob. The bob may introduce a new rhyme, or, as in the case of the original *Christis Kirk*, the bob and the line following it may rhyme with the last line of the preceding octave or be unrhymed; and this bob-wheel was further simplified, in the case of Ramsay and later Scottish poets, by the substitution of a refrain consisting of an unrhymed line of two accents. The special bobwheel of *Sir Tristrem* was no doubt derived from the French.   An approximate example occurs in an Anglo-Norman stave, quoted in Arch-bishop Langton's Sermons, and dating probably from the beginning of the thirteenth century :—

> 'Bele Aliz matin leva,
> Sun cors vesti e para
> Enz un verger s'entra
> Cink flurettes y truva
> Un chapelet fet en a
>   De rose flurie ;
> Pur Deu, trahez vus en la
>   Vus ki ne amez mie.'

More elaborate forms of the bobwheel were made by

doubling, or, as in *The Pistill of Swete Susan* (p. 36),
trebling the first section of the wheel.

Next to Thomas of Erceldoune in date comes the
poet named by Wyntoun, Huchown of
the Awle Ryale:— Huchown
of the Awle
Ryale.

> 'That cunnand wes in literature.
> He made the gret gest off Arthure,
> And the Awntyre off Gawaine
> The Pystyll als off Swete Swsane ;   also
> He wes curyws in hys style,
> Fare of Facund, and subtile,   eloquence
> And ay to plesans and delyte
> Mád in metre mete his dyte :   writing
> Lytil or nocht nevyrtheles   nothing
> Waverand fra the suthfastness.'   truth

Of the three works here mentioned by Wyntoun,
the last, *The Pistill of Susan*,[1] is that alone about
whose identity there has been practically
no dispute, and it therefore supplies an   ' The Pistill
                                                of Susan'—
important basis for further conclusions   its value as
                                                evidence
regarding Huchown and his other works.   regarding
                                                Huchown,
The earliest MS. of *The Pistill*, that in the who was
                                                probably Sir
Bodleian Library, Oxford, dates about   Hew of
                                                Eglinton.
1380; but the many evident corruptions
it contains indicate that it was very far from
being a first-hand copy of the original, which
therefore must have been of considerably earlier
date. Further, notwithstanding the prevalence of
Midland and Southern spellings in all the five extant

---

[1] Published in Laing's *Select Remains of the Ancient Poetry of
Scotland*, 1822 (2nd ed. 1885) ; since which the best of several
editions are those of Kösler (Strassburg, 1895) and of the Scottish
Text Society in *Scottish Alliterative Poems*, ed. Amours, 1896-97.

MSS., the Northern origin of the poem can be clearly established by the rhyme endings. We are thus able to conclude, first, that the author flourished about the middle of the fourteenth century; second, that he was a northern poet; and thirdly, since he is so circumstantially lauded by Wyntoun, and at the same time referred to familiarly as 'Huchown of the Awle Ryale,' that he was a Scot. But if he was a Scot, his name could scarce have been omitted from the death-roll of Dunbar's stately *Lament for the Makaris*, and therefore he is usually identified with the Sir Hew of the *Lament* :—

> 'The gude Syr Hew of Eglintoun,
> Ettrik, Heryot, et Wyntoun
> He hes tane out of this cuntré :
> > *Timor mortis conturbat me.*'

taken

Some have identified him with Clerk, or rather the Clerk, of Tranent, referred to in the lines :—

also

> 'Clerk of Tranent eik he has tane,
> That made the anteris of Gawane';

but it is unlikely that 'Huchown' could have two such different designations. Moreover, a Sir Hew, Lord of Eglinton—married to Egidia, half-sister of Robert II.—died about 1375, and was therefore a contemporary of Huchown, whoever Huchown may have been.

But Mr. Amours, the latest editor of *The Pistill*, surmises that there were two contem-porary Sir Hews of Eglinton—the one a knight, and the other a priest. The epithet 'gude' has also been adduced in support of the

Were there two Sir Hews of Eglinton?

theory that Sir Hew was a priest, although it is also commonly used by the poets, not to designate priestly, but knightly, qualities. Mr. Amours' special objection against the knighthood of Sir Hew is that ' it is incredible that Wyntoun should have called a nobleman of high rank by the curt and familiar name of Huchown in a passage meant to be as eulogistic as Wyntoun could make it.' But the objection surely is as valid if Huchown were a priest; and in any case, it loses its cogency if we reflect that Sir Hew may himself in the character of poet have adopted the title of ' Huchown of the Awle Ryale'; and, on the whole, it is more credible that there was only one Sir Hew of Eglinton than two contemporaries of that title—the one a nobleman, and the other his parish priest. The phrase ' Awle Ryale'—or in one MS., ' Auld Ryall'—is of uncertain signification; but the interpretation ' Royal Palace' is as feasible as any that has as yet been suggested.

The identification of the two other works of Huchown mentioned by Wyntoun is rendered difficult by the number of existing romances that would fit the titles. Internal evidence, based on a comparison with *The Pistill*, is specially deceptive in the absence of northern copies; but Dr. Trautmann[1] has adduced reasons—based mainly on the use made of it by Wyntoun in his *Chronicle*, and specially on the fact that it contains

Other works of Huchown.

[1] *Der Dichter Huchown und seine Werke*, in *Anglia* (1877), pp. 109-188.

the very mistake of mentioning Lucius Tiberius as
emperor instead of procurator, to which Wyntoun
specially refers—for identifying *The Gest of Arthure*
with the non-rhyming alliterative poem *Morte
Arthure*.[1] Further, notwithstanding the contrary
opinion of Dr. Trautmann, Mr. F. J. Amours adduces
strong reasons for identifying *The Awntyre of
Gawaine* with a rhyming alliterative poem, *The
Awntyrs of Arthure at the Terne Wathelyne*.[2]
Other poems attributed to Huchown are the long
unrhymed alliterative *Geste Historiall of the Destruction of Troy*, translated from Guido delle Colonne's
Historia Troiana;[3] *Sir Gawain and the Green
Knight*;[4] and *Golagros and Gawaine*.[5] The first of
these Dr. Trautmann endeavours, from internal
evidence, to show could not, though the work of a
Scots translator, have been the work of the author of

[1] In the Thornton MS. at Lincoln, ed. Halliwell, 1847 ; and also
published by the Early English Text Society, ed. E. Brock, 1865.

[2] Published in Pinkerton's *Scottish Poems*, 1792, under the title
Sir Gawain and Sir Galaron of Galloway ; by David Laing in
Select Remains, 1822 (2nd ed. 1885) ; by the Bannatyne Club, ed. Sir
F. Madden, 1839 ; by the Camden Society, ed. Robson, 1842 ; and
by the Scottish Text Society in *Scottish Alliterative Poems*, ed.
Amours, 1896-97.

[3] Early English Text Society, ed. Donaldson and Panton, 1869-74.

[4] Bannatyne Club, ed. Sir F. Madden, and Early English Text
Society, with three religious poems from the same MS., and by the
same author, ed. Morris, 1864. Abridged ed. by Jessie L. Weston, 1898.

[5] Printed with other Scottish pieces by Chepman and Myllar,
Edinburgh, 1508 ; facsimile reprint by David Laing, 1827 ; included
in Pinkerton's *Scottish Poems*, 1792 ; published also by the
Bannatyne Club, ed. Madden, 1839, by Dr. Trautmann, in *Anglia*,
1879, and by the Scottish Text Society in *Scottish Alliterative
Poems*, ed. Amours, 1896-97.

The Pistill and *The Morte Arthure*; as for the second,
notwithstanding various objections suggested by the
versification and vocabulary, it has some claims to be
regarded as a rival to *The Awntyrs of Arthure* for
identification as *The Awntyre of Gawaine*, and these
claims are strengthened by the fact that at the beginning of the MS. is the name 'Hugo de'; and as to
the last, an adaptation from the French, though
there is no convincing evidence that it is, as some
editors hold, of later date, it differs utterly in style
from the two undoubted works of Huchown.   There
is some probability that it is the *Anteris of Gawaine*
ascribed by Dunbar to Clerk of Tranent; but nothing
can be inferred as to his date from Dunbar's mention
of him, Dunbar's chronology in the three previous
stanzas being quite promiscuous.

All these works—whether Huchown's or not—
appear to us now more or less bizarre.   Though lin-
guistically of great interest, and though
metrically they left traces of their influence on later poetry, they are rather of
interest to the scholar and antiquary than
to the general reader;[1] but both *Sir Gawaine* and the
Awntyrs of Arthure have a good deal of graphic force.
All the four assigned to Huchown—two being his
without doubt, and two having rival claims to be

*Metrical
characteristics
of the
Alliterative
Romances.*

---

[1] It may be that a Cymric tradition lent, in Cumbria, a certain
special interest to these romances; but the *Awntyre of Gawaine* has
been traced to a French source, and when Huchown wrote, the
Arthurian legend was the common property of the romancists of all
countries.

reckoned his—are in different metres.   In *Morte Arthure* the metre is unrhymed alliteration, but in

The stave of
' The Pistill.'

the others alliteration is combined with rhyme.   Of the stave of *The Pistill* — which is merely a versified paraphrase of the story of Susanna and the Elders in the Vulgate—here is an example :—

> ' Thenne the folk of Israel fel vppon knes [1]
> And loued that louely lord, that hire the lyf lent ;
> Alle the gomes that hire goode wolde gladen and glees
> This prophete so pertly proues his entent,
> Thei trompe bifore this traitours and traylen hem on tres
> Thorwout the citee, be comuyn assent.
> Ho so leeueth on that lord, thar hym not lees,
> That thus his seruaunt saued that schuld ha be schent
> In sete.
> This ferlyes bifel
> In the dayes of Daniel.
> The pistel wittenes wel
> Of that prophete.'

The stave thus consists of an interwoven octave of lines rhyming alternately, followed by a complex bobwheel; the bob of one accent, introducing a new rhyme, being followed by three short lines each rhyming only with each other, after which comes a short line rhyming with the bob.   Various examples of the

---

[1] ' Then the people of Israel fell upon their knees, and loved that lovable lord that granted her life.   All the knights that would her welfare celebrate and sing (this prophet so openly proves his case), they sound the trumpet before these traitors and drag them on trees throughout the city by common assent.   Whoso trusteth in that lord, need not be lost, that this his servant saved, who should have been injured in his place.   These marvels happened in the days of Daniel.   The book of that prophet testifies to their truth.'

same bobwheel are to be found in other poems of the fourteenth century. In *The Awntyrs of* The stave of *Arthure* we have an admirable example 'The Awntyrs.' of the most common form of rhymed alliterative romance. Here is a stave :—

> 'Bare was hir body, and blake to the bone [1]
> Alle by-claggede in claye, vn-comlyly clede ;
> It weryit, it waye-mettede lyke a womane,
> That nowther one hede, ne one hare, hillynge it hade.
> It stottyde, it stounnede, it stode als a stane.
> It marrede, it mounede, it moyssede for made.
> Vnto that grysely gaste Sir Gaweayne es gane :
> He raykede to it one a rase, for he was neuer rade ;
> For rade was he neuer, nowe who that rychte redis.
> One the chefe of the cholle,
> A tade pykit one hir polle ;
> Hir eghene war holkede fulle holle,
> Glowand als gledis.'

It begins, as does *The Pistill,* with an interwoven octave rhyming alternately ; but this is followed by a ninth line, introducing a new rhyme, and to this succeeds three hemistichs rhyming only with each other, the stanza being concluded with a half hemistich rhyming with the ninth line. But the most notable feature of the poem is the device of iteration ; the ninth line generally beginning with the repetition

---

[1] 'Bare was her body, and black to the bone, all clagged with clay and uncomelyly clad. It cursed, it lamented like a woman, so that it had a covering for neither head nor hair. It halted, it was astonished, it stood as a stone. It was demented, it moaned, it mused as if mad. Unto that grisly ghost Sir Gawayne is gone. He went to it with a rush, for he was never afraid, for afraid was he never, now who that reads right (believe me). On the upper part of the jaw a toad pecked on her head ; her eyes were sunken full hollow, glowing as burning coal.'

of the last half of the eighth in a kind of inverted
order, while the one stanza is connected with its
successor by the transference to it of the last line.
Thus the stanza following the one quoted begins :—

> ' Alle glowede als gledis the gaste whare scho glydis.'

The *Awntyrs* furnishes the chief extant example
of the persistent use of this device. Gradually, however, the author lost patience, as he well might, and
in the latter portion of the poem it occurs only
intermittently.

Sir Gawain and the Green Knight, whether by
Huchown or another, West Midland or Northern,
poet, is, if a more poetical, metrically
a less elaborate, achievement than *The
Awntyrs.* It consists of non-rhyming alliterative
lines separated, as the exigencies of the situation
suggest, by a rhyming bobwheel, of which the wheel
of one accent continues the previous line, the four
following hemistichs rhyming alternately. Here is
an example of the bobwheel :—

Metre of 'Sir Gawain.'

> ' A hundreth of hunters ; as I haf herde telle
> > Of the best
> > To trysteis vewters zod : [1]
> > Couples huntes ofkest,
> > Ther ros for blastez gode
> > Gret rurd in that forest.'

Certain romances, as *Sir Gray-Steel,* and *Roswall*

---

[1] 'To the stations the keepers went ; the huntsmen cast off the
couples ; by good blasts [of the horn] a great noise rose in the
forest.'

and Lillian, both in the octo-syllabic metre, which were long popular in Scotland, exist only in modernised languages, and may be of English origin. There are also Scoto-English translations of Other Romances. French romances, as *Lancelot of the Lak*,[1] and part of the *Romaunt of the Rose*; but of the translators nothing is known.

[1] Maitland Club, ed. Madden, 1839, and Early English Text Society, ed. Skeat, 1865.

III

HISTORICAL POETRY

IT is with *The Bruce* of Barbour that Scottish
vernacular literature, as a distinctive national product, first begins to take shape. The old
national rounds and songs were, as we
have seen, very rude and simple, and all
but a few fragments of them have perished.
Then the ancient romance poetry was a general
product of the early Middle Ages, created by a
strange commingling of different races and civilities.
By the conditions of its birth it represented a merely
temporary phase of sentiment; it was concerned
mainly with a remote past, and towards the close of
the fourteenth century it began to lose its hold on
human interest. But *The Bruce*, by its very scope
and intent, is linked to generations yet unborn; it
portrays the triumph of a splendid struggle for
independent nationality—a struggle which, for good
or evil, was successful, and therefore enshrined for
ever in the nation's memory; and if not entitled to

*Scottish litera-
ture properly
begins with
Barbour's
'Bruce.'*

40

rank as a great national epic by virtue of qualities essentially poetic, it yet celebrates the daring and victorious career of a national hero in a manner not unworthy of the stirring theme.

Of John Barbour (1320 ?-1395), its author, scarce anything is known except what is official. The surname indicates that, like the Bruce, he was of Norman origin; and the family John Barbour (1320 ?-1395). may well have come to Scotland in the train of one of Bruce's ancestors. But neither of his parents, nor of the date or place of his birth, is there any record, the first mention of his name, 13th August 1357, being as Archdeacon of Aberdeen. To his very special accomplishments the varied allusions in his poem *The Bruce* bear testimony; and the zeal with which he cultivated his scholarly tastes is shown by safe-conducts granted him during several successive years to go both to Oxford and to France for purposes of study. In 1372 he became clerk of audit of the king's household, and he also during various years acted as auditor of the Exchequer. He finished *The Bruce* in 1375. That he was high in favour with the king is proved by a gift to him, 14th March 1377-78, of ten pounds; by a grant, 29th August 1378, of an annual pension of twenty shillings to 'our beloved clerk,' and his heirs and assigns for ever; by a gift in 1380-81 of a ward of a minor; and by a grant, 5th December 1388, of a yearly pension of ten pounds—'pro suo fideli servicio nobis impenso.' He died 13th March 1395.

Besides *The Bruce,* Barbour, according to Wyntoun, was the author of two poems now lost—*The Brut*

Works attributed to Barbour. and *The Stewartis Oryginalle.* Certain fragments also of a translation of *The Siege of Troy* are attributed to him by the fifteenth - century transcriber of the MS. in Cambridge University Library; but it has been argued from internal evidence that they could not have been written by Barbour. He has further been credited, but on insufficient evidence, with the authorship of the *Legends of the Saints,* which have been published, from the MS. in the University Library, Cambridge, by Horstmann at Heilbronn, 1881-82, and by the Scottish Text Society, ed. Metcalfe, 1887-1896. The literary interest of these *Legends* is but slight, and they present no features calling for special comment.

The Bruce[1] is the main Scottish authority for the events it records, John of Fordun not having com-

'The Bruce,' a poetic narrative. How far is it trustworthy? pleted his Latin Chronicle further than the death of David I. (1153), and Wyntoun—in view of Barbour's *Bruce*—resolving to 'lightly overpass the story of these years.' How far *The Bruce* is accurate history

---

[1] Printed first at Edinburgh in 1571; reprinted by Hart at Edinburgh in 1616, and more or less erroneously, at different succeeding dates, from Hart's edition; edited by Pinkerton, 1790, from a MS. in the Advocates' Library, Edinburgh, written by John Ramsay in 1489; by Jamieson, 1820, from the same MS.; by Innes for the Spalding Club, 1856, from the collation of this MS. with another in St. John's College, Cambridge, written also by John Ramsay in 1487; by Skeat for the English Text Society, 1870, from a collation of these MSS. with Hart's edition; and by the same editor for the Scottish Text Society, 1894.

it would be rash to assert. It was written six-and-
forty years after the death of its hero; and although
for some of the incidents Barbour had the vouchers
of eye-witnesses, he no doubt got many of his stories
from tradition or from second-hand testimony. But
in many details he is corroborated even by English
chroniclers; and Scottish State documents, so far as
they are available, on the whole substantiate his
declaration that to the best of his wit his aim
was—

> 'To put in wryt a suthfast story.'   true

Still, *The Bruce* is intended to be a poetic narrative,
not a mere prose narrative in metre. Something
must be allowed for imaginative embellishment even
of what is 'suthfast,' for the artistic need to fill in
vague outlines with effective colouring, and to round
off a story with adequate impressiveness. Since,
moreover, the theme was essentially patriotic, facts
were bound to be more or less distorted by prejudice
or enthusiasm, especially when dealt with poetically;
for even your modern war correspondent, how un-
poetical soe'er he be, can scarce resist the craving
to fight, if only in description, on his country's
side. But Sir Herbert Maxwell's insinuation[1]
that Barbour, contrary to his strong professions
of regard for 'suthfastness,' may have suppressed
or modified the truth from mere sordid motives,
can scarce be given heed to on mere conjecture.
Such an hypothesis seems, in fact, superfluous.

[1] *Robert the Bruce*, p. 8.

Bruce was the object of the nation's wild idolatry; and Barbour, sharing in that idolatry, depicted him *con amore* from the standpoint of national adoration. Neither the grant, nor the hope, of a royal dole, a thousand times greater than the pittance he received—but as matter of fact he was not in the receipt of a royal bounty while writing *The Bruce*—could have so well inspired him to glorify Bruce as the ambition to do honour to a national hero, and so to celebrate his deeds that they should 'last aye furth in memory.'

In *The Bruce*, as we now have it, there is, however, one glaring error. Bruce at the beginning of the romance proper is referred to as 'The Bruce I spak of ayr.' Now the Bruce spoken of in the introduction was not the patriot, but his grandfather; and it has therefore been assumed that Barbour had recourse to the extraordinary device of confounding the deliverer of Scotland with his grandfather, in order to put King Edward outrageously in the wrong, and further because—as Cosmo Innes expresses it in the introduction to his edition of *The Bruce*—his hero was 'not to be degraded by announcing that he had sworn fealty to Edward, and once done homage to Baliol, or even joined any party but that of his country and freedom.' No doubt this is a most plausible explanation, but is it the only possible one? And unless it be the only possible one, ought Barbour to be lightly credited with so glaring and deliberate,

Curious genealogical error in 'The Bruce.'

and at the same time so foolish and vain, a falsehood ?
Is there not at least the faint chance that Barbour
may have made an accidental slip, or that the error
was the work of some copyist ? This last alternative
obtains some corroboration from the fact that in the
portion of *The Bruce* preserved by Wyntoun, instead
of the lines—

> 'This lord the Brwss, I spak of ayr,
> Saw all the Kynryk swa forfayre,'

before
kingdom so
forlorn

we have—

> 'Quhen all this sawe the Brwss Robert
> That bare the crowne soone efftirwart.'

And even if Wyntoun has merely altered his copy
of Barbour, the fact that Wyntoun has not, at least,
accepted the accidental or intended fiction, indicates
that there was no general desire among the Scots to
bolster up either their cause or that of Bruce by such
a stupid artifice. Further, Barbour had no need to
have recourse to it, for his theme did not include the
years in Bruce's life when, perhaps, his patriotism was
stifled by his rivalry with Baliol; and to have introduced him simply as the grandson of him he 'spak
of ayr' would equally well have suited his purpose.
Lastly—and this seems conclusive,—if Barbour did
wilfully falsify facts, how could he have set himself
to expose his own falsification by compiling the
genealogy of the Stewarts, ending with Robert II. of
Scotland ?

But here we are less concerned with the historic trustworthiness of *The Bruce* than with its merits as

Barbour's aim in 'The Bruce.'

literature. Written in the octo-syllabic couplet, it extends to about 12,500 lines, and thus in mere bulk is a considerable achievement. Its aim, according to its author, is to tell the story of Robert the Bruce and his companion in arms, the good Sir James of Douglas :—

strong   'That in thar tyme war wycht and wyss,
             And led thar lyff in gret trawail,
tumult   And oft in hard stour off bataill
             Wan richt gret price off chewalry,
void of   And war woydyt off cowardy.'
cowardice

Rightly to appraise it as a literary achievement, we must take into account that it was an original

'The Bruce' an original venture in literature.

venture in literature—the first poetical effort in Scotland to break away from the wonders of the old romances. Like the greater Chaucer, Barbour had no poetic predecessor worthy of the name. Though Chaucer was his contemporary, he was in no way Chaucer's disciple; and indeed *The Bruce* was written before the bulk of Chaucer's best work. Barbour is virtually the father of Scottish literature, just as Chaucer is the father of English literature; but with the proviso that he is not in the same plane of greatness with Chaucer, who further was regarded as their master by certain later Scottish poets.

Barbour's language is that current in the lowland Scotland of his time, as well as in northern England.

As for the octo-syllabic couplet—afterwards a favourite measure of Scottish poets for chronicles and tales —we have no evidence regarding its previous use in Scotland. It was common in French verse, and was used by Mannyng, and also by Chaucer. Several examples also exist in earlier English poems; but in these the rhythm is looser and more uneven than that of Barbour, who, for his time, is a most correct, if not remarkably musical, metrist.

Barbour's language and metre.

The poem relates the thrilling tale of Bruce and his comrades as champions of Scottish freedom: their distresses, jeopardies, toils, hairbreadth escapes, subtle stratagems, heroic combats, until, from being a houseless wanderer in the mountains of Galloway, Bruce becomes the victor of Bannockburn, and the immutable sovereign of a nation emancipated by his prowess. Necessarily, the interest of the story culminates with Bannockburn; but though the narrative of the Irish and other wars is poetically an anti-climax, than the final incidents in Bruce's life no better close is conceivable: his resolve that since he had been unable—by reason of his stern struggle for his crown and for Scottish freedom—to fulfil an early vow to embark in the Crusades, his heart should be borne on 'goddis fayis' by that one whom his lords should deem most worthy. That the Douglas should be chosen; that the Douglas should die in the act of performing his great leader's behest; and that the bones of Douglas

The story of the poem.

and the heart of Bruce, rescued from the Infidel, should be brought back to mingle with the dust of the fatherland, to whom both had rendered such imperishable service, is also, we discern, a consummation uniquely blessed.   Whether or not Barbour's portrait of Bruce harmonises with actual fact in all its details, matters, on the whole, comparatively little.   One who so strove and achieved, and nobly vowed and finely bequeathed, was — whatever the inconsistencies of his earlier years—one of the elect among heroes.

For a Scottish poet there could be no more excellent theme than Barbour's; and in intent and purpose, at least, his treatment is not inadequate.   His tact is subtly perfect, his tone and temper beyond all praise. Naturally and inevitably he exaggerates the exploits of Bruce and his fellow-champions; but the exaggeration, though in some instances gross—especially as regards the numeration of their foes—is on the whole that of the artist, not that of the empty braggart or foolish fanatic.   Neither does he fall into the artistic blunder of reviling or belittling the enemies of Bruce.   On the contrary, Sir Edward Caernarvon is commended as one of the 'starkest' men to be found in 'any country'; Sir Aymer de Valence is described as 'wyss and wycht,' and by virtue of his own nobility and bravery, sincerely appreciative of the feats of Bruce; Sir Ingram de Umfraville was, we are told, renowned for his 'high prowess'; Sir Henry de

Barbour's treatment of his theme.

Bohun, the champion whom Bruce vanquished and slew in sight of the two armies at Bannockburn, was the 'worthy' Sir Henry

> 'That was ane gud knight and hardy';

King Edward's host at Bannockburn, its 'multitude' and 'beauty,' is exhibited to us in all its formidable magnificence; and the heroic death of Sir Giles de Argentine—who, when he saw King Edward preparing for flight, bade him 'gud day,' and turning his bridle, rode single-handed on the foe—is recorded with sympathetic sorrow: 'Of his ded was great pittye.' King Edward had, of course, in Barbour's view, a bad cause; he fought for 'might' only, Bruce and the Scots for their lives, their children and wives, and the freedom of their land; but Englishmen and Scots alike met foemen worthy of their steel, and both with kindred ardour devoted themselves nobly to 'do chivalry.'

But *The Bruce* is not a mere record of adventures and combats: as a political master-piece it occupies an exceptional place in literature; and much of its effect is gained by the vein of noble sentiment that animates it. The keynote is struck by the famous eulogy of freedom, beginning :—

'The Bruce' a political masterpiece. Its lofty idealism.

> 'A! fredome is a noble thing !
> Fredome mayss man to haiff liking ;
> Fredome all solace to man giffis,
> He levys at ess that frely levys !
> A noble hart may haiff nane ess,
> Na ellys nocht that may him pless,

makes pleasure

Nothing else

D

> Gyff fredome failzhe ; for fre liking
> Is zharnyt our all othir thing.
> Na he, that ay hass levyt fre,
> May nocht knaw weill the propyrte,
> The angyr, na the wrechyt dome,
> That is cowplit to foule thryldome.'

yearned for above

nor

And the same lofty idealism pervades the whole poem. Here, for example, is an excellent commendation of loyalty :—

> 'Leavte to luff is gretumly ;
> Throuch leavte liffis men rycht wisly ;
> With a wertu of leavte
> A man may zeit sufficyand be :
> And but leawte may nane haiff price,
> Quhethir he be wycht or he be wyss ;
> For quhar it failzeys, na wertu
> May be off price, na off valu,
> To mak a man sa gud, that he
> May symply gud man callyt be.'

Loyalty

without
strong

Then the efficacy of love is thus persuasively set forth :—

> 'For luff is off so mekill mycht
> That it all paynys makes lycht ;
> And mony tymis maiss tendir wychtis
> Of swilk strength and swilk mychtis,
> That thai may mekill paynys endure
> And forsakis nane aventure.'

great

fellows
such
many

And apropos of love, here is a naively excellent couplet on the service of women :—

> 'In wemen mekill comfort lyis
> And gret solace in mony wiss.'

much
ways

Again, the value of fearless decision is thus admirably presented :—

> 'For gude begynning and hardy,
> And it be followit vittily,

It

> May ger oftsiss onlikely thing   *make oft-*
> Cum to right fair and just endying.'   *times*

And, to conclude these quotations, from a glowing eulogy of 'vorschip' (*i.e.* valour), here is a most happy definition of the thing itself :—

> ' For hardyment with foly is wice   *vice*
> Bot hardyment, that mellit is   *mingled*
> With vit, is vorschip ay, per de :   *wit ; valour*
> For but vit, vorschip may not be.'

Thus though *The Bruce* is primarily a patriotic epic, it at the same time presents us with a living picture of chivalry more vivid, through *Chivalric spirit* its generous patriotism, than that of *of 'The Bruce.'* *Barbour the* Froissart. It glows with the true *precursor of* *Sir Walter* chivalric spirit of romance and adven- *Scott.* ture, not summoned, as in the case of most poets, from the mere imaginative past, but inspired by sympathetic regard for actual warriors, scarce a generation removed from that of the writer, and by the very moral atmosphere of a time identical in sentiment with theirs. Thus it is that Barbour is the main poetic progenitor of Sir Walter Scott. Scott 'kindled at his flame'; indeed, without Barbour's flame to kindle at, he might never have written his poetic romances, and he would certainly not have written them as we now have them. He was content to model himself in a great measure after the poet of *The Bruce*, or, in other terms, Barbour is a primæval, a half-articulate Scott. Barbour's vocabulary is somewhat stinted and monotonous, his artistic elaboration rude and incomplete, his intellectual standpoint very primitive, but in outline, in embryo, he has all the qualities of an artist intrinsically akin to Scott; and as regards romantic poetic narrative, he is, allowance being made for his so different circumstances, not so greatly inferior to his successor.

The great merits of *The Bruce* are its absolute clearness, its masterly selection of facts and details, its cunning regard for the picturesque, and its graphic compression. Notwithstanding his inevitable tendency to exaggerate the exploits of the Scottish heroes, Barbour particularly excels in the description of adventures and combats; and here especially Sir Walter wisely placed himself under his tutelage, for Barbour was theoretically a master in the art of war as practised by the ancients, and had listened to the recital of knightly feats by the tongues of famous warriors.

Literary merits of 'The Bruce.'

Here is part of a fight in which 'the King slew the three men that swore his death':—

Barbour as a depicter of combats.

    ' Thai abaid till that he was
      Entryt in ane narow place,
      Betuix a louchside and a bra ;
      That wes sa strait, ik wnderta,
      That he mycht nocht weill turn his stede.
      Then with a will till him thai gede ;
      And ane him by the bridill hynt :
      But he raucht till him sic a dynt,
      That arme and schuldyr flaw him fra.
      With that ane othir gan him ta

hill

on each side

to; went
seized
reached to
him; blow

take

> Be the lege, and his hand gan schute
> Betuix the sterap and his fute :
> And quhen the King felt thar his hand,
> In sterapys stythly gan he stand,   straight up
> And strak with spuris the stede in by ;
> And he lansyt furth delyuerly,
> Swa that the tother failzeit fete ;
> And nocht-for-thi his hand was zeit   nevertheless
> Wndyr the sterap, magre his.'

As to the sequel, it must suffice to state that
though the third combatant suddenly leapt on
Bruce's horse from behind, Bruce was equal to the
occasion, turning instantly round, dragging him
forward and killing him, and then sending the
reeking sword into the 'felon foe' at his stirrup.

Wonderfully vivid are also the descriptions of the
various fights and stratagems of Bruce
while pursued in the mountains by a   At the ford.
'sleuth-hund,' especially his adventures during a
moonlight night, when, watching alone, he heard

> 'A hundis quhistlyng apon fer,
> That ay com till him ner and ner,'   to

which was followed by the 'haill rowt' of his foes,
whom he resolved to withstand at the pass of the
ford, where they could meet him only one by one;
and, according to Barbour, he withstood them with
such success that :—

> 'In litill space he left lyand
> Sa feill, that the vpcom wes then   so many
> Dittit with slayn hors and men ;   closed up
> Swa that his fayis, for that stopping,
> Micht nocht cum to the vp-cummyng.'

But of course the classic combat is that of Bruce on his grey palfrey, 'littil and joly,' against the English champion De Bohun on his war-steed—'the first strak of the ficht' at Bannockburn. Indeed, the whole portrayal (Books XI. and XII.) of the eventful Bannockburn is, after its own fashion, a masterpiece. It could only have been accomplished after the most careful investigation and the most patient pondering of facts; and the knowledge—which clearly forms the substratum of the description—is so admirably animated with patriotic prejudice, with ingenuous admiration of every thought and act of Bruce as the one heaven-born commander, and with an unerring sense of the dramatically appropriate—whether the incidents of the drama be invented or embellished, or merely selected,—as to be almost irresistible in compelling sympathetic belief. The whole panorama of incident from the time that King Edward with his mighty host—their burnished arms glancing in the sun, so that 'all the felde ves in ane leyme,' and their 'baneris richt freschly flawmand '—took his way from Berwick, until

Barbour as the poet of Bannockburn.

> ' That he with sevintene in a bat
>   Wes fayne for to hald hame his gat,'

is set before us with full circumstantiality of detail, enlivened with apt and frequent anecdote. We realise the scenes with something of the vividness of actual pageantry and battle; we are made to

share in the uncertainties and fears, the resolves and
hopes, and final triumph of the Scots; so that in
truth Bannockburn, as described by Barbour, has
done more to perpetuate the sentiment of Scottish
nationality than even Bannockburn as fought and
won by Bruce.

But properly to appreciate Bannockburn as an
achievement of Barbour's hero, it is necessary to
know the 'nobill king'—his hardihood, Barbour's por-
audacity, hopefulness, courtesy, supreme traits.
wisdom in council, and unmatched prowess in arms
—as portrayed with such adoring skill throughout
the whole poem.   All Barbour's heroes are, in truth,
admirably drawn—drawn, it is evident, from the life,
that is, from well-verified tradition, and with an
appreciation at once intelligent and sincere.   Generally we have no formal portrait; but here, in conclusion, is one of the Black Douglas:—

> 'He wes in all his dedis lele ;   loyal
> For him dedeynzeit nocht to dele   he deigned
> With trechery, na with falset.   falsehood
> His hart on hey honour wes set ;
> And hym contenyt on sic maner,   he demeaned
> That all him luffyt that war him ner.   him ; such
> Bot he wes nocht sa fayr, that we
> Suld spek gretly off his beaute :
> In wysage wes he sumdeill gray,   something
> And had blak har, as ic hard say ;
> Bot off lymmys he wes weill maid,
> With banys gret and schuldrys braid.
> His body wes weyll maid and lenye,
> As thai that saw him said to me.
> Quhen he wes blyth, he wes lufly,
> And meyk and sweyt in cumpany :

> But quha in battaill mycht him se
> All othir contenance had he.
> And in spek wlispit he sum deill ;
> Bot that sat him rycht wonder weill.'

Andrew of Wyntoun's *Orygynalle Chronykil of Scotland* [1] is, like *The Bruce* of Barbour, the pro-

Wyntoun's 'Chronicle'— its aim. duct of the exulting sense of nationality inspired by the permanent triumph of Robert the Bruce. It is indited to set forth the glory and honour of Scotland as an independent kingdom. But while the aim of Barbour is to quicken the sentiment of patriotism by a recital of the illustrious achievements of Scotland's deliverer, Wyntoun's main purpose—like that of his contemporary Latin chronicler, Fordun—is to justify the claims of Scotland to an independent nationality by an appeal to the authority of antiquity, by a recital of the history of the Scottish nation from the earliest dawn of tradition.

Of the author scarce anything is known beyond what may be gathered from his own *Chronicle*. By

Andrew of Wyntoun (fl. c. 1395-1424). baptism, he tells us, he was Andrew of Wyntoun, and this seems to imply that he was a cadet of a good family of that name, of which several are mentioned in Scottish documents of the period. Further, he mentions that Sir John of the Wemyss, at whose instance he compiled his *Chronicle*, had his 'service in his ward'; but he says nothing more of his obligations to the

---

[1] Published, ed. Macpherson, 1795 ; and in *The Historians of Scotland* series, ed. Laing, 1872-79, from the collation of numerous MSS.

laird of Wemyss. Originally a canon regular of St.
Andrews, Wyntoun was, by the grace and favour of
his fellow-canons, elected, some time before 1395,
prior of St. Serf's Inch in Lochleven, where—with
much the same outlook of water, wood, and hill as
that which, blent with the gloomy memories of a
prison, was to become stamped on the brain of Mary
Stuart—he continued to pass the uneventful days
of a scholar and recluse until probably his death.
This must have taken place not long after the conclusion of his *Chronicle*, between 1420 and 1424; for
in his prologue to the last book he refers to 'sudden
and fierce maladies' with which he was sorely troubled,
and which admonished to 'see for a conclusion,' for,
says he, with the conviction of pious humility—

> ' Wal I wate, on schorte delay　　　　Well I wot
> At a court I mon appeire　　　　　　must
> Fell accusationis thare till here.'　　Dire; to

Like *The Bruce*, Wyntoun's *Chronicle* is written in
the octo-syllabic couplet, but it is in no proper sense
a poem. Even as a mere metrist Wyn-　Characteristics
toun is inferior to Barbour; nor is his　of the 'Chron-
narrative—except by widely isolated fits　icle.'
and starts—warmed with anything of Barbour's
patriotic glow. Rarely, except in reporting mythological marvels, does he show symptoms of enthusiasm; and on the whole he keeps very much to the
commonplace conventional level of contemporary
chroniclers. No more than they had he any just
and sufficient conception of history as it was later

understood.   His aim is neither faithfully to picture
nor thoroughly to expound the past, although he
intermittently relieves the tedium of the narrative
by a certain anecdotical garrulosity.   His most
marked want is that of individuality.   Thus his
character-sketches are often very much a mere
summary of conventional virtues, and smack mainly
of the funereal eulogy.   Here is how he panegyrises
Alexander III. :—

charitable
To

> ' He honryd God and Haly Kirk,
>   And medful dedys he oyswd to wyrk.
>   Till all prestys he dyd reverens
>   And sawffyd thare statys wyth diligens.
>   He was stedfast in crystyn fay ;
>   Relygyows men he honoryde ay.
>   He luivyd all men that war wertuows ;
>   He lathyd and chastyd all vytyows.'

And the perfections of Sir Andrew Moray are cata-
logued thus :—

> ' He wes a Lord of gret Bowntè
>   Of sobyr lyf and of chastytè ;
>   Wyse and wertuows of cownsale ;
>   And of his gudis liberale.
>   He wes of gret Devotyown
>   In Prayeris and in Orysown ;
>   He wes of mekil Almows-dede ;
>   Stowt and hardy of manhede.'

The standpoint of Wyntoun is in fact essentially
that of a Churchman and recluse.   The animating

Wyntoun's
standpoint
that of a
Churchman.

events of the past, the glorious achievements of great warriors, the stir and
struggle of battle, have not for him quite
the same   puissant   charm   that   they   possess   for

Barbour. Though he does not disdain to mention jousting tournaments—everything is fish that comes to his net—chivalry was not for him, as for Barbour, a name to conjure with. In his antipathy to the English he is therefore something more virulent. While Barbour expresses mild astonishment that King Edward, who had so little mercy on captured Scots, could 'trastly' ask mercy of God, Wyntoun does not scruple to give his decisive ghostly verdict against Edward's salvation :—

> 'The sawlys that he gert to slay down thare   made
> He sent quhare his sawle nevyrmare
> Wes lyk to come, that is the blys
> Quhare alkyn joy ay lestand is.'   every

And he thus roundly asserts the starkly unprincipled conduct of the English in regard to their most solemn obligations :—

> 'It is of Inglis natioune
> The commone kend conditioune   known
> Of Trewis the wertu to forget,   Truces
> And rekles of gud Faith to be.
> Quhare thai can thare Avantage se
> Thare may na Band be maid sa ferm
> Than thai can mak thare Will thare term.'

Wyntoun entitles his *Chronicle* ' orygynall ' because, as he himself explains, it begins at the beginning, namely, with mans creation, and with a   Subject and
history of man as an inhabitant of the   Sources of the
                                          'Chronicle.'
world in general, or so much of it as was
known to Wyntoun. In the adoption of such a
pedantic comprehensiveness, he and other chroniclers

were, it may be, partly influenced by scriptural example, but no doubt it was also Wyntoun's aim to emphasise the dignity of the Scottish nation as possessing annals which were interwoven with the world's history. After a general outline of the more wondrous events of the half-mythical ages, Scotland is seen gradually emerging from the obscurity of the past; but not till the reign of King Ewan in 724— commencing with the sixth book of the *Chronicle* —is its history related with much detail. For all his events Wyntoun is careful, so far as possible, to give the year; and while well acquainted with the standard authorities on ecclesiastical and European history, he had clearly access to various Scottish monastic records which are now destroyed. Several portions of a Latin chronicle were also utilised; and he further incorporated a Scottish chronicle, written, like his own, in octo-syllabic metre, and embracing the years from the birth of David II. to the death of Robert II. Besides this he took the liberty of borrowing some 300 lines of Barbour's *Bruce*, bringing events down to the time when Bruce slew the Comyn; but for the remainder of Bruce's career he modestly refers the reader to Barbour, who, he says,

made
> 'In Brws hys Bwk has gert be sene
> Mare wysely tretyd into wryt
> Than I can thynk with all my wyt.'

It is clear that Wyntoun was, according to his lights, a conscientious and painstaking chronicler;

and even the credulity which he shares with other writers of his time gives a certain piquant flavour to much that is otherwise tedious, and increases rather than not the historic value of his rhymes, for it at least sup- plies us with interesting outlines of superstitious belief. Who, for example, would wish to lose his version of the wondrous story of the Sheepstealer, and the striking exposure of his prevarication by the dead beast itself? The thief, it would appear, had already devoured it, or the most part of it, and with portions of its members in the process of digestion was so brazenly bold as, when summoned before St. Serf, to deny the theft, whereupon

Wyntoun's credulity—the Sheepstealer.

   'The schape thare bletyd in hys Wame.   Belly
    Swa wes he taynted schamfully
    And at Saynt Serf askyd mercy.'

Then we have the great theological tilt between St. Serf and the Devil, recorded with the delicate appraisement of metaphysical niceties which stamps the scholastic connoisseur. Wyntoun had also, it is plain, a special pride in recording this august encounter, from the fact that it took place on the very 'Inch' where he was penning his *Chronicle*. So mortified, he vauntingly narrates, was the arch-enemy by the superior astuteness of the Saint, that in disgust he suddenly vanished,

St. Serf and the Devil.

   ' And nevyr wes sen thare till this day.'

Akin to this we have an elaborate version of Pope
Sylvester's infatuated treaty with the Devil, whose
spiritual dominion he finally eluded by
delivering up to him, one by one, his
fleshly members.

Pope Sylvester.

But the most interesting of all the traditions is the
original version of the interview between Macbeth
and the weird sisters, which, as embellished by Boece, forms the basis of
Shakespeare's great tragedy :—

The Weird
Sisters.

'A nycht he thowcht in hys dreming
That sittand he was besyd the King
At a sete in hwntyng, swa
In-till a leysh had grewhundys twa.
He thowcht quhile he was swa sittand
He sawe thre wemen by gangand,
And thai wemen than thowcht he
Thre werd systrys mast lyk to be.
The fyrst he hard say gangand by,
"Lo yhondyr the Thayne off Crwombawchty" !
The tothir woman sayd agayne,
"Off Morave yhondyre I se the Thayne."
The thryd than sayd, "I se the Kyng."
All this he herd in his dremyng.
Sone efftyre that in his yhowthad
Off thyr thayndomys he Thayne was made ;
Syne neyst he thowcht to be Kyng
Fra Duncanys dayis had tane endyng.'

going
those

Cromarty

Historically the most valuable part of the *Chronicle*
is that from the death of Bruce ; and for these eighty
or ninety years it is the most important and trustworthy record we possess.

Although *The Actes and Deidis of the Illustre and*

Vallzeant Campioun Schir William Wallace, by Henry the Minstrel,[1] belongs to a considerably later date than Barbour's *Bruce,* or Wyntoun's Blind Harry's *Chronicle,* its historic theme suggests the 'Wallace.' propriety of dealing with it in the present chapter.

According to the historian John Major, Henry the Minstrel, who was blind, Major says, from his birth, composed the whole book of William Blind Harry, Wallace during Major's infancy, that is, or Henry the Minstrel (fl. c. between 1470 and 1480. In the Lord 1450-1492). High Treasurer's *Accounts* there are several entries of small sums paid to 'Blin Hary' for recitations given before James IV., the last entry being in 1492 ; and it is almost certain that he died in that or the following year, for in Dunbar's *Lament for the Makaris* his name precedes that of Patrick Johnstoun, who died not long after 12th June 1494. In his catalogue of the deceased 'Makaris,' Dunbar does not adhere to chronology with absolute strictness in every case, but he seems to profess an adherence to it in the stanza in which Blind Harry and Patrick Johnstoun are introduced, and apparently means to affirm that the 'schot of mortal haill' reached Johnstoun after it had struck Blind Harry and Sandy Traill.

---

[1] MS. in the Advocates' Library, written in 1488 by John Ramsay; printed about 1508 (but only fragments of a copy of this edition exist), 1570 (copy in the British Museum), 1594, and at different periods down to 1790; edited from the original MS. by Dr. Jamieson, 1820, and by Mr. James Moir for the Scottish Text Society, 1884-89.

Both Blind Harry and his poem are something of a conundrum. Harry was professionally a minstrel, and his chief theme seems to have been Wallace; for Major informs us that by the recitation of his book on Wallace *coram principis* (*i.e.* in the halls of the nobles or gentry) he deservedly obtained food and raiment. Of himself Blind Harry says: 'It is well known I am a burel' (*i.e.* boorish, or unlearned) 'man'; he also describes his poem as 'but a rurall' (*i.e.* rude or unpolished) 'dytt'; and he further thus apostrophises it :—

Major on Blind Harry the Minstrel, and Blind Harry on himself.

> ' Go nobill buk, fulfillyt off gud sentens,
>   Suppose thow be baran off eloquens ;
>   Go worthie buk fullfillyt off suthfast dede,
>   But in language off help thou has gret ned.' [1]

true exploits

This, it may be said, is but the conventional pose of graceful modesty; and in a modern writer it might even be accepted as symptomatic of the modesty which is the blossom of culture. Moreover, the merits of the poem are not quite those of the modern rustic bard; and in his own time Harry may be ranked next to Henryson. As a mere metrical achievement the poem is a great advance on Barbour's *Bruce*; and although Harry is not usually classed as a Chaucerian, there can be no doubt that he shared, directly or indi-

Harry as Chaucerian.

[1] In this envoy Blind Harry was doubtless inspired either by Chaucer (*Troilus and Criseyde*), Lydgate (*Temple of Glas*), or James I. (*The Kingis Quair*). It most closely resembles the last :—

> ' Go litill tretise, nakit of eloquence
>   Causing simplese and pouertee to wit.'

rectly, in the Chaucerian influence. It is significant, not merely that for the bulk of his poem he chose the heroic couplet—possibly the earliest extant example of its use in Scotland,—but that in the two instances in which he varied his metre he made choice of Chaucerian staves, introducing in Book II. 170-354 a nine-line stanza, aab, aab, abb (occasionally bab), identical with that of Chaucer's *Compleynte of Faire Anelida upon False Arcyte* and with Dunbar's *Goldyn Targe,* and at the beginning of Book VI. the ballat royal or French octave of three rhymes— ab, ab, bc, bc—in its five accented form. Of course Harry may have got these metres from another than Chaucer, and indeed the ballat royal was in common use in England from the fourteenth century,[1] but Chaucer, we know, wrote to be publicly 'red,' or 'elles songe,' and it is not improbable that he was recited, if not by Harry, at least in Harry's hearing. Anyhow, Harry employs the ballat royal in such a manner as to show that he had an admirable perception of its proper poetic function. Here, for example, are two stanzas forming part of a nobly pathetic strain, not unworthy of either Henryson or Dunbar:—

'Now leiff thi myrth, now leiff thi haill plesance ;
   Now leiff thi bliss, now leiff thi childis age ;
Now leiff thi zouth, now folow thi hard chance ;
   Now leiff thi lust, now leiff thi mariage ;
   Now leiff thi luff, for thow sall loss a gage
Quhilk neuir in erd sall be redemyt agayne,
   Folow fortoun, and all hir fers owtrage ;
Go leiff in wer, go leiff in cruell payne.

whole

Which; earth

---

[1] Wright's *Political Poems, passim.*

E

> Fy on fortoun, fy on thi frewall quheyll ; [1]
>   Fy on thi traist, for her it has no lest ;
> Thow transfigowryt Wallace out off his weill
>   Quhen he traistyt for till haiff lestyt best ;
>   His plesance her till him was bot a gest
> Throw thi fers cours, that has na hap to ho ;
>   Him thow ourthrew out off his likand rest,
> Fra gret plesance, in wer, trawaill, and wo.'

frail

to
here
no constancy
pleasant
into

Harry's classical allusions, astronomical lore, and use of French words and phrases have also been adduced as proof that ' he was by no means an unlearned man.' Further, since he affirms that he composed his poem

The argument for Harry's learning.

> ' Eftir the pruiff geyffin fra the Latin buk
>   Quilk master Blayr in his tym vndertuk,'

Which

it has been supposed that he had Latin sufficient to enable him to paraphrase a Latin *Life* of Wallace, now unknown, written by a person, now equally occult—a certain John Blair, whom Harry declares to have been Wallace's chaplain. Moreover, the composition of so long, so complicated, and, after its own fashion, so meritorious a poem, has been pronounced beyond the powers of one born blind; for in the days of Harry the blind were not taught the art of reading, which forms the basis of education.

But notwithstanding this accumulative array of specious argument, the hypothesis that best fits the whole circumstances of the case is that Harry—otherwise nameless except as ' Blind'—was, as Major states, blind from

Harry most probably blind and unlearned.

---

[1] The wheel of Fortune is frequently alluded to by Chaucer, and is elaborately depicted in *The Kingis Quair.*

his birth, and, as he himself records, a 'burel' or
unlearned man. Of course, he neither could have
been blind nor unlearned if he did himself read or
translate Blair's Latin *Life* of Wallace. But so far
from affirming that he had either seen or read the
aforesaid book, Harry does not even affirm that it
then existed; and if he does not actually imply that
it no longer existed, he refrains from stating where,
or from whom, he had access to it. Further, nothing
whatever is now known of this Latin *Life*; for the
so-called *Relationes Arnoldi Blair*, even if authentic
and the original of the *Scotichronicon* account of
Wallace, instead of being derived from it, supply but
the slightest materials for an account of Wallace.
Nor was the existence of Blair's book known to
Major, who gives only partial credit to Harry's stories;
nor to Wyntoun, who wrote of Wallace :—

> ' Off his gud dedis and manhead
> Gret gestis I hard say are made,
> But sa mony, I trow nocht
> As he intill his dayis wrocht' ;

not
during his
lifetime

nor, in fact, to any writer—except Harry—previous to
the inventious Dempster (1627), who, further, does
not scruple to assign to Blair an admirably selected
companion volume, *De Tyrannide*. The truth, therefore, seems to be that Harry's main sources were the
'gestis' mentioned by Wyntoun; nor is it at all
unlikely that the mythical Latin *Life* was the invention of one of those earlier bards.

But if Harry knew not Latin, whence, it may be

asked, those classical allusions of his? To this the sufficient reply is that there are allusions and allu-

Harry's education as Minstrel.

sions, and that those of Harry are in no degree identical in kind with those of Barbour, or Wyntoun, or other learned writers, but merely the common counters of the romancists. Nor as a symptom of education is more stress to be laid on his employment of French terms not now in use in Scotland, for, as we have already seen, the Scottish vernacular, even in its spoken form, has now lost many French words and idioms which at one time had been almost woven into the language; and besides, Harry, while frequenting courts and castles, had many opportunities of picking up French phrases. The truth is, that though uneducated, as we now understand the term, Harry, as a professional minstrel, must have undergone a special literary training. We must disabuse our minds of precon-ceptions of education as solely derivable from books; for Harry and his brother minstrels and reciters were to their generation very much what the printed book is to ours. Born blind, Harry, in all likelihood, was dedicated to the office of minstrel from boyhood, and instructed for it by accomplished minstrels. Like other minstrels, he would presumably learn by heart much of the traditional and current poetry of his day; for originally poetry was composed solely for recital, nor did the art of writing ever become so complete a substitute for recital as the art of printing.

But, of course, being but a minstrel, Harry has the special defects of the minstrel's qualities. Compare the *Wallace*, for example, with Barbour's *Bruce* or Henryson's *Fables*, and the general inferiority of calibre proclaims Harry to have been but a 'burel' man. An accomplished minstrel, it is true—though representing minstrelsy in its decadence, minstrelsy divorced from chivalry,—and saturated with various poetic influences and traditions; also, it is clear, of robust personality, and animated with much rough poetic ardour, but devoid of true intellectual discipline as of consistent moral dignity; wofully, if not wilfully, heedless of patent historic facts; childishly credulous, and combining with a certain rugged pathos a braggardism that is frankly, and even fervently, brutal.

(margin: Harry only a Minstrel.)

The Wallace of Blind Harry is, in truth, the mere hero of a pantomime. Witness, for example, his really burlesque encounter with Percy and his horsemen at the Water of Irvine, when he was engaged in fishing, and had no other weapon at hand than the pole of a drag-net. On one of the horsemen approaching him with drawn sword, to compel him to give up his fish,

(margin: Harry's hero, Wallace.)

> ' Willzham was wa he had na wappynis thar   *sorry*
> Bot the poutstaff, the quhilk in hand he bar.   *netpole;*
>   *which*
> Wallas with it fast on the cheik him tuk
> Wyth so gud will, quhill of his feit he schuk.   *until*
> The suerd flaw fra him a fur breid on the land. *breadth*
> Wallas was glaid, and hynt it sone in hand ;   *took*
> And with the suerd awkwart he him gawe
> Wndyr the hat, his crage in sondre drawe.   *neck*

By ; the
others

if

That ; both
other

Be that the layff lychtyt about Wallas ;
He had no helpe, only bot Goddis grace.
On athir side full fast on him thai dange ;
Gret perell was giff thai had lestyt lang.
Apone the hede in gret ire he strak ane ;
The sherand suerd glaid to the colar bane.
Ane ither on the arme he hitt so hardely
Quhill hand and suerd bathe on the feld can ly.
The tither twa fled to thar hors agayne ;
He stekit him was last apon the playne.
Thre slew he thar, two fled with all thair mycht
Efter thar lord, bot he was out off sicht.'

And this is but a very mild sample of the hero's
' acts of prowess eminent.' As Harry says of him—

  ' It was his lyff, and most part of his fude,
    To se thaim sched the byrnand southrone blude.'

Or at least it was the 'lyff' and 'maist part of the
fude' of Harry so to depict him; for the poem is
really a mirror of Harry's Scottish audience, of Scotland after the age of chivalry had gone, and now for
generations at bitter feud with England.

Of course, poetic justice, and even probability,
demanded that such a resistless champion should,
whatever his final fate, taste, at least
once, the crowning triumph of bringing
Edward and England to their knees.
Harry, therefore, presented his hearers with the
mythical march on London—a twin conception to
that which must have haunted the brain of Prince
Charlie on the eve of his famous fiasco—when 'in
awful fer' Wallace and his wild host travelled
'throuch the land' of the Southron. The Commons

Wallace's
mythical
march on
London.

of England urged their mesmerised monarch to make
some effort against the resistless Scots, but, asseverates
the unblushing Harry,

> 'Awfull Eduuard durst nocht Wallace abid
> In playn battaill for all England so wid.'

The recreant English king—erstwhile *Malleus Scoto-
rum*—having thus in trembling terror retired within
the battlements of the Tower, Wallace, The terror of
shortly before reaching St. Albans, des- Edward.
patched a message to the effect that unless overtures
of peace were immediately proferred he would assail
him 'at Londonis zettis.' Naturally such a menace
greatly perturbed the 'awfull Eduuard':—

> 'With gret wness apon his feit he stud,   difficulty
> Wepand for wo for his der tendyr blud';

and at last he did accept the advice of his council 'to
take pees in tyme.'

But a new difficulty arose:—

> 'Na man was thar that durst to Wallace wend,'   The Queen
>   sent as
for the mere sight of an Englishman ambassador
'moyis him ay to wer.' But, happily, the to Wallace.
queen herself was already, so says Harry, a little
enamoured of the conqueror

> 'For the gret woice off his hie nobilnes';   fame

and having, therefore, a laudable curiosity to behold
the wondrous hero, she volunteered to be the
messenger. All the lords at once seconded her
proposal; and to stay the wrath of this terrible

Achilles the king had nothing for it but 'with awkward will' to give his consent.

One beautiful summer morning, therefore, when Wallace and two knightly attendants were sauntering near St. Albans 'atour the feyldis green,' they saw coming riding soberly from the south none other than the Queen of England with a great train of ladies and old priests, who when they reached Wallace's pavilion, conspicuous by the effigy of the Scottish lion,

Wallace and the Queen.

then

> 'To ground thai lycht, and syne on kneis can faw,
> Prayand for pece thai cry with petous cher.'

Wallace received the distressful queen with gracious courtesy :—

> 'Quhen scho him saw, scho wald haiff knelyt doune ;
> In armys sone he caucht this queyn with croun,
> And kyssyt hyr withoutyn wordis mor ;
> Sa dyd he neuir to na sotheron befor.'

But, of course, the incorruptible patriot was proof against her promises, her prayers, her bribes,

made ; for that purpose

> ('Thre thousand pound, off fynest gold so red,
> Scho gert be brocht to Wallace in that sted.
> "Madam," he said, "na sic tribut we craiff ;
> Anothir mendis we wald off England haiff"') ;

and even her soft confessions of love :—

reputed

> '"Wallace," scho said, "yhe war clepyt my luff :
> Mor baundounly I maid me for to pruff ;
> Traistand tharfor your rancour for to slak ;
> Methink ye suld do sum thing for my saik."'

Though much flattered, he warily and wisely declined

to enter into political understandings merely with
ladies : he would treat only with the King :—

> ' All the hail pass apon himselff he sal tak
> Off pees or wer quhat hapnyt we to mak.'

whole business

All, therefore, that was left for the queen was, on her
return, to advise the king and his lords

> ' To purches pees, with outyn wordis mar :
> For all Ingland may rew his raid full sayr.'

And Edward had nothing for it but to agree to the
terms dictated by Wallace—to give up Roxburgh,
Berwick, and other castles, and to renounce his claims
to a Scottish overlordship.

For much of the preposterousness of Harry's stories
—especially his amazing accounts of combats—his
blindness must be held responsible. He
could not recognise the sheer impossibility
of many of his glosses or inventions. Some
have indeed argued, from what is termed

Defects of the poem due partly to Harry's blindness.

his ' feeling for nature,' that he must at one time have
possessed the faculty of sight. But this ' feeling ' is
shown merely in his references to the influences of
the seasons, and to the charms of a spring or summer
morning—influences and charms to which the blind
are specially susceptible ; and indeed the very general
character of his recorded impressions of nature is
almost proof positive that he was born blind. His
descriptions of Wallace's wanderings display, for
example, no more detailed topographical knowledge
than is contained in a mere map of names.

Yet gross travesty of the truth though *Wallace* be, it no doubt embalms a considerable modicum of fact. The Wallace It even records important facts—such as of Harry, and the visit of Wallace to France—not to the Wallace of fact. be found in Wyntoun or Bower. The original 'gestis,' on which the poem is partly founded, must have had their foundation in actual occurrences, however much these occurrences may have been embellished, or even transformed, by successive minstrels; and although to 'tickle the ears of the groundlings' was ever Harry's main aim, we may nevertheless be certain that the leading features of so great a personality as Wallace would—so far as the common crowd could understand it—be preserved under all the external accumulation of fable. Nor, allowance being made for national partialities and prejudices, does Wallace, as portrayed by Harry, differ essentially from the robber chief, the freebooter, the murderer, the malicious incendiary, of the English chroniclers.   Clearly a hero who—even when there was no war with England—was only too pleased to take an Englishman at a disadvantage and assassinate him, and who, when closely pursued by sleuth-hounds, did not scruple to slay his companion, of whose fidelity he was nothing more than doubtful, and did so with probably, as Harry more than hints, a view of providing something that would prove a 'great stoppage' of the hounds,—clearly such a hero was not possessed of a specially scrupulous sense of honour, and may very well have been the 'le Wallas' who in his youth was guilty at Perth of robbing a widow of her ale. It is, in fact, more probable than not that Wallace was a warrior very much after the type of Rob Roy: that his audacity, his skill in arms, and his other great qualities as a leader were perfected in the course of his experiences as a freebooter. But this augments rather than diminishes the greatness and glory of his actual achievements. The bare, undisputed facts of his marvellous career—his rise from obscurity into unrivalled eminence, even when feudalism was at its strongest, as the marshaller of the nation against the might of England, and the stand he made in the name of the people as the champion of the country's freedom, when king and nobles were succumbing to Edward's diplomacy—sufficiently attest not merely his political insight, and his ability and prowess in war, but the stupendous power of his personality.

IV

THE SCOTTISH FABLIAU AND THE DECAY OF ROMANCE

' ANE BALLAT OF THE NINE NOBLES '—' RAUF COILZEAR '
— ' COLKELBIE'S SOW ' — ' KING BERDOK ' — ' THE
GYRE-CARLING '—' LORD FERGUS'S GHOST.'

THE great crucial struggle of Scotland with the
Edwards, which issued in its triumph over the
gigantic efforts of England to effect its
conquest, naturally tended to lessen the
interest of the people in the half-mythical stories of
the old romances. For the fables of the romancists
Barbour sought to substitute 'suthfast' stories about
Scotland's own heroes; and 'gret gestis' of the deeds
of Wallace were, as we have seen, current among the
people long before Blind Harry began, in that hero's
behalf, to make the round of the Scottish castles. A
curious example of the preference of the Scots for
their own heroes to the old traditional ones is found
in *Ane Ballat of the Nine Nobles*.[1] The ballad, after
devoting a stanza to each of the nine heroes of

The Nine Nobles.'

---

[1] Printed in Laing's *Select Remains*, 1822 (second ed. 1885), from a
MS. copy at the conclusion of a MS. copy of Fordun's *Chronicle* in
the University Library, Edinburgh.

antiquity—Hector, Alexander, Cæsar, Joshua, David, Maccabeus, Arthur, Charlemagne, and Godfrey—concludes thus:—

> ' Robert the Brois throu hard feichtyng,
>   With few venkust the mychthy Kyng   *vanquished*
>   Off Ingland, Edward twyse in fycht,
>   At occupyit his realme but rycht ;   *Who; without*
>   At sumtyme wes set so hard
>   At hat nocht sax till hym toward ;   *six on his side*
>   Ze gude men that ther balletis redis   *these*
>   Deme quha dochtyast was in dedis.'   *Decide*

Thus although the fourteenth century saw the completion of several important tales of romance, for the bulk of the nation the old romance poetry was losing its charm; *The Humorous Tale.* and before the influence of Chaucer had reached Scotland, the mirthful or humorous tale began to obtain that special place in Scottish vernacular poetry which it has never ceased to hold.

That the *Taill of Rauf Coilzear, how he harbreit King Charles*,[1] is, like the famed *Sir Thopas* of Chaucer, intended as a direct caricature *'Rauf Coilzear,'* of minstrels or romances, is not quite *akin to the romantic* evident; for the old legends concerning *ballad.* Charlemagne are not here burlesqued as they were by Ariosto and other Italian poets, the marvellous being merely superseded by the humorous. But the

---

[1] Published at St. Andrews in 1572 (copy, the only one known, in the Advocates' Library, Edinburgh); republished in Laing's *Select Remains of Ancient Popular and Romance Poetry*, 1822 (second ed. 1885); for the English Text Society, ed. Herrtage, 1882; by Tonndorf, Berlin, 1894; and for the Scottish Text Society, in *Scottish Alliterative Poems*, ed. Amours, 1894-97.

very introduction of such a plain personage as a
collier or charcoal merchant, with his panniers, is
inconsistent with the dignity of the old romances.
Properly, the poem is akin rather to the romantic
ballad than the romance proper; and a similar theme
figures in many later English and Scottish ballads,
as *King Alfred and the Shepherd, Edward IV. and
the Tanner, King James I. and the Tinker, Henry
VIII. and the Cobbler,* etc.   There is also a nearly
contemporary English ballad, *John the Reve,*[1] which
long enjoyed in Scotland a rival popularity with
Rauf. Both are bracketed together by Dunbar and
Douglas.   Contrasting the rewards which those
worthies received from their respective monarchs
with his own neglect by James IV., Dunbar, in *Schir
Remember,* refers to

> 'Gentle and semple of every clan,
> Keyne of Rauf Colzear and John the Reif.'

Douglas gives the two knights a place cheek by jowl
in his *Palice of Honour* :—

> ' I saw Rauf Colzear with his thrawin brow
> Crabit John the Reif and auld Cowkellpis sow.'

But the growth of the romance ballad marked the
decline of the old metrical romances.   Further, the
author of *Rauf* uses a stave specially
associated with the serious romances,
and the mere utilisation of it for the
purposes of mirth or humour inevitably
suggests burlesque.   Some have indeed surmised,

A parody of the old romances, and a Norman tale with a Scottish setting.

Kin

---

[1] Percy folio MS., printed by the Ballad Society, ed. Furnivall,
1867-68.

from the fact that *Rauf* begins after a similar fashion
to *The Awntyrs of Arthur* (p. 37), and is in the same
stave, that it also may have been written by Huchown, but it is unlikely that Huchown would seek to
parody himself. Besides slightly parodying *The
Awntyrs, Rauf* is probably derived from some old
Norman tale. In any case, the poet has really given
it a Scottish setting. Though the scene is laid in
France, the muir is a Scottish muir; the snowstorm is
a right Scottish snowstorm; the collier is an honest,
but rude, dour, unmannered Scot; and the humour
of the vividly dramatic scenes is Scottish to the core.

One day, while journeying to Paris, Charlemagne,
through the oncome of a snowstorm, got   *The King
meets the
collier.*
separated from his train.

> ' The wind blew out of the Eist, stiflie and stoure,
> The deip¹ durandlie draif in mony deip dell ' ;   *keen
continuous
drift*

he lost his way, and when almost in despair, he, ' on
the wild muir in blinding storm,'

> ' Sa come thair ane cant carll chachand the gait
> With ane capill and twa creillis cuplit abufe.'   *cheerful fel-
low; trudg-
ing the road
horse; pan-
niers*

On the king asking the ' cant carll ' to bring him
to ' sum herbery,' the collier told him there was none
in the neighbourhood, but made him welcome to his
own dwelling ' amang the fellis hie.' As the king
was clad in travelling attire, the collier, taking

¹ It has been supposed that ' deip' is a misprint for some word
meaning drift or snow. Drift is not, however, an old Scots word,
and it is at least possible that ' draif' may here mean drift—that
which is driven.

him for a common wayfarer—if not a highwayman
—treated him with the familiarity of an equal,
modified at first by wary suspicion. On arriving at
the door, after stabling their horses, the collier
motioned to him to enter first; and when the king
ceremoniously insisted that the collier should precede
him, the collier, unversed in the punctilios of polite-
ness, and not quite easy in his mind as to the
stranger's purpose, took him by the cuff of the neck
and shoved him forward, saying—

If; ready   ' Gif thow at bidding suld be boun or obeysand,
knew   And gif thow of courtasie couth, thow hes forzet it clene.'

The collier, in fact, claimed sovereignty in his own
house, and unhesitating compliance with the slightest
indication of his wishes :—

Since else;   ' Sen ellis thow art vnknawin
ignorant how   To mak me Lord of my awin,
angry   Sa mot I thriue I am thrawin,
quarrel   Begin we to threip.'

But the king was insufficiently heedful of this
plain warning. When, therefore, on supper being
ready, the collier invited him to take his
wife by the hand and sit down at the
board, he again politely suggested that the collier
should first take his seat. This second exhibition
of gross ill manners was too much for the choleric
collier :—

Supper is
served.

without   ' He let gyrd to the King, withoutin ony mair,
more ado   And hit him under the eir with his richt hand.

> Quhill he stakkerit thair with all,　　Until
> Half the breid of the hall.　　breadth
> He faind neuer of ane fall　　felt the
> 　　Quhill he the eird fand.'　　ground

On the king recovering himself, the collier called
on his wife to take the guest by the hand and lead
him to the board.　The king submitted in silence,
whereupon his host thus admonished him:—

> ' "Schir, thow art vnskillfull, and that sall I warrand,
> 　Thow byrd to haue nurtour aneuch, and thow hes nane ;　ought;
> 　　enough
> Thow hes walkit, I wis, in mony wyld land,　guess
> 　The mair vertew thow suld haue, to keip the fra blame
> Thow suld be courtes of kynd, and ane cunnand courtier.
> 　Thocht that I simpill be,　Though
> 　Do as I bid thee :
> 　The house is mine pardie　by my faith
> 　And all that is heir." '

Though never in his life 'thus-gait leird' (taught
in this way), and rather amazed at the collier's notions
of courtesy, the king took the collier's　Supper and
rebuke in seeming good part, which at　conversation.
once restored the collier's good-humour.　The fare
was of the best—rabbits, venison, and game from the
king's own forests, with wine of quite an excellent
vintage—and as the evening advanced they 'fure into
fusion.'　Sitting round the blazing fire, the collier
entertained his guest with stories of hunting feats in
the king's own forest, where, he affirmed, he brought
down the fattest of the deer ; and having at last
exhausted the budget of his confidences, he began to
show some curiosity as to the name and pursuits of his
guest, and inquired as to his 'maist wynning,' that is,

F

his usual place of residence.   The king informed him
that he was a groom in the Queen's Chamber, and at
the palace was known as Wymond of the Wardrobe.
On leaving in the morning, he further advised his
host to bring a load of coals to the palace and
inquire for him, when he would be certain of a ready
sale at a good price.   This advice the masterful
collier—much against the counsel of his wife, who
could not believe that the stranger had forgotten all
about the blow—resolved to accept; and his adventures at the palace are told with not a little of the
same admirable verve and humour which characterise
the narrative of the great supper scene in his own
dwelling.

A knight, Sir Roland, whom the king had directed
to watch for the collier, told him he had orders to
bring him before the king; but the sturdy
collier declined to be at the service of
any one until, in accordance with his
promise, he had brought his load of coals to Wymond
of the Wardrobe.   Both were obstinate, but of necessity the determination of the collier triumphed, who
further at parting challenged Sir Roland to meet him
on horseback for single combat at the same place
and at the same hour on the morrow.   On the collier
inquiring at the palace gate for Wymond of the
Wardrobe, he was by the king's orders admitted; and
pushing his way unceremoniously through the throng
of courtiers into the royal hall, he at last got a sight
of his guest, when he mused thus:—

The collier's
adventures at
the palace.

' " I ken him weill, thocht he be cled in vther clething   *know;*
  In clais of clene gold, kythand zone cleir.   *though*
      glittering
     *   *   *   *   *   *brightly*
      yonder
In faith he is of mair stait than euer he me tald.   *more*
  Allace, that I was hidder wylit,
  I dreid me sair I be begylit ! "   *sorely*
  The King preuilie smylit,
    Quhen he saw that bald.'   *bold one*

Then, while the collier stood lost in perplexity and
wonder, the king began, greatly to his alarm, to relate
his adventures of the previous night, and concluded
by asking the company what they thought should be
done to one who had treated him in this fashion.
The 'courageous knights' suggested that he should
be hung, but the king took a different and more
human view of the collier's character and conduct:—

' " God forbot," he said, "my thank war sic thing   *my thanks*
      were such
  To him that succourit my lyfe in sa euill ane nicht !   *a*
Him semis ane stalwart man and stout in stryking,
  That carll for his courtasie salbe maid knicht ;   *fellow*
I hald the counsall full euill that Christin man slais,
  For I had myster to haue ma,   *need; more*
  And not to distroy tha   *those*
  That war worthie to ga
    To fecht on Goddis fais." '   *fight*

Raised to his new rank, and provided with a horse
and a suit of rich armour, Sir Rauf, therefore, on
the morrow sallies out to keep his ap-   *The collier*
pointment with Sir Roland. As he nears   *as knight.*
the place of tryst he sees approaching a gigantic
knight riding on a camel, whom, taking him for
Sir Roland, he attacks at full speed. At the
first shock the spears of both are splintered and

their steeds killed; and when they are engaged in a desperate fight on foot, Sir Roland himself appears and separates them, when the opponent of Sir Rauf is found to be Magog, a great Saracen knight, sent to proclaim war against France. A speech of Sir Roland suddenly converts the Saracen to Christianity, and the three knights over their swords swear eternal friendship. Magog marries the Duchess of Anjou, and Sir Rauf finally becomes Marshal of France, when, to mark his gratitude to the king, he causes to be erected a hostel for wayfarers on that spot on the muir where he first met him.

In *Sir Rauf* the old metrical romance forms are utilised to exhibit one of the great heroes of romance mainly from a humorous point of view. In the rude and grotesque production called *Colkelbie's Sow*,[1] a remarkable picture of ancient rustic manners, the alliterative stave of the romances is discarded; and although the author also incorporates with his story a tale of chivalry, he gives it merely on the authority of his grandame Gurgunnald:—

'Colkelbie's Sow'—its character.

> ' Scho knew the lyfe of mony faderis ald,
> Notable gestis of peax and weiris in storye,
> Fresche in hir mynd and recent of memorye.'

peace; wars

The author had also made the acquaintance of Chaucer's poetry, for he refers to that chanticleer—

> ' Of quhome Chaucer treitis in to his buke.'

---

[1] Bannatyne MS. ; also published in Laing's *Select Remains*, 1822 and 1885.

Like that of the poet Skelton, the rhyme of *Col-kelbie* is 'ragged, tattered, and gagged,' and, according to the poet himself, designedly so:— Metre of the poem.

> 'Bot, for Godis luve and his appostill Peter,
> Pardoun the fulich face of this mad metir.
> Sen the sentence to feill is fantastike
> Lat the lettir and langage be such like.'

Since; know

The rough and ready metre is the appropriate vehicle of the boisterous merriment which pervades most of the story, and secured it a lasting popularity rivalling that of *Rauf Coilzear*.

The tale, which is preceded by a short Prohemium in irregular heroic couplets, consists of three parts or fyttes. The first is in similar short coup-lets to those of Skelton's *Colin Clout*; but since *Colkelbie's Sow* is entered as having been included in the Asloan MS., and is referred to both by Dunbar and Douglas as a well-known Scottish classic, the poem must be older than *Colin Clout*, and the author, of his own impulse, must have adopted the device of treating the octo-syllabic couplet in a somewhat more unceremonious fashion than his predecessors. Divisions of the poem: the first fytte.

Once upon a time there was a 'merry man' called Colkelbie, who had 'a simple black sow,' which he sold for three pennies, and these pennies he disposed of thus:— The subject of the poem.

> 'The first penny of the thre
> For a girle gaif he;

ford (of a
stream)
hoard

> The secund fell in a furde ;
> The third he hid in a hurde.'

The poet then puts the query, 'Which of the pennies was best bestowed?' and he proceeds to give the answer, beginning with the second penny, that which 'fell in a furde.' It was found by some one, who bought with it a little pig; but a harlot who lived hard by, wishing to give a great feast to her patrons, and having 'no substance at all,' resolved that the little pig should grace the board. To the feast she invited the whole *élite* of contemporary blackguardism :—

Story of the
second penny:
the harlot and
her guests.

One

experienced
beggar
witch;
weaver
cheat;
sponger

carter

castrater

> ' On apostita freir,
> A peruerst perdonair,
> And practand palmair,
> A wich and wobstare,
> A milygant and a mychare
> A fond fule, a fariar,
> A cairtar, a cariar,
> A libbar and a lyar,' etc.

When this select company had convened, they proceeded to kill the victim; but the poet informs us that, unlike dogs, swine are 'lovand beastis' towards each other, and that—

The vain at-
tempt to kill
the pig.

If one

learns

> 'And on of thame be ourthrawin,
> That his cry may be knawin,
> All the remanent that leiris
> Cumis in thair best maneiris,
> To reskew as thay may :
> So did thay this day.'

Then we have a picturesque roll of the names of the valiant rescuers :—

> 'Wrotok and Writhneb,
> Hogy evir in the eb,
> With the halkit hoglyn,   hacked
> Suelly Suattis Swankyn,
> Baymell bred in the bog,
> Hog hoppit our hog,' etc.

All this great horde came

> 'With sick a din and a dirdy,   bustle and
> A garray and a hirdy girdy,   confusion
> The fulis all afferd wer,
> And the harlot hurt thare
> With bair Tuskyis tuth.
> And for to say the verry suth,   truth
> In that fellon affray
> The littill pig gat away,
> And ilk bore and ilk beest   every
> Defoulit the fulis of the feest.'

But this was not the worst. The several owners of
the pigs hearing the uproar, and afraid   The muster of
that so 'curst a company' designed to   the swine-
owners; the
steal their live-stock, raised an alarm by   dance; the
the blowing of stock-horns, and with   attack.
minstrels and dancers, as knights of old were wont,
issued forth to the rescue:—

> 'Gilby on his gray meir,
> And Fergy on his sow fair,
> Hoge Hygin by the hand hint,   led
> And Symy that was sone brint,   sun-struck
> With his lad Lowry,
> And his gossep Gloury,'

and many heroes more, in higgledy-piggledy confusion. As they advanced with banners flowing and
pipers blowing, they saw approaching them a similar
company, whom they at first took for enemies, but

found to be allies aroused by their alarm. In the joy of meeting each other, the two companies forgot for a time the serious matter which had called them to arms, and with one accord commenced dancing :—

at once

cow-herds

stepped out

'And all the menstralis attonis
Blew up and playit for the nonis ;
Schiphird, nolt hirdis,
And swyn hirdis outgirdis
For to dance merily.'

From the exhaustive list of dances of every variety that were performed, we gather that the merriment must have lasted an unconscionable time ; but at last one of the leaders called to them, as both minstrels and dancers were getting exhausted, to remember for what purpose they were assembled. They therefore at once hurried to the house of the harlot :—

'Fyll on the foirsaid Sottis,
And ourthrew all the ydiottis
Both of the swyne and the men.'

Little glory was, however, gained by either party ; for, as the poet sagely observes, the only real victor was the little pig :—

great

Yet

'And all this grit brawling,
Babling and vthir thing,
Wes for a pig as ze hard sayn,
Zit he eskapit onslane.'

The extravaganza forming the first part is the only portion peculiarly and characteristically Scottish. In the second part the poet sounds an entirely dignified note; and, on the authority of his grandame, proceeds in

The story of the first penny: a tale of chivalry.

Chaucerian couplets to narrate a tale of chivalry,
changing Colkelbie, without so much as a word of
warning, for the nonce into a Frenchman. With the
first penny Colkelbie bought from a blind man a
girl, whom he gave in marriage to his own son
Flannisie. Flannisie was a skilful archer; and the
King of France having lodged one night at Colkelbie's
hostelry, was on the morrow so impressed with the
feats of Flannisie at a 'great shooting,' that he made
him his body squire. Finally he became a knight,
his fair lady Adria—whom Colkelbie had bought
from the blind beggar for a penny—being made one
of the queen's chamber ladies. Both grew more and
more in favour with the king and queen—the lady
by her beauty and goodness, and the husband by his
deeds of valour, until the king resolved to create for
them an earldom, which, by a union of portions of
their two names, he termed Flandria (Flanders).

The story of the third penny is less romantic, but
also sufficiently edifying. After keeping it hoarded
for some time, Colkelbie bought with it
twenty-four hen eggs, of which he made
a gift to his godson Colkalb; but the
mother disdainfully declining this gift, this 'simple
thing,' Colkelbie sent them to his hen-wife, charging
her to ' do her care' and 'make them fruct.' The
'fruct' was twelve male and twelve female chickens,
whose names and qualities the poet sets forth in
thorough fancier fashion; and by and by Colkelbie
was able, in a solemn assembly of relations, to

Story of the
third penny :
practical and
edifying.

present his godson with no less a sum than £1000, saved with 'grace divine' from the twenty-four eggs. Finally—

> 'This Colkalb grew efter to grit richess
> Throw this penny : he grew the michtiest man
> In ony realme.'

A more direct burlesque of the romances is the curious fragment *King Berdok*,[1] which relates the adventures of the great king of Babylon, Berdok, who in summer dwelt 'in till ane bowkail stok' (cabbage stock), and in winter in ' a cokkil shell.' He wooed the 'golk' (cuckoo) 'sevin zeir of Maryland,'[2] and after going over sea and land to visit her, saw her 'milkand her myderis ky,' and put her in 'a creil upon his back' to carry her home to his own country, but on his return found he had nothing but a 'howlat's nest.' The fact was, he was being circumvented by her father, 'the king of Fary,' who afterwards, calling to his assistance the kings of Pechtis and Portugal, of Naippilis and Navern, besieged King Berdok in a killogie (the air-hole of a lime-kiln), where he had taken refuge. There they attacked him with guns ammunitioned with 'raw daich' (dough); but the gracious god Mercury turned him into a 'braikane buss' (fern bush).

The tale of King Berdok.

> 'And quhen thay saw the buss waig to and fra,
> Thay trow'd it wes ane gaist, and thay to ga ;

a ghost; left

---

[1] Bannatyne MS. ; published also in Laing's *Select Remains*, 1822 and 1885.

[2] Merryland or Fairyland.   Cf. Dunbar's *In Secreit Place* :—
> 'Wylcum ! my golk of Maryland.'

Thir fell kingis thus **Berdok** wald haif slane, Those mighty
All this for lufe, luveris sufferis pane :
Boece said, of poyettis that wes flour,
Thocht lufe be sweit, aft syiss it is full sour.' ofttimes

This light and graceful skit strikingly contrasts with the weirdly gross love-tale of *The Gyre-Carling*,[1] the mother-witch of Scotland, with stories of whom Sir David Lyndsay used to 'comfort' the young king, James v. 'The Gyre-Carling.' The tale is written in the rhymed alliterative staves of the *Awntyrs of Arthur* and other romances.[2] The Gyre-Carling dwelt in 'awld Betokis bour' in the Tinto Hills, where she lived on Christian men's flesh and raw hides. Near by her there lived one Blasour, who, we are told, for love of her 'lawchane' (gaping) 'lips,' 'walit and weipit,' and since he was unable to soften her hard heart, resolved to make her his by force :—

'He gadderit ane menzie of modwartis to warp doun the tour ; multitude of moles ;
The Carling with ane yrne club, quhen that Blasour sleipit, undermine iron
  Behind the heill scho hatt him sic ane blaw, hill ; such a blow
    Quhill Blasour bled ane quart That
    Of milk pottage inwart.'

The Carling laughed at his discomfiture, and during her merriment, in quite unconventional fashion, produced North Berwick Law. But her exultation was short-lived, for the king of Fary, with his elfs,

---

[1] Bannatyne MS. ; published also in Laing's *Select Remains*, 1822 and 1885.

[2] An alliterative romance, *The Warres of the Jewes* (Warton's *History of English Poetry*, ed. Ritson, etc., ii. 147), begins like the *Gyre-Carling* thus :—
    'In Tyberus' tyme the true Emperour.'

proceeded to besiege her, and all the dogs from
Dunbar to Dunblane, with all the tykes of Tervey
—wherever that may be—gathered to the fray. The
dogs began to gnaw 'doun with thair gomes mony
grit stane'; but when the case seemed hopeless for
the Carling, she changed herself into a sow, and went
'gruntlyng our the Greek sie' to Asia, where she became
'quene of Jowis' (Jews), and married Mahoun. But
her expatriation from Scotland was not unmourned :—

Since then	'Sensyne the cokkis of Crawmound[1] crew nevir a day,
sorrow	For dule of that devillisch deme wes with Mahoun mareit,
since then	And the hennis of Hadingtoun sensyne wald nocht lay,
savage witch who; troubled; worried	For this wyld wilroun wich thame widlit sa and wareit.'

Another of these mock tales of wonder is the
'gentill geist' of *Lord Fergus's Ghost*.[2] Since there
'Lord Fergus's Ghost.' is a reference in this tale and *The Gyre-Carling* to 'Betokis bower,' it has been
rashly surmised that both are by the same author.
But from *The Gyre-Carling* you gather that the story
of Betok, bred of an acorn, was well known in Scotland. There is a further suggestion that the author
of both was James Wedderburn, the author of certain plays against the Papists. Wedderburn, we are
told by the historian Calderwood, counterfeited 'the
conjuring of ane goust which was indeed practised
by Friar Lang';[3] but there is nothing to show any

---

[1] Cramond is a village five miles west of Edinburgh, but the
name is merely introduced for the pun's sake.

[2] Bannatyne MS.; printed by Scott in his *Minstrelsy of the
Scottish Border*, and in the 1885 edition of Laing's *Select Remains*.

[3] *History*, vol. i. p. 142.

connection between Lord Fergus and the friar. After various misdemeanours—such as stealing God's 'whittle,' a ring and other ornaments, from 'piteous Abraham,' and a pair of 'awld yrn schone' from the man of the moon, besides strangling an old chaplain —the ghost was finally conjured by a little Spanish fly—

> 'That with her wit and ingyne,   cleverness
> Gart the gaist leif agane ;   Made ; live
> And syne mareid the gaist the fle,   then
> And cround him kyng of Kandelie ;
> And they gat thame betwene
> Orpheus king and Elpha quene.'

Of others of these old tales mention may be made of the *Tailis of the Fyue Bestis*,[1] if only because the Hart's tale has reference to the fortunes of Sir William Wallace.

----

[1] Asloan MS. Printed in Laing's *Select Remains*, ed. Small, 1885.

V

THE EARLY CHAUCERIANS, Etc.

JAMES I.—ROBERT HENRYSON—JOHN CLERK—RICHARD
HOLLAND—PATRICK JOHNSTOUN—MERSAR—SIR
JOHN ROULL—QUENTINE SCHAW.

WHILE the old romance poetry was being superseded
by 'gestis' concerning Scotland's own heroes, by such
patriotic epics as *The Bruce* and *Wallace*,
and by comic tales after the type of the
ancient *fabliau*, a new impulse was given
to Scottish poetry through contact with
the master influence of Chaucer. The honour of
introducing Chaucer to Scotland has usually been
assigned to James I. There is no evidence of his
earlier introduction; and if, as Bower states, James
was in the habit of giving much of his time to
the cultivation of literature; and if, as Major—
corroborated by all subsequent Scottish historians,
including Buchanan, who professes to criticise from
personal knowledge — affirms, he actually wrote
poetry, he could just as little avoid, while in England,
becoming a disciple of Chaucer as he could abstain
from making Chaucer known to those who cultivated

Chaucer probably introduced to Scotland by James I.

94

the art in Scotland. This, apart from the question
whether James I. was the author of the *Kingis
Quair*,[1] which has, for the first time, been seriously
disputed by Mr. J. T. T. Brown in *The Authorship of
the Kingis Quair*, 1896.

For crediting James I. with its authorship, the
original authority is the historian John Major (1518),
who says that James 'wrote an ingenious
little book about the Queen while he was
yet in captivity, and before his marriage.'
Nothing further was known of this

'The Quair'—
argument
against the
authorship of
James I.

'little book' until in 1783 a note by Bishop Tanner
drew Tytler's attention to the MS. in the Bodleian,
where, also, the authorship of the poem is attributed
to James I. But Mr. Brown proposes to discredit both
authorities, and to adopt the only other possible theory
—that the poem was an ingenious forgery. His main
arguments are in substance these: (1) Major wrote
his history about eighty years after the death of
James I., and his testimony therefore is of very little
value; (2) the transcriber of the MS. is in error as to
the authorship of five out of ten other poems in the
MS., and therefore the chances are at least equal that
he errs in regard to the authorship of *The Quair*;
(3) James I. does not appear in Dunbar's *Lament for
the Makaris*, and it is therefore almost certain that
he was not known to Dunbar as a poet; (4) in the

---

[1] Published (ed. Tytler) 1783, from the only known MS.—that
in the Bodleian Library, Oxford; and frequently reprinted, the
best and only satisfactory edition being that edited by Professor
Skeat for the Scottish Text Society, 1884.

poem the age of James I., when he was captured by
the English, is given as ten, whereas we now know
he was eleven, and since Wyntoun states he was
captured in 1405 instead of 1406, the poem must
have been partly forged from Wyntoun; (5) the
poem is written in an artificial dialect by some
Scotsman who sought to counterfeit the dialect of
Chaucer, and belongs to the same class of poems as
part of *The Romaunt of the Rose,* as *The Court of
Love* and *Lancelot of the Lak,* regarding the authorship of which no proper explanation is possible; and
(6) various sentiments in *The Kingis Quair* are borrowed from *The Court of Love,* a poem presumably
of later date than the time of James I.

It may be admitted that if Mr. Brown has not
established his case, it is simply because it cannot
be established; for he lacks nothing in
ingenuity, and his learning is employed
to the best advantage possible in such a
cause. But (1) Major, though writing over eighty
years after the death of James I., was fifty years
of age when he so wrote, and was not severed
from the reign of James I. by more than one
generation; he also prided himself on his critical
incredulity, and he had plainly seen and read this
little book whose authorship he, as a matter of
course, assigns to James. (2) The transcriber of
the MS.—which may have been written before 1488,
and must before 1513, and was long in the possession
of the noble family of Sinclair—was a Scot, and

*The argu-
ments for the
authorship of
James I.*

therefore by no means so likely to be mistaken regarding the authorship of a famous Scottish poem as the authorship of English ones of much earlier date. (3) The testimony of Major and that of the transcriber ought not to be disposed of separately; they agree, and their agreement incalculably strengthens both. (4) The absence of James I. from Dunbar's *Lament* is at the best merely negative evidence; and its value as such is further greatly discounted by the universal testimony of Scottish historians that James I., whether he wrote *The Quair* or not, was a 'makar.' Moreover, the omission may be explained by the fact that distinctively he was king rather than 'makar,' and by the distressing circumstances of his death. (5) It is absurd to attach the smallest importance to the possible mistake of one year in the statement of the king's age at the time of capture. What more vitally concerns the question of forgery is the fact that Wyntoun, from whom the forger is supposed to have got his facts, states that the capture took place, not in March, as the poem affirms, but in April. Further, it would appear that the inference of Sir William Hardy[1] that the capture took place in the end of February, or beginning of March, is founded on an error of one month in his calculation. The first entry of payment for the king's expenses in the Tower, on 14th August 1406, amounts to £44, 7s. 10d., which, at the rate of 6s. 8d. a day, implies an imprisonment there of only 133 days,

[1] Burnet's preface to *The Exchequer Rolls of Scotland*, vol. iii.

and seems to show that he was sent to the Tower about the beginning of April; and as we know his father, Robert III., died on 4th April, shortly after the son's capture, all the probabilities point to about the middle of March as the date, and thus corroborate the poem; although, of course, a poet can choose an arbitrary date. (6) The language and grammar of the poem—a combination of the Northern speech with the Midland dialect of Chaucer—exactly corresponds with what might be expected if James I. was its author; for the probability is that, mingling largely with companion prisoners from Scotland, he retained his early knowledge of the Northern speech, and never thoroughly mastered the Midland dialect. (7) To say the least, it cannot be affirmed that dependence on *The Court of Love* is proved; some of the resemblances are accidental, and others have a common source. But unless the resemblances absolutely demonstrate that *The Court of Love* was written before *The Quair*, there is no reason for doubting the authorship of James I.[1] (8) Unless James was known as a poet, no one would dream of passing off a forged poem as his; and if he did write poetry, as he is reputed to have done, he is by far the most likely author of *The Quair*. Further, no motive for the forgery is apparent; and the emotion of the poem—this each reader can decide for himself—seems to be thoroughly genuine, and the record of an actual experience.

[1] See on this subject, especially, Professor Skeat's introduction to *The Court of Love*, in *Chaucerian and other Poems*, 1897.

The poem is a classic example of the love allegory developed in Italy and France, and disseminated in England through Chaucer's translation of the *Roman de la Rose* and his *Troilus and Criseyde*. It is written in the seven-line stanza of *Troilus*—ab, abb, cc—known since the time of Gascoigne as *rime royal*.

'The Quair,' a classic example of the love allegory, but represents also a personal experience.

But though the author, besides closely modelling his style and method after Chaucer, borrows unconsciously portions of his phrases and turns of expression, the poem is not a mere servile imitation of the English master: it has a special individuality of its own. Through all the artificial imagery and traditional love mechanism there is ever present the note of a peculiar personal experience, supplying an emotional warmth and tenderness which are absent from Chaucer, and are not fully attained either in Lydgate's *Temple of Glas* or in *The Court of Love*. The poet's own case—if the poet was James I.—furnished a quite ideal theme for chivalrous allegory. To him in captivity love was an exceptional joy and solace; it was also the means of deliverance from it; and through love his cup of bliss became so absolutely full, that he was ready to praise even the place of his captivity and the day when he was taken prisoner:—

> ' And thankit be the fairë castell wall,
>   Quhare as I quhilome lukit furth and lent.
> Thankit mot be the sanctis marciall
>   That me first causit hath this accident.'

It has, however, been too rashly assumed that the poet was actually a strict prisoner in a tower after the fashion described in the poem; that he first saw Jane Beaufort by accident in the garden of the castle—usually supposed to be Windsor—while looking from his lattice. As matter of fact, he was not at Windsor when introduced to the lady; and we may believe that they first met under different circumstances, for the marriage was promoted by Henry of England from reasons of state. The lattice scene must be regarded as merely figurative, although embodying the essence of an actual experience; it is modelled after that of Palamon and Emelye in Chaucer's *Knight's Tale.*

Scene of meeting merely figurative.

But it is only in the environment that the two scenes resemble each other. Chaucer's is a light external description of love at first sight, but than the scene in *The Quair*, notwithstanding the traces of an artificial mode, no more consummate description of the dawn of love exists in verse; and we must almost inevitably conclude that it represents the poet's own experience:—

Love at first sight—as described by Chaucer and James I.

> ' And there-with kest I doun myn eye ageyne,
>   Quhare as I sawe, walking vnder the·toure,
> Full secretly new cummyn hir to pleyne,
>   The fairest or the freschest zongë floure
>   That euer I sawe, me thoght, before that houre,
> For quhich sodayn abate, anon astert
> The blude of all my body to my hert.

play

instigation; started

And though I stude abaisit tho a lyte,   *then a little*
   No wonder was ; for-quhy my wittis all
Were so ouercom with plesance and delyte,
   Onely throu latting of myn eyën fall,
   That sudaynly my hert became hir thrall,
For euer, of free wyll ; for of manace
There was no takyn In hir suetë face.

And In my hede I drewe ryght hastily,
   And eft-sonës I lent It forth ageyne,   *soon after-*
And sawe hir walk, that verray womanly,   *wards*
   With no wight mo, bot onely wommen tue**yne**.   *person*
   Than gan I studye in my-self and seyne,   *said*
" A ! suete, ar ze a warldly creature,
Or hevinly thing in likenesse of nature ?

" Or ar ze god Cupidis owin princesse,
   And cummyn are to louse me out of band ?
Or ar ze verray nature the goddesse,
   That haue depaynted with zour hevinly hand
   This gardyn full of flouris, as they stand ?
Quhat sall I think, allace ! quhat reuerence
Sall I minster to zour excellence ?

" Gif ze a goddesse be, and that ze like
   To do me payne, I may It noght astert ;   *avoid*
Gif ze be warldly wight, that dooth me sike,   *maketh me*
   Quhy lest god mak zou so, my derrest hert,   *sigh*
   To do a sely prisoner thus smert,   *pleased*
That lufis zow all, and wote of noght bot wo ?   *knows*
And therefor, merci, suete ! sen It is so." '

This fair creature is, of course, depicted as attired,
not in the apparel of an English gentlewoman, but
in the figurative bravery of a queen of
love. For the description, all that can   The poet's
be said is that it is admirably done ac-   description
cording to the accepted mode, but the poet attains   of the lady.

to more than artistic artificiality in the passion-inspired lines :—

know

> ' And, aboue all this, there was, wele I wote,
> Beautee eneuch to mak a world to dote,'

and in the stanzas detailing the lady's gifts and graces of character as shadowed in her mien, concluding thus :—

> ' Throw quhich anon I knew and vnderstude
> Wele, that sche was a warldly creature ;
> On quhom to rest myn eyë, so mich gude
> It did my wofull hert, I zow assure,
> That It was to me Ioye without mesure.'

The allegorical description of the means whereby the lover attains to success in his suit—his visits to Venus, Minerva, and Fortune,—though ornate and artistic, and informed throughout by emotional earnestness, fails, through its antiquated method, to secure the full sympathy of the modern reader. The poem ends with stanzas of thanks to the goddesses who, by their 'might celestial,' had brought his suit to a happy ending, to the nightingale who sang that song of love in the garden where his lady walked, to the flowers as emblems of her innocence and beauty, to the castle wall where he 'lukit furth and lent' when the vision of her loveliness first met his gaze, to the saints of the month of March who brought about the captivity which led to such perfect bliss, and to the 'grene bewis bent,' under which his heart's remedy and comfort first appeared to him.

The allegorical visits to Venus, etc., and the close of the poem.

Besides *The Kingis Quair*, Major ascribed to James 'alium artificiosum cantilenum ejusdem' (that other song in elaborate metre) *Yas Sen*; and 'jucundum artificiosumque illum cantum' (that mirthful poem in elaborate metre) *At Beltayne*. The title of the former of these is plainly incorrect; 'Yas,' which has no meaning, being a clerical error for some term unknown. Pinkerton[1] printed an anonymous song from the Maitland MS., beginning,

Other poems attributed to James I.: 'Sen that Eyne,' and 'Sen throu vertew.'

> 'Sen that eyne that workis my weilfair,'   *since; eyes*

as probably that referred to by Major; but the resemblance of its initial words to those quoted by Major is too faint to justify the ascription of it to James I. In *The Gude and Godlie Ballates* (see *post*, p. 270), a poem of three stanzas in *rime royal*, beginning,

> 'Sen throu vertew encressis dignite,'

is assigned to James I.; and the poem is printed in the Scottish Text Society's edition of *The Kingis Quair*. As in both the Cambridge MS. and the Bannatyne MS. it appears anonymously, the editor of *The Gude and Godlie Ballates* may have had no special authority for ascribing it to James I.; but though in the Northern dialect, and though there is nothing except the initial word 'Sen' to show it is the song referred to by Major, its sentiment and style

---

[1] *Ancient Scotish Poems*, 1786, p. 214.

is not unlike that of *The Kingis Quair*, and it may well have been written by James I.

As to the third poem, the mirthful *At Beltayne*, there is almost no doubt that Major, rightly or wrongly, meant to ascribe to James I. the humorous poem *Peblis to the Play*,[1] beginning,

'At Beltayne':
Professor
Skeat's views.

each person
prepares to
go

'At Beltane quhen ilk bodie bownis.'

The only reason for doubting that this was Major's intention is that he adds in reference to *At Beltayne*, 'quem alii de Dalkeith et Gargeil mutare studierunt.' How, or in what way, or for what reason, some persons of Dalkeith and of Gargeil sought to change the poem, Major does not say. No such place as Gargeil is now known, but a possible interpretation of the words is that some persons of Dalkeith and Gargeil sought to make the poem apply to these places instead of to Peebles. The theory of Professor Skeat is, however, that certain poets of Dalkeith and Gargeil—though it is difficult to believe that these places contained several poets of reputation—sought to parody the king's poem, and that in all likelihood it is one of these parodies, and not the original poem, which has survived. To clinch his argument finally, he also boldly proposes to make a statement in Major, usually interpreted as referring to the king, refer to the poem : he would shut up the mirthful poem instead of the disconsolate king in the castle where the lady dwelt with her mother. Why any one—

[1] Maitland MS.; printed in Pinkerton's *Select Scotish Ballads*, 1783.

whether the king or his executors—should shut it up
in the company of the two ladies, or how, if it were so
shut up, the Dalkeith and Gargeil poetasters could
have got hold of it to parody it, or why they should
be seized by such a mania to parody in a mirthful
manner a poem that was already mirthful, he does
not explain. In any case, Major must have been
permitted to look at it; and the poetasters, both
of Dalkeith and Gargeil, must somehow have got
copies, which, however, they would no doubt destroy
after they had completed their parodies. But if the
mirthful poem were not shut up, as Professor Skeat
asserts, nor destroyed by the poetaster rivals of the
king, the chances are that the original *At Beltayne*,
reputed in Major's days to have been written by
James I., would survive any parody by obscure
village versifiers if such parodies there were. Certain
Scottish poets may, of course, have clothed it in a
Scottish dialect; but this is very improbable, since if
James I. knew Scots, he would inevitably use it in
depicting such specially Scottish scenes.

Once, however, you admit that *Peblis to the Play* is
the *At Beltayne*, or even a parody of the *At Beltayne*
mentioned by Major, it becomes im- 'At Beltayne'
possible to relegate it, as has been done, ('Peblis to the
to the sixteenth instead of the fifteenth Play') and
century. Whether the work of James I. Kirk': mutually
or another, it could not, if it came into evidence for the
existence only in the sixteenth century, James I.
have been ascribed by Major, writing in 1518, to

James I., who died in 1437. More than this, Major's
mention of it in such a fashion is almost proof
positive that it belongs to the earlier half of the
fifteenth century, or at least that it can't be later
than the first quarter of the last half; for Major
was born in 1469, and he could not so write of
At Beltayne unless the tradition that it was by
James I. dated from his youth. Further, the mere
mention of *At Beltayne* by Major—if *At Beltayne*
has any connection with *Peblis to the Play*—makes
it impossible—a fact totally ignored by Professor
Skeat and others—for it to have been the work of
James V., for when Major wrote James V. was but
six years of age. This is a most important point
when considered in connection with the companion
poem *Christis Kirk on the Green.*[1] They are in the
same rollicking metre; and their style and humour
are so absolutely similar, that they are universally
ascribed to the same author. Now in the Bannatyne
MS. *Christis Kirk* is attributed to James I.[2] True,
a later tradition grew up that it was written by
James V., and it is assigned to him by Bishop
Gibson and by Watson; but if we trace back that
tradition, we find that it derives solely from the

[1] Bannatyne and Maitland MSS. ; printed by Bishop Gibson, 1691 ;
by Watson in his *Collection*, 1706 ; by Tytler, along with the *Kingis
Quair*, 1763 ; by Pinkerton in *Select Scotish Ballads*, 1783 ; and
frequently in various collections.

[2] Bannatyne's testimony has been scouted because he accidentally
represents Dunbar's *Dregy* as sent to James V., not to James IV. ;
but James IV. and James V. were, of course, successive sovereigns,
whereas James I. preceded James V. by about a century.

fabling Dempster (1627); and if any value at all
attaches to Major's statement about *At Beltayne,*
Christis Kirk, if by the same author as *At Beltayne*,
could not have been the work of James V. Further,
the Bannatyne MS. and Major—two excellent authorities both—must be regarded as corroborative of each
other; for while Major affirms that the mirthful *At
Beltayne* is by James I., the Bannatyne MS. ascribes a
very similar poem to the same king, while there is a
general consensus of tradition that one or other of
the two kings was the author of the poems. It has,
indeed, been pointed out that the *Justing of Barbour
and Watson* by Sir David Lyndsay begins in a similar
strain to *Christis Kirk*:—

> 'In Sanct Androis on Witsoun Monanday
> Was never sene sic Iusting in no landes.'

And it is further true that these expressions in *Christis
Kirk*—

> 'His lymmis were lyk twa rokkis. . . .   distaffs
> Ran vpoun otheris lyk rammis. . . .
> Bet on with barrow trammis'   shafts

are found interwoven in the same poem thus:—

> 'Quod Iohne, "Howbeit thou thinkis my leggis lyke rokkis. . .
> Zit, thocht thy braunis be lyk twa barrow-trammis,   calves
> Defend the, man!" Than ran thay to, lyk rammis.'

From this circumstance Professor Skeat draws
what he terms 'the obvious conclusion' that '*Christis
Kirk* belongs to the reign of James V.'; but surely
the only absolutely 'obvious conclusion' is that
Lyndsay had read *Christis Kirk*; and it is further

probable, if not 'obvious,' that *Christis Kirk* was earlier than the reign of James v., for Lyndsay was more likely to incorporate lines from an ancient than from a contemporary writer.

All the reliable external evidence, therefore, points to James I. as the author of those poems; and this being so, the internal evidence by which mainly it has been proposed to deprive him of their authorship requires very careful scrutiny. Chiefly from deference to the authority that justly attaches to Professor Skeat's opinion, I have hitherto disbelieved in the authorship of James I., and entered on this inquiry strongly biassed against his claims; but more minute consideration convinces me that there is no evidence against them. What is the internal evidence on the subject?

External evidence favours the authorship of James I.

1. There is what may be termed the moral objection, thus expressed by Guest, and adopted by Skeat: 'One can hardly suppose those critics serious who attribute this song (of *Christis Kirk*) to the moral and sententious James the First.'[1] This merely means that a poet cannot be a poet of strikingly contrasted moods; or, in other terms, that the human personality is an absolutely simple and consistent individuality instead of a curious conjunction of contrarieties. How, on such a theory, could we even conceive of James, the refined, sentimental, poetic artist, as the most energetic ruler of his time?

The internal evidence: the moral objection.

[1] *English Rhythms*, ed. Skeat, p. 624.

But let the question be confined to poetry. If, for example, we accept Shakespeare as the creator of the moral and sententious Hamlet, must we then rob him of the sententious but inimitably immoral Falstaff? Or to go to Scotland for an illustration: let us take the case of Burns, like James I., both an English and a Scottish poet, like him influenced by two distinct poetic traditions. From Burns illustrations may be obtained in almost bewildering profusion: enough that he who has given us the matchless presentment of blackguard revelry in *The Jolly Beggars* is the same who did the admirably conventional sketch of peasant piety in *The Cotter's Saturday Night*.

2. There is the question of language. It is not, of course, denied that James I. retained some knowledge of the Northern dialect in captivity, or The language that he regained his knowledge of it question. when he returned to Scotland.[1] Indeed, Professor Skeat argues that he knew this dialect, and he prints along with *The Kingis Quair* a poem in it. All, therefore, that we have to decide is whether the language of these poems belongs to an earlier or later date than the time of James I. But here the evidence is almost wholly of a negative kind; for lateness of transcription so tends to alter the phraseology, that it is impossible to draw any certain conclusion except in the case of the rhyming words.

[1] Not by Professor Skeat, though it has been—without evidence —by Mr. J. T. T. Brown.

Nor does Professor Skeat profess to point out more
than one instance of 'obvious lateness.' In stanza
xix. of *Peblis* 'stokks' is made to rhyme with 'ox,'
whereas with James I., we are told, the plural of
stok is 'stokkis.' But is this not to take too solemn
a view of this amusing stanza? The curious thing
is that the transcriber in the same stanza makes
'Lockkis,' not 'Locks' or 'Lockks,' to rhyme with
'ox'; and may it not well have been the aim of the
poet's mirthful muse to make 'ox' for the nonce
rhyme with 'stokkis' and 'lokkis'? But besides the
plural 'is' is constantly used not only in other
stanzas of *Peblis*, and of *Christis Kirk*, but by
David Lyndsay, to name no more. In truth, even
had James I. lived in Lyndsay's day, his natural
impulse would, as much as ever, have been to write
'stokkis.'

3. As to the metre: Professor Skeat contents himself by affirming that 'it will be found by no means
easy to point out any undoubted example
of the use of the rollicking metre of this
poem anterior to the year 1450; whereas James I.
died in 1437.' This is a very guarded statement—so
guarded that it is insufficient for Professor Skeat's
purpose. Even to admit that a specimen of this
metre of as early a date as 1450 has come down to
us, goes a far way to prove that the metre is of earlier
date; for the poetry of this early period that survives
is but a fraction of the whole. It is also very difficult
to date anonymous poetry; but amongst the anony-

The metre.

mous poetry in this metre which has not perished
are the old ballads of *The Battle of Otterbourne* and
The Hunting of the Cheviots, the originals of which
probably date from the beginning of the fifteenth
century, if not earlier. Here is a stanza of *The Hunting of the Cheviots* as 'carefully printed from the
Ashmole MS.' in Professor Skeat's own *Specimens of
Early English*:—

> ' The dryvers thorowe the woodes went
>   For to reas the dear ;
> Bomen byckarte vppone the bent
>   With ther browd aros cleare ;
> Then the wyld thorowe the woodes went
>   On every syde shear ;
> Grea hondes thorowe the grevis glent
>   For to kyll thear dear."

As matter of fact, this rollicking metre was
intended to be chanted or sung: and this may
explain why so few early specimens of it exist; for
scarce any of the songs of the minstrel were committed to writing; and of the numerous songs whose
names have been preserved in the writings of ancient
Scottish authors almost none survive.

Apart from authorship, to prove the possible
antiquity of these poems is of some importance, for
metrically they seem to form a curious
blend of the old ballad and the alliterative
romance. The stanza may, indeed, be
described as a sort of ballad variation of
that of *Sir Tristrem*—*Sir Tristrem* changed into
rollicking metre, and the bobwheel simplified, but

The metre a blend of the ballad and the metrical romance.

the alliteration—which survived much longer in Scotland than in the south—preserved as elaborately as ever. Here, as an example, is the admirable second stanza of *Christis Kirk*:—

> 'To dans thir damysellis thame dicht,
>   Thir lassis licht of laitis,
> Thair gluvis wes of the raffel rycht,
>   Thair schone wes of the straitis[1];
> Thair kirtillis wer of lynkome licht,
>   Weill prest with mony plaitis.
> They wer so nyss quhen men thame nicht
>   Thay squeilit lyk ony gaitis,
>   So lowd,
>   At Chrystis Kirk of the grene that day.'

(marginal notes: those; dressed; gay of manners; doeskin; Lincoln; skittish; nighed; goats)

The poems are further classic specimens of the utilisation of the combined ballad and romantic methods in depicting the humours of everyday life; and their influence on the after vernacular poetry can scarce be over-estimated, this apart from direct imitations of their method. Another poem in the same stanza, of probably about the same date, but whether earlier or later it is impossible to say, is the ecclesiastical satire of *Symmie and his Bruder* (p. 286), the heroes of which were two palmers who used to stand begging in the ' old grey cathedral city' by the sea. A later piece is the amusing *Justing and Debait vp at the Drum,* by Alexander Scott (p. 248). *Christis Kirk* was published by Allan Ramsay with a second part added by himself, and this second part is one of the

(marginal note: Their characteristics, and their place in Scottish poetry.)

---

[1] This is explained by some as coarse woollen cloth ; and also as the Straits of Gibraltar, on the way to Morocco.

best of Ramsay's humorous pieces. *Christis Kirk*
and *Peblis* are also the models metrically and poetically of Fergusson's *Leith Races* and *Hallow Fair* and
of Burns's *Holy Fair* and *Ordination*. Neither as
poems nor as pictures of the humours of rustic life
are they equalled by Fergusson, nor without them
would we probably have had much that is best in
Burns. They necessarily suffer from the flight of
time; for besides that the customs, modes, and
manners which are the subject of their wit have
passed away, the niceties of the old language can no
longer be fittingly apprehended by the most learned
and Scottish of the Scots; but their vividness and
truth still penetrate even these obstacles to appreciation. In *Peblis* the humours of the old village fair
of four centuries ago are reproduced with a colour
and life not yet faded beyond recognition. It is not
so vigorous a production as *Christis Kirk*, but as a
study of rustic manners it is equally good, and it is
plainly the work of the same 'makar.' As for
Christis Kirk, which depicts the wild revels and
disorders rather than the humours of the fair, its
fervour and *abandon* are irresistible. Near the beginning of the poem we have a most arch and
amusing glimpse of the distresses and whims of a
love-lorn damsel:—

> 'Off all thir madynis myld as meid   mead
>   Wes nane so gympt as Gillie,   slim
> As ony ross hir rude wes reid,   rose; cheeks
>   Hir lyre was lyk the lillie :   skin

H

Fow yellow yellow wes hir heid,
    But scho of lufe wes sillie.
Thocht all hir kin had sworn hir deid,
    Scho wald haif bot sweit Willie
              Allone,
At Chrystis Kirk of the grene.

Scho skornit Jok and skraipit at him,
    And mvrionit him with mokkis ;
He wald haif luvit, scho wald nocht lat him,
    For all his yallow loikkis :
He chereist hir, scho bad ga chat him,
    Scho compt him nocht twa clokkis ;
So schamefully his schort goun set him,
    His lymmis wes lyk twa rokkis,
              Scho said
At Chrystis Kirk of the grene.'

Marginal glosses: Full / Though; death / jibed / derided / hang / beetles / distaffs

But the fun soon begins to get fast, and after passing through various phases of the absurd, finally becomes furious :—

'Twa that wes heidmen of the heird,
    Ran vpoun vtheris lyk rammis,
Than followit feymen rycht onaffeird,
    Bet on with barrow trammis ;
But quhair thair gobbis wes vngeird,
    Thay gat vpoun the gammis ;
Quhill bludy berkit wes thair beird
    As they had wirreit lammis,
             Maist lyk
At Chryst Kirk of the grene.

The wyvis kest vp ane hiddouss yell,
    Quhen all thir yunkeris yokkit,
Als ferss as ony fyr-flaucht fell,
    Freikis to the feild thay flokkit :
Tha cairlis with clubbis cowd vder quell,
    Quhill blud at breistis out bokkit.
So rudly rang the commoun bell,
    Quhill all the stepill rokkit
             For reird,
At Chrystis Kirk of the grene.'

Marginal glosses: madmen; unafraid / Beaten / mouths; unguarded / gums / Until; clotted / worried / youngsters / set to / lightning / terrible / Stout fellows / men / Until; belched / noise

This final scene is indeed one of mere blind, rude, rustic savagery; but the verve and spirit of the piece are wholly admirable.

After James I. the most notable name in Scottish poetry in the fifteenth century is that of Robert Henryson (1425 ?–1506 ?), second among the old Scots bards only to Dunbar, who belongs to both centuries. As in the case

Robert Henryson (1425 ?-1506 ?)

of most poets of this century, only the faintest outline of his history survives. Of his parentage there is no record, and the tradition that he was progenitor of the Hendersons of Fordell seems to rest more on fanciful imagination than on fact. There is no evidence that he studied at the University of St. Andrews; and Glasgow University, not founded until 1451, was probably not in existence in his student days. He was therefore, most likely, educated abroad. In any case, his name is found among the incorporated members of Glasgow University, 10th September 1462, as 'the venerable Master Robert Henryson, licentiate in arts, and bachelor in decrees,' which implies that he graduated somewhere in law; and if he was not a lecturer in law in the University, he must have been deemed a person so eminent in learning that his enrolment was intended as an honour either to the University or to him. On the title-page of his *Fables* he is designated 'Schoolmaster in Dunfermline'; and he is no doubt also the *Magister Robertus Henrison, notarius publicus*, whose name appears as a witness to certain deeds in March 1477-78

and July 1478. Whether he was in priest's orders
is unknown; but he seems to have been, as a certain
John Henderson was in the sixteenth century,
'master of the grammar-school within the Abbey of
Dunfermline.'

Sir Francis Kynaston, who in his Latin translation
of *Troilus and Criseyde*, 1635, was the first to point
out that Henryson was the author of
The Testament, states that 'being very
old, he dyed of a diarrhea or fluxe,' regarding which
he relates a 'merry, though somewhat unsavoury
tale.' It is about a wise woman or witch who, when
he was a-dying, entered his house and told him that
if he would be cured, he must go to a whikey tree
at the end of his orchard and walk round it three
times repeating the rime:—

> ' Whikey tree, whikey tree,
> Take away this fluxe from me.'

This, Henryson affirmed, he was too weak to do,
and he jocularly proposed instead to repeat certain
words to the oaken table in his room. To adapt it to
this new divinity it was necessary to vary the wording
of the request, but it must suffice to state that he
proposed to make it rhyme with ' Oaken burd, Oaken
burd.' The proposed compromise was naturally
unpleasing to the wise woman, who, we are told,
' seeing herself derided and scorned, ran out of the
house in a great passion, and Mr. Henderson within
half a quarter of an hour departed this life.' The
anecdote is quite credible of the author of *Sum*

His death.

Practysis of Medecyne, and if true, shows that Henryson retained his cheerful spirit to the last. He probably died not long before 1506, when Dunbar wrote thus of Death in his *Lament for the Makaris*:—

> 'In Dunfermelyne he has done rovne
> With gud Maister Robert Henrisoun.' [1]

just whis-
pered

In Henryson the Chaucerian influence is at its strongest, and in part supersedes the old Scottish tradition. His favourite stave is either Henryson's the *ballat royal* (or French octave) in staves. three rhymes—ab, ab, bc, bc—in its four accented or five accented form, with a refrain, or the seven-line stanza in *rime royal*; and he also introduced the nine-line and ten-line interwoven stanza from Chaucer's *Faire Anelida and False Arcite.* But the rollicking metre of *Robene and Makyne, The Garmond of Gud Ladyis,* and *The Bludy Serk* was no doubt derived from the ballads of the older minstrels; while in *Sum Practysis of Medecyne* we have his one solitary example in the rhymed alliteration of the old romances. Again, the stave of *The*

---

[1] The poems of Henryson—Bannatyne, Maitland, Asloan, Gray, Harleian, and Makculloch MSS.—were first published in a collected form, ed. David Laing, in 1865. The sixteenth-century editions of his poems are *Orpheus and Eurydice,* with the ballad on *The Want of Wise Men,* printed by Chepman and Myllar, Edinburgh, 1508 ; *The Moral Fables,* by Lekprevick, St. Andrews, 1570; and *The Testament of Cresseid* in Chaucer's *Works,* London, 1532, and separately by Henry Charteris, Edinburgh, 1593. Numerous subsequent editions of these were published, and pretty full selections from his works appeared in Ramsay's *Evergreen,* 1724, and in the collections of Lord Hailes, 1770, Sibbald, 1804, etc.

Salutation of the Virgin—ab ab, ba ab, ba ab—was probably derived from the old Latin Hymns.

Robene and Makyne, while it is the most characteristically Scottish, is also the gem of Henryson's 'Robene and Makyne.' productions; and indeed one of the most perfect, because one of the least artificial, pastorals in literature. Never has the ingenuous naturalness of rustic love been suggested in verse more deftly or with less intimation of caricature. The theme is a slight one. We are introduced to Robene ' on gud grene hill' besieged by the love-lorn Makyne. He, however, nothing knows of love; and her endeavours to instruct him in 'luvis lair' (learning) proving vain, he, quite at a loss to understand her pleadings, answers her—

> ' " I wait nocht quhat is lufe ;
> But I haif mervell incertaine
>   Quhat makis thé this wanrufe.
> The weddir is fair, and I am fane,
>   My scheip gois haill aboif,
> And we wald play us in this plane
>   They wald us bayth reproif." '

wot

unrest
happy
in good
health
If

But too late he suddenly discovers that he in turn has become the victim of the passion. When, on seeing Makyne again, he follows after her and calls that all his 'luve it salbe' hers, she tells him, half sadly, half scornfully—

> ' " Robene, that warld is all away,
>   And quyt brocht till ane end ;
> And nevir agane thairto, perfay,
>   Sall it be as thow wend." '

to

by my faith
thinketh

And the poet is too remorselessly faithful to truth to gratify the sentimental reader with the usual happy ending :—

> 'Makyne went hame blyth anewche   *enough*
>   Attour the holtis hair.   *over the grey uplands*
> Robene murnit, and Makyne lewche ;   *laughed*
>   Scho sang, he sichit sair :   *sighed*
> And so left him bayth wo and wreuch,   *sad ; wretched*
>   In dolour and in cair,
> Kepand his hird under a huche   *crag*
>   Among the holtis hair.'

It is a rustic episode, not idealised, still less carica-tured, in any way, but etched in its simplicity, its rude truthfulness, and its lugubrious faliance, as it actually happened 'on gud grene hill.'

Most of the other minor poems are of a meditative, moral, and semi-religious cast; reflecting, no doubt, a very prevalent mood of the author, especially in his old age. In *The Gar-mond of Gud Ladyes* allegory is em-ployed with quaint effect to depict the excellences that are desirable in woman.   It is an ingenious example of the allegorical methods then in vogue, and though antiquated in form, is both tasteful and spirited.   Here are two stanzas :—

'The Gar-mond of Gud Ladyes.'

> 'Hir gown suld be of gudliness,
>   Weill ribband with renowne,
> Purfillit with plesour in ilk place,   *each*
>   Furrit with fyne fassoun.   *fashion*
>
> Hir belt suld be of benignitie,
>   About hir middill meit ;
> Hir mantill of humilitie
>   To tholl bayth wind and weit.'   *endure ; rain*

And he concludes:—

> 'Wald scho put on this garmond gay,
>   I durst sweir by my seill,
> That scho woir nevir grene nor gray
>   That set hir half so weill.'

became

The Bludy Serk, on the other hand, is an adaptation of the ballad form for the purposes of religious 'The Bludy Serk.' allegory. The story agrees very much with one of the *Gesta Romanorum,* and the poem is chiefly of interest as indicating that the ballad stanza, since it is here used for parody, must have existed before Henryson's time. The ballad begins in this romantic fashion :—

last

> 'This hindir yeir I hard be tald,
>   Thair was a worthy King;
> Dukis, Erlis and Barronis bald,
>   He had at his bidding.
> The Lord was anceane, and ald,
>   And sexty yeiris cowth ring;
> He had a Dochter, fair to fald,
>   A lusty lady ying.'

embrace

And this is how the *Moralitas* begins:—

> 'This King is lyk the Trinitie
>   Baith in hevin and heir.
> The Manis saule to the Lady:
>   The Gyane to Lucefeir.
> The Knycht to Chryst, that deit on tre,
>   And cost our synnis deir:
> The pit to hell, with panis fell;
>   The syn to the woweir.'

Of the unallegorical and emotionally reflective there are two, *The Abbay Walk* and *The Prais of*

Age, each in its own way beautiful and touching
expressions of a particular mood, and both
remarkably fine examples of musical versification in the octave of three rhymes.

'The Abbay
Walk,' and
' The Prais of
Age.'

Here, for instance, is a nobly dignified stanza from
The Abbay Walk :—

> 'Thy Kindome and thy grit empyr,
>   Thy ryaltie, nor riche array,
> Sall nocht endeur at thy desyre,
>   Bot, as the wind, will wend away ;
> Thy gold, and all thy gudis gay,
> Quhen fortoun list, will fra thé fall :
>   Sen thou sic sampillis seis ilk day,
> Obey, and thank thy God of all.'

Shall not

Since; such;
each

The poem specially sets forth the bliss of content-
ment with one's inevitable lot.   But in *The Prais of
Age* another note is struck, a note of sadness and
despondency, inevitable in the case of a simple un-
worldly man living in such corrupt and calamitous
times.   That it was only a mood is, however, shown
by representing *The Prais of Age* as sung by an
aged minstrel:—

> 'In tyl ane garth, under ane reid roseir,
>   Ane auld man, and decrepit, hard I syng ;
> Gay wes the noit, sweit was the voce and cleyr ;
>   It wes grit joy to heir of sic ane thyng.
>   "And to my doume," he said, in his dytyng,
> "For to be young I wald nocht, for my wyss,
>   Of all this warld to mak me lord and King :
> The moyr of aige the nerar hevynnis bless.

Into a gar-
den ; rose

such a
As ; fate ;
song
not ; because
of my know-
ledge

> "Fals is this warld, and full of varyance,
>   Oureset with syt and uther synnys mo ;
> Now trewth is tynt, gyle hes the governance,
>   And wrachitness hes turnyt al fra weill to wo :

Overcome;
sorrow ;
grievances
more
lost

expelled

> Fredoume is tynt, and flemyt the Lordis fro.
> And cuvattyce is all the cause of this :

gone

> I am content that yowthheid is ago ;
> The moyr of aige the nerar hevynnis blis."'

The evils of the times are also more specifically

Other reflec-
tive poems.

dealt with in *The Want of Wyse Men*, with the curious refrain—

Since

> 'Sen want of wyse men makis foulis sitt on binkis.'[1]

Another poem in a similar vein is that *Aganis Haisty Creddence of Titlaris. The Ressoning Betwixt Aige and Youth* and *The Ressoning Betwixt Deith and Man* tell also much the same tale of the vanity of life. The latter is almost wholly didactic, and of small poetic value; but the former gives a striking series of contrasted portraits of youth and age according to their respective methods of regarding the same aspects of life. Here are two stanzas :—

enclosed
grounds;
decked

Those

tell

> 'Quhen fair Flora, the goddess of the flowris,
>   Baith firth and feildis freschely had ourfret,
> And perly droppis of the balmy schowris,
>   Thir woddis grene had with thair watter wet ;
>   Musand allone in mornyng myld, I met
> A mirry man, that all of mirth cowth mene,
>   Syngand the sang that richt sweitly wes sett,
> "O yowth be glaid in to thy flowris grene !"

faded
eyes; hol-
,ow ; hoarse
coughing
Shrivelled

true without
lies

very

> I lukit furth a litill me befoir,
>   And saw a catiff on a club cumand,
> With cheikis leyne, and lyart lokis hoir ;
>   His ene was howe, his voce was hace hostand ;
>   Wallowit and wan, and waik as ony wand ;
> Ane bill he beure upoun his breist abone,
>   In letteris leill but les, with this legyand,
> "O yowth thy flowris faidis ferly sone !"''

---

[1] Benches ; as judges or governors.

But the poet concludes by adopting the burdens of both as true :—

> ' O youth, be glaid into thy flowris grene ;
> O youth, thy flowris faidis ferly sone.'

In *Orpheus and Eurydice*, an allegorical adaptation from Boethius of some 630 lines, the classical learning has almost quite smothered the poetic inspiration ; but the *Testament of Cresseid* —intended to complete Chaucer's tale of *Troilus and Criseyde* in a manner more consistent with moral if not poetic justice—is by traditional criticism regarded as Henryson's masterpiece. He here claims comparison with Chaucer, and some think not entirely to his disadvantage. Yet the poem is merely an imperfect amalgam of Chaucer and Henryson, the complete effect being rather mixed, for the temperaments of the two were essentially different. Still, largely imitative though it be, and while imitative, not only quite at variance with the tone of Chaucer's story, but by the very strenuousness of its morality in some degree both poetically and morally repulsive, it is interesting as a poetic *tour de force*, and is also sprinkled with passages of richly ornate beauty. In the portraits of the seven deities who sat in judgment on Cresseid's sin the poet reaches the very acme of the old allegorical art. Here the piquantly vivid realism—the peculiar realism of the Scottish muse—triumphs over the artificial methods, the portraiture being both strongly

marginal note: 'Orpheus and Eurydice,' and 'The Testament of Cresseid.'

graphic and delicately felicitous.   In the case of
Saturn the Scottish method is specially victorious :—

frosted	' His face frosnit, his lyre was lyke the leid,
shivered	His teith chatterit, and cheverit with the chin
eyes ; hollow	His ene drowpit, how, sonkin in his heid,
moisture	Out of his nois the meldrop fast can rin,
blue	With lippis bla, and cheikis leine and thin,
icicles	The iceschoklis that fra his hair doun hang,
wondrous	Was wonder greit, and as ane speir als lang.
Out over ; grey	
tangled ;	Atouir his belt his lyart lokkis lay
spangled	Felterit unfair, ovirfret with froistis hoir,
attire	His garmound and his gyis full gay of gray,
withered dress	His widderit weid fra him the wind out woir ;
strong	Ane busteous bow within his hand he boir,
sheaf of cruel arrows	Under his girdill ane flasche of felloun flanis,
Feathered	Fedderit with ice, and heidit with hailstanis.'

In quite a different vein is the portrait of Jupiter.
Here is a stanza :—

eyes	' His voice was cleir, as cristall wer his ene,
	As goldin wyre sa glitterand was his hair ;
	His garmound and his gyis full gay of grene,
edges ; slash	With golden listis gilt on everie gair ;
burly	Ane burelie brand about his middill bair,
sharpened	In his right hand he had ane groundin speir,
	Of his father the wraith fra us to weir.'

But the leprous scene at the close of the poem is—
except perhaps the silent meeting between Troilus
and Cresseid—scarce more than grimly forbidding : a
strenuous morality has extruded not merely adequate
emotional pathos, but even true poetic art; and apart
from the repulsiveness little remains but wearisome
didactic prosing.

The true individuality of Henryson is to be found, not in such laboured and ambitious efforts as *Orpheus* or *The Testament*, but in the wholly simple and ingenuous *Robene and Makyne*, and the naively humorous naturalism of the *Moral Fables*. While Henryson but for 'Chaucer, glorious' could not have been what he was, he perhaps allowed his admiration for the 'flower' of 'Makaris' to override too much his own personality; indeed, it must further be confessed, that while Scottish poetry gained incalculably from the comprehensive genius of Chaucer, it suffered not a little in freedom and spontaneity from the stiffening artificiosity of various Chaucerian conventionalisms. But in *Robene and Makyne* Henryson writes as if Chaucer had never written; and in the *Moral Fables* (paraphrased from Æsop) we have some of the most delightful examples of allegory in literature. Both *Robene* and the *Fables* show that his strength lay not in the old allegorical love-tale, or the old allegorical morality: that just as Chaucer is truly great—great almost as Shakespeare—in various and penetrating knowledge of the world, so Henryson is at his best as an interpreter of rustic character or animal life—or, in other terms, when his poetry is inspired by the experiences of his own quiet days.

The *Fables* have by some been pronounced prolix, but they will be found so only by those who can discover nothing of their humour (delicate but shrewdly wise), whose sympathy with the

The true individuality of Henryson to be found in 'Robene,' and in the 'Moral Fables.'

'The Fables.'

fresh and artless aspects of nature is but tepid, and to whom the world of animal life is a virtual blank. As an animal allegorist Henryson has no superior : by no fabulist is the human in the animal better realised, while the special animal characteristics are admirably preserved and indicated. Incidentally, also, an old phase of Scottish life, as it existed in this ancient ecclesiastical city and its rural surroundings, looms peacefully out of the mists of the past with a charm all the more enticing because of a certain indistinctness.

The slightest of the *Fables* is *The Cock and the Jasp*; but the picture of the cock is truthful and spirited. Much fuller of incident and adventure, as well as of allegorical significance, is the *Uplandis Mous and the Burgess Mous.*

'The Cock and the Jasp,' and 'The Uplandis Mous and the Burgess Mous.'

> ' This rurall mous in to the wynter tyde,
>> Had hunger, cauld, and tholit greit distress ;
> The uther mous that in the burgh can byde,
>> Wes gild-brother and maid ane free burgess :
>> Toll fre als, but custum mair or less,
> And fredome had to ga quhair ever scho list,
>> Among the cheis in cask, and meill in kist.'

suffered

also, without

chest

The burgess mouse went on a visit to her sister in the country, whose humble home is thus prettily described :—

> ' As I hard say, it was ane sober wane,
>> Of fog and fairn full febilie wes maid,
> Ane sillie scheill under ane steidfast stane,
>> Of whilk the entres wes nocht hie nor braid ;
>> And in the samyn thay went but mair abaid,
> Withoutin fyre or candill birnand bricht,
>> For commounlie sic pykeris luffis not licht.'

dwelling
moss and fern
frail shelter
not
without more delay

such pickers

The country mouse entertained her sister with 'nuttis and peis,' but the epicurean burgess lady could not 'accord' with such 'rude diet,' and proposed that her rustic sister should leave 'this hole,' and come to her 'place' in town, where was to be had all the choicest gustatory dainties. They therefore hied them thither, creeping now under rank grass and corn, now under bushes 'privily' until they 'fand the town,' when they took their 'herberie' in a well-stored spence. But while sumptuously dining on all 'the coursis that cuikis culd defyne,' they were suddenly disturbed by a visit of the butler, which caused the timorous rural mouse to swoon for very dread. However, he left without discovering the 'pykeris'; but hardly had they sat down again to the banquet, when Gib-Hunter, the 'jolie cat,' looked in on them. The sharp-witted burgess mouse, quick as 'fyre of flint,' darted into her hole; but alas! her rustic sister was unequal to the emergency, and Bawdrons, pouncing on her, caught her by the back :—

> 'Fra fute to fute he kest hir to and fra,
>   Quhylis up, quhylis down, als cant as ony kid ;   *Now; playful*
> Quhylis wald he lat hir run under the stra,
>   Quhylis wald he wink, and play with her bukhid   *hide-and-seek*
> Thus to the selie mous greit pane he did,
> Quhill at the last, throw fortune and gude hap,   *Until*
> Betuix ane burdë and the wall scho crap.'

Happily she escaped, more frightened than hurt. But the fright was enough; the choicest delicacies ceased to be enjoyable when danger seemed to lurk in every morsel; and as soon as Gib-Hunter took his baffled departure she leapt down from her concealment, and took instant leave of her sister and of the 'mangerie' so 'myngit all with cair':—

> 'Bot I hard say, scho passit to hir den,
> As warme als woll, suppose it wes nocht greit,
> Full benely stuffit, baith but and ben,
> Of beinis and nuttis, peis, ry, and quheit;
> Quhen ever scho list scho had aneuch to eit,
> In quyet and eis, withoutin ony dreid,
> Bot to hir sisteris feist na mair scho geid.'

As ; wool comfortably; in kitchen and parlour

enough

went

Of *Schire Chanticleir and the Foxe*, perhaps the most deliciously humorous stanzas are those setting forth the sorrowful and other reflections of the three widowed hens, Bertok, Sprutok, and Tappok:—

'Schire Chanticleir and the Foxe.'

> '"Allace!" quod Pertok makand sair murning,
> With teiris greit attour hir cheikis fell,
> "Yone wes our drowrie, and our dayis darling,
> Our nichtingaill, and als our orlege bell;
> Our walkryfe watche, us for to warne and tell
> Quhen that Aurora, with hir curcheis gray,
> Put vp hir heid betuix the nycht and day.

out over
That one; love
clock
wakeful
head-dress

> "Quha sall our lemman be? quha sall us leid?
> Quhen we are sad, quha sall unto us sing?
> With his sweit bill he wald brek us the breid
> In all this warld wes thair ane kynder thing?"'

lover

But Sprutok deems such extreme sorrow quite uncalled for, finding in her bereavement sufficing consolation in the proverb that 'as gude luve cummis as gaes'; while Tappok, again, is neither sad nor glad, but simply self-righteously content:—

> 'Than Tappok lyke ane curate spak full crous,
> "Yon wes ane verray vengeance fra the hevin;

conceitedly

He wes sa lous, and sa lecherous ;
  He had," quod scho, "Kittokis[1] ma than sevin ;   *more*
  Bot rychteous God, haldand the ballandis evin,   *balance*
Smytis richt sair, thocht he be patient,   *sorely*
For adultrie that will thame nocht repent."'

The various other fables, in which the Fox or Wolf
(or both) figures, are all admirably droll, the wit
being both barbed and tempered with
the writer's shrewd wisdom; while con-   *Other fables
temporary political or social depravations*   *of the Fox or
Wolf.*
are indicated and satirised with great skill and
subtlety. *The Tod's Confession to Freir Wolf* is
perhaps the most caustic of any. This stanza is
delightful :—

  ' " Art thow contrite, and sorie in thy spreit
    For thy trespas ?" "No, schir, I can nocht dude ;   *not do it*
  Me think that hennis are sua honie sueit,
    And lambis flesche that new are lettin bluid,
    For to repent my mind can nocht concluid,
  Bot of this thing, that I haif slane sa few."
  "Weill," quod the Wolf, " in faith thow art ane schrew."'   *rascal*

The Preaching of the Swallow indicates perhaps
more than any of the others the poet's keen sympathy with the animal creation, and his
delight in the sights and sounds of   *'The Preaching of the*
Nature. In *The Testament of Cresseid*   *Swallow':
a spring*
he has given us a glimpse of himself   *morning.*
sitting down in a winter night to read Chaucer :—

  ' I mend the fyre, and beikit me about,
    Than tuik ane drink my spreitis to comfort,   *warmed*
  And armit me weill fra the cauld thairout,' etc.

---

[1] A common name for a loose woman.

I

In the following stanza from *The Swallow* we see
him, as, leaving the cloisters of the old Fife city, he
'passit forth' one fine spring morning to ramble
amongst the fields and woods :—

      'That samin seasoun, in to ane soft morning,
gone Richt blyith that bitter blastis wer ago,
      Unto the wod to se the flouris spring,
other birds   And heir the maveis sing, and birdis mo,
then   I passit furth, syne lukit to and fro,
      To se the soyll, that was richt seisonabill,
Moist; fit   Sappie, and to resaif all seidis abill.

this way   Muving thus gait greit mirth I tuke in mynd,
      Of lauboraris to se the besines,
stone fence   Sum makand dyke, and sum the pleuch can wynd,
      Sum sawand seidis fast, from place to place,
      The harrowis hoppand in the saweris trace :
loved   It wes greit joy to him that luifit corne,
      To se thame laubour, baith at evin and morne.

abode; com-
fortable   And as I baid under ane bank full bene,
      In hart greitlie rejosit of that sicht,
      Unto ane hedge, under ane hawthorne grene,
wondrous   Of small Birdis thair come ane ferlie flicht,
therewith   And doun belyif can on the leifis licht
every
side   On everilk syde about me quhair I stude,
large   Richt mervelous ane mekill multitude.'

Here also is a companion summer picture from
the *Prologue* to *The Lyoun and the*
Mous :—

A summer morning.

      'Sweet wes the smell of flouris quhyte and reid,
      The noyis of birdis richt delitious,
boughs
broad   The bewis braid blomit abone my heid,
grasses   The ground grawand with gersis gratious ;
      Of all plesance that place wes plenteous
      With sweit odouris, and birdis harmonie,
stronger   The morning myld, my mirth wes mair firthy.

> The roisis reid arrayit on rone and ryce,
>   The prymerois, and the purpour viola ;
> To heir it wes ane poynt of Paradice,
>   Sic mirth the mavis and the merle couth ma.
>   The blossummis blyith brak upon bank and bra,
> The smell of herbis, and of foullis cry,
> Contending quha suld haif the victorie.'

bough and branch

Such ; blackbird ; make slope

As a poet of Nature, Henryson is a kind of pioneer: the traditional realism of the north enabling him, at least intermittently, to escape from the old hackneyed classical imagery, and to record his impressions in the language of simple sincerity. Passion he has none, but he can be nobly emotional; and if seldom or never strongly pathetic, he frequently attains to a stately seriousness which is not unimpressive. Except in *Robene and Makyne* the theme of love has scarce a place in his poetry, for in *The Testament of Cresseid* love becomes merely a text for a sermon. Among modern poets he is most akin to Cowper and Wordsworth, and more to the former than the latter ; but he is more graphic, perhaps more really poetic than Cowper, and although he has none of the comprehensive reflectiveness or essential greatness of Wordsworth, his love of Nature is indicated with less insistent obtrusiveness, while his humour, more various, idiomatic, and constant, if less frolicsome than that of Cowper, tends to redeem even his occasional excesses in sermonising, and guards him against the worst Wordsworthian lapses into almost fatuous commonplace.

As a poet of Nature, Henryson is a pioneer. Compared with Cowper and Wordsworth.

As we gather from Dunbar's *Lament*, and from references by Gavin Douglas, David Lyndsay, and others, there were several contemporaries of James I., Blind Harry, and Henryson not quite without repute in their day, although in some cases their works have wholly perished, and all that survives of the whole of them is, taken together, comparatively insignificant in quantity, although not so in quality.

Contemporary poets.

Of James Afflek and John Clerk, distinguished for 'balat making and trigidë,' nothing very certain is known. Afflek may possibly be a certain James Auchinleck who was 'servitor to the Earl of Rosse,' and died while holding the chantry of Ross, sometime in or about 1497. It has further been supposed that he was the author of a poem in the Selden MS., *The Quair of Jealousy*, to which the name Auchin is attached; but necessarily all this is little more than surmise.

James Afflek (d. 1497 ?).

John Clerk is presumably he whom Dunbar in *The Testament of Mr. Andro Kennedy*, represents as obtaining from Kennedy the bequest of 'God's braid malison and mine.' In the Bannatyne MS. there are five poems which are assigned to Clerk, but in the only case in which they are assigned by the writer of the MS. the name is erased. The five are (1) *My wofull Hairt me stoundis throw the vanis*, a religious ballad in the French octave of four accents with a refrain (assigned to Clerk by another than the writer of the MS.), in which Christ

John Clerk.

is represented as detailing the events of the Passion;
(2) *Sons hes bene ay exilit owt of sicht*, in *rime royal*
(assigned to him by Ramsay), a lament on the growth
of pride among the lords and barons; (3) that remarkably witty but somewhat broad ballad *In Secreit
Place*, in seven-line stanzas—aa, bb, cbc—with a
refrain (assigned to him by Ramsay), but in the
Maitland and Reidpath ms. assigned to Dunbar; (4)
even that fine antique, *The Wowing of Jok and Jynny*
(see p. 289), prototype of many songs in the same
vein, including the three dedicated to the fortunes
of Duncan Gray (in this case the name inserted by
the writer of the ms. is deleted); and (5) another song
in a five-line stave—aa, bab—of four accents, *Fane
wald I luve, but quhair abowt* (assigned to him by
Ramsay, but possibly by Dunbar), partly humorous
but wholly moral, and ending thus:—

> ' Bot quha perfytly wald imprent,
> Sowld fynd his luve moist permanent :
> Love God, thy prince, and freind, all thre ;
> Treit weill thy self, and stand content,
> And latt all vthir luvaris be.'

If Clerk was the author of any of the three last, he
was possessed of no small sprightliness and wit, while
all show very high metrical accomplishment.

Sir Richard Holland—bracketed by Dunbar along
with Barbour, and a priest and a follower
of the Douglases, who, for rebellion, was, **Sir Richard
Holland**
while in England in 1482, excepted **(fl. 1482).**
from pardon—is the author of a curious political

allegory, *The Howlat*,[1] written for Elizabeth Dunbar, Countess of Moray It is mainly interesting as a curious and solitary example of the engraftment of allegory on the old alliterative romance stave. At the time it was composed the allusions may have been pretty well understood and appreciated, but for us the allegory has now wholly lost its point. It is a sort of variation of the tale of the Jackdaw in borrowed plumage, the borrower in this case being the Owl or Howlat. Being dissatisfied with his shape and appearance, he applies to the Peacock, the Pope of Birds, to cry upon Christ to reshape him; but this being impossible, the Peacock and Eagle (the Emperor) apply to Dame Nature, who decrees that 'ilk fowl of the firth' should send him a feather. Becoming 'flour of all foulis throw fettern so fine,' he grows so insolent that it is found necessary to deprive him of all his false finery, and his final plight is thus described:—

'Than this Howlat, hideous of hair and of hyde,
Put first fro poverty to pryce, and princis awin peir ;
Syne degradit fra grace, for his grit pryde,
Bannyt bittirly his birth bailfully in beir.
He welterit, he wrythit, he wareit the tyd
That he wes wrocht in this warld in wofull weir ;
He criplit, he cryngit, he cairfully cryd
He solpit and sorrowit, in sichingis seir ;
He said, "Allace, I am lost, lathest of all,
Bysyn in bale beft ;

Marginal glosses:
praise
Then
with clamour cursed the season made; fear
sobbed (?); sighings loathsomest monster; woe

[1] Bannatyne and Asloan MSS., printed by Pinkerton in a *Collection of Scottish Poems*, 1792, vol. iii.; in the Bannatyne Club, ed. Laing, 1823; by Arthur Diebler, Chemnitz, 1893; and by the Scottish Text Society in *Scottish Alliterative Poems*, ed. Amours, 1897.

> I may be sample heir eft   example
> hereafter
> That pryd yit nevir left
> His feir but a fall." '   companion
> without

The poem contains a few vigorous stanzas, and, besides other interesting references to the Douglases, quotes the lines:—

> ' O Dowglass, O Dowglass,
> Tender and trewe !'

embroidered on the coat-armour of the pursuivant. But the allegory is so complicated by a great variety of under plots that it loses its unity, and the whole becomes a puzzle which it is impossible, even if it were worth the trouble, to decipher.

Patrick Johnstoun, who was unable to escape the 'shot of mortal hail' which slew Blind Harry, is no doubt the same Patrick Johnstone to whom there are various references in   Patrick Johnstoun (d. 1494 ?) *The Exchequer Rolls* and *The Treasurer's Accounts* as performing plays before the king, and who died not long after 12th June 1494. He is the disputed author of a poem in the French octave, *The Three Deid Pows*, assigned to him in the Bannatyne MS., but in the Maitland MS. to Henryson. It is, of course, impossible to decide which of the two was the author. It may well have been written by Henryson — although only in the leprous scene in *The Testament* does he compass a mood of such ruthless severity. The three death's-heads are supposed to address mankind in a strain of which this opening stanza may suffice as a sample :—

‘ “ O sinfull man ! in to this mortall se
    Quhilk is the vaill of mvrnyng and of cair
With gaistly sicht behold oure heidis thre,
    Oure holkit ene, our peilit pollis bair
As ye ar now, in to this warld we wair
Als fresche, als fair, als lusty to behald :
    Quhan thow lukis on this swth examplair
Off thy self, man, thow may be richt vnbald.” ’

Which

hollow eyes

true

unbold

Following the reference to Johnstoun, Dunbar in
the *Lament* pays this high encomium to
a dead ‘makar’:—

Mersar.

    ‘ He [Death] hes reft Merseir his endite
    That did in luf so lifly write,
      So schort, so quyk of sentence hie :
      Timor mortis conturbat me.’

Mersar is further mentioned in Lyndsay's *Papyngo*
as one of six poets who

*Though;
writings*

    ‘Thocht they be deid their libels been levand,’

but so far as the facts of his life are concerned he is
now to us little more than a name; and it is impossible to single him out from among several Mersars
mentioned in the *Treasurer's Accounts,* or indeed
to tell whether he really is mentioned there. He
is usually referred to only as the author of one
authenticated poem, *The Perell of Paramours,* but
in addition to it other two are assigned him in
the Bannatyne MS.: (1) *Off Luve quhay Lyikis to
haif Joy,* and (2) *Thir Billis are Brevit*; and all
three exactly tally with Dunbar's eulogy of him,
for they are by no means bad examples of the
aphoristic love-ballad. *Off Luve quhay Lyikis,*

partly in the French octave of five accents, partly in *rime royal,* is occupied with advice in the art of love, and begins thus:—

'Off luve quhay lyikis to haif joy or confort,
   Ye man begin and leir this A. B. C.   *learn*
Heireftir writtin ; quha will it rycht repoirt ?
   First to be courtess, wyiss, gentill and fre,
   Lairge, honest, gentill, bayth secreit and prevë
And of him self na vantour, as I wene :   *deem*
   Be sobir, trew and every day lustë,
   And quhair thow luvis se thow be senedill sene.'   *seldom seen*

Here also is a sample of its particular advice:—

'Gif mony luvaris thi lady will persew,
   Swa at thow leif nocht in jolesy ;   *See*
Scho is the bettir swa that scho be trew :   *so*
   Non wald hir luve was scho nocht womanly.   *not*
   Repair nocht till hir ay oppinly,
   Bot in all tyme be reddy hir to pleis,
   Howbeit thi hairt thow think sumtyme at weiss.'   *opposed*

The Perell of Paramours, in the French octave of four accents with a refrain, takes, however, a much severer view of love, as may be judged from this opening stanza:—

'Allace, so sobir is the micht
   Of wemen for to mak debait,
Incontrair menis subtell slicht,   *skill*
   Quhilk ar fulfillit with dissait.   *Who are*
   With tressone so intoxicait   *filled full*
Ar mennis mowthis at all houris,
   Quhome in to trest no woman wait :   *knows*
Sic perrell lyis in paramouris.'

The last, *Thir Billis,* in *rime royal,* is intended for the special behoof of ladies, and concludes:—

'Be war for weir, latt nevir your wit go wyld,   *Beware of*
   For every day ane sample may ye se ;   *trouble*

young man

without
goodness ;
pin

Scho that is farest fra tyme hir fame be fyld
    Thair will no berne be blyth of hir bewte,
    Bot ay are skornand bayth he and he.
Thus I conclude, suppois my wit be grene,
    Bewty but bonty is nocht wirth a prene.'

Of the two Roulls thus lamented by Dunbar—

'He has tane Roull of Aberdene
    And gentill Roull of Corstorphine ;
Twa better fallows did no man se
    Timor mortis conturbat me'—

nothing is known, though one or other must have been
the author of *The Cursing of Sir Johne
Rowlis Upon the Stelaris of his Fowlis*,[1]
a sort of mock excommunication of those who had de-
frauded him of his religious dues. Written in the octo-
syllabic couplet, it is a curious compound of jest and
earnest, blasphemy, and, apparently, piety, and amid
much of the merest Billingsgate contains some passages
of real denunciatory vigour.   Here is a sample:—

Sir John Roull.

loathsome ;
toad

ill-will

'Deip Acheron zour saulis invaid
    As blak, as mich as ony taid ;
Snaykis, serpentis and eddeirs
    Mott stuff zour bellyis and zour bledderis,
In hellis hoill quhair nevir is licht,
    Nor nevir is day, bot evir nicht,
Quhair nevir is joy evin and morrow,
    Bot endles pane, dule and sorrow ;
Quhair nevir is petie nor concord,
    Nor amitie, bot discord,
Malice, rancour and invy,
    With magry and malancholy ;

---

[1] Bannatyne and Maitland MSS., printed in Lord Hailes' *Collection*,
1770 ; Pinkerton's *Ancient Scotish Poems*, 1786 ; and Laing's *Select
Remains*, 1822, second ed. 1885.

> Quhair thair is hunger, cald, and thirst
> Dirknes, mirknes, rouk, and mist,   *exhalation*
> And Cair, but consolatioun   *without*
> With eternal damnation.'

The only other poet mentioned in *The Lament*—
known to be the author of any poems that survive,
is Quintyne Schaw, whom Kennedy in   Quintyne
his *Flyting* with Dunbar calls his 'cousing   Schaw
Quintine,' and who, Dunbar in his *Flyting*   (d. 1504?)
states, composed with Kennedy a poem in their own
praise. He and Kennedy belonged to Ayrshire,
Schaw being the son of a certain John Schaw of
Hails, who in 1467 was an ambassador for the
marriage of James III. with Margaret of Denmark.
He died some time after 8th July 1504. Since he
was in receipt of a pension of £10, and occasionally
got other gifts, it is probable that like Dunbar he
frequented the court, and this obtains some corroboration by the only poem, known to be his, that has
come down to us. It is entitled *Adveyce to a Courtier*,[1] and if not remarkable as poetry, is soundly
sensible in its counsel. The stave consists of
five lines of four accents, aa, bab. Here are two
stanzas :—

> 'Gif changes the wynd, on force ye mon   *If; of neces-*
> Bolyn huke, haik, and scheld[2] hold on.   *sity you*
> Thairfor bewar with ane scharpe blawar :   *must*
> Gif ye be wys avyce heiron ;
> And set your sale a litle lawar.

---

[1] Maitland MS., published in Pinkerton's *Ancient Scotish Poems*,
1786.

[2] A technical description of the handling of a vessel, not now
ully understood, although 'Bolyn' of course means bowline.

if ; too tight   For gif ye hauld your sale ouir strek
blasts   Thair may cum bubbis ye not suspek ;
                          Thair may cum contrair ye not knaw ;
                        Thair may cum stormes and caus a lek,
must ; wave   That ye man cap by wynd and waw.'

Other poets mentioned by Dunbar—Heryot, Mungo
Lockart, Sandy Traill, Sir John the Ros, 'Gentill

Poets whose   Stobo'—have left nothing known to be
works are not   theirs, although some anonymous poetry
now known to   in the Bannatyne or Maitland or other
survive.   MSS. may have been written by one or other of
them. Sir Gilbert Hay, alluded to rather curtly, is
only known as the 'makar' of translations—several
in prose, and a very long one in verse, *The Buke of
the Conqueror, Alexander the Great*.[1] It is unlikely
that Dunbar, though he made no mention of James I.,
omitted other dead poets of note ; but no doubt there
were in this as in all other centuries a number of
very minor bards, as one Glassinbery, a dull set of
verses by whom is printed in Laing's *Early Metrical
Tales* (1826, 2nd edition 1885). Of the large bulk of
anonymous poetry (see *post,* p. 277) that survives
much must belong to the fifteenth century, and various
poets of note who wrote in the following century
produced much of their best work in the fifteenth.
Except Dunbar, none of these old Scots poets can
claim to rank as great ; but the general level of
excellence—especially as regards form—is very high.
Nearly all already alluded to cultivated poetry with

[1] MS. at Taymouth Castle—extracts printed by the Bannatyne
Club, 1834.

the most strenuous endeavour after metrical excellence; and while the Chaucerian influence assisted
to widen and elevate their aims, the strong realism
of the native tradition tended to prevent that
Chaucerian degeneration which in England was in
such marked contrast with the rise of the vigorous
Scottish school, whose great master was Dunbar.

VI

DUNBAR AND WALTER KENNEDY

WALTER KENNEDY, the antagonist of Dunbar in *The Flyting*, enjoyed in his day a poetic fame only second, if second, to that of Dunbar. In Gavin Douglas's *Palice of Honour* he is entitled 'Greit Kennedie' and bracketed with 'Dunbar yit undeid'; and Sir David Lyndsay celebrates his 'terms aureate,' which no one can 'now counterfeit.' Born about 1460 — probably in the same year as Dunbar—Kennedy was of noble descent, being the third son of Gilbert, first Lord Kennedy, who was heritable bailie of the Carrick district of Ayr. He was educated at the University of Glasgow, where he matriculated in 1475, and took his Bachelor's degree in 1476, and his Master's in 1478. From Dunbar's allusions in *The Flyting* one gathers that he was rather a needy younger son, and lived a rude country life; but he himself asserts that he had 'stores and stakkis,' and that Dunbar would be glad to gnaw stinking bones under his board behind the dogs' backs. Whatever may be the truth as to his 'stores,' little is known of him, except that in 1481 he was one of the examiners in Glasgow University, in 1492 was bailie-depute of Carrick, and in 1504

Walter Kennedy (1460?-1507?)

142

acquired the lands of Glentigh. Occasionally, to quote the invective of Dunbar, he 'brought the Carrick clay to Edinburgh corse'; but Dunbar derides him as a mere countryman, whose 'lippis' could 'blabber' only the 'Ershry' (the Erse language) of the Strathclyde Welsh. He was tall, and not improbably well enough looking, for Dunbar, conscious of his own short, and it may be rotund, figure, makes special mockery of his length and leanness:—

'The larbar lukis of thy lang lene craig,   *lazy; neck*
  Thy pure pynit thrott, pelit and owt of ply, *starved; bare*
Thy skolderit skin, hewd lyk ane saffrone bag *shrivelled*
  Garris men dispyt thar flesche, thow spreit of Gy : *makes; contemn*
Ffy feyndly ffront; ffy! tykis face, ffy! ffy!
Ay loungand, lyk ane loikman on ane ledder ; *hangman*
  Thy ghaistly luke fleys folkis that pas thé by, *scares*
Lyke to ane stark theif glowrand in ane tedder.' *strong; staring; halter*

Unless the illness—under which he suffered when Dunbar wrote his *Lament*—resulted otherwise than was apprehended, Kennedy died probably in 1507, for he is the subject of this touching stanza:—

'Gud Maister Walter Kennedy
In poynt of dede lyis veraly ; *death*
Gret ruth it wer that so suld be:
  Timor mortis conturbat me.'

This stanza would seem to indicate that Dunbar held Kennedy in high esteem, and the next that he even regarded him as his last remaining contemporary brother; but it does not follow that *The Flyting* between the *'The Flyting,' was it wholly jest?* two poets—though sanctioned by ancient custom— was a merely playful duel in metrical skill and repartee. Even at the present day the Eastern Scot

rather contemns (no doubt unjustly) his brother of
the West; and in Dunbar's time the old antagonism
between the Saxon of Lothian and the Welsh Celt
of Cambria was more than latent, although not so
active as between the Saxon and the uncivilised
Celt of the Highlands. We may therefore infer that
The Flyting indicates, if not direct enmity, a certain
racial jealousy; but Dunbar was never one to cherish
mere personal animosity, and perhaps enjoyed what
he got almost as much as what he gave.

Kennedy's part in *The Flyting* cannot quite compare with that of Dunbar in metrical ease, in masterly
alliteration, in sumptuousness of ribaldry,
in variety of ridicule, or in impetuosity
of invective; but it is not much awanting
in any of these attributes, and in Dunbar's not uneventful career Kennedy had a richer supply of
satirical material. More genealogical, historical, and
specifically personal, he at least holds his own as regards asserted facts, and his final salute, though by no
means his deadliest, and but a feeble reflex of Dunbar's
metrical effects, is not without perorative power:—

Kennedy's part compared with that of Dunbar.

'Deulbere, thy spere of were, but feir, thou yelde,
    Hangit, mangit, eddir-stangit, stryndie stultorum,
To me, maist hie Kenydie, et flee the felde,
    Pickit, wickit, conwickit, Lamp Lollardorum.
Defamyt, blamyt, schamyt, Primas Paganorum.
Out! out! I schout, apon that snowt that snevillis.
Tale tellare, rebellare, induellar wyth the deuillis,
    Spynk,[1] sink with stynk ad Tertara Termagorum.'

Devil-born; war; with-out doubt

offspring of fools

Select

---

[1] Spynk = Finch, and is used of course as a term of reproach, but
the exact meaning is now lost.

Owing, it may be, to his Western connection, few of Kennedy's other poems have been preserved, and we may well believe that none of these are the most characteristic, all of them being somewhat didactic.[1] Perhaps the best is that *Againis Mowth Thankles*. It is in the French octave with refrain, and shows a certain refinement of style. It begins—

Other poems of Kennedy.

> ' Ane aigit man twyss fourty yeiris,
>   Eftir the halydayis of Yule,
> I hard him say, amangis the freiris
>   Of ordour gray, makand grit dule,
>   Rycht as he wer a fowriwss fule ;
> Oft syiss he sicht and said, "Allace,
>   Be Chryst, my cair ma nevir cule,
>   That evir I scherwit mowth thankles." '

A Christmas lamentation
Ofttimes he sighed
served the thankless mouth

Like Kennedy, Dunbar was probably a scion of the nobility; for Kennedy taunts him with descent from Cospatrick, Earl of March, generated betwixt a she-bear and a 'deill,' and callit 'Dewlbeir and nocht Dumbar'; it has also been conjectured that he was the son or nephew of William, third son of Sir Patrick, who was the fourth son of George, tenth Earl of Dunbar; but there is no evidence on the point, beyond the fact that he was a native of Lothian born about 1460.

William Dunbar (1460?-1520?).

Intended for the Church from his 'nurse's knee,' Dunbar was educated at the University of St. Andrews, where he took his Bachelor's degree in 1477 and his Master's in 1479. From the fact that he dates one of his poems 'at

Dunbar as a novice.

---

[1] Five are printed in Laing's ed. of Dunbar.

K

Oxinfurde,' it has been supposed that he continued
his studies at Oxford University; but the poem
indicates rather a mere casual visit to Oxford. It is
much more certain that he studied at Paris. At some
unknown date he entered the order of St. Francis,
and while still in his noviciate went on a preaching
and mendicant tour, and after making 'good cheir'
in every 'lusty town and place'

> 'Off all Yngland from Berwicke to Kalice,'

and preaching 'eik in Canterbury,' he—so he rehearses
in his poem *How Dunbar wes desyred to be ane Freir*
—crossed from Dover and continued his wanderings
through Picardy, where he not only the 'peple techit,'
but engaged, as was indeed then almost the conventional habit of his profession, in quite contrarient
practices:—

bear
God knows
falsehood
expelled

> 'As lang as I did beir the freiris style
>   In me, God wait, was mony wrink and wyle,
>   In me was falset with every will to flatter,
>   Quhich mycht be flemit with na holy watter :
>   I wes ay reddy all men to begyle.'

On his return from his wanderings, he felt unable
to refuse the world and accept the monastic habit—
the offer of it scared him, he affirmed,
At the court
of James IV. as if he had been frightened by a ghost,
—but he became a secular priest. In 1491 he
accompanied the embassy sent to negotiate for the
marriage of James IV. with a princess of France,
and this failing, it would seem that he also went

with the deputations to various other countries, for in his verses on *The World's Instabilitie,* he ventures to remind the king that he had served him also in Germany, Italy, and Spain, this in addition to England and Ireland. An allusion in *The Flyting* shows that he was also on one occasion wrecked on the coast of Norway. From at least as early as 1500—and it may be from or before 1491—he was a recognised official at court, probably a notary, for it was in this capacity that in 1501 he was included in the embassy to England for arranging the marriage of James IV. with the Princess Margaret. A favourite with Queen Margaret from the time that he celebrated the royal marriage in *The Thrissil and the Rois,* he was also on easy terms with the accomplished, manly, chivalrous, dissolute, superstitious, headstrong, and entirely human James IV.; and the society at the court of this characteristic Stewart king —its jovial freedom, its eager greed, its motley crowd of 'solicitaris,' its amusements, revelries, and coarse indecorums—is mirrored in the facets of his many-sided verse.

At the court he never held more than a comparatively humble post. His constant hopes of a benefice were doomed to disappointment; and though one can't accept the satires of *His disappointments.* Kennedy in *The Flyting* with perfect seriousness, we may, without doing great injustice to Dunbar, infer that his reputation was not quite consistent with his grave ambitions:—

> ' Ane benefice quha wald gyve sic ane beste,
>   Bot gif it war to gyngill Judas bellis,[1]
> Tak thé a fidill, or a fleyt et geste [2]
>   Wndought, than art ordanyt to not ellis.'

On 15th August 1500 he, however, obtained a
pension of £10 for life, and this in 1507 was increased
to £20, and in 1510 to £80. His poetic
gifts were no doubt his main passport to
the favour both of the king and queen,
and if his designation as 'the rhymer of Scotland' in
the grants to him by Henry VII. in 1501 is not to be
taken as implying that he was formally recognised in
Scotland as 'poet laureate,' he probably owed his pension chiefly to his poetry. At the same time he based
his claims to a benefice, not on his poetical accomplishments, but on his personal services to the king.[3]
How he fared after the death of James IV. at Flodden
in 1513 there is no record: he may have retained the
pension of £80 until his death; but he never attained
to any position at all commensurate with his ambition
or his talents. Making a false step at the beginning
of his career, he was all his after years in conflict
with his circumstances; and the nut of life conceded
to him no satisfying kernel:—

His pension,
last years,
and death.

> ' I seek abowte this world onstable
>   To find a sentence convenable ;

---

[1] To betray Christ as Judas did.

[2] Take a fiddle or a flute and recite stories (as the minstrels did).

[3] Mr. Oliphant Smeaton (*William Dunbar*, p. 50) suggests that
Dunbar was confidential agent of the king both in politics and love.
The surmise is perhaps feasible, but no sufficient evidence is adduced
to warrant the acceptance of the surmise as fact.

> Bot I can not in all my witt
> Sa trew a sentence find of it
> As say it is dissavable.'

He died probably in 1520; but not even his place
of burial is known.

Dunbar's poetry[1] is almost as full of self-revelation
as that of Burns.   With a candour that is entirely
naive he paints the picture of his novitiate   Dunbar's self-
in its unedifying completeness, and un-   revelation.
feignedly proclaims his preference for the charms
of secular licence to the 'holy weid' of the monk;
if less scientifically skilled in the 'Hevins glory'
of gastronomy than a Brillat-Savarin, or a Ber-
choux, he dilates on its blissful results with an
equal enthusiasm; drink and good fellowship he sings

---

[1] Dunbar's poems are preserved in the Asloan, Bannatyne,
Maitland, and Reidpath MSS., and there are individual poems in
the Mackulloch MS. in the University of Edinburgh, in three MSS. in
the British Museum, and in a MS. in the Town Clerk's Office,
Aberdeen.   Seven were printed in Dunbar's lifetime by Chepman
and Myllar, Edinburgh, 1508.   Selections were included in Ramsay's
Evergreen, 1724, and were also published by Lord Hailes, 1770,
Pinkerton, 1786, Sibbald, 1802, etc.; but the first collected
edition was that by Laing, 1824, second edition with supplement,
1865.   Of an edition by James Paterson, 1863, little can be said
by way of commendation.   The Scottish Text Society's edition,
1884-1893, is elaborate as regards introductions, vocabulary, and
notes, but the most complete as regards text is that of Professor
Schipper, Vienna (in the *Memorials* of the Imperial Academy of
Sciences), 1892-93.   Dr. Schipper has also published *William
Dunbar sein Leben und seine Gedichte*, 1884, in which he gives
specimens of Dunbar translated into German; and he has
treated of Dunbar's metres in *Englische Metrik*, Bonn, 1882-1888,
and *Grundriss der Englischen Metrik*, 1895.   *William Dunbar* by
Oliphant Smeaton ('Famous Scots' Series), 1898, gives some new
particulars about Dunbar's earlier years.

with much of the devil-may-care fervour of 'rantin Robin':—

> 'Now all this tyme let vs be merry,
>   And set nocht by this world a cherry:
>   Now, quhile thair is gude wyne to sell,
>   He that does on dry breid virry
>   I give him to the devill of hell';

not

worry

his own characteristic capers at *The Dance in the Quenis Chalmer* he parades with unaffected laughter at himself; he vies with Burns in allusions to the carnal; regarding his ambitions and disappointments he also gives you his full confidence; and in fine he hides from you none of his varying moods: neither his profound persuasion of his own deserts, nor his general contempt for human nature, his sincere respect for occasional human worth, his poignant melancholy, his patience and blythe resolutions, his strong desires, his equally strong conviction that all is vanity, his overwhelming sense of the might and his dread of death, 'the strong unmerciful tyrand,' his more noble aspirations, his orthodox piety, his conventional hopes of heaven.

The peculiar virtue of his verse is that it palpitates with reality.   It is an intensely true and living record of himself, and certain aspects of the court and burgess life of Scotland at the close of the Middle Ages; and no criticism of this strange and strong poet—not even Lowell's comparison of his works to a mere field of thistles—seems to me more hopelessly and delightfully inappropriate than the verdict

His reality.

of Professor Courthope—usually careful and judicious —who, preferring to Dunbar's vivid verse the elaborate prolixities of Gavin Douglas, asserts that 'though his works are of great importance to the antiquary, he rarely touches those notes of human interest which are a passport to the sympathy of the general reader.' Here by one generalising sweep you have the human race apportioned into the two great orders of antiquaries and general readers, and you are further almost given to understand that 'the sympathy of the general reader' is the one criterion of 'notes of human interest.' But make of your 'general reader' what you will, Dunbar—who in life was quite other than dry-as-dust—is less than most of the old poets a fit companion for the mere antiquary. As for his 'notes of human interest,' he touches them if anything too often and too variously rather than too seldom. They are not all, it may be, a passport to modern sympathy; but if even the 'general reader' can find no congenial 'note of human interest' in, say, *The Lament for the Makaris*, *The Petitioun of the Gray Horse*, or *Meditatioun in Wyntir*, to name but three poems out of many similar ones, then the blame is not in Dunbar but in 'the general reader,' and 'the general reader' is also a much duller person than his worst enemies suppose.

In considering more specifically the characteristics of Dunbar, one is at once arrested by the ease and artistic finish of nearly all his productions. As a mere master either of metre or language, he is not

surpassed even by Chaucer, as he is not approached
by any of his predecessors except in a degree by
James I. or Henryson. The immense
variety of his staves, and his almost
uniform success in each, stamp him as
quite an exceptional expert in the artistic use of words.
For purposes of rhythm or rhyme language is in his
hands an absolutely ductile material. Trace of effort
in his verse there is little or none, and very rarely
any faintest glimpse of the sacrifice of thought to
form or form to thought. Most likely half or more of
his poems have perished, for few were printed in his
lifetime, and none known to be in his handwriting survive. But in the some ninety pieces that may fairly
be ascribed to him, he attempted a greater variety
of metrical form than any predecessor. Besides
excelling in Chaucer's special metres, he profited
somewhat by Lydgate, but he seems also to have
studied nearly every form of the old English stave;
and while, moreover, he did not disdain to use the
unrhymed alliteration as well as the rhymed stave
of the old northern romances, he also utilised his
familiarity with the French poetic methods to introduce new metrical effects, especially in the case
of refrains.

His one surviving poem in unrhymed alliteration
is the more than Swiftian *The Twa Merrit Wemen
and the Wedo*. Here is an example, in the
beautiful lines describing the dawn of
the summer morning which gladdens you, while the

A master of metre and language

Unrhymed alliteration.

'gay wyffis,' having just concluded the baring of their hearts to one another, are 'cooling their mouths with comfortable drinks':—

> ' The morow myld wes et meik, the mavis did sing
> And all remuffit the myst, et the meid smellit ;   meadow
> Siluer schouris doune schuke, as the schene cristall,   bright
> And berdis schoutit in schaw, with thair schill notis ;   the woods
> The goldin glitterand gleme, so gladit ther hertis,
> Thai maid a glorius gle amang the grene bewis.
> The soft souch of the swyr, et soone of the stremys,   sighing of
> The sweit sawour of the sward, and singing of foulis ;   the wind in hollows
> Myght confort ony creatur of the kyn of Adam ;
> And kindill agane his curage thocht it wer cald sloknyt.   though ; quenched
> Than rais thir ryall wivis, in ther riche wedis
> And rakit hame to ther rest, through the rise blwmys.'   underwood

While in this short specimen the alliterative conventions of the older poets are broken—though broken rather by way of richness than of poverty of alliteration—not merely the perfect rhythmical flow, but the musical melody and suggestiveness of the lines indicate an admirable sense of the poetry of words.

In much of his rhymed verse, also, Dunbar makes skilful use of alliteration, and by lavish recourse to it in the more denunciatory passages of *The Flyting* immensely enriches their ludicrous effect; but the only surviving

The old rhymed alliterative stave.

example of his—it is most probably his—in the rhymed alliterative stave of the old romances, with the bobwheel, is the ballad detailing in such daring terms the quenchless thirst of *Kynd Kittok*. Its stave differs somewhat from any of the examples of rhymed alliterative verse previously quoted (see pp. 36-38) in the formation of the bobwheel, the bob, which introduces a new rhyme, being a full hemi-stich.   Here is an example:—

> ' And for to brew and baik :
> Friendis I pray you hertfully,
> Gif ze be thirsty or dry,
> Drink with my gud dame as ze ga by
> Anys for my sake.'

heartily
If

Once

On one solitary occasion—in that rapid rush of denunciation *The Epitaph for Donald Owre* (the Highland rebel, Donald Dubh) —he appropriates the old romance bobwheel to form a complete stave, as thus :—

The romance bobwheel as a stave.

> ' In vice most vicious he excellis
> That with the vice of tresone mellis ;
> Thocht he remissioun,
> Haif for prodissioun,
> Schame and suspissioun,
> Ay with him dwellis.'

meddles
Though
Have

Unless we regard the *Freiris of Berwick* as indu-bitably Dunbar's, only once—in the wholesome contrast to *The Twa Merrit Wemen and the Wedo*, the lines in *Prays of Women*—does he adopt Chaucer's heroic couplet; but he writes the octo-syllabic couplet of Barbour and Chaucer with ease and spirit, as well as with orna-mental touches which lend to it additional point and vivacity.   He employs it in nearly all the several ritualistic divisions of *The Dregy*, in his picturesque catalogue of *The Solisitaris in Court*, and both in

The couplet: heroic, and octo-syllabic.

his *Complaint* and his *Remonstrance to the King.*
In *The Dregy* he, however, introduces variations in
the responses, adopting from the French what was
then known as the common rondeau, in imitation of
a peal of bells inviting to the services of the church :—

> 'Tak consolatioun
>   in zour pane ;
> In tribulatioun
>   tak consolatioun ;
> Out of vexatioun
>   cum hame again :
> Tak consolatioun
>   in zour pane.' [1]

Of the French octave—ab, ab, bc, bc—both in its
four accented and five accented form, Dunbar makes
large use. Unlike Chaucer, he occasion-   The French
ally enriched it—as in several stanzas of   octave, with
The Flyting—by the device of internal   refrain.
rhymes, and, unlike Chaucer, he never made use of
it in the complete French ballade form, where the
identical rhymes of the whole first stanza are repeated
throughout the poem, but except in the solitary
instance of *The Flyting* he introduced the refrain.

[1] Response No. 2 has two final lines in couplets, and Professor
Schipper (*Altenglische Metrik*, p. 382) therefore regards it as a form
of *rime couée*—ab, aa, bb—with internal rhyme. Mr. G. P.
M'Neill (Scottish Text Society's edition of *Dunbar*, III. clxxxix)
justly observes that the final couplet ' is not an integral part of the
strophe'; but it has further no right to a place in the response,
the title—*Iube Domine benedicere*—having been omitted. Two
other examples of this rondeau in old Scots poetry are *Polwart, zee
peip*, etc., in Montgomerie's *Flyting* (p. 257), and an anonymous
piece, *Thus I propone* (p. 298), in the Bannatyne and Maitland
MSS., printed in Pinkerton's *Ancient Scotish Poems*, p. 211.

This device was not, however, as editors have stated, a free adaptation by Dunbar of the French ballade; for (1) the octave without refrain, as written by the Scots 'makaris,' is as common in French poetry as the ballade; (2) the French ballade has the refrain, and it is found in Chaucer's English ballades; and (3) the octave with refrain as written by Dunbar was not only used by French poets—as by Villon in his double ballade,[1]—but besides being frequently found in Early English poetry,[2] was used by Henryson and the Scots poets of the fifteenth century. Nevertheless, Dunbar utilised it with special ingenuity and with great variety of effect: in elegies, as in that on Lord Bernard Stewart, where the changes are impressively rung on the 'flower of chivalrie'; in the celebrations of 'the blyth and blissful burgh of Aberdein,' and of London, 'the flower of cities all'; in the enforcement of special moral maxims, as that 'without gladness availis no tresour'; in personal eulogies, as that on Lord Bernard Stewart on his return to England 'With gloire and honour, lawd and reverence,' and on Queen Margaret—'Gladeth thou Quenye of Scottis regioun'; in religious pieces, the refrain being usually a Latin quotation, as in *Done is a Battell*—'Surrexit Dominus de sepulchro'; and in the enforcement of petitions, as in *Sen that I am a Prisoneir*, where only the last word 'prisoneir' is common to all the refrains throughout the poem.

---

[1] *Œuvres*, ed. Prompsault, Paris, 1835, pp. 150-153.
[2] See Wright's *Political Poems*, passim.

But in the bulk of Dunbar's other poems the refrain is also a prevailing form. For the French kyrielle — aa, bb — he shows a special partiality, using it in the stately *Lament for the Makaris,* with its melancholy burden 'Timor mortis conturbat me'; in the remonstrance *Of James Dog,* with the humorous recapitulated warning, 'Madam, ye heff a dangerous Dog'; in the whimsical *Amendis to the Tailzours and Sowtaris,* with the ludicrous iteration, 'Tailzours and Sowtaris blest be ze'; and in some other dozen pieces with an equally admirable discernment of its relation to particular effects.

The Kyrielle.

He also adapted the refrain to the five-line stave, of four or five accents, derived from the French rondeau. This stave, either aa, bb, a, without the refrain, or aa, bab with the refrain,[1] is responsible for more than a third of Dunbar's pieces. Here is the stave as exampled in part of a rondeau of Villon :—

The five-line stave, with refrain.

> 'Sire, clarté perpétuelle,
>   Oui vaillant, plat n'y escuelle
>   N'eut oncques, n'ung brin de percil.
>   Il fut rez, chef, barbe, sourcil
>   Comme ung navet qu'on racle et pelle.'

Here is a stanza of unrefrained Dunbar, from *My Heid did Zak* :—

---

[1] For an example of a stave thus arranged, but without refrain, see *Adveyce to a Courtier,* by Quintyne Schaw, *ante,* p. 139.

'Full oft at morrow I wprise
Quhen that my curage sleipeing lyis,
   For mirth, for menstrallie and play,
sport   For din, nor dancing, nor deray
not awake   It will nocht walkin me no wise.'[1]

And here are two stanzas—from *Of Ane Blak-Moir*
—as modified by Dunbar's special device of the
refrain:—

'Quhen scho is claid in reche apperrall
smiles   Scho blinkis als brycht as ane tar barrell;
suffered   Quhen scho was born, the sone tholit clippis
eclipse
gladly   The nycht he fain faucht in hir querrell:
big   My ladye with the mekle lippis.

W   Quhai for hir saik, with speir and scheld,
most   Preiffis maist mychtelye in the feld,
         Sall kiss, and withe hir go in grippis
thence   And fra thyne furth hir luff sall weld;
         My ladye with the mekle lippis.'

We have also two examples—*The Petitioun of the
Gray Horse*, and *Now Culit is Dame
Venus Brand*—of a stave of six four-
accented lines—aaa, bbb—the last two
forming a double refrain, thus:—

Six-line stave
with double
refrain.

'Quhen I was zoung and into ply,
in condition And wald cast gammaldis to the sky,
capers   I had beine bocht in realmes by,
bought;   Had I consentit to be sauld.
adjoining   Schir, lett it nevir in toun be tald,
Christmas   That I sould be ane zuillis zald.'[2]

---

[1] This is the *In Memoriam* stave of Tennyson, plus an additional
line at the beginning.

[2] Zald, yald, or yaud = an old, worn-out horse, not worth being
cared for.

Another instance of a double refrain is found in *The Satire of Edinburgh,* which is properly a development of the five-line stanza with refrain, an additional line being added to the beginning, and an additional line of refrain being introduced in the form of a bob, the refrain thus taking the form of a bobwheel, and the stanza being composed of seven lines—aaa, bbab—six of four accents, and one of two, thus:— *The double refrain in the form of a bobwheel.*

> 'At your hie Croce, quhair gold and silk   high Cross
> Sould be, thair is bot crudis and milk;   curds
> And at zour Trone[1] bot cokill and wilk,   whelk
> Panches, pudingis of Jok and Jame:
>   Think ze nocht schame,   not
> Sen as the world sayis that ilk   Since; that same
> In hurt and sclander of zour name!'

It should be noted, however, that the word 'name,' alone, is common to the last lines of refrain throughout the poem.

In the seven-line stave of Chaucer—ab, abb, cc—named by Gascoigne *rime royal,* Dunbar wrote *The Thrissil and the Rois,* and other serious pieces, but he never fitted it as some early English poets do (e.g. *Lament of the Duchess of Gloucester* in Wright's *Political Poems,* i. 205, and Lydgate in that rollicking variety of the stave, the *London Lyekpenny*) with a refrain, using instead a stave thus arranged—aa, bb, cbc—a development of the five-line stave (see *ante,* p. 157). *The seven-line stave without and with refrain.*

[1] The Trone was the public weighing-beam, which occupied the site of the present Tron Church.

All his verse in this stave is of a more or less humorous, often coarsely humorous, kind. Here is an example in two stanzas from *Of a Dance in the Quenis Chalmer*, the broad buffoonery of the one stanza piquantly contrasting with the devoted sentiment of the other :—

Poet

nimbler
disorderly
dance

until;
slipper

'Than cam in Dunbar the Mackar,
    On all the floore thair was nane frackar,
    And thair he dannset the dirrye dantoun ;
    He hoppet lyke a pillie wantoun,
        For luff of Mwsgraeffe,[1] men tellis me ;
    He trippet, quhill he tint his pantoun :
        A mirrear Dance mycht na man se.

taught; the
others

Than cam in Maestriss Mwsgraeffe ;
    Scho mycht hef lernit all the laeffe ;
    Quhen I saw hir sa trimlye dance,
    Hir guid convoy and countenance,
        Than, for hir saek, I wissit to be
    The grytast erle, or duik in France :
        A mirrear Dance mycht na man se.'

Dunbar's solitary example of a nine-line stave — aab, aab, bab—is *The Goldyn Targe*. This stave was

The nine-line
stave.

used by Blind Harry and Robert Henryson, and also by Chaucer in *Faire Anelida and False Arcyte*.

There is also a solitary example of the very old octave stave in lines of four accents rhyming

Imperfect
macaronic
stave.

alternately—ab, ab, cd, cd (occasionally ab, ab, ab, ab, and ab, ab, ac, ac)—in *The Testament of Mr. Andro Kennedy*, a

Latin line alternating with the English one, thus

[1] The wife of Sir John Musgrave, who accompanied Queen Margaret to Scotland. Dunbar's jocular reference has been taken very seriously by some critics.

forming an imperfect variety of macaronic verse.
Here is a stanza:—

> '*Nunc condo testamentum meum*
>   I leiff my saull for euermair,   leave
> *Per omnipotentem Deum*
>   In to my lordis wyne cellare ;
> *Semper ibi ad remanendum,*
>   Quhill domisday, without disseuer,   Until; ceasing
> *Bonum vinum ad bibendum*
>   With sueit Cuthbert that luffit me never.'

This blended Latin and vernacular poetry is of very
early date. A long example in lines of three accents
is a *Song on the Times*, 1388.[1]

In that superb piece of word music and rhymal
ingenuity, *Ane Ballat of Our Lady*, Dunbar makes
use of an octave of alternating rhyming
lines of four and three accents respec-   Octaves with
tively, but enriches it in the four accented   bobwheel refrain.
lines by two internal rhymes, and fits it with a
Latin refrain introducing a bobwheel of three lines.
Here is an example:—

> 'Haile sterne superne ! Haile in eterne,
>   In Godis sicht to schyne !
> Lucerne in derne, for to discerne   darkness
>   Be glory and grace devyne !   By
> Hodiern, modern, sempitern,
>   Angelicall regyne !
> Our terne infern for to dispern   fierceness
>   Helpe rialest rosyne.
>   *Aue Maria, gratia plena !*
> Haile, fresche flour femynyne !
> Zerne ws, guberne, wirgin matern   Yearn toward
>   Of reuth baith rute and ryne.   pity; stem

> .   .   .   .   .

[1] Wright's *Political Poems*, i. 270.

Imperiall wall, place palestrall
  Of peirless pulcritud ;
Trywmphall hall, hie tour royall
  Of Godis celsitud ;
Hospitall riall, the lord of all
  Thy closet did include ;

rose

Bricht ball cristall, ross virginall,
  Fulfillit of angell fude.
    Aue Maria, gratia plena!
  Thy birth has with his blude,
Fra fall mortall, originall,

cross

    Ws ranusound on the rude.'

For *rime couée* Dunbar shows no great partiality,
but what varieties of it he has recourse to he uses with
Rime couée— his accustomed mastery.   An example
six-line stave. of it, in a modification of its simplest
form, is his *Sir Thomas Norray*, plainly suggested
by Chaucer's *Sir Thopas* ; but instead of the
Chaucerian six-line stave built on two rhymes—aab,
aab—he uses a six-line stave built on three rhymes
—aab, ccb—the head lines having four accents and
the tail lines three :—

listen
strong

    ' Now lythis of ane gentill knycht,
      Schir Thomas Norray wyse and wicht
        And full of chivalrie :
      Quhais father was ane grandë Keyne,
      His mother was ane Fairë Queen

begotten

        Gottin be sossery.'

The stave is derived from the Latin, but the minstrels whom Chaucer burlesqued got it from the
Anglo-Norman.[1]

By the device of repeating the rhyme of the tail
line, two six-line staves are linked together to form

[1] For Anglo-Norman example, see Wright's *Lyric Poetry*, p. 55.

the twelve-line stave of *The Dance of the Sevin Deidly Synnis* and *The Turnament*, aab, ccb, ddb, eeb. Numerous examples of this stave are to be found in Early English, and there is a curious variation on it in Latin—*Against the Lollards*, 1381,[1] made by interchanging the rhyme of the head and tail lines, thus: aab, aab, bba, bba. In *The Turnament* it admirably conveys the regular succession of incidents, and in *The Dance* the regular movements completing the dance of the several sins, a stanza being allotted to each sin, thus:—

Rime couée—twelve-line stave.

> 'Than Yre come in with sturt and strife ;
> His hand wes ay vpoun his knyfe,
>   He brandeist lyk a beir :
> Bostaris, braggaris, and barganeris,
> Eftir him passit in to pairis,
>   All bodin in feir of weir ;
> In iakkis, and stryppis and bonettis of steill,
> Thair leggis wer chenzeit to the heill,
>   Ffrawart wes thair affeir :
> Sum vpoun vdir with brandis beft,
> Sum jaggit vthiris to the heft,
>   With knyvis that scherp cowd scheir.'

Then Ire

bear
wranglers

clad in garb of war

covered with chain armour
Frowart; gait
beat
handle
cut

Dunbar supplies only one example of the common eight-line stave divided into two equal sections, *Quha will behold of Luve the Chance*, which is built on two rhymes only, aaab, aaab, the head lines being of four accents, and the tail lines of two only; but we have two instances of a sixteen-line stave, *The Fenzeit Freir*, and—if it be Dunbar's—*Ane Littill Interlud*

Rime couée—eight-line stave.

[1] Wright's *Political Poems*, i. 231.

built on four rhymes, aaab, cccb, dddb, eeeb.   In
The Fenzeit Freir the tail lines have three accents,
and the first and concluding staves are of twenty-
four lines.   In *Ane Littill Interlud* the tail lines
have two accents only.

The only remaining example of *rime couée* is *Thir*
Ladyis Fair, of twelve lines built on four rhymes,

Rime couée— aab, aab, ccd, ccd, the head lines
twelve-line having only two accents and the tail lines
stave of short three.   It is formed by doubling a six-
lines. line stave fashioned on the imperfect Iambic tetrameter,[1] of which there are examples in Early Norman,
and which became very common in England in the
sixteenth century.   The six-line stave is used by
Alexander Scott (see *post,* p. 244) both singly and as
part of a compound stave.

But apart from his mere achievements in rhyme
and rhythm, Dunbar is a special master of the art
Dunbar as a of expression, and if not a greater, a more
master of curious master than Chaucer.   In such
'terms aureate'
—'The Thrissil excessively allegorical poems as *The*
nd the Rois.' *Goldyn Targe* and *The Thrissil and the*
Rois—where the influence of the English 'makaris'
is at its strongest—he exhibits wonderful expertness
in the floridly ornamental style which was deemed
the fitting convention for such themes.   It is all
elaborately artificial—for even the 'intense sense
of colour,' which some critics praise, is a mere
mechanical intensity assumed for the nonce and

[1] See Guest, *English Rhythms,* p. 587.

resulting in the production of a landscape which, instead of glorifying, gives the lie to Nature—but the effect, if really cold, is at least nobly melodious. Here is an example from *The Goldyn Targe* :—

> ' Full angellike thir birdis sung thair houris   those
>> Within thair courtyns grene, in to thair bouris,
>>> Apparlit quhite and red, with blumys suete ;
>> Anamalit was the felde wyth all colouris,
>> The perly droppis schuke in silvir schouris,
>>> Quhill all in balme did branch and levis flete ;   float
>>> To part fra Phebus, did Aurora grete,
>> Hir cristall teris I saw hyng on the flouris,
>>> Quhilk he for lufe all drank vp with his hete.'   Which

In deference, it may be, to the English convention, Dunbar thought fit to celebrate the praise of London in the same highly decorative fashion. But, all the same, the poem indicates a special   London. mastery in the art of eulogy, and if occasionally the imagery be too formal and traditional, yet to what stately music has he set his numbers !

> ' Aboue all ryuers thy Ryuer hath renowne,
>> Whose beryall stremys, pleasaunt and preclare,
> Under thy lusty wallys renneth down,
>> Where many a swanne doth symme with wyngis fare ;
>> Where many a barge doth saile, and row with are,
> Where many a ship doth rest with toppe-royall,
>> O ! towne of townes, patrone and not compare :
> London, thou art the floure of Cities all.'

Yet excellent, in their own way, though these samples of Dunbar's 'terms aureate' be, they are mainly an echo of other 'makaris,' and moreover the echo of an affectation : they represent Dunbar as the disciple, the imitator, the masquerader, not

Dunbar as himself, as a new poetic force, as the
assimilator of many poetic influences — English,
Scottish, French—to his own growth in
individual skill and grace. Never, of
course, is his individuality entirely hid
amongst the profusion of his 'terms aureate': even
in *The Goldyn Targe*, besides the rhythmical music
and the polished diction, we have occasional examples of the condensed vividness of phrase and
epithet in which he excels all his predecessors (*e.g.*
'The skyis rang for schouting of the larkis,' 'Ane
saill as quhite as blossom vpon spray,' 'The schour
of arrowis rappit on as rayn,' 'For reird it semyt that
the raynbow brak'); but these are mere isolated
violations of his 'terms aureate,' violations that prove
the rule. It is only when he departs from the
allegorical and mannered method of his predecessors, and trusts to his own artistic instincts—to his
personal observations of nature and man, and to the
racy vernacular of which he had such limitless
command—that he does suitable justice to his gifts.
Happily his lapses into the allegorical and artificial
were only occasional. Indeed it is one of his chief
merits that he was not content to be merely imitative
even in manner, that he bent his energies to the
discovery of the mediums best fitted for the direct
and apt expression of each particular theme.

In no preceding poet does the verse, even in its
rhythmical form, more exactly mirror the sentiment
or thought. In the specially poetic quality of terse-

Dunbar greatest when he forsakes 'terms aureate.'

ness he outvies all his contemporaries or predecessors. Even Chaucer is chargeable with the prolixity which is the prevailing sin of all the early English poets from Chaucer to Lydgate; but in the *His terseness.* case of all Dunbar's more characteristic pieces, not a stanza, not a line, not even a word is superfluous. In this matter we may assume the influence of his French predecessors and contemporaries, which is further manifest in the polished perfection of his stanzas, and he also owed not a little to the racy vigour of the Scots vernacular; but only by his own sincerity and strength could he have achieved his own individual triumphs. Yet the triumphs were achieved at a certain cost. He is perhaps too succinct, too unexpansive. His genius was, it may be, 'cabin'd, cribb'd, confin'd' by his metres, by his mere love of form, as it was by the peculiarities of his career and circumstances; but at least within his own sphere he is, by virtue of his strong originality and the perfection of his art, fully entitled to a place among the worthiest.

The main theme of Dunbar is human nature, as found in himself and the world around him, and especially human nature represented from the humorous or satirical point of view. His view is comprehensive, and his method absolutely thorough and sincere. Whatever, for example, may be thought of his choice of such a subject as *The Twa Merrit Wemen and the Wedo*—however strange its coarse Rabelaisism may appear to modern eyes—there can

scarce be two opinions as to its remarkable qualities
as literature.   The great poetic beauty of several
passages, the cunningly executed contrasts between
appearances and reality, the vivid vigour of the narrative, the entire matter-of-fact air that pervades
the indelicate gossip of the ladies—all contribute to
the deadliness of the satire.   Analysis of the poem is
almost impossible, and quotation difficult; but the
following lines from the introduction, though rather
in Dunbar's ornate manner, will show how skilfully he
indicates the painting of the outside of the cup and
platter :—

'I saw thre gay ladeis sit in ane grene arbeir,

<table>
<tr><td>decked with</td><td>All grathit in to garlandis of fresche gudelie flouris ;</td></tr>
<tr><td></td><td>So glitterit as the gold wer thair glorius gilt tressis,</td></tr>
<tr><td>That ;
grasses</td><td>Quhill all the gressis did gleme of the glaid hewis ;</td></tr>
<tr><td>Combed</td><td>Kemmit was thair cleir hair, and curiouslie sched</td></tr>
<tr><td>Out over</td><td>Attour thair schulderis doun schyre, schyning full bricht ;</td></tr>
<tr><td>kerchiefs ;
fine cloth ;
beautiful</td><td>With curches, cassin thame abone, of kirsp cleir and thin ;</td></tr>
<tr><td></td><td>Their mantillis grein war as the gress that grew in May sessoun,</td></tr>
<tr><td>Fastened</td><td>Fetrit with thair quhyt fingaris about thair fair sydis :</td></tr>
<tr><td>marvellous</td><td>Off ferliful fyne favour war thair faceis meik,</td></tr>
<tr><td></td><td>All full of flurist fairheid, as flouris in June ;</td></tr>
<tr><td></td><td>Quhyt, seimlie, and soft, as the sweit lillies ;</td></tr>
<tr><td>opened</td><td>New vpspred vpon spray, as new spynist rose ;</td></tr>
<tr><td>verdure</td><td>Arrayit ryallie about with mony rich wardour,</td></tr>
<tr><td></td><td>That nature, full nobillie, annamalit fine with flouris</td></tr>
<tr><td>every ; man</td><td>Of alkin hewis under hewin, that ony heynd knew :</td></tr>
<tr><td></td><td>Fragrant, all full of fresche odour fynest of smell.</td></tr>
<tr><td>those</td><td>Ane marbre tabile coverit was before thai thre ladeis,</td></tr>
<tr><td>cups</td><td>With ryale cowpis apon rawys full of ryche wynys.'</td></tr>
</table>

Two of the fair ladies were married to lords and
the third was a widow, 'wantoun of laitis.'   The
more they 'wauchtit at the wicht wyne,' the more

unvarnished became their confidences to each other,
until they 'sparit no materis,' the matters they did
not spare being especially those of love and matrimony.
The two noble ladies' opinions of their husbands are
too expressive for quotation, and the experiences,
'wayis,' and 'wonderful gydingis' of the widow are
expounded with still greater liveliness. As for the
poet, his attitude is entirely neutral: he merely
reports 'thair pastance most mery,' and contents
himself with the ironical query:—

> 'Ze Auditoris, most honorable, that eris has gevin
> Onto this vncouth aventur, quhilk airly me happinit;
> Of ther thre wantoun wiffis, that I haif writtin heir,
> Quhilk wald ze waill to zour wif, gif ze suld wed one?'

those Which; choose; if

In somewhat piquant contrast to this gorgeous
picture of candid voluptuousness is the
daguerreotype of the two mutually dis-
sembling old women, who, in affected
dread of Lentern 'leanness,' are seen early on Ash
Wednesday in earnest methodical bibulation:—

'Rycht airlie on Ask Weddinsday.'

> 'Rycht airlie on Ask Weddinsday,
> Drynkand the wyne satt cumeris tway;
> The tane cowth to the tother complene,
> Graneand and suppand cowd scho say,
> "This lang Lentern makis me lene."

gossips two could Groaning lean

> On cowch besyd the fyre scho satt,
> God wait gif scho wes grit and fatt!
> Zit to be feble scho did hir fene;
> And ay scho said, "Latt preif of that:
> This lang Lentern makis me lene."'

God knows Let me taste

Both are equally concerned about the debilitating
effects of Lentern, and each with ready deference to

the other's judgment recognises the virtue that lies in
wine as a sovereign antidote, and so :—

> ' Off wyne owt of ane choppyne stowp,
>   Thai drank twa quartis sowp and sowp,
>   Sic drowthe and thirst was thame betwene,
>   Bot than to mend thai had gud howp :
>   That Lanterne sould not mak them lene.'

sup
Such

Another—still more impressive—instance of female
thirst is that recorded in *Kynd Kittok* — usually
assigned to Dunbar,—detailing the experiences of the alewife of Falkland Fells
in the other world. Though she died of ' thirst,'
she set out to heaven without misgiving, and, after
wandering a little, met a newt riding on a snail,
who permitted her to sit behind him until they
reached the inn at heaven's gate. Here she had
an opportunity of quenching her thirst, and on the
following morning eluded St. Peter and got into
heaven privily. ' God,' we are told, ' lukit and saw
her lattin in, and lewch his hert sair ' ; but for seven
years she lived quite soberly as Our Lady's hen-wife,

' Kynd Kittok.'

> ' And held Sanct Petir in stryfe,
>   Ay quhile scho wes in Hevin.'

But happening one day ' in an evil hour ' to look out,
the sight of the alehouse revived the old thirst :—

highway ; go

> ' And out of Hevin the hie gait cowth the wyfe gang
>   For to get ane fresche drink, ze aill of Hevin was sour.'

Nothing doubting, she again returned and rang the
bell for re-entrance, but St. Peter was this time on

the look-out, and drove her away with his club, so that she had nothing for it but to go back to her old occupation—the 'pitcheris to pour,' to 'brew and to baik'—in this other-world alehouse, where the Poet recommends his friends to call, on their way heaven-wards, and

> 'Drink with my gud dame as ze ga by
> Anys for my sake.'   Once

All these three sketches of female frailty are qualified by a certain humorous mirth. In that grim imagery of the recreations of Satan, *The Dance of the Sevin Deidly Synnis*, the mood is wholly saturnine. Suggested by the pageant of the *Dance of Death*, and by traditional conceptions of the seven deadly sins—such as those of Langland and Chaucer—the poem is yet a great individual achievement. It has been compared, to its disadvantage, with Langland's portrayal of the sins, but Langland is not so strictly poetical as expository, whereas Dunbar presents us with rapid kaleidoscopic scenes of startling vividness. The stanza on Ire has been already quoted (p. 163), and here is a compendious spectacle of 'sweirness' or sloth :—

'The Dance of the Sevin Deidly Synnis.'

> 'Syne Sweirnes, at the secound bidding
>   Come lyke a sow out of a midding,
>   Full slepy wes his grunzie :
>   Mony sweir bumbard belly huddroun
>   Mony slute daw and slepy duddroun,
>   Him serwit ay with sounzie ;

Then Sloth

snout
stupid ;
sloven
sluttish slug
gard ; drab
hesitation

chained
together

loins

motion

He drew thame furth in till a chenzie,
And Belliall, with a brydill renzie,
Evir lascht thame on the lunzie :
In dance they war so slaw of feit,
They gaif thame in the fyre a heit
And maid thame quicker of counzie.'

The grimness of the horrid pageant is slightly relieved by the ludicrous episode of Piper Macfadyane
and the Highlandmen; but the noise of the outlandish
crew proved too much for the nerves even of Satan,
and with the gruesome stoppage of it the poem
concludes:—

Gaelic began

croak

deafened

smothered

' Thae tarmegantis, with tag and tatter
Ffull lowd in Ersche begowth to clatter,
And rowp lyk revin and ruke :
The Devill sa devit wes with thair zell
That in the depest pot of hell
He smorit thame with smvke.'

Other general satires are the *Ballat against Evil
Women*; *The Dream*, directed against corruptions in
Other general
satires.
Church and State; and those indictments
of contemporary society, *Devorit with
Dreme*, and *Quhome to sall I complene my Wo*, the
latter filled with scathing stanzas like the following:—

every single

eye

In

' Fra everilk mowth fair wirdis proceidis,
In every hairt disceptioun breidis ;
Fra everylk E gos luke demure,
Bot fra the handis gois few gud deidis :
Into this world may none assure.'

And ending with solemn reminders of a judgment
other than that of man:—

> ' O ! quha sall weild the wrang possessioun,   who
>   Or the gold gatherit with oppressioun,
>   Quhen the angell blawis his bugill stoure,   strong
>   Quhilk vnrestorit helpis no confessioun ?   Which
>   Into this warld may none assure.'

Satires of more specific application are *Tidings from the Sessioun* and the *Ladyis Solisitaris at Court,* both dealing—and the latter somewhat suggestively — with the corruptions of the law-courts; *The Satire on the Trades,* *or the Devil's Inquest,* directed against the asseverations of tradesmen as to the quality of their goods; *Solisitaris at Court,* a succinct summary of the expedients employed to win the royal favour; the *Satire on Edinburgh,* a graphic but unflattering picture of the street scenes of old Edinburgh, of its smells and squalor, its craftsmen, minstrels, street sellers, and shouting crowds of sturdy beggars; and *How Dunbar was desyrit to be ane Friar,* which is mainly biographical, and concludes with the revelation that his tempter was not St. Francis but the Devil:—

Satires of specific application.

> ' He vaneist away with stynk and fyrie smowk
>   With him me thocht all the househend he towk
>   And I awoik as wy that wes in weir.'   one; trouble

Some satirical pieces have particular persons for their theme, as *The Flyting* (*ante,* p. 142); the picturesque *Testament of Andro Kennedy* (*ante,* p. 160), suggested, it may be, but nothing more, by the testaments of Villon; that amazing parody of ancient combats, *The Turnament,*

Satires on individuals.

a mock heroic account—the Devil being patron and referee—of an actual set-to betwixt a certain tailor and a certain shoemaker; the stinging *Epitaph* 'on the fell strong traitour,' Donald Owre (*ante*, p. 154); the ballad on the peculiar knightly adventures of Sir Thomas Norray (*ante*, p. 162); *We Lordis hes chosin a chiftane mervellous*, which 'chiftane mervellous' was the Regent Albany; *The Wowing of the King Quhen in Dunfermline*, in which the 'ferly case' of his Majesty in the character of a tod (fox) is set forth in caustic but unedifying detail; and *The Fenzeit Freir of Tungland*, inspired by the doings of a scientific quack, the Lombardian John Damian—promoted by the king to be Abbot of Tungland,—and especially by his futile attempt by artificial wings to rise into the air at Stirling.

Some of the stanzas of this exuberant and brilliant production are a sort of anticipation of Burns's *Death and Dr. Hornbook*; but its main feature

'The Fenzeit Freir of Tungland.'

is the realistic picture of the attack on this new and strange bird by the different fowls of the air, the flight, movements, and cries of the birds being suggested with great skill.   Here is one round of the combat:—

cloud
merlins;
hawks; sea-
mews
dashed

shout

'Thik was the clud of kayis and crawis,
Of marlezonis, mittanis and of mawis,
That bikkirt at his berd with blawis
   In battell him about;
They nybbillit him with noyis and cry,
The rerd of thame raiss to the sky;
And evir he cryit on Fortoun "Fy!"
   His lyfe was in to dowt.'

Finally he only escaped death by slipping out of the 'feddreme' (feathering) into a bog up to the eyes. His assailants thereupon 'dang' at the 'feddreme,' sending all the feathers into the air, while he lay scarce daring to breathe :—

'And he lay at the plunge evirmair
So lang as any ravin did rair ;
The crawis him socht with cryis of cair
In every schaw besyde.   bush
Had he reveiled bene to the rwikis,
Thay had him revin all with thair clwikis ;
Thre dayis in dub amang the dukis   mire ; ducks
He did with dirt him hyde.

The air was dirkit with the fowlis   darkened
That came with zawmeris and with zowlis   lamentings ;
With skryking, skrymming and with scowlis,   howls
To tak him in the tyde.   screeching ;
                                                                          screaming
I walknit with the noyis and schowte,   awoke
So hiddowis beir was me abowte ;   uproar
Sensyne I curss that cankerit rowte   Since then ;
Quhair evir I go or ryde.'   irritated

As to the satiric tale *The Freiris of Berwick,* with its curious glimpse of the ancient hostelry, and its deftly humorous sketches of friar human nature, there is no evidence that it was 'The Freiris of Berwick.' written by Dunbar; and though quite worthy of his powers, it seems to lack the special savour of his salt. It is therefore dealt with under ANONYMOUS POETRY (see p. 277).

Although so specially addicted to satiric humour, Dunbar was, as eulogist, at least the Eulogistic Pieces. equal of most poets laureate. The classic stanzas on London have been already alluded to

(p. 165); and *Blyth Aberdein,* commemorative of the queen's visit to that city in 1511, is a delightfully cheerful sketch of ancient burghal pageantry. Again, the ballad of *Lord Bernard Stewart,* if a little too ornate and high-flown, is skilfully attuned to the pomp and circumstance of war; and while the several pieces in honour of the queen are seemingly written *con amore,* the warmth of their loyalty is so tempered with discretion as never to verge on fulsomeness, although a certain poem, *To the Queen,* written on Fastern's Eve, startlingly reveals that the discretion of those days was different from that of our own.

Most of Dunbar's poems addressed to the king take the form of requests; but there is one exception, *A New Year's Gift,* a faultlessly graceful expression of good wishes. It begins:—

'A New Year's Gift.'

give thee

> ' My prince in God gif thé guid grace,
>   Joy, glaidness, confort, and solace,
>   Play, pleasance, mirth, and mirrie cheir
>   In hansell[1] of this guid new zeir.'

Specially interesting are those pieces in which Dunbar directly or indirectly deals with himself: his personal circumstances or his particular moods. Some are strongly Epicurean. Thus, in that strange parody of the Romish funeral service, *The Dregy to the King bydand too lang in Stirling,* he humorously invokes the whole spiritual hierarchy that the king may be delivered from his penitential sorrows to the jovial bliss of

'The Dregy.'

[1] Hansell = the first gift, the gift on New Year's Day.

'meriness' with Dunbar and the court at Edinburgh :—

> 'Patriarchis, profeitis, and appostillis deir,
> Confessouris, virginis, and marteris cleir
> And all the saitt celestiall,   tribunal
> Devotely we vpoun thame call,
> That sone out of zour painis fell,   dire
> Ze may in hevin heir with ws dwell,
> To eit swan, cran, pertrik, and plever   crane ;
> And every fische that swymmis in rever ;   partridge
> To drynk with ws the new fresche wyne,
> That grew upoun the rever of Ryne,
> Ffresche fragrant clairettis out of France
> Of Angerss and of Orliance,
> With mony ane course of grit dyntie ;
> Say ze amen for cheritie.'

We cannot suppose that this admirable—if rather
scandalous—parody was actually sent to the king at
Stirling, for James was serious enough when the fit
was on him, but we may well believe that by the
jovial 'company of lordis and knychtis,' in whose
name Dunbar writes, its recital would be received
with much merry approbation.

There is every reason to suppose that Dunbar himself devoutly practised the doctrines which he thus
enticingly expounded. In his naive   'Sanct
complaint as to the 'painfulness' of his   Saluatour.'
purse, *Sanct Saluatour: Send Siluer Sorrow*, he
thus laments :—

> 'Quhen men that hes pursiss in tone,   tune (well
>   Passis to drynk or to disione,   filled)
>   déjeûner
>   Than mon I keip ane grauetie,   must ; a
> And say, that I will fast quhill none :   until noon
>   My panefull purss so pricliss me.

M

such
coin stay

lose

> 'My purss is maid of sic ane skyn,
>   Thair will na corss byd it within ;
>   Fra it as fra the Feynd thay fle,
>   Quha evir tyne, quha evir win ;
>   My panefull purss so pricliss me.'

It is indeed only too probable that his many importunate addresses to the king, for promotion to a benefice, were prompted by constantly recurring pecuniary difficulties due in part to his jovial habits. They are curiously outspoken, and abound in shrewd aphorisms, partly bitter, partly humorous, and expressed with much cleverly varied felicity. In *The Petitioun of the Gray Horse* humour is subtly mingled with pathos :—

'The Petition of the Gray Horse.'

> 'I am ane auld horss, as ze knaw
>   That evir in duill dois drug and draw ;
>   Great court horss puttis me fra the staw
>   To fang the fog be firthe and fald ;
>   Schir, latt it nevir in toun be tald
>   That I sould be ane zuillis zald.' [1]

pull
stall
catch

Christmas

It is mainly when he touches on human life—its follies and delights, its mischances, griefs, uncertainties and vanity—that he kindles into true poetic warmth. In none of his few love-poems does he attain to passionate emotion; he does on one occasion refer to 'a deadlie passioun dolorous,' and in another makes use of the Language of Flowers to illustrate to a lady that she has every virtue except pity; but we probably possess none of

Love-poems.

---

[1] A worn-out horse, not worth being cared for.

his youthful verses on the passion, none written
before he had acquired such convictions as the
following :—

> 'Discretion and considerance
> Ar both out of hir gouirnance ;
> Quhairfoir of it the short plesance
>   May nocht indure ;   *not*
> Scho is so new of acquentance,
> The auld gais fra remembrance :
> Thus I gife our the obseruanss   *give over*
>   Of luvis cure.'

But apart from passion his outlook on life is
strongly emotional.   Such pieces as   *His outlook*
Meditatioun in Wyntir and *The Changes*   *on life—his*
                                            emotional
of Life indicate a special susceptibility   *moods.*
to the influences of the weather and the seasons :—

> 'Quhen that the nycht dois lenthin houris,
> With wind, with haill and havy schouris,   *troubled*
>   My dule spreit dois lurk for schoir,   *spirit ;*
>   My hairt for languor dois forloir   *cower for*
>   *dread*
> For laik of symmer with his flouris.   *wearies*
>
> .   .   .   .   .
>
> Zit, quhone the nycht begynnis to schort,
> It dois my spreit sum part confort,
>   Off thocht oppressit with the schouris.
>   Cum, lustie symmer ! with thy flouris
> That I may leif in sum disport.'   *live*

Sometimes his mood is recklessly jovial, as in *He*
that His Gold, ending 'Now all this time let us be
merry,' etc. (see *ante*, p. 150), and in *Man*
                                            Jovial mood.
sen thy Lyfe is ay in Weir, with the re-
frain, 'Thyne awin gud spend quhill thou has space.'
Yet he never attains to the light-hearted levity of

Villon, and indeed he most commonly advocates a merely cheerful stoicism :—

not

> 'Be mirry man ! and tak nocht far in mynd
>   The wavering of this wrechit warld of sorrow
> To God be hvmill, and to thy freynd be kynd,
>   And with thy nychtbouris glaidly len and borrow ;
>   His chance to-nycht it may be thyne to-morrow.
> Be blyth in hairt for ony aventure,

aforetime

>   For oft with wysmen it hes beene said aforrow
> Without glaidness awailis no tressour.'

But occasionally—from illness or special disappointments—his mood is much more sombre. In *The Lament for the Makaris* the poignancy of the pathos is intensified, and the melancholy deepened, rather than relieved, by the very nobleness and sincerity of the eulogy, and by his proud reverence for the vocation in which he, like those he lamented, had 'played his pageant.' His respect for the Muse was kin to that of Burns, and equally with him he was convinced that he had earned a lasting title to his country's remembrance. No contemporary worker—no architect, builder, goldsmith, lapidary, or other artificer at the court—had, he declares in his *Remonstrance to the King*, accomplished anything which would outlast what he had done :—

'The Lament for the Makaris.'

remembrance complete

Without wearing

> 'Als lang in mynd my wark sall hald !
>   Als haill in every circumstance,
>   In form and matter and substance,
>   But wering, or consumptioun,
>   Roust, canker, or corruptioun,
>   As ony of thair workers all,
>   Suppois that my rewarde be small !'

The *Lament* was no doubt more than suggested by Villon's ballads on the 'dames' and 'seigneurs' of olden time; but while Dunbar's thoughts concentrate on his poetic predecessors, Villon contrasts himself with those of whom he sings, and his mood is lightly defiant rather than melancholy.[1]

Sometimes Dunbar's own hard lot made him, as we have seen, specially bitter against the unrighteously prosperous, and it begot an occasional melancholy which revealed itself in such refrains as 'All erdly joy returns in pane.'

Dunbar's melancholy.

[1] Dunbar's final stanza, 'Sene for the deid remeid is none,' may be held to express only the conventional view of the priest; but let us take these two :—

> 'Onto the ded gois all Estatis,
> Princis, Prelotis, and Potestatis
> Baith riche and pur of all degre;
>   *Timor mortis conturbat me.*

poor

> .   .   .   .   .
>
> Sen he has all my brether tane
> He will nocht lat me lif alane;
> On forse I man his nyxt pray be:
>   *Timor mortis conturbat me.*'

Since; taken
not
Of necessity; must

The first of the stanzas reads like a mere echo of the first four lines of Villon's *Huitain*, xlii.; but the whole tone of the poem, as is more especially seen in the second stanza now quoted, is in absolute contrast with that of Villon as evidenced in the latter part of the *Huitain* :—

> ' Puys que Papes, Roys, filz de Roys
>   Et conceux en ventre de Roynes,
> Sont enseveliz mortz et froidz;
>   En aultruy mains passent les Reynes;
>   Moy, pauvre mercerot de Renes
> Mourray Je pas? Ouy se Dieu plaist;
>   Mais que J'aye faict mes estrenes :
> Honneste mort ne me desplaist.'

Compare also Dunbar's much inferior *Momento, Homo, Quod cinis es!*

Necessarily also with advancing years—years spent,
it may be, in penury and neglect, and, at any rate,
saddened with the defeat of many hopes—melancholy
tended more and more to prevail, and it occasionally
assumed a hortatory form, as in *Vanitas Vanitatum*:—

> ' Walk furth pilgrame, quhill thow hes dayis lycht,
>   Dress fro desert, draw to thy dwelling-place ;
> Speid home, for-quhy anone cummis the nicht
>   Quhilk dois thé follow with ane ythand chaise !
> Bend up thy saill, and win thy port of grace ;
> For and the deith ourtak thé in trespas
>   Then may thou say thir wourdis with allace !
> *Vanitas Vanitatum, et omnia Vanitas.*'

Forth from

constant

those

Such pieces are usually classed as moral or religious,
but they represent rather the sapience of old age.
Widely human as a moralist, Dunbar was
no ardent religionist. Thus his hymns
and other strictly religious pieces, apart from impressive references to the shortness and uncertainty of
life, are sonorous and stately, but little more. He
remained nominally true to a great time-honoured
faith which, though it impressed his imagination, had
not much hold of his intellect, but for whose imposing machinery he seems to have entertained a strong
traditional respect, and whose mysteries and observances he celebrated in nobly musical stanzas, embodying sentiments and beliefs which were mainly
mechanical.

Religious pieces.

A place among poets of the first rank has been
claimed for Dunbar by Sir Walter Scott, who asserts
that ' in brilliancy of fancy, in force of description, in

the power of conveying moral precepts with terseness, and marking lessons of life with conciseness
and energy, in quickness of satire and in   His place
poignancy of humour,' he may 'boldly   among poets—
                                          verdict of Sir
aspire to rival' Chaucer.[1] This strong   Walter Scott.
verdict—even if allowance be made for patriotic prejudice—should at least have assured to Dunbar
more careful, if not respectful, consideration than
some modern critics have bestowed on him.

By the late J. Russell Lowell [2] the very notion that
Dunbar was a poet at all was received with mere
derision. In his 'serious verses' he could   The late
find nothing that was not 'tedious and   J. Russell
                                           Lowell.
pedantic,' and his melodious and polished stanzas
he could only liken, for all the world, to 'unwieldy
hay-stacks of verse.' His humour was to Lowell only
the 'dullest vulgarity'; his satire, he conceded, 'would
be Billingsgate if it could,' but, failing, becomes 'a
mere offence in the nostrils.' Professing to regard
Dunbar with the same horror as he would a haggis,
he 'puts his handkerchief to his nose, wonders, and
gets out of the way as soon as he civilly can.' The
only excuse for such uncivil, if amusing, language—
language which would apply equally to much of the
poetry, not merely of the old classical writers, but of
Chaucer, and even Shakespeare, which confounds
poetry with convention, takes no account of the fact
that Dunbar merely wrote as it was then customary

[1] *Memorials of George Bannatyne* (Bannatyne Club, 1829), p. 14.
[2] *The English Poets*, in the Camelot Series, London, 1888, pp. 13-17.

to talk, and belittles or ignores all his admirable verse
that might be read without offence in the precisest
of drawing-rooms :—the only excuse for such sportive
mockery of a great writer is that, Dunbar being somewhat difficult reading, Lowell allowed himself to be
scared from a systematic perusal by abnormal moral
delicacy.

But once a process of detraction is begun it is
bound more or less to run its course, and echoes of
Professor Lowell's criticism may be found rever-
Courthope. berating noisily or faintly in almost every
recent allusion to the old Scottish 'makar.' Thus
Professor Courthope[1] proposes, as we have seen, to
confine Dunbar mainly to the care of the antiquary.
Taking what he regards as a 'cooler estimate of his
genius' than earlier critics, including Sir Walter, and
led astray by the initial mistake that Dunbar's
'talents were always employed in satisfying the
momentary taste of his patrons,' he confines his
reader's attention to *The Goldyn Targe, The Thrissil
and the Rois, Bewty and the Prisoneir,* and *The
Sevin Deidly Synnis*; the first three being introduced
as special instances of allegory, and the last in order
to point out that in the one instance in which, it
would seem, 'original genius' is claimed for him, he
is 'hardly entitled to it.'

No recent critic has more fully recognised the
merits of Dunbar as a metrist than Mr. Gosse,[2] who

[1] *History of English Poetry*, i. 370-74.
[2] *Modern English Literature*, pp. 48-51.

also does justice to other qualities, but withholds the
'first rank to his gorgeous talent,' and this solely on
the ground that 'he never escapes from
the artificial in language,' that he is
'defective in taste—rhetorical, over-ornate.'   But Mr.
Gosse has failed to recognise that Dunbar has two
styles—the artificially ornate, and the rich and racy
vernacular Scots.   One of his chief claims to greatness is, in fact, his subtle and comprehensive mastery
of expression : while such pieces as *The Goldyn Targe*
show that, as Lyndsay expresses it, he 'language had
at large,' the bulk of his best poetry really consists of
' escapes from the artificial in language.'

Dunbar was the disciple of Chaucer—his greatest
disciple, but he was something more.   So far as he
was a mere Chaucerian, or only the
ingenious contriver of varieties of traditional allegory, he has not much claim
to 'first rank,' notwithstanding his 'gorgeous talent.'   Such claim must be based mainly on the
belief that he got from Chaucer, from nearly contemporary French poets, and from the Scottish tradition
a peculiar and varied artistic training, which tended
only the more perfectly to develop his own poetic
idiosyncrasy.   He could be truly great neither as
Chaucerian nor as Scoto-Frenchman, but as essentially
a Scottish poet.   How far he is great is another
matter ; but uniting to his mastery of expression a
rare command of metrical effects, almost as rich and
brilliant a humorist as Burns, and an equally caustic

Mr. Gosse.

Dunbar more
than the
disciple of
Chaucer.   His
claim to 'first
rank.'

and more various satirist, strongly emotional and
illumined by a vivid and daring imagination,—if he
cannot be ranked with the greatest of English poets
it is less for lack in himself than in his circumstances.
Certainly these were far from propitious. His very
priestly profession was a great handicap; and though
he succeeded as poet—partly because he was an
unsuccessful, an abortive priest—the result was that
his life remained 'bound in shallows,' if not in
'miseries.' Then he was the poet of 'times that were
out of joint'; he lived on the borderland of change;
mediævalism was passing away, and the new era had
not quite arrived, nor was it fully to arrive in
Scotland for many generations. But as fully and
truly as Chaucer, he is the poet of his own time and
country, such as they were; more various, if more
fragmentary, in his methods, he is as effective in
depicting whatever comes within the range of his
experience; equally sincere and penetrating, he is, if
less genial and comprehensive, more succinct and
intense. His genius was never perhaps so fully
kindled, but that he has failed to obtain similar, if
not equal, appreciation is mainly part of the same
bad luck which dogged him while alive. The
poetic school of which he was the great master became presently smitten as with sudden palsy; the
veil of Biblical obscurantism descended on his
countrymen; for generations he was as extinct to
them as the Dodo; and now his vocabulary is to
many almost as effective a veil as the ancient insen-

sibility. Isolated very soon as regards Scotland, he remained totally unknown in England, and had no connection with the creation of the new poetic era that was to dawn in England some half-century after he went to his forgotten grave; but this again was rather his misfortune than his fault. His brilliant genius became buried for a time in complete oblivion, but that very oblivion of him, and of the poetic school of which he was the chief, was to be the means of only the more signally attesting its vitality; for this forgotten school of old Scots 'makaris' was, more than two centuries and a half after the death of Dunbar, to culminate in Burns.

VII

GAVIN DOUGLAS AND SIR DAVID LYNDSAY

In marked contrast with the fortunes of Dunbar were those of his contemporary—though some fifteen years **Gavin Douglas** younger—Gavin Douglas. Like Dunbar **(1475?-1522).** the cadet of a noble house, he was the third son of Archibald, fifth Earl of Angus, known by the expressive sobriquet of 'Bell-the-Cat,' and also as the 'Great Earl'—the great earl of a race that had long posed as rivals of even the royal line,—and became, by virtue of his abilities and his training as ecclesiastic, the political counsellor of his illustrious family in all its ambitious intrigues. He was born about 1475, and being designed for the Church, studied, like Dunbar, at the University of St. Andrews, where he matriculated in 1489, and graduated M.A. in 1494. An allusion of Major shows that he continued his studies at Paris; and it is more than likely that he somewhere completed a course of civil law. But as early as 1496 he had taken priest's orders, and was presented to Monymusk, Aberdeenshire, after which he became parson of Linton and rector of Hauch, or Prestonhauch (now Prestonkirk), near Dunbar.

Here in 1501 he wrote *The Palice of Honour*, in which he makes mention of 'Dunbar zit undeid'; and if the two poets up till then had never met, they doubtless did meet shortly afterwards when Douglas was preferred to the important dignity of Provost of the Collegiate Church of St. Giles, Edinburgh.

For twelve years or more the two poets walked the same streets, worshipped before the same altar, and mingled in the same modish society, but the one as a great ecclesiastical dignitary, the other as a penurious hanger-on of the *Douglas and Dunbar in Edinburgh.* court, soliciting in vain for 'ane kirk scant coverit with heather.' On 20th September 1513, Douglas— his translation of Virgil having been completed in the previous July—was 'without charge' also made a free burgess of the city—whether for political or literary reasons is uncertain ; but, anyhow, the older and greater poet, whose genius, like that of Burns, was perhaps in his own day as much dreaded as admired, and whose *Satire of Edinburgh* was scarce fitted to commend him to the powers that were, is not known to have lured from them any souvenir of literary approval.

Flodden, 9th September 1513, which put an end to all Dunbar's hopes of further favours from at least James IV., only opened up to Douglas new possibilities of preferment. Greatness *Douglas as candidate for a bishopric.* was virtually thrust on him. Appointed one of the new Lords of Council to give special guidance to the widowed queen, faithfulness to his house

demanded that he should make all possible use of
this rare opportunity of advancing its interests. He
it was, mainly, who effected the match between the
queen and his nephew and chief, the sixth Earl of
Angus; and after the marriage, 6th August 1514, his
ecclesiastical promotion became a matter of prime
consequence to his patrons. When asking from the
Pope confirmation of his appointment, the queen commended him, no doubt justly, as worthy 'of the very
highest ecclesiastical authority, even the Primacy.'
It so happened, also, that before the matter of the
abbacy was settled, the archbishopric of St. Andrews
actually fell vacant, 25th October 1514, and immediately both the queen and her brother, Henry VIII.,
sent earnest entreaties to the Pope on Douglas's
behalf. They were, however, ineffectual; and he
even lost the abbacy of Arbroath, which was conferred on Archbishop Beaton of Glasgow, the chief
opponent of Angus and the Douglases. In the
spring of 1515 he obtained the see of Dunkeld, but
the return of Albany from France in May entirely
checkmated the ambitious schemes of Angus, and
Douglas shared in his fall. He was thrown into
prison on the ground that the Papal confirmation of
his appointment had been procured by the illegal
interference of Henry VIII., and was not set at liberty
until a year afterwards, when Angus, for reasons of
his own, came to terms with Albany.

On obtaining his liberty, Douglas, by various humi-
liating apologies to his old ecclesiastical opponents,

obtained consecration and access to his see. For
some time he enjoyed in his beautiful Highland retreat the lettered ease which he probably Political
preferred to either ecclesiastical state intrigues,
exile, and
or political intrigue, but he could not death.
escape the destiny appointed for him by his family
connection. While Albany was still in Scotland he
was sent in 1517 to complete a treaty at Rouen
between France and Scotland against England; but
no sooner had Albany, in the same year, returned
to France than Douglas became engaged in new
intrigues for his nephew's return to power. For a
time Angus and the Douglases triumphed, but their
triumph wasn't final. Douglas did his utmost to
warn Wolsey and Henry VIII. to take precautions
against Albany's return in 1521, but in vain; and
when he did arrive in November, Douglas and Angus
had no resource but immediate flight to England.
There, though Douglas retained the respect both of
Wolsey and the king, and the special friendship of
Lord Dacre, he found himself latterly deserted by the
'unworthy Earl of Angus.' Deprived of his bishopric,
and disdaining to return to Scotland so long as Albany
remained there, he continued to reside in London,
making acquaintanceship, among other learned men,
with Polydore Vergil, to whom he supplied some
traditional information on the early history of Scotland—opposed to certain critical statements of Major
—which Vergil embodied in his *History of England*.
He never saw Scotland again, but died of the plague

in September 1522, and was buried in the Hospital Church of the Savoy.

Notwithstanding various conjectures and assertions, Douglas is not known as the author of other poetry than *The Palice of Honour, King Hart,* to which is attached some stanzas on *Conscience,* and *The XIII. Bukes of Eneados of the Famous Poete Virgile Translated out of Latyn Verses into Scottis Metir.* The *Palice* was written while he was still at Linton, the *Translation* was completed some months before Flodden, and *King Hart* is supposed to be of intermediate date: so that his nine years of political prominence were barren of any literary fruit.[1]

The works of Douglas.

Douglas represents almost solely an extreme development of the allegorical method introduced by James I., practised variously by Henryson, cultivated most likely by 'Greit Kennedie'

As allegorist.

---

[1] An edition of *The Palice of Honour* appeared at London some time before 1579, when an edition appeared at Edinburgh, in which there is also references to copies of the work 'set furth of auld amang ourselfis.' The Edinburgh edition was reproduced in Pinkerton's *Ancient Scotish Poems,* 1786, republished at Perth 1787, and reprinted in 1829 by the Bannatyne Club with variations from the London edition. *King Hart,* preserved in the Maitland MS. at Cambridge, was also published by Pinkerton in 1786. The *Virgil* was printed at London by William Copland in 1553, and reissued 1710, ed. Ruddiman, with corrections from the Ruthven MS. in the Edinburgh University Library; and an edition based on the MS. in Trinity College, Cambridge, was printed for the Bannatyne Club in 1839. Other MSS. are the Elphinstone in Edinburgh University Library, that in the Lambeth Library, and that belonging to the Marquis of Bath. Douglas's *Works,* ed. Small, were published at Edinburgh 1874, in four volumes.

—whose 'terms aureate' are specially lauded by Sir David Lyndsay—and exampled in several highly ornate productions of Dunbar. As allegorist, Douglas may have been the pupil of Kennedy, and he was partly the pupil of Dunbar; but his two poems are more laboured and extensive examples of pure allegory than any that survive in Scottish verse.

As for his language, though he is the first to regard himself as a 'Scottis' not an 'Inglis' makar, and though in the first prologue of his *Æneid* he professes to have taken special pains *His language.* to be vernacular—to 'mak it braid and plane,' and to keep 'na Sudroun but our own language,'—he had yet to confess that 'Scottis' was sometimes insufficient for his needs:—

> 'Nor zit so clene all Sudroun I refuse
> Bot some word I pronounce as neychtbour doise,
> Lyk as in Latyne bene Grew terms sum,
> So me behovit quhilum, or than be dum,
> Some bastard Latyne, French, or Inglis oiss
> Quhair scant war Scottis—I had na wther choiss.'

Southern
do
are Greek;
some
behoved
sometimes
use

The racy and rough vernacular was in fact unsuited for artificial verse; and—*King Hart* excepted—not only does Douglas have more frequent recourse than Dunbar to the southern speech, but he quite outvies him in the multiplicity and variety of his coinages from French and Latin, his language being often as incongruous as much of his allegorical imagery.

The distinctive note of *The Palice of Honour* is the intermixture of Sacred History and the Christian Faith with Heathen Mythology. It represents the

Catholic theology and morality humanised, only in part and unconsciously, by Greek and Roman poetry,

'The Palice of Honour.' Its distinctive note.

and clothed in an imagery incongruously compounded of Christianity and ancient Paganism. Even if it had been essentially poetic, its fantastic framework was bound to be fatal to its permanent popularity; but not only does it represent a merely artificial phase of sentiment, a temporary conjunction of streams of tendency bound in opposite directions: it is loaded with such a super-fluity of learned allusion as could not but be fatal to poetic inspiration.

Written partly in the nine-line stave of *The Goldyn Targe*—aab, aab, bab,—partly in a variation of it—aab, aab, bcc,—*The Palice of Honour*

Its subject.

is an allegorical representation of the difficulties and dangers attending the journey to true glory and honour, and in several ways antici-pates Bunyan's *Pilgrim's Progress*, whether Bunyan borrowed from it or not. According to the approved fashion, the poet having in a garden fallen into a swoon finds himself in a 'desert terrible' near by a horrible river, roaring in flood and swarming with yelling monsters. All around is only the waste wilderness, and he is beat upon by wild tempests of rain. Suddenly he hears the stamping and cry of a herd of beasts, and hides him in a clump of bushes, whence looking forth he sees pass successively before him the courts of Minerva, Diana, and Venus, the latter goddess attended by Mars and Cupid, and having in her train all the famous lovers—men and women—of sacred and classic story: some in hope, some in 'greit thirlage' (bondage), some in despair, some in perfect happiness and joy. Greatly commoved, he begins to sing a ballad on the 'inconstancy of love,' in which he curses the 'world's felicity, fortune, and all his pleasures,' which so enrages the goddess that he is seized and brought before her for judgment; but as sentence of condign punishment is about to be passed, the Court of the Nine Muses, attended by the great poets of ancient and modern times, arrives on the scene. Calliope interposes, and at her suggestion he composes and recites 'a ballad for Venus' plasour,' which mollifies Venus, 'and instant scho and her court was hence.' Under Calliope's protection, and on a splendid courser, the poet, with his fellow-followers of the Muses, then, swift as thought, traverses all the most famous countries of the world to the Castalian Fount, where, at a great feast, Ovid recites the deeds of ancient heroes, Virgil 'plays the sportes of Daphnis and Corydone,' Terence the comedy of Parmeno, etc. Then on their swift horses the company set forth on their journey to the Palace of Honour. Dismounting at the foot of the hill, the poet proceeds to climb it guided by an attendant nymph. Near the summit they are faced by a terrible abyss, from which rise the smoke of brimstone, pitch, and burning lead, and the wailing cries of unworthy pretenders who had vainly attempted to cross it. While he stands before it almost paralysed, his guide seizes him by the hair of the head, and brings him to the top of the hill. Here he sees below him the storm-tossed sea of the world, on which rides the carvel (ship) of the State of Grace; and looking above he beholds the Palace of Honour, standing in 'a plane of peerless pulchritude.' Entering the outer gate of its enclosure, he stands for a time rapt in admiration of its beauty, and is then conducted to Venus' Mirror, where he views the great events of Eternity and Time, and the 'deeds and fate of every earthly wight.' Next he is brought to the 'crystal palace white,' on the walls of which are engraven the wondrous sights of the universe, after which his guide discourses with appalling prosiness on 'Virtue as the only way to Honour, and not riches or hie blud.' Then bethinking her that after such an ordeal of wonders the poet would be benefited by 'taking the air,' she proceeds to conduct him to the garden, when in crossing the narrow bridge he falls into the moat and awakes. The poem then concludes with a ballad in commendation of Honour and Virtue, introducing inner rhymes in the manner of Dunbar. Here is the last stanza :—

'Haill rois, maist chois, till clois thy fois greit micht,
Haill stone quhilk schone vpon the throne of licht,
  Vertew, quhais trew sweit dew ouirthrew al vice,
Was ay ilk day, gar say the way of licht ;
Amend, offend, and send our end ay richt.
  Thow stand, ordant as sanct, of grant maist wise,
  Till be supplie, and the hie gre of price.
Delite thé tite me quite of site to dicht,
For I apply schortlie to thy deuise.'

to
which

each ; made

To ; degree
soon; shame;
cleanse

Less ambitious and grandiose than *The Palice of Honour*, *King Hart* is not so digressive and incoherent.   Its theme is more strictly moral and its method more direct, the cumbrous mythological imagery being altogether dispensed with.   It opens with this description of King Heart (the heart of man) :—

> ' King Hart, into his cumlie castell strang
>   Closit about with craft and mekill vre,
> So semlie wes he set his folk amang,
>   That he no doubt had of misaventure :
>   So proudly wes he polist, plane and pure,
> With zouthheid and his lustie levis grene ;
>   So fair, so fresche, so likelie to endure,
> And als so blyth as bird in symmer schene.
>
> For wes he never zit with schouris schot,
>   Nor zit ourrun with rouk, or ony rayne ;
> In all his lusty lecam nocht ane spot,
>   Na never had experience into payne,
>   Bot alway into lyking, nocht to layne,—
> Onlie to love, and verrie gentilnes
>   He wes inclynit cleinlie to remane,
> And wonn vnder the wyng of wantownness.'

Marginal glosses: 'King Hart.' Its theme. — toil — leaves — also — mist — body; no — Nor — to tell the truth — dwell

In this castle he is waited on by a troop of attendants — Strength, Rage, Wantonness, Green Lust, Disport, and many more—who, while they appear to minister to his wants, really have him under their control.   He has also five servitors—the five senses —to guard him from enemies without and within, but they occasionally betray him.   They show special hostility to the entrance of Honour, who, however, manages to enter by scaling the wall, and proceeds to the great tower which he adorns with ' mony florist

floure.' But near by the castle is the palace of Dame
Pleasaunce, and on her passing by the castle, the
king sends out Youthheid and Fresh Delight to
reconnoitre, who are immediately taken captive, as
are also various other succeeding scouts. Thereupon
King Hart resolves to give battle to the Dame, but is
defeated, wounded, and taken prisoner. Being attended also by Dame Beauty, he of course gets worse,
but by the treachery of Dame Pity he is set at liberty,
and then makes Dame Pleasaunce a prisoner in her
own palace. At last, however, Old Age gets admission, and his youthful attendants thereupon deserting
him, Conscience and Sadness intrude, and so vex
Dame Pleasaunce that she leaves her own palace.
Left alone in this 'empty pleasure house,' he is
advised by Wisdom and Reason to return to his own
castle, but has scarce reached it before Decrepitude
with attendant ailments gets entrance, and inflicts on
him a mortal wound—only sufficient strength being
left him to make his will, by which he bequeathes to
Dame Pleasaunce his palfrey Unsteadiness, to Fresh
Beauty, Green Appetite, and so on.

The theme is a representation of human life from
the traditionally Catholic point of view, and the trite-

*Its char-
acteristics.* ness of the theme is not redeemed by
exceptional vigour or brilliancy of treatment. The language is, however, simpler and purer
than that either of *The Palice of Honour* or *The
Æneid*, the narrative clear and comparatively concise,
and the versification—in the French octave—flowing

and melodious. What is mainly wanting is poetic afflatus. Eloquent and rhetorical Douglas often is; but though also a thorough proficient in poetical technique, he remains only a highly accomplished versifier.

The main performance of Douglas is his translation of *The Æneid* into heroic couplets, a remarkable achievement for his 'barbarous age,' and a not inconsiderable one in itself; for though his language is an incongruous blend of the familiar and the ornate, though his, on the whole accurate, renderings are achieved with excessive effort, and though he does not scruple for the sake of being better understood to clothe occasionally the old ideas in modern garb—representing Virgil, for example, as a baron, and the Sibyl as a nun—he is thoroughly interpenetrated with the Virgilian atmosphere, and succeeds in communicating this to the reader.

Translation of 'The Æneid.'

His prologues to the several books have also been much admired, especially the seventh, twelfth, and thirteenth, describing respectively Winter, May, and June. Douglas here shows that he had almost kindled at the flame of Virgil, the Virgil of the *Georgics.* They indicate at least great accuracy of observation: he records what he knows, and records it with a certain vigour and picturesqueness, but the redundancy of detail is fatally inconsistent with true poetical effect. Here is a short passage—one of his best—which may have suggested Burns's description of the flooded Ayr, but which needs only to be com-

pared with that vivid picture that its lack of poetic
inspiration may be felt :—

> ' Reveris ran reid all thair bankis downe,[1]
> And landbrist rumbland rudely with sic bier,
> So loud ne rummist wyld lioun or beir.
> Fludis monstreis, sic as meirswyne or quhailis
> For the tempest law in the deip devallyis.
>
> . . . . .
>
> Soure bittir bubbis, and the schowris snell,
> Semyt on the sward ane similitude of hell,
> Reducyng to our mynd, in every steid,
> Goustly schaddois of eild and grisly deid,
> Thik drumly scuggis dirknit so the hevyne.
> Dym skyis oft furth warpit feirfull levyne,
> Flaggis of fyir, and mony felloun flawe,
> Scharp soppis of sleit, and of the snypand snawe.
> The dowy dichis war all donk and wait,
> The law vaille flodderit all with spait.
> The plane stretis and every hie way
> Full of fluschis, doubbis, myre, and clay.
> Laggerit leys wallowit farnys schewe
> Broune muris kithit thair wysnit mossy hewe,
> Bank, bra, and boddum blanschit wolx and bair ;
> For gurll weddir growyt bestis haire ;
> The wynd maid wayfe the reid weyd on the dyk
> Bedovin in donkis deyp was every syk.'

---

[1] Rivers ran red down all their banks, the breakers rumbling
rudely with a noise louder than the bellowing of wild lion or bear.
Sea monsters, such as porpoises and whales, remained on account of
the tempest low in the deep. . . . Sour bitter blasts seemed on the
sward a similitude of hell, creating to our imagination, in every place,
ghostly shadows of eld and grisly death—thick gloomy shadows
darkened so the heavens. Dim skies frequently sent forth fearful
lightning, flashes of fire and many a dreadful blast, sharp blasts of
sleet and of the biting snow. The dreary ditches were all dark and
wet, the low valley flooded with overflow. The plain streets and
every highway full of overflowing water, pools, mire and clay.
Mud-covered pastures showed decayed ferns, brown muirs showed
their wizened mossy hues. Bank, incline, and level became white

Read as prose the passage is not without considerable merit.   It is full of a kind of picturesque
gloom.   The whole description is, however, a mere
catalogue of facts accurately and minutely observed,
but not grouped so as either to indicate their
relative significance, or to lead to any proper poetic
climax.

Several of the prologues are written in stanzas:
the second in *rime royal*, the third in the less frequent variety of the nine-line stave, the   Metres of the
fourth in *rime royal*, the fifth in the   Prologues.
nine-line stave of the third, the sixth in the French
octave, the eighth in the alliterative romance stave
with the bobwheel, the tenth in the five-line stave
of Dunbar—aa, bb, a,—and the eleventh in the
French octave.

Sir David Lyndsay of the Mount, Lyon King-at-
Arms, the only one of the older Scots 'makaris'
whose popularity remained unbroken   Sir David
by the Reformation, and survived to   Lyndsay
modern times, was the son of David   (1490-1555). His
                                       early life.
Lyndsay, who possessed two estates—The Mount in
Fife, and Garmylton, near Haddington.   On account
of this duality, the son's birthplace, as well as place
of education—Haddington or Cupar Grammar-School
—is a matter of doubt.   That he attended St.
Andrews University is inferred from the name 'Da.

---

and bare.   On account of the stormy weather the cold beasts
shivered.   The wind made the weed wave on the stone fence.
Filled with deep water was every rill.

Lindesay' in the roll of incorporated students of St. Salvator's College, 1508-9—immediately above that of 'Da. Bethune' (afterwards Cardinal); but the student at St. Andrews could scarce have been the Lyndesay who, as equerry of the young prince, received in 1508 a certain sum for 'his fee and his horse's keep.' In any case, the poet had in 1511-12 a pension of £40 a year as a member of the Royal Household, though a blank in the Treasurer's Accounts from 1508 renders it impossible to state when the pension began.[1] Since, also, a sum of £3, 4s. was on 12th October 1511 paid for a play coat to him, for a play performed at Holyrood, he was probably at first employed chiefly as an actor or musician; and confirmation of this seems to be supplied by his own statements. On the birth of James V., 10th April 1512, he was 'appointed the Keeper of the Kingis Grace's person'—not his tutor, but his attendant and companion; and in his *Epistle to the Kingis Grace* he mentions that he was accustomed, 'lute in hand,' to sing the young prince to sleep; and that he amused him sometimes with dancing, sometimes 'with play- and farces on the floor.'

> ' And sumtyme, lyk ane feind transfigurate,
>   And sumtyme lyk the greislie gaist of Gye,
> In divers formis oft tymes disfigurate ;
>   And sumtyme dissagysit full plesandlye.'

---

[1] It should also be noted that in *The Dialog* (ll. 597-8), Lyndsay regrets that he hadn't 'the tongues,' and seems even to imply that he was ignorant of Latin. His lack of a University education would also account for the fact that he was merely the attendant not the tutor of the young prince.

These accomplishments partly explain Lyndsay's appointment in 1529 to be Lyon King-at-Arms, for this implied official charge of what Knox terms the 'farcings, maskings, and other prodigalities,' then such an essential feature of royal fêtes. A pretty accurate notion of the pageantry on these occasions may be gathered from Lyndsay's own sorrowful lament, in the *Deploratioun of the Death of Queen Magdalene*, over the preparations for her coronation, thus rendered abortive. Of the arrangements for the reception of Mary of Guise at St. Andrews in May 1538 he had also special charge. She was received, Lyndsay of Pitscottie tells us, with ' greit joy and mirriness, of fearssis and plays maid and prepared for hir'; and first at the New Abbey Gate there was erected a triumphal arch ' be Sir David Lyndsay of the Mont, Knight, alias Lion King of Armes, who caused ane great cloud to cum doun out of the heavines abone the yett: out of the quhilk cloud came doun ane fair ladie, most like ane angell, having the keyis of Scotland in hir hand, and delyvered them to the queines Grace in signe and tokin, that all the heartis of Scotland war oppin for ressaving of hir Grace.'

As Lyon King Lyndsay compiled a *Register of Scottish Arms* (published in 1820). He was also often sent on embassies to foreign courts; and while at Brussels in 1531 was witness of a great tournament, of which he wrote for the king a description, ' in

As Lyon King.

His later years. Was he a ' Protestant Reformer'?

articles,' which is now lost. In May 1546 he was
intrusted by Parliament — where he sat as Com-
missioner for Cupar — with the official duty of
summoning the murderers of Cardinal Beaton to
surrender the Castle of St. Andrews, which in
December he did, but without result. Perhaps
about the same time he was privately engaged
in penning his *Tragedy of the Cardinal*, printed
in London, 1546-7; and, according to Knox, he
was in close communication with the Reformers,
and advised that Knox should take upon him
the office of preaching. But he can scarce be held
responsible for what Knox did actually preach,
and there is no evidence that he ever formally
joined the Reformers, or even once attended the
preaching of Knox. The fact that he remained
formally a Catholic, and that he ceased to satirise
between the death of James v. in 1542 and the
murder of Cardinal Beaton in 1546, largely accounts
for his escape from prosecution, and his retention of
office till his death, 18th April 1555.

Lyndsay was married in 1522 to Jonet Douglas,
who was probably a female attendant on the young

His wife.

prince, and at anyrate, even after her
marriage, received various sums for sew-
ing the 'kingis sarkis.' They had no children; but
that their married life was unhappy is a mere inference from the 'terms in which he commonly talks
of the sex.'

Lyndsay's[1] poetical relations to his time are in a
measure paralleled by those of Dunbar to the immediately preceding period; but the contrasts   Lyndsay com-
are greater than the similarities. Dun-   pared with
                                             Dunbar. His
bar's satires were prompted partly by his   coarseness.
chronic dissatisfaction with his lot; but only once,
and just before he became Lyon King, does Lyndsay
—*Complaynt to the King*—express special discon-
tent at lack of reward for his services. Unlike that
of Dunbar, his verse is less the utterance of accidental moods than of permanent convictions. Versifier rather than poet, and influenced by a definite
practical purpose, he is both narrower and more
superficial in his judgments—his point of view being
that of the average man, his art that specially fitted
to tickle the crowd. Yet moralist though he professes to be, he quite outvies Dunbar, if not in the
candour, in the coarseness of his allusions, and this,
in part, because not otherwise could he amuse and
gratify the gross multitude he sought to convince.

[1] Lyndsay's *Complaynt of the Papyngo* appeared at London in
1538; *The Tragedy of the Cardinal* at London c. 1546-47; *Ane
Dialog betuix Experience and ane Courteour* at Copenhagen (? St.
Andrews), probably in 1554; editions of his *Poems* at Paris, 1558,
Copenhagen (? St. Andrews), 1559, and London, 1566; *The Pleasant Satyre of the Thrie Estaitis* was first published at Edinburgh in
1602; the interludes, more fully than in the 1602 édition, are
preserved in the Bannatyne MS. It was included in subsequent
editions of his *Poems*, many of which appeared in the seventeenth
as in the sixteenth century, but fewer in the eighteenth. The
modern editions are those of Chalmers, 3 vols., London, 1806; the
English Text Society, 1865-71; and David Laing, 3 vols., Edinburgn,
1879. Laing gives a pretty full bibliography of previous editions.

To select ribald buffoonery as the special medium for
the promulgation of a strict conventional morality,
may strike a modern reader as the very acme of the
preposterous; but lacking ribaldry all the satiric
verse of this period in Scotland would have been
almost wholly ineffective. Still, Lyndsay and his
fellow-satirists themselves partly shared in that special
penchant for ribaldry, which is the efflorescence of a
disordered social system; and that being so, the free
course permitted, for generations, to the poetry of
Lyndsay amongst a community too Puritan to peruse
the best secular poetry of England, is an impressive
example of the, at least occasional, irrationalities
of ecclesiastical opinion. Lyndsay's method, effective
for the time being, was bound in the long-run rather
to defeat than further that portion of his purpose
which concerned specially the laity ; and it may be
that his sustained popularity among the mass of the
people has some connection with the specially fescen-
nine character of much of the Scottish folk poetry.

As satirist a superficial pupil of Dunbar, Lyndsay
also largely utilised the allegorical machinery which
His practical   Dunbar and Douglas had done so much
aim.   to elaborate. Like Douglas and unlike
Dunbar he was a poet with a purpose, and, as in
Douglas, the strenuous moral aim is more manifest
than the poetic inspiration. Douglas, the poet of the
old Catholic morality, curiously blended with chivalry
and classicism, was primarily meditative and abstract.
Lyndsay, the precursor of Puritanism, depicts the

Catholic morality in its decay, and is above all things practical. For Douglas he had a special esteem as the 'lamp' of 'this land,' and 'in our Inglis rethorick the rose,' and no doubt obtained from him valuable hints in the construction of his peculiar variations of the traditional allegory; but though *The Dialog* is as comprehensively pedantic as *The Palice of Honour*, even it is by no means so exemplary; while nothing could be in stronger contrast with Douglas's irreproachable allegories than some of Lyndsay's plain, practical, and ribaldly moral medleys.

It may be that in his earlier years Lyndsay practised various forms of poetry for the amusement of the young prince; and it seems His relation to to have been largely his special interest the Clergy. in the young king's welfare that moved him, as late as 1528, to make his formal appearance as a serious poet. If he specially satirised the clergy, it was because he regarded them as largely responsible for the political and social mischiefs of the time. Taking an essentially common-sense view of human conduct, he had no difficulty in exposing the glaring contrast between the ecclesiastical ideal and the ecclesiastical reality. He represented in part the resentment of the nobles and gentry at the grasping ambition of the Church, in part the derision of the people at the Church's open violation of its own moral code; but he was further specially incensed at the injurious influence exercised by the clergy over the king.

Lyndsay's productions have sometimes a curious biblical or theological framework, and even when the biblical influence is not, as it is in *The Dialog,* paramount, they frequently teem with theological allusions ; but except as satirist he is dull and commonplace, and much of his effect as satirist is due to the fact that the subject lent itself so easily to satire. Merely to state the truth, and nothing but the truth, was almost satire sufficient. Still, to state it as he has stated it implied at least an ardent and strong, if not quite poetic, personality ; and though his wit too often sinks into mere buffoonery, the buffoonery is not without cleverness, and the wit was no doubt thoroughly enjoyed by the rude community to whom it was addressed.

As Satirist.

The earliest of Lyndsay's pieces, *The Dreme* (1528), is comparatively exemplary and only partially satirical. Written in *rime royal,* it is a kind of allegorical medley, bringing within the compass of its survey Hell, Purgatory, the Starry Firmament, Heaven, the Earth, Paradise, and Scotland, and all this to impress on the king his obligations as ruler of the nation. It opens with an *Epistle to the King,* full of personal reminiscences, such as those already quoted (p. 202), after which, in his prologue, he details how one bleak day of January he wandered to the seashore, and falling after the accustomed manner asleep in a cave, dreamed the 'marvellous vision' he sets himself to record.

'The Dreme.'

The poem contains the story of his adventures with Dame Remembrance, who, to cure him of his melancholy, proceeded to conduct him on a tour through the Universe, beginning with the Lowest Hell. Here his attention was first engrossed by the shoals of ecclesiastics, from popes and cardinals down to 'cunning clerkis' and 'priestis secularis,' who for 'covatyce, lust and ambition' were doomed

Its story— visit to Hell.

> 'eternallie [to] dwell
> Into this painefull poysonit pytt of Hell.'

But heretics innumerable were also to be seen, 'with carefull cryis girning and greityng,' as well as 'princes, lordis temporal, and caitive kings,' all well represented, and even many noble ladies,

> 'Lyk wod lyonis, were carefullie cryand   *mad*
> In flame of fyre richt furiouslie fryand.'

Nor was the 'pain that is perpetuall' reserved alone for the learned and powerful, for

> 'mony ane thousand
> Common pepill lay, flichterand in the fyre,
> Of everilk stait there was ane bailfull band.'   *every*

After this 'dolorous dungeon,' Purgatory failed to greatly impress him, but he viewed with some interest the Place of Perdition tenderly 'reserved' for 'unbaptised infants'! and also that mild dungeon of our 'forefathers,' termed the Lympe.

Purgatory.

Emerging through the bowels of the earth from
'these places perrelous,' they ascended beyond Earth,
Water, Air, and Fire, and made the
round of the Seven Planets (learnedly
described after the lore of the 'cunnyng
astrologis' of the time).   Beyond their melodious
harmony, they then mounted up through the 'Chris-
tallyne' Heaven, until they entered Heaven itself,
peopled according to the accepted theological arrangements.

The Seven
Planets and
Heaven.

On his way down through the 'spheres of the
Heavens' he was then granted a view of the Earth,
'all at one sight,' after which he was permitted to behold the original Paradise,
which, in lines faintly anticipatory of those of Milton,
is thus described :—

Paradise.

> 'The countre closit is aboute, full rycht
> With wallis hie, of hote and birnyng fyre,
> And straitly kepit be ane Angell brycht,
> Sen the departyng of Adam, our grandschyre ;
> Quhilk, throw his cryme, incurrit Goddis yre,
> And of that place tynte the possessioun
> Baith from hymself and his succession.'

Since
Who
lost

From Paradise he proceeds to Scotland, whose
advantages and 'great commodoties'—its lochs and
rivers teeming with fish, its fruitful
mountain pastures, its lusty vales for
corn, its forests of deer, its metals and precious
stones, its wholesome fruits, and its fair and ingenuous people—prompt the query as to its strange
poverty.   To this the reply is want 'of justice, policy,

Scotland.

and peace,' due to the negligence of the 'infatuate heidis insolent,'—that is, the bishops and those of the nobles who were usurping the functions of government.

But while the poet and his guide were thus 'talking to and fro,' they

> 'Saw a bousteous berne cum ouir the bent
> But hors, on fute, als fast as he mycht go,
>   Quhose rayment wes all raggit, revin and rent ;
> With visage leyne, as he had fastit Lent :
> And fordwart fast his wayis he did advance,
> With ane rycht melancolious countynance.'

vigorous fellow; moorland Without a

This was John the Commoun Weill, who, having been maltreated in every district of the country, was 'with scrip on hip, and pyik staff in his hand,' hastening to leave it. Asked when he would return, he answered not until the court was guided by the wisdom of 'ane gude auld prudent king' :—

John the Commoun Weill.

> 'Als yit to thee I say ane uther thyng :
>   I see rycht weill, that proverbe is full trew :
> "Wo to the realme that hes ouer young ane king"—
>   With that he turnit his bak and said "Adew."'

too ; a

The Complaynt to the King—in the octo-syllabic couplet—written in celebration of the king's escape from the Douglases in 1529, is, while reminiscent, congratulatory, denunciatory (of the king's advisers), and admonitory (of the king himself), in substance a plea on the poet's part for some recognition of his past services. The manner of that recognition he leaves to the king himself,

'The Complaynt to the King.'

but is rather inclined to suggest the loan of one or
two thousand pounds, which he undertakes to pay on
conditions having plainly a satirical reference to the
all too ready oaths of indigent borrowers :—

> ' Quhen the Basse and the Yle of Maye
> Beis sett vpon the Mont Senaye ;
> Quhen the Lowmond, besyde Falkland,
> Beis lyftit to Northumberland ;
> Quhen kirkmen yairnis no dignitie,
> Nor wyffis no soveranitie ;
> Wynter but frost, snaw, wynd, or rane ;
> Than sall I geve thy gold agane ;
> Or, I sall mak the payment
> Efter the Daye of Jugement,
> Within ane moneth at the leist,
> Quhen Sanct Peter sall mak ane feist
> To all the fycharis of Aberladye,
> Swa thow have myne acquittance reddye ;
> Failyand thareof, be Sanct Phillane,
> Thy grace gettis never ane grote agane.'

without

a

So
by

The following year Lyndsay wrote the much more
pungent *Testament and Complaynt of our Soverane
Lordis Papyngo* (parrot).   It opens with
a prologue—in the nine-line stave, aab,
aab, bcc—in which, after a warm eulogy
of several famous ' makaris,' from Chaucer
to his own day, he humorously declares that

' Testament
and Complaynt
of the Papyn-
go.'   The Pro-
logue.

> ' in all the garth of eloquence
> Is no thyng left, bot barrane stok and stone
> The poleit termes are pullit everilk one,
> Be thir fornamit Poetis of prudence ' ;

garden

every single
By those

and that since he could find ' none uther new
sentence,' he had resolved to record the ' complaynt

of ane woundit Papyngo.' He then utilises the impalement of the king's parrot on a stake by a fall from a lofty tree for the exposition, in the parrot's name, of his own views on Church and State. After lamenting—in *rime royal*—her rashness in climbing to such a giddy height, the dying bird proceeds—also in *rime royal*—to 'breve' her counsel (1) to the king, and (2) to her 'Brether of courte'; and this is followed by (3) the 'commonyng betuix the Papyngo and hir holy executouris.'

The first epistle is a shrewd and outspoken address on kingcraft, in which his Majesty is reminded that of his fivescore and five predecessors on the Scottish throne, no less than five-and-fifty had been slain, The first epistle.

> 'And moist parte, in thair awin mysgoverance.'

The second epistle illustrates by interesting examples from Scottish history—such as the cases of the Duke of Rothesay, Murdoch, Duke of Albany, Cochrane, the favourite of James III., the dowager Queen Margaret herself, Archbishop Beaton, and the Earl of Angus—the 'over-leaping' of that 'ambition' which seeks either to usurp the sovereignty or to make the sovereign its bondman. The second epistle.

But it is in the 'commonyng' of the wise bird with her 'holye executouris'—the pyot (a canon regular), the raven (a black monk), and the gled (a holy friar), that the satire is most biting. Though their professional visit to the dying bird was 'The Commonyng.'

avowedly dictated by concern for its ghostly interests, their solicitude was all centred on its 'goods and chattels.' The pyot recommended itself as executor, because it was 'ane holye creature'; but the immediate arrival of the raven and the gled changed the situation. The three worthies combined in the general interests of the Church and of one another, and the gled in their name vowed that if the dying bird made a 'memorial of its gear,' they would make its funeral feast, burying its bones with 'great bliss,' and afterwards twenty masses all at once :—

> 'And we sall syng about your sepulture
>   Sanct Mongois matynis and the mekle creid :
> And syne devotely saye, I yow assure,
>   The auld Placebo bakwart and the beid ;
> And we sall weir, for yow, the murnyng weid :
> And, thocht your spreit with Pluto war profest,
> Devotely sall your Diregie be addrest.'

larger
then

clothes
though

To this the Papyngo replied with many acute observes on ecclesiastical worldliness; and though, having no other option, she accepted them as executors, she bequeathed her personality thus: her 'gay galbarte of grene,' her 'brycht depurit ene,' her 'burneist beik,' her 'music' and 'voce angellycall,' her 'toung rhetoricall,' and her 'bones,' respectively to the owl, the bat, the pelican, the cuckoo, the goose, and the phœnix, and her heart to the king, leaving to the executors only her 'trypes,' with her 'luffer and lowng to part equale' among them. But instead of giving faithful effect to her wishes, hardly had she said *In Manus*

The Will.

Tuas when all three began incontinently to devour her body, and when nothing was left but the heart, away flew the gled with it hotly pursued by the other two.

To some of Lyndsay's counsel the king made reply in pretty scurrilous verse; for in *The Answer to the Kingis Flyting* — in *rime royal* — he retaliates with some rather abusive admonition, the more piquant portions of which are, however, too graphic for quotation. Other short pieces, written in the lifetime of James v., are *Ane Publict Confessioun of the Kingis auld Hound callit Bagsche*—in the French octave,—a satire on the intrigues and quarrels of the courtiers; *The Deploratioun of the Death of Queen Magdalene*, in *rime royal*; *The Justing betuix James Watsoun and Jhone Barbour*—in the heroic couplet,—an account, mildly modelled after Dunbar's *Turnament*, of a mock encounter between two 'medicinaris' of the court; *Kitteis Confessioun*—in couplets,—a more than witty exposure of the misuses of auricular confession; *Ane Supplicatioun againis Syde Taillis*, one of the coarsest, yet one of the most diverting of his skits, and a most lively sketch of contemporary female fashions. Here are a few decorous lines :—

> 'Bot, I lauch best to se ane Nun
> Gar beir hir taill abone hir bun,
> For nothing ellis, as I suppois,
> Bot for to schaw hir lillie quhyte hois ;
> In all thair Rewlis, they will nocht find
> Quha suld beir up thair taillis behind.

Short pieces written during the lifetime of James V.

a
Make bear

not

Poor draggled-tail wenches
Who

Kittie; last night
To-morrow

ewes

houghs

cow-house; stay
Unless
burghs
longest

vexation

nose
eyes

Bot I have maiste into despyte
Pure claggokis cled in roiploch [1] quhyte,
Quhilk hes skant twa markis for thair feis,
Will have twa ellis beneath thair kneis :
Kittok, that clekkit wes yestrene,
The morne, wyll counterfute the Quene :
Ane mureland Meg, that milkit the yowis,
Claggit with clay abone the howis,
In barn, nor byir, scho wyll nocht byde
Without her kyrtyll taill be syde.
In burrowis, wantoun burges wyiffis,
Quha may have sydest taillis stryiffis,
Weill bordourit with velvoit fyne :
Bot following thame it is ane pyne,
In somer quhen the streittis dryis,
Thay rais the dust abone the skyis ;
None may ga neir thame at thair eis,
Without thay cover mouth and neis,
Frome the powder to keip thair ene :
Considder gif thair cloiffis be clene !'

But the most characteristic and the cleverest of Lyndsay's productions is *Ane Pleasant Satyre of the Thrie Estaitis in Commendatioun of Vertew and Vituperatioun of Vyce.* An adaptation to current political and social questions of the old morality play, it is a nearer approximation to the regular drama than any contemporary English production. The idea was not of course original, for in England John Heywood's merry interludes against the Papists preceded — some of them, at least—Lyndsay's *Pleasant Satyre,* and John Bale, who utilised the morality play for the same purpose, was his contemporary. Further, a Scottish friar

'Ane Pleasant Satyre.' The Drama in Scotland.

[1] Coarse undyed woollen cloth.

named Kyllour 'set forth,' in 1535, a play 'against
the Papists'[1] at Stirling. But the interludes of
Heywood were mere single acts; and while the plays
of Bale differ little from the old moralities, Kyllour's
play, which has not been preserved, was a mere adaptation of *The History of Christ's Passion*. It may be,
however, that apart from Lyndsay, Scotland was at
this time slightly in advance of England in drama,
as she also was in poetry. That strange fragment,
the *Interlude of the Droichis Part of the Play*—
preserved in the Asloan and Bannatyne MSS., dating
from at least the earlier years of the sixteenth century, and supposed by some to have been the work of
Dunbar,—seems to indicate the existence, even in the
reign of James IV., of some better examples of drama
than possibly even Lyndsay's *Pleasant Satyre*. We
are also told by the historian Calderwood[2] that James
Wedderburn, about 1540, 'made divers comedies and
tragedies,' wherein 'he nipped the abuses and superstitions of the time,' among them 'The History of
Dionysius the Tyrant, in form of a comedy which was
acted in the playfields' of Dundee. Robert Birrel also
mentions that, on 17th June 1568, a play by Robert
Sempill was performed before the Lord Regent,[3] but
we know nothing of its character. Playgoing seems,
however, to have been common for some time after
the Reformation, for James Melville records that John
Davidson, one of the Regents of St. Andrews Univer-

---

[1] Knox, *Works*, i. 62.   [2] *History*, i. 142-3.
[3] Diary in Dalyell's *Fragments*, p. 14.

sity, made a play at the marriage of John Colvin,
which was played in Knox's presence, 'wherein,
according to Knox's doctrine, the castell of Edinburgh
was besieged, taken, and the Captain, with an or twa
with him, hangit in effigie.' In Melville's time it was
also customary to have declamations, banquetings, and
plays at graduation time.[1]

In 1575 the Kirk, while it prohibited altogether
the performance of clerk plays upon the 'canonical
parts of Scripture,' advised that such as 'confer
upon the policy' should make provision 'that
comedies, tragedies, and other profane plays, which
are not made upon authentic parts of Scripture,'
might be considered before they were acted publicly.
More consistent, perhaps, in its rigour than any cen-
sorship that now exists, this method was, we may
infer, so effective that secular equally with sacred
plays were gradually suppressed; and in any case
Lyndsay's *Pleasant Satyre* is the only example of the
older Scottish drama which now survives.[2]

---

[1] *Diary* (Bannatyne Club edition), p. 22.

[2] In 1599 a company of English comedians visited Edinburgh,
and after playing before the king, obtained a precept to the bailies
of Edinburgh to obtain for them a house for performances. One
was got in Blackfriars Wynd. But the clergy, says Calderwood,
'fearing the profanitie that was to ensue,' convened the four sessions
of the Kirk, who passed an Act that 'none resort to these profane
comedies, for eschewing offence of God' (*History*, v. 765). Called
before the king, the clergy sought refuge in an Act passed against
'slanderous and undecent comedies.' The king, however, remaining
firm, they were compelled to rescind their Act; and a proclamation
was issued by the Privy Council ' in favour of the English comedians
now playing in Edinburgh,' in which the inhabitants were informep

From certain references to the Rex Humanitas of the play as unmarried, it has been inferred that *The Pleasant Satyre* was written and produced before the marriage of James v., and probably in 1535; and from the references in certain interludes it has also been argued that this first performance took place at Cupar Fife; but the earliest authenticated performance is that before the king at Linlithgow on the Feast of Epiphany, 6th January 1540.[1] It was also acted on the Castle Hill at Cupar at some unknown date, and at Greenside adjoining Edinburgh in 1554, before the Queen Regent.

A notable feature of the *Pleasant Satyre* is the

Performances of ' The Pleasant Satyre.'

---

that they were at liberty to attend the performances without incurring ' ony pane, skaith, censuring, reproche, or sclander,' or being found fault with by the ' ministeris, magistratis, or sessionis of the said burgh' (*Register of the Privy Council of Scotland*, vi. 39-43). After the accession of James to the English throne several English companies visited Scotland ; and in 1603 was published at Edinburgh a comedy written in the vernacular and in stanzas— *Ane verie excellent and delactibill Treatise entitled Philotus* : qvhairin wee may persave the greit inconveniences that fallis out in the Marriage betwene Age and Youth.' (Reprinted in Pinkerton's *Scotish Poems*, 1792, vol. iii.) It has been suggested that this was Robert Sempill's play, but the theory is unsupported by evidence, external or internal.

[1] Of the effect produced by its performance in 1540 a record has been preserved in a letter of Sir William Eure to Cromwell, 26th January 1540. 'The king,' he states, ' did call upon the Bishop of Glasgow, being chancellor, and other bishops, exhorting them to reform their fashions and manners of living, saying that unless they so did, he would send six of the proudest of them unto his uncle in England, and, as they were ordered, so he would order all the rest that would not amend.'

variety of its metres.[1]   The poem begins with a
stanza (spoken by Diligence, the master

Its metres.

of the ceremonies) in the rhymed alliterative measure of the old romances with the bobwheel;
and in the same speech we have stanzas of sixteen
lines—ab, abb, cbc, ded, cc, fef—of which there are
both early Latin and French examples, and also
stanzas of eight lines in *rime couée*—aaab, cccb—of
which there are very early examples in English, and
which is found in Towneley *Mystery Plays*, sometimes with a bobwheel.   The bulk of the dialogue of
the *Pleasant Satyre* is either in this measure, or in
the octo-syllabic couplet; but he introduces also the
heroic couplet, as well as other forms of *rime couée*:
the six-line stave—aab, aab—and several occasional
variations including the six-line stave used in Burns's
Address to the Deil[2]—aaa, bab,—which is not to be
found in any earlier Scottish poetry that is not
anonymous.   The kyrielle and the French octave are
also represented.

No production of any old Scottish 'makar' gives
such a detailed picture as does the *Pleasant Satyre*,

A picture of
the period.

not merely of the customs and manners,
but of the inner life and thought of the
period.   We are transported back to the years when
the old religious system was tottering to its fall; the

---

[1] Professor Schipper (*Altenglische Metrik*, vol. i. pp. 522-31) has
devoted much serious attention to Lyndsay's rhythm ; but most of
Lyndsay's peculiarities were mere imperfections, Lyndsay being a
very careless metrist.

[2] See *post*, p. 244.

crisis of the struggle is pictured in the play, and those concerned in the crisis are personified, so far at least as to enable us to know the main types. The excessive frankness—not to say coarseness—of much of the dialogue, and especially the rude buffoonery of the interludes, enhances the value of the play as a representation of the old social life. We obtain a deeper insight into the character of the times than we could otherwise compass. In modern plays the realities of human nature are greatly veiled by conventions, but Lyndsay's play deals with society at a time when the old conventions had broken down, and human nature disported itself very much according to the moods of its lawless instincts.

The play is constructed with considerable skill, even judged by modern standards: it is evidently not the work of a novice; and we must infer from it that Lyndsay had at least *Its construction.* much previous experience in the construction of farces, masks, and other pieces. Dramatically, the interludes are much the better portions; but if in the play proper the serious characters are mere wax figures, the less reputable personages are very distinctly realised.

Part I., divided into two Acts, represents the Temptation of Rex Humanitas by Sensualitie, who is introduced and recommended to the King by Wantonness, Placebo, and Solace, the *Part I.* eloquence of the last in praise of her charms being coloured by the liquor he has consumed. Sensualitie,

attended by her two maidens Homeliness and Danger,
then enters, and to her insinuating address the King
replies :—

> 'Welcum to me peirles in pulchritude ;
>> Welcum to me thow greiter nor the lamber,[1]
>> Quhilk hes maid me of all dolour denude.
>> Solace, convoy this Ladie to my chamber.'

than
Who

When the stage is cleared of the disreputables,
Gude Counsall appears, but is immediately followed
by the three Vices, Flatterie, Falset, and
Dissait, in the guise respectively of Devo-
tioun, Sapience, and Discretioun. On the entrance of
the King the three step forward and salute him ; and
after they have flattered and beguiled and cozened
according to their several methods, he gives them
cordial welcome as ' three men of gude.' Meanwhile
Gude Counsall is standing modestly near the door,
and the King, espying the stranger, sends his three
newly discovered friends to bring him forward ; but
instead of doing so they ' hurl' him out with the
direst threats, and on returning to the King tell him
that the fellow is a detestable housebreaker whom
they have ordered to be sent to the thief's hole.
Sensualitie and her ladies now begin to sing a song,
and the King sits down among them ; but hardly has
he done so ere Veritie enters, who, however, at the
instance of Spiritualitie, the Abbot, and the Parson,
is immediately put in the stocks. Chastitie then
makes her appearance, but the Lady Prioress, Spiritu-

Act I. of Part I.

---

[1] Amber used for the making of images.

alitie, the Abbot, and the Parson all in turn disown her acquaintance with marked rudeness, and the curtain falls whilst even Temporalitie is advising her that she had best be gone.

After Act I. followed the first Interlude. It represents a coarse and uproarious scene between the Sowtar and Tailor and their two Wives, who surprise the two worthies soberly entertaining Chastitie in an alehouse. Chastitie they chase away with foul abuse, and then, as the stage direction expressively puts it, the two termagants 'speik to their gudemen and ding them'; and the Interlude ends with the Sowtar's Wife 'lifting up hir clais (clothes) abone hir waist,' and entering 'the water' on her way to the town for wine to celebrate the victory.

The first Interlude.

Act II. opens with the introduction of Chastitie— by Diligence, the master of the ceremonies—to the King, but Sensualitie plainly tells the King that he can't have both of them. Thereupon Chastitie is put into the stocks by the three guardian Vices; but on the sudden arrival of Correctioun's Varlet they immediately recognise that the game is up. Flatterie hastily bids farewell to his two friends; but Dissait and Falset are determined not to leave empty-handed, and while the King is sleeping resolve to steal his box. This Falset does, but claiming on that account the larger share of the money, is attacked by Dissait, who finally runs away with the box through the 'water.' Immediately

Act II. of Part I.

thereupon Divine Correctioun enters, by whom Gude
Counsall and Veritie are set free from the stocks,
and Sensualitie is dismissed. She affirms that she
does not care 'twa strais' for the King, and will fare
much better among bishops and cardinals: as she
does, being welcomed by Spiritualitie as their 'dayis
darling.' The King then receives into his service
Gude Counsall, Veritie, and Chastitie, and embraces
with 'a humble countenance' Correctioun, who also
graciously pardons Wantonness, Placebo, and Solace,
provided they 'do no other crime':—

> 'For quhy ? as I suppois,
> Princes may sumtyme seik solace
> With mirth, and lawful mirriness
> Thair spirits to rejoyis.'

The first part being over, the audience are dismissed
by Diligence to make 'collatioun,' with a variety of
pleasant advice, as:—

> 'Tarie nocht lang, it is lait in the day ;
> Let sum drink ayle and sum drink claret wine.
> Be gret Doctors of Physick, I heare say,
> That michtie drink comforts the dull ingine.'

spirit

Part I. was followed by the Interlude of the Poor
Man and the Pardoner, in which pathos, drollery, and
other qualities are blended with no little
The second
Interlude.   skill.   Entering the empty apartment
tired and footsore, the Pauper, who is on his way to
St. Andrews for legal redress against his ecclesiastical
oppressors, climbs up to the King's chair to rest him,
but is driven away by Diligence, who, however, is so

struck by his exclamation that 'thair is richt lytill play at my hungrie hart,' that in real concern he asks him to tell the story of his 'unhappy chances.' The 'blak veritie' he recounts is the utter ruin both of his father and him by the funeral dues demanded by the Church. Then while the Pauper lies down to rest him, a Pardoner enters, and proceeds to vaunt the merits of his wares:—

'My patent Pardouns, ye may se,
Cum fra the Cane of Tartarie,
   Weill seald with oster-schellis.
Thocht ye have na contritioun,   *Though*
Ye sall have full remissioun,
   With help of buiks and bellis.
Heir is ane relict, lang and braid,   *a; broad*
Of Fine Macoull[1] the richt chaft blaid,   *true jawbone*
   With teith, and al togidder :
Of Colling's cow, heir is ane horne,
For eating of Makconnal's corne,
   Was slaine into Baquhidder.   *Balquhidder*
Heir is ane coird, baith great and lang,
Quhilk hangit Johne the Armistrang :[2]
   Of gude hemp soft and sound :   *Which*
Gude, halie peopill, I stand for'd
Quha ever beis hangit with this cord,
   Neids never to be dround !
The culum of Sanct Bryd's kow,   *tail*
The gruntill of Sanct Antonis sow,   *snout*
   Quhilk buir his haly bell :   *Which bore*
Quha ever he be heiris this bell clinck,
Gif me ane ducat for till drink,   *a; to*
   He sall never gang to hell,   *go*

---

[1] One of Ossian's heroes.
[2] The freebooter hanged in 1529. 'Iohnne ermistrangis dance' is mentioned in *The Complaynt of Scotland*, and Ramsay published a traditional ballad on him.

Without he be of Baliell borne :
Maisters trow ye, that this be scorne !
Cum win this Pardoun, cum.

not
to

Quha luifis thair wyfis nocht, with thair hart,
I have power thame for till part :
Methink yow deif and dum !
Hes naine of yow curst wickit wyfis,

into ; vexa-
tion

That halds yow intill sturt and stryfis ?
Cum tak my dispensatioun ;

gossip
to blame

Of that cummer, I sall mak yow quyte,
Howbeit your selfis be in the wyte,
And mak ane fals narratioun.
Cum win the Pardoun, now let se,
For meill, for malt, or for monie,

young pig

For cok, hen, guse, or gryse.
Of relicts, heir I haif ane hunder ;
Quhy cum ye nocht ? this is ane wonder !
I trow ye be nocht wyse !'

Then follows a lively scene between the Sowtar, the
Sowtar's Wyfe, and the Pardoner, who, after grant-
ing them divorce on certain unspeakable conditions,
addresses them thus :—

' Dame, pas ye to the east end of the toun ;

a

And pas ye west, evin lyke ane cuckald loon ;

broad

Go hence ye baith, with Baliel's braid blissing !
Schirs, saw ye ever mair sorrowles pairting ?'

The interview between the Pardoner and the Pauper
is not so satisfactory. The Pauper having received
for his groat nothing except a promise—of 'ane
thousand years of pardouns'—demands it back
again :—

' Quhat say ye, Maisters ? call ye this gude resoun,

a

That he suld promeis me ane gay pardoun,
And he resave my mony, in his stead ;

Then

Syne mak me na payment till I be dead ?'

The Pardoner refusing, Pauper attacks and routs him: 'Heir,' says the stage-direction, 'sall they fecht with silence; and Pauper sall cast doun the buird, and cast the relicts in the water.'

Part II. is more complicated—if not confused—in plot than Part I.; but if the modern reader will find it tedious, this is solely because he cannot realise the situations as Lyndsay's audience did. This part, dealing less with abstractions than Part I., and indeed wholly with 'burning questions,' bristles with points which must have kept the audience in a constant simmer of excitement. Absolutely candid in exposing the abuses in Church and State, Lyndsay employs all the resources of his art to incite the nation to drastic remedies. The three Estates of Parliament—Spiritualitie, Temporalitie, and Merchand —make their entrance on the stage walking backwards, 'led by the Vices': Spiritualitie by 'Covetice and careless Sensualitie,' Temporalitie by Publick Oppressioun, and Merchand by Falset and Dissait. At the instance of Correctioun the Vices are put in the stocks, greatly to the sorrowful indignation of Spiritualitie, who bids Sensualitie and Covetyce farewell with much show of feeling, and hopes they will do their utmost to return soon :—

Part II.

'Want I yow twa, I may nocht lang endure.'

two; not

Temporalitie and Merchand manifest, however, no such regrets, and, on the advice of John the Commoun Weill, send instead for Gude Counsall, on whose

arrival John proceeds to detail to the Estates the
evils that demand urgent attention; his complaint
dealing chiefly with all sorts of idlers, specially

> 'great fat Freiris,
> Augustenes, Carmleits, and Cordeleirs;
> And all uthers, that in cowls bene cled,
> Quhilk labours nocht, and bene well fed,' etc.

are
Who; not

Temporalitie and Merchand are much impressed by
the address, and promise amendment; but since
Spiritualitie declines to come to terms with Commoun Weill, the various representatives of the Church
are finally summoned before Correctioun to give an
account of their stewardship.   Spiritualitie boasts:—

> 'I gat gude payment of my Temporall lands,
> My buttock-maill,[1] my coattis,[2] and my offrands,
> With all that dois perteine my benefice,
> Consider now, my Lord, gif I be wyse.
> I dar nocht marie, contrair the common law,
> Ane thing thair is, my Lord, that ye may knaw.
> Howbeit, I dar nocht plainlie spouse ane wyfe,
> Yit concubeins I have had four or fyfe.
> And to my sons I have givin rich rewairds,
> And all my dochters maryit upon lairds,' etc.

offerings
if
dare not
a
landowners

The Abbot extols himself in a speech of which this is
the kernel:—

> 'Thare is na monke, from Carrick to Carraill[3]
> That fairs better, and drinks mair helsum aill.'

wholesome
ale

The Parson, while admitting that he does not
trouble to preach, affirms that he is more zealous in

[1] Fine for fornication.
[2] Testament dues.
[3] Carrick in Ayrshire, on the west coast, to Crail in Fifeshire, on
the east coast

the discharge of other, perhaps more important, duties of his office:—

> ' Thocht I preich not, I can play at the caiche ;   hand-ball
> I wait thair is nocht ane amang yow all,   wot
> Mair ferilie can play at the fut-ball ;   cleverly
> And for the carts, the tabils, and the dyse,   cards
> Above all persouns, I may beir the pryse.'   parsons

And the Lady Prioress, asked why she would not give 'harberie' to Lady Chastitie, calmly replies that her 'complexion would not assent.'

Correctioun then directs that Doctour should preach a sermon 'in Inglish tongue land folk to edifie,' much to the disgust of the Abbot and the Parson; and it being observed that a certain Friar is about to leave to set 'the toun on stir' against the preacher, he is stripped of his habit, and found to be none else than our old friend Flatterie. The Prioress is also stripped of her habit, when lo! she is seen to have been wearing beneath it a kirtle of silk. The three Prelates—who are also stripped of their habits, which are put on three young licentiates—go to confer with Sensualitie and Covetyce, but being now renounced by them with scorn, set out to discover a means of earning an honest living. John Commoun Weill is then clothed 'gorgeously' and given a seat in Parliáment; and finally Flatterie is pardoned on condition that he consent to act as executioner of his two old friends, Falset and Dissait, with whose execution and that of Commoun Thift—a Border reiver who had unwarily come into the meeting to obtain information about the Earl of Rothes's 'best hacknay,' and is betrayed by his old master Oppressioun—and their dying speeches, Part II. is brought to an edifying close

Part II. is followed by an after-piece—Interlude III.—containing the 'Sermon of Follie,' a buffoon who, after a ludicrous account of his adventures on the way to the playhouse, proceeds to preach a sermon on a saying of Solomon —*Stultorum numerus infinitus est,*—and after a definition of various kinds of folly, goes on to indicate these supremely foolish persons whom he deems to have worthily earned one of his 'Follie Hattis or Hudes.'

Interlude III.

Of the other productions of Lyndsay little need be said. The satirical *Tragedy of the Cardinal,* 1547— suggested as to form by Boccaccio's *De Casibus Virorum Illustrium,* which he professes to be reading when the wounded ghost of the cardinal appears to him and recounts the cardinal's own history—is one of the dullest of his short pieces. *Pedder Coffeis* gives an amusing sketch of seven varieties of contemporary cheats. *The Historie of Squire Meldrum* narrates, after the fashion of the old romances, and with no small sprightliness, the amorous and heroic adventures of that famous Fife laird. As for *The Dialog,* it is a sort of portentous application of biblical history to contemporary events, concluding with dissertations on Death, Antichrist, and the General Judgment.

Other works of Lyndsay.

On the whole, Lyndsay was greater as man than poet. Had opportunity and scope been granted him, he had the makings of a great statesman; and as it is, his influence on the immediate future of Scotland was only second, if second, to that of Knox. His poetic gift was hampered rather than benefited by his absorption in ecclesiastical and social questions; but he was at least a clever, and more than clever, playwright, and, indeed, at a later period his dramatic ability must have won him high distinction.[1]

More a dramatist than a poet.

[1] Lindsay had at least one poetic disciple in William Lauder (1520?-1573), minister of Forgandenny, etc., whose *Compendious and Breve Tractate*, ed. Hall, was published by the Early English Text Society in 1864, and his *Minor Poems*, ed. Furnivall, by the same Society in 1870; but though displaying much of Lindsay's zeal for political and social reform, they are wellnigh destitute of any qualities entitling them to rank as literature.

VIII

MINOR AND LATER POETS OF THE SIXTEENTH CENTURY

BELLENDEN—INGLIS—KYD—STEWARTE—STEWART OF
LORNE—HENRY STEWART—KING HENRY STEWART
— BALNAVES — FETHY — FLEMING — SIR JOHN
MOFFAT—STEIL, ETC.—ALEXANDER SCOTT—ALEX-
ANDER MONTGOMERIE—SIR RICHARD MAITLAND—
JAMES VI., ETC.—THE WEDDERBURNS AND 'THE
GUDE AND GODLIE BALLATES'—ROBERT SEMPILL
AND THE REFORMATION SATIRISTS.

AMONG contemporary poets of Douglas and Lyndsay
there are none of peculiarly distinctive merit.

John Bellenden, Archdeacon of Moray, whose
translations of Boece and Livy (see *post*, p. 304) are
John Bellenden among the most characteristic examples
(fl. 1533-1587). of old Scots prose, is, though designated
by Lyndsay 'ane plant of poetis,'

'Quhose ornat workis my wyitt can nocht defyne,'

known poetically merely as an exemplary disciple of
Gavin Douglas. To his prose translations he wrote
'prohemiums,' mainly devoted to the exposition and

232

enforcement of excellent moral maxims by means of learned classical allusions; and none other of his verses survive except 'a godly and lernit work callit *The Banner of Pietie,*[1] and descriptive of the Incarnation.

It may be that Sir James Inglis—on whom Mackenzie in his *Writers of Scotland* fathers, without evidence, that curious prose work *The Complaynt of Scotland*—deserves all the commendation given him by Lyndsay for his 'ballates, farses, and plesand playes,' but none of these have survived—the *General Satyre*, with which he is credited in the Maitland MS., being in the Bannatyne MS. much more credibly assigned to Dunbar. The pieces referred to by Lyndsay were written while he was a hanger-on at the court, where, the Treasurer's Accounts indicate, he was employed in connection with the theatrical and other entertainments; but Lyndsay laments that his promotion to the abbacy of Culross had made impotent his pen.

Sir James Inglis (d. 1531).

Of Kyd, described by Lyndsay as 'in cunnyng and practick, rycht prudent,' nothing is known beyond the fact that in the Bannatyne MS. his name is attached to *The Richt Fontane of hailfull Sapience*, written in the French octave, and intended seemingly for the edification of the young king. Exactly coinciding with Lyndsay's allusion, it is excellent rather as advice than as poetry. Here is a specimen:—

Kyd.

---

[1] Bannatyne MS.

communing

> 'Thy pastyme suld oft be in commonyng
>> With profound clerkis of science and prudens ;
> For cunnying termes afferis in a king,
>> Quhilk sald be polyt and of eloquence.
>> In hering wysmen men gettis sapience,
> Without the quhilk is no stabilitie ;
>> Thairfoir in tyme thow get intelligence
> Or elles thy wisdome sall in seeking be.'

are fitting
Who

which

Of Stewarte, whose personal history is also an absolute blank, except that he is mentioned in Rolland's *Seven Sages* as a court poet, but who, Lyndsay tells us, 'desyreth ane stately style' and

Stewarte.
'First Lerges.'

> 'Full ornate workis daylie does compyle,'

we have more various examples than of any other minor bard of the period, some dozen of his productions having been preserved in the Bannatyne MS. He was plainly a disciple of Dunbar rather than Douglas; and a curious ballad on the New Year's 'Lerges' (bounty) indicates that, like Dunbar, he was a not extremely successful 'solisitar.' It begins :—

bounty
Who

> 'First lerges the king my cheife,
>> Quhilk come als quiet as a theif,
>>> And in my hand sled shillingis twa,
>> To put his lergnes to preif
>>> For lerges of this New Yeirday.'

From most of his other possible patrons—the Bishop of Galloway, the Abbot of Holyrood, the secretary, the treasurer—he also got little but fair words, so that he was moved to exclaim :—

'Fowll fall this frost that is so fell,   Foul befall
It hes the wyt, the trewth to tell,   blame
   Baith handes and purs it bindis sway   so
Thay may gife ne thing, by thame sell,   of their
For lerges of this New Yeirday.'   freewill

There was but one exception to the general stingi-
ness, ' My Lord of Bothwell,' who gave him

'ane cursour gray,
Worth all this sort that I with mell,   meddle
For lerges of this New Yeirday.'

The tailor and shoemaker—those favourite butts
of the old ' makaris '— supplied Stewarte with a
theme for several pieces, on the whole   His ' Flyting.'
more ribald than witty.   His *Flyting*   *Mots* on tailors.
betuix the Soutar and the Tailyour is an average
specimen of the orthodox Billingsgate of the period;
and he also wrote several *mots* on tailors, of which
this one may serve as a characteristic sample of that
age's wit :—

'Betuix twa foxis a crawing cok,
  Betuix twa freiris a maid in hir smok,
  Betuix twa cattis a mowis,
  Betuix twa telyeouris a lowiss :
Schaw me, gud schir, nocht as a stranger,   not
Quhilk of thais four is grittest in danger ?'   Which

Stewarte is further one of the few amatory poets
among the old Scots ' makaris,' but he possesses little
of the grace and ease of the later school   As amatory
of which Scott is the chief.   *For to declare*   poet.
the he (high) Magnificence of Ladies—in the French

octave, with refrain—is an ardent outburst, ending in this effusive fashion :—

'War all the erd papir and perchmyne,
    And pennis wer all treis, herbis and flouris,
And all the sternis in the lift dois schyne,
    War in this erd moist ornat oratouris,
    The se were ynk, with fresche fludis and schouris—
All wer to small ane buk to edify,
    For to contene of ladeis the honouris,
And factis that thair fame dois fortefie.'

earth *stars; sky* *sea* *a* (marginal glosses)

In the Bannatyne MS. are three other of Stewarte's amatory pieces.

Lyndsay also makes mention of Stewart of Lorne, who 'wyll carp rycht curiously.' This was most likely W. Stewart, who, in the Maitland MS., is credited with *This hinder Nycht neir by the Hour of Nine*—also in the Bannatyne MS. —giving the revelation of Dame Virtue as to when Scotland, 'sin Flowdoun field,' shall again enjoy 'peace and rest and plenty.' Another Stewart (Henry) appears in the Bannatyne MS. as author of *Be Gouernour baith Guid and Gratious*; and there is further King Henry Stewart (Lord Darnley) to whom the Bannatyne MS. assigns a love-song in the French octave, somewhat in the manner of Scott. It is scarcely necessary to add that, although James v. enjoyed some repute in his day as a poet, no verses with his colophon survive, and that his title to the authorship of *The Gaberlunzie Man* and *The Jolly Beggar* is based on mere unverified tradition.

Other Stewarts. (marginal note)

Certain other poets, not mentioned by Dunbar or Lyndsay, who figure in the Bannatyne MS., clearly belong to the later school of Scott and Montgomerie. Balnaves—presumably not *Balnaves.* Henry Balnaves of Halhill (d. 1579), the Scottish Reformer, and author of a *Comfortable Treatise on Justification*—is credited with *O Gallandis all I cry and call,* containing some rather piquant advice to gallants, written in Scott's favourite six-line stave in *rime couée*[1]:—

> 'Huntarres adew,
> Gif ye persew
> To hunt at every beist,
> Ye will it rew,
> Thair is anew : *enough*
> Thairto haif ye no haist.'

A certain Fethy[2] appears as the author of two love-songs—*My Trewth is Plicht,* in *rime royal,* and *Pansing in Hairt,* in the *Fethy.* French octave of three accents with a curious double refrain:—

> 'Cauld, cauld, culis the lufe
> That kendillis our het.' *too hot*

To Fleming we are indebted for *Be mirry Bretherne,*

---

[1] See *ante*, p. 164.
[2] In all likelihood Sir John Futhy, a priest who, according to the manuscript of Thomas Wode, or Wood, in Dublin University Library, composed a song beginning 'O God abufe,' with words and music, and was 'the first organist that ever brought in Scotland the curious new fingering and playing on organs.' See David Laing's Introduction to Stenhouse's *Notes to Johnson's Musical Museum,* p. xxxi.

a clever and amusing, indeed quite modern, exposition of the plague of evil wives, which is also of some interest for its stave, the first section being *Fleming.* sometimes in the *rime couée* of Scott, but occasionally dropping the internal rhymes, so as to form a quatrain in the old ballad measure; and the last section being a kind of bobwheel, the inner lines of which are occasionally in tumbling metre. Here is an example:—

> 'Than wad scho say, "Allace this day
>   For him that wan this geir,
> Quhen I him had, I skairsly said,
>   'My hart ains mak gud cheir.'
> Or I had lettin him spend a plak,
> I lever haif wittin him brokin his bak,
> Or ellis his craig had gottin a crak,
>   Our the heicht of the stair."'

Then would money · *once Before known neck*

Sir John Moffat, who is credited by another than Bannatyne with the classic tale, *The Wyfe of Auchtirmwchty*, is also credited by *Sir John Moffat, and Steil.* Bannatyne with a rather sprightly piece, *Brother, Bewar I rede you Now*, in the five-line stave — aab, ab — with refrain; and Steil, known otherwise as the author of a political poem, *The Ryng of the Roy Robert*,[1] has his name attached to two love-poems, *Lanterne of Lufe* and *Absent*, neither of much account, and both rather 'aureate' of language.

[1] Maitland MS., reprinted in Watson's *Choice Collection*, part iii., and in Laing's *Fugitive Scottish Poetry*, 1823-25, and *Early Metrical Tales*, 1826.

To the same late school belongs the Clapperton who, in the Maitland MS., appears as the author of *Wa Worth Maryage,* beginning :— **Clapperton.**

> In Bowdoun, on blak Monunday
> Quhen all was gadderit to the Play,
>   Bayth men and women semblit thair,
> I hard ane sweit ane sich, and say—
>   " Wa worth maryage for evermair." '

Monday

sigh
Woe befall

Other still more minor names in the Bannatyne MS. are Lichtoun Monicus, Robert Norval, and Henry Scogan.[2] John Blyth, Allan, and Allan Matson are clearly pseudonyms.[3] **Minor names.**

In Lyndsay we have seen the beginning of that theological absorption which was to infect, and for a time destroy, the nation's poetic sentiment; but at first the infection was only partial, and it was slightly counteracted either by **The later Scottish School.**

---

[1] Published in Pinkerton's *Ancient Scotish Poems*, p. 135.

[2] Henry Scogan, an Englishman, was tutor to the sons of Henry IV. A poem by him is published in Skeat's *Chaucerian and other Poems*, 1897.

[3] George Bannatyne (1545-1608), the transcriber of the Bannatyne MS., was the son of James Bannatyne of Kirktown of Newtyle, Forfarshire. He became a merchant in Edinburgh, and during an outbreak of the plague there in 1568 took refuge in his native place, where he amused his enforced leisure by compiling, mostly, he states, from 'copies awld, markit and vitillat,' that treasury of old Scots poetry, the Bannatyne MS., which, with the Maitland MS., was the chief means of preserving the bulk of the work of the old Scots 'makaris' from oblivion. From the Bannatyne MS. Allan Ramsay got the material for his *Evergreen*, 1724, and it was drawn upon by late editors both for general *Collections* and for editions of individual poets; but the whole MS. was first printed *verbatim et literatim* through the enterprise of the Hunterian Club, 1873-1896. Bannatyne prefixed certain poetical introductions to the MS., and also contributed to it a few other pieces of his own, but they are of no poetic merit.

direct contact with the poetic revival in England represented by Tottel's *Miscellany*, 1557, or by contact with influences similar to those which produced that revival. Of this later Scottish school, which tended to become more and more assimilated to that of England, the two chief names are Alexander Scott and Alexander Montgomerie.

Of Alexander Scott—his parentage and personal history — we know no more than of the obscurest of the old Scots 'makaris.' Laing conjectured that he may have been the second of two sons of Alexander Scott of the Chapel Royal, Stirling, who were legitimated on 21st September 1549; but the Scotts are so numerous a clan that the conjecture can scarce rank as even a faint probability. It is as likely that he was the Alexander Scott, burgess of Edinburgh, who in 1581 was joint cautioner with Mungo Scott for George Scott of Synton, and Robert Scott of Hanying, then in ward in Edinburgh Castle, and who in 1584 became caution for the loyalty of James Thomsoun.[1] It is worth noting that this Alexander Scott is designated a burgess merely, not merchant or any kind of tradesman. It is almost certain that Scott was an Edinburgh resident, the whole tone of his poetry, apart from poetical references to Edinburgh and its neighbourhood, being that of a town gallant; and we know from an allusion to him

Alexander Scott (fl. 1547-1584).

---

[1] *Register of the Privy Council of Scotland,* vol. iii. p. 396; *ib.* vol. iii. p. 696.

in a sonnet of Montgomerie to Hudson that he was
alive in 1584:—

> 'Yourself and I, old Scott and Robert Sempill,
> Quhen we are deid that all our dayis but daffis,   larks
> Let Christian Lyndsay write our epitaphs.'

This quotation also, if it does not imply that Scott
had no stated employment, is rather inconsistent
with the supposition—from his use of two law-terms,
'blanche-ferme' and 'quyt-cleme'—that he was a
lawyer, at least in constant practice.

Scott's *New Zeir Gift to the Quene Mary* expresses
the current anti-Catholic feeling of Edinburgh in
1562; but notwithstanding this piece, and
his two translations from the *Psalms*, he   Unchanged
by the
represents a mode of sentiment which it   Reformation.
need hardly be said is alien to that of the Kirk.
Most likely, indeed, the bulk of his verse that now
survives was written before the 'Evangel' was
established in Scotland. We possess none of later
date than 1568, and it is inferred that *Departe,*
written 'of the Master of Erskine,' lover of the Queen-
Dowager, slain at Pinkie in 1547, dates from shortly
after the Master's death; while that characteristic
piece *Of May* celebrates, among other old customs,
the representation of Robin Hood and Little John
prohibited by Act of Parliament in 1555. But the
reference of Montgomerie further shows that the
Reformation effected no radical change in Scott's
habits; and the fact that none of his verses are
known to survive, except what Bannatyne tran-

scribed, betokens rather that he continued to write in the old vein, than that he either ceased to write or devoted himself specially to serious verse.

The whole of Scott's productions that survive, under his signature, number only thirty-six,[1] and with the exception of the *New Zeir's Gift, The Justing and Debait,* and the translations of the first and fiftieth *Psalms,* they are wholly devoted to love—a subject which seems to have had as much practical interest for him as it had for Burns :—

A love poet.

' The blenkyne of ane e
 Ay gart thé goif and glake ' ;

smiling ; eye made thee look sillily and foolishly

but while his verses plainly represent his own experience, and are the effluence of a strong lyric impulse, their sentiment and manner has much in common with the English lyrical school represented chiefly by Skelton, Wyatt, and Surrey.

Doubtless Scott knew Skelton's poetry, and made acquaintance with the later school of Wyatt and Surrey in Tottel's *Miscellany,* 1557, if not before this in MS. ; but if influenced by some of the English school in his preference for short-lined staves, he had little to gain from it as regards rhythmical excellence. We have only to compare his finished and musical versification

An accomplished metrist. Compared with Surrey.

---

[1] They are all contained in the Bannatyne MS. A few were published by Ramsay, 1724—very incorrectly—Lord Hailes, 1770, and Sibbald, 1802 ; but the first complete edition is the somewhat Bowdlerised one by David Laing, 1821. An edition was printed for private circulation at Glasgow, 1882 ; and one was edited for the Scottish Text Society by Dr. James Cranstoun, 1896.

with the jolting doggerel of even Wyatt, to recognise how far the Scots 'makaris' were in advance of the English, until Surrey; and as regards correctness of accent, management of the pause, and purity and exactness of rhyme, he is hardly to be regarded as Surrey's inferior.

Though addicted to short-lined staves, Scott also used many of Dunbar's, but did not in these confine himself to iambics. He was partial to the French octave, which he wrote not only in its five- and four-, but in its three-accented form, as in *Oppressit Hairt*:— *A disciple of Dunbar. Use of the French octave.*

> 'Oppressit hairt, indure
>   In dolor and distress,
> Wappit without recure
>   In wo remidiless ;
>   Sen scho is merciless,
> And caussis all thy smert,
>   Quilk suld thy dolor dress,
> Indure, oppressit hairt.'

Wrapped round; cur

Since

Who; redress

For that ecstatic celebration of love, *Vp, Helsum Hairt*, he uses a ten-line stave formed by the addition of a couplet to the French octave:— *Ten-line stave.*

> 'Vp, helsum hairt ! thy rutis rais, and lowp ;
>   Exalt and clym within my breist in staige ;
> Art thow not wantoun, haill, and in gud howp,
>   Ffermit in grace and free of all thirlaige
>   Bathing in bliss and sett in hie curaige ?
> Braisit in joy, no falt may thé affray,
>   Having thy ladies hart as heretaige
> In blenche ferme ffor ane sallat every May
>   So neid thow nocht now sussy, sytt, nor sorrow
>   Sen thow art sure of sollace evin and morrow.'

joyful; leap

hale

confirmed ; bondage

Enveloped

tenure

not; fret; grieve
Since

He has also several examples of *rime royal*, including that curious fantasia on the heart
beginning :—

> 'Haif hairt in hairt, ze hairt of hairtes haill ;
>   Trewly, sweit hairt, zour hairt my hairt sal haif,' etc.

Of the three examples of the five-line stave of
equal lines, two, *Of May* and *The Answer
to Hairts*, are arranged in the refrain
form of the stave, and the third, *To Luve Vnluvit*,
has the refrain :—

Five-line
stave.

> 'To luve vnluvit it is ane pane :
>   For scho that is my soverane,
> Sum wantoun man so he hes set hir,
>   That I can get no luf agane,
> Bot brek my hairt, and nocht the bettir.'

a

nothing

Only once, in the witty *Of Womenkynd*, does he
use a six-line stave with double refrain ;
but instead of the Dunbar form built on
two rhymes, he borrows from the English
lyrists that built on three rhymes, and known as the
'ballade' (see *post*, p. 258):—

Six-line stave
with double
refrain.

> 'I muse and mervellis in my mynd,
>   Quhat way to wryt, or put in verss,
> The quent consaitis of wemenkynd,
>   Or half thair havingis to reherss :
>   I fynd thair haill affectioun
>   So contrair thair complexioun.'

behaviour
whole

More partial than Dunbar to *rime couée*, he supplies
two examples— *A Complaint agains
Cupeid* and *On Paciens in Life*—of that
six-line form of it which, the troubadours
having adapted to it their love-songs, and the monks

Rime couée
in the stave of
the 'Address to
the Deil.'

their exemplary Latin rhymes, became common, through the early English minstrels, all over England, whence it later found favour with the Scots, but only partially, until, having been revived by Sir Robert Sempill in 'Standard *Habbie*,' it finally obtained a lease of immortality through Robert Burns.[1] Here is a stave of Scott more after the manner of Burns than most of the pinchbeck imitations of the latter bard :—

> ' Quhat is thy manrent bot mischeif :   homage
> Sturt, angir, grunching, yre, and greif,   vexation;
> Evill lyfe, and langour but releif   grumbling without
>   Off woundë wan,
> Displesour, pane, and he repreif   high
>   Off God and man ? '

In *On Paciens* the stave is adapted to a single refrain, ' Bot paciens,' or ' With paciens,' and in that candid exposition of the poet's own love-code, *It cumis zow Luvaris to be Laill*, he introduces with much effect a double refrain of one accent, thus :—

> ' It cumis zow luvaris to be laill,   becomes;
> Off body, hairt, and mind alhaill ;   loyal entirely
> And thocht ze with zour ladyis daill—   though
>   Ressoun ;
> Bot and zour faith and lawty fail—   loyalty
>   Tressoun.'

Scott has also examples—*A Luvaris Complaint* and *Leif, Luve, and Lat me leif Allone*— of a seven-line stave in *rime couée*, of two rhymes, formed from this six-line stave by the addition of a head-line to the last section;

    Seven-line stave in rime couée.

[1] For a complete history of this stave, see *The Centenary Burns*, vol. i. pp. 336-42.

but in both cases the last line takes the form of a
refrain, and in the latter the tail-lines are of three
accents :—

> ' Leif, Luve, and lat me leif allone
> At libertie, subject to none,
> Ffor it may weill be sene vpone
> My bludless blaikn'tt ble :
> The tormenting in tym bygon,
> That skerss hes left bot skin and bon
> Throw fremitness of thé.'

complexion (gloss for "My bludless blaikn'tt ble")

perverseness (gloss for "Throw fremitness of thé")

But the special stave of Scott in *rime couée* is that
fashioned on the imperfect Iambic tetrameter.[1] In his
Translation of the First Psalm, and in
Ladeis Fair, he uses it in its common
six-line form ; while in *Quha is Perfyte,
In June the Jem,* and *Quha lykis to
Luve,* he adds a bobwheel :—

*Rime couée
fashioned on
the imperfect
Iambic
tetrameter.*

> ' Quha lykis to luve,
> Or that law pruve,
> Lat him beleif this lyfe to leid :
> His mynd sall moif,
> But rest or ruve
> With diuerss dolouris to the deid :
> He sall tyne appetite
> And meit and sleip gife quyte
> And want the way perfyte
> To find remeid.'

*Without ;
stay
to death
lose*

remedy

Of this six-line stave in *rime couée* he uses in
Favour is Fair a modification formed by rhyming
the first half of the third line with the second, and
the first half of the sixth with the fifth, so as to form
an eight-line stave :—

---

[1] See *ante*, p. 164.

> ' Favour is fair
>   In luvis lair,   *learning*
>   Zit Friendship mair   *more*
>   Bene to commend ;   *is to be commended*
>   Bot quhair despair
>   Bene adversare,
>   Nothing is thair
>   Bot wofull end.'

Of this stave there are examples in the *Coventry
Mysteries.* Scott has also two examples of *rime couée*
in eight-line staves—*Departe,* the head-   **Eight-line
lines of which are of three accents and   stave in
the tail-lines of two, and *I will be Plane,* rime couée.**
the head-lines of which are of two accents, the tail-
lines of one three-syllabled accent, assuming the
form of a double refrain :—

> ' I will be plane,
>   And lufe affane   *sincerely*
>   Ffor as I mene   *mean*
>   So take me ;
>   Gif I refrane   *If*
>   For wo or pane,
>   Zour lufe certane ;
>   Forsaik me.'

The other staves of Scott are (1) the old bobwheel
stave of *Christis Kirk* in *The Justing*; (2) in *Langour
to Leive,* a four-line stave of alternate   **Other staves.**
rhymes, the rhymes of the second and
fourth lines being repeated throughout its thirteen
stanzas, with the burden of ' again '; and (3) a variety
of the roundel, *Lo! qhat it is to Luve* (p. 249).

The New Zeir Gift, of small merit poetically, is of
some interest as representing the views of a shrewd
man of the world on the political pro-
blems of Scotland in 1562. But though
filled with grave political advice, it begins with a
stanza of elaborate compliments after the approved
'aureate' fashion, and the Envoy and Lectori are
utilised for a display of those crowning accomplishments of the old 'makar,' internal rhyme and alliteration. Here is the quaint close :—

'The New
Zeir Gift.'

note
writing
Sent by

'Noblest natour, nurice to nurtour, not
 This dull indyte, dulce, double dasy deir,
 Send be thy sempill servand Sanderris Scott,
  Greting gret God to grant thy Grace gude zeir.'

*The Justing and Debait vp at the Drum betuix
Wā. Adamsone and Johne Sym* is modelled as
to form after *Peblis* and *Christis Kirk,*
and as to subject-matter after Dunbar's
Turnament and Lyndsay's *Justing.* With the former
two pieces it cannot compare in realistic vivacity, nor
with Dunbar's in breadth—apart from the question
of grossness—of humour, but the fun is not so strained
as Dunbar's, nor is there any suggestion of burlesque.
The incidents are described with quite a naïve simplicity: the ludicrous cowardice of Will, who

'The Justing
and Debait.'

stronger ;
body
knit

'wichter was of corss
Nor Sym and better knittin,'

in its contrast with the dapper coolness of the pigmy
but 'better sittin' Sym, affording opportunity for
much slily effective wit.

But the special praise of Scott is that he is the chief
lyrist of the old Scots 'makaris'—more essentially
a lyrist than Dunbar or Montgomerie, *The chief old
and among English contemporaries the *Scots lyrist—
fellow of Surrey. Yet Scott is peculiarly *but the dis-
the disciple of Dunbar, and the influence *Dunbar.
ciple of
of that master is seen not merely in the artistic finish,
but in the succinctness, the aphoristic vigour of his
verse.

For all these qualities his supreme example is
undoubtedly *The Roundel of Love*:— *'The Roundel
Love.'*

> 'Lo ! quhat it is to lufe
>   Lerne ze, that list to prufe,
> Be me, I say, that no wayis may   By
>   The grund of greif remvfe,
> Bot still decay, both nycht and day ·
>   Lo ! quhat it is to lufe.
>
> Lufe is ane fervent fyre,   a
>   Kendillit without desyre :
> Schort plesour, lang displesour,
>   Repentance is the hyre ;
> Ane pure tressour without mesour   poor
>   Lufe is ane fervent fyre.
>
> To lufe and to be wyiss,
>   To rege with gud adwyiss,   rage at
> Now thus, now than, so gois the game,
>   Incertane is the dyiss :
> Thair is no man, I say, that can
>   Both lufe and to be wyiss.
>
> Fle alwayis from the snair,
>   Lerne at me to be ware :
> It is ane pane and dowbill trane   snare
>   Of endles wo and cair ;
> For to refrane that danger plane
>   Fle alwayis frome the snair.'

Elsewhere he also manifests some of the coarser aspects of the old Scottish realism, curiously mingled with the graceful amorous frivolity of the school of Surrey. As to his asserted lack of earnestness, fervour, passion, surely *Vp, Helsom Hairt,* and its companion piece, *My Hairt is High Above,* the latter unsigned but engraven all over with his subscription, are fervent and passionate enough, though erotic rather than sentimental; and is not this exquisitely simple stanza—as imagined coming from the lips of the dying Master of Erskine —as expressive a symbol of passionate regret as the loudest of protestations ?—

His asserted 'lack of earnestness.'

own

> ' Adew my awin sueit thing,
>   My joy and conforting,
>   My mirth and sollesing
>   Of erdly gloir ;
>   Ffair weill, my lady bricht
>   And my remembrance rycht,
>   Ffair weill and haif gud nycht :
>   I say no moir ! '

earthly glory

At the same time Scott is not a poet of the domestic affections, but the poet chiefly of gallantry. The bulk of his verse that has been preserved is of the light, gay, and even frivolous, rather than serious, order. A wit more than humorist or satirist, his wit plays over all the superficial aspects of love with a certain sparkling, if not dazzling, brilliancy. His maxims and experiences are those of the gallants of his time; but such as they are, they are detailed with much artful cleverness

The poet o gallantry.

and vivacity, as also with an ease and elegance unequalled by any of the old Scots 'makaris,' and by
none of the earlier English lyrists except Surrey.

Alexander Montgomerie, properly the last of the
Scots 'makaris,' was, like Dunbar and Douglas,
closely connected with one of the great
Scottish families, being the younger son
of Hugh Montgomerie of Hazelhead, Ayrshire, descended from a younger branch of the
Montgomeries, Earls of Eglinton. By intermarriage
the family was also variously related to the poetic
Sempills. He himself states that he was born on
'Easter day at morne,' but the year is unknown,
though it was probably about 1540. Nor, though
he was highly accomplished, do we possess any information about his education; the story of Hume
of Polwart in *The Flyting* as to his being sent to
Argyle to learn 'leir' being so plainly meant in mere
scorn that nothing can be inferred from it. Most
likely he visited Argyle in some military capacity, for
Dempster states that he was vulgarly called 'the
Highland trooper.' That he had some special intercourse with Highlanders, and possessed at least a
sprinkling of Gaelic, is clear from his *Answer to
ane Helandmanis Invective*; and if he also wrote
How the Helandman was made [1]—which, however, is
more like the work of an earlier poet—most likely he
had reasons for a special grudge against the Argyle
Highlanders.

Alexander
Montgomerie
(1540 ?-1610 ?).
His early life.

[1] Bannatyne MS.

A sonnet by Barclay of Ladyland is addressed to Montgomerie as 'Captain,' but he is not to be con- founded with Captain Robert Mont- gomerie, who was one of the king's bodyguards. Though in some special sense he served the Regent Morton and King James VI., the exact nature of his office is unknown. But, for some years, he was a *persona grata* at the curious court of the young prince, an intimate of some of the more powerful nobles, a friend of many fair dames, an avowed gallant after the manner of his time, and for some time the favourite poet, and it may be the poetic instructor, of his pedantic patron, whose bound- less literary vanity he did not scruple to feed with the gross flattery which alone would have satisfied it :—

At the Court of James VI.

'So quintessence of Kings, when thou compyle,
Thou stainis my verses with thy stately style.'

In 1583 Montgomerie obtained a pension of 500 merks a year, chargeable on the rents of the Arch- bishop of Glasgow, but some difficulty as to the payment led to legal proceed- ings, which apparently terminated in his favour, the grant of the pension being confirmed in 1588. Meanwhile, during a foreign tour, for which he obtained leave of absence in 1586, he is stated to have been sent into a foreign prison; but where, or why he was imprisoned, or even how or when he was set at liberty, is unknown.[1] Be that as it may, he latterly

His retirement from Court.

[1] Irving, in his *Life* of Montgomerie in Laing's edition, states that 'an authentic document informs us that he was detained in a

so completely lost the favour of the king that he had to retire from the court, and there is no evidence that he was ever again permitted to return. No light on the cause of his disgrace is to be obtained from his poetry, except that he regarded himself as very ill used, but it is sufficiently explained if he be the Alexander Montgomerie, brother of the laird of Hazelhead, who, a neglected entry in the *Register of the Privy Council*[1] informs us, 'having failed to appear to answer for being art and part with the late Hew Barclay of Ladyland in the treasonable enterprise for the taking of Ilisha for the use of the Spanish, is'—14th July 1597—'to be denounced rebel.' This Hew Barclay, who, on being surprised at Ailsa, rushed into the sea and drowned himself, was a poetic acquaintance of Montgomerie's,[2] and, moreover, the old laird of Hazelhead, the supposed brother of Montgomerie, was still alive, so that the Alexander Montgomerie accused of having been art and part in this foolish enterprise seems to have been none other than the poet. Nothing is known as to his later years. The tradition that he settled at Compstone Castle, Kirkcudbrightshire, near which, at the junction of the Dee and the Taffe, is supposed to be the scene of *The Cherrie and the Slae*, is quite unverified; and

---

foreign prison,' but he quotes no reference. The poems of Montgomerie usually affirmed by editors to refer to his foreign imprisonment could, from the context, only refer to his imprisonment in this country.

[1] Vol. v. p. 402.

[2] A sonnet of Ladyland to Montgomerie, Montgomerie's answer, and Ladyland's reply, are included in Montgomerie's *Poems*.

not only was *The Cherrie and the Slae* written before
he lost the king's favour, but there is no reason to
suppose that he ever acquired means sufficient to
enable him to occupy such a residence. Though his
sonnets and poems represent a varied love acquaintanceship, he was apparently more a languishing than
a successful suitor. It has been taken for granted
that the 'maistres' of most of his sonnets and poems
was Lady Margaret Montgomerie, to whom, we are
told, he 'plied his suit with equal poetic skill and
courtier-like grace'; but Lady Margaret, who became
the wife of the Master of Seton, afterwards Earl of
Winton, must have been over twenty years his junior,
and his verses to her are more fatherly than amatory
in tone. There is no evidence that he ever married.
He was alive in 1605, and died some time before 1615.

A disciple of Scott, Montgomerie was, however,
more inventive in his metres and also more akin to
The sonnet of   the English school in language as well as
Montgomerie.   method.[1] His susceptibility to the new
influences is especially seen in his preference for the
sonnet, of which he has left no fewer than seventy

[1] Montgomerie's *Cherrie and the Slae*, first printed in 1597, and
an edition 'newly altered, perfyted,' etc., by Montgomerie before his
death, was published by Andro Hart, 1615. This edition was
known to and partly used by Ramsay for his *Evergreen*, but no copy
is now known to exist. Various other separate editions have been
published. The *Flyting* first appeared in 1621, and *The Mindes
Melodie* in 1605. The collected editions of his *Poems* are those of
Laing, 1821, and the Scottish Text Society, ed. Cranstoun, 1887.
The MSS. are the Bannatyne, the Maitland, and the Drummond
(University Library, Edinburgh).

examples. To this form of verse he may have been
introduced through Tottel's *Miscellany,* 1557, but it
is further clear that he was greatly influenced by
Ronsard, several of his sonnets being merely translations of those of the French poet.[1] Although (1) he
uses the occasional Wyatt (and common Sidney) form
—abba, abba, cd, cd (in one instance dd), ee—and
(2) the more common Wyatt form—abba, abba, cdd,
cee—he never uses the Surrey and Shakespeare form
of three alternately rhyming quatrains, but by linking
the third quatrain to the second as the second is
linked to the first, he introduces (3) a variation—ab,
ab, bc, bc, cd, cd, ee[2]—and (4) he avoids in one or
two instances the final couplet by adopting, from
Ronsard, the arrangement abba, abba (in one instance
abab), ccd, eed, the nearest approach to the Petrarchian
before Sidney and Milton. The following example
will also show that he understood something of the
special poetic use of the sonnet, the change in the
tenor of the thought at the ninth line being very
clearly marked, while its whole direction is towards
the final conclusion :—

> ' Bright amorous ee vhare Love in ambush lyes,   eye
>   Cleir cristal tear distilde at our depairt,   departure
>   Sueet secreit sigh more peircing nor a dairt,   than
>   Inchanting voice, beuitcher of the wyse,

---

[1] This fact was first pointed out by Dr. Hoffmann in *Studien zu
Alexander Montgomerie*; Altenburg, 1894.

[2] Dr. Hoffmann points out that Spenser, who is the first English
poet to use this form, must have got it from the *Essayes of a Prentise,*
by James VI., 1584, Montgomerie being the inventor of the form.

Quhyt ivory hand, vhilk thrust my fingers pryse—
I challenge zou, the causers of my smarte,
As homiceids, and murtherers of my harte,
In Resones Court to suffer ane assyse.
Bot oh ! I fear, zea rather wot I weill,
To be repledgt ze plainly will appeill
To Love, whom Resone never culd command :
Bot since I can not better myn estate,
Zit vhill I live, at leist I sall regrate
Ane ee, a teir, a sigh, a voce, a hand.'

which

know

while
eye

But the metrical form with which Montgomerie's
name is chiefly associated is the quatorzain of *The
Bankis of Helicon,* in which he also wrote
that very popular piece *The Cherry and
the Slae,* as well as the emotional farewell,
Adieu, O Daisy of Delight. That *The Bankis of
Helicon,* preserved in the Maitland MS., is the earliest of
the productions in that measure, is proved by the fact
that Sir Richard Maitland's *Ballat of the Creatioun of
the World,* in the Bannatyne MS., is said to be 'maid
to the tone of *The Bankis of Helicon.*' It is also in
the Bannatyne MS. that mention is first made of
this tune, and Montgomerie's authorship of the words
is as clearly proved as, from mere internal evidence,
it can be.

The quatorzain of ' The Bankis of Helicon.'

Montgomerie's metrical invention consisted in adding to a ten-line stave, very common in England from
the beginning of the fourteenth century, a peculiar
wheel borrowed from a stave of the old Latin hymns.
It may be that the song was written to fit some old
sacred tune, or the tune may have been written by
some court musician. Its popularity gave the stave

a considerable vogue, other examples besides Mont-gomerie's and Maitland's being *Ane Ballat of ye Captain of ye Castle*, Burel's *Passage of a Pilgrim*, and *The Dumb Wyff*—none of them, however, of the slightest poetic merit. Revived by Ramsay, the stave became a favourite one of Burns, whose most effective use of it is in the recitatives of *The Jolly Beggars*.

With the exception of the French octave—named by James VI. the *ballat royal*, and recommended by him for 'heich and grave subjects,' espe-cially drawn out of 'learnit autors'—and the *rime royal*, Montgomerie shows little partiality for the favourite staves of the old 'makaris.' In *The Flyting* he, however, introduces the old rhymed alliterative stave of the romances, which he also makes use of in *Ane Answer to ane Helandmanis Invective*; and in the introductory verses of *The Flyting* he applies the common rondeau (in triple measure) to Polwart with some effectiveness :—

His use of the old staves.

> 'Polwart zee peip
> Like a mouse amongst thornes,
>   Na cunning zee keepe.
>   Polwart zee peip,
>   Ze look like a sheipe
> And zee had twa hornes.
>   Polwart ze peip
> Like a mouse amongst thornes.'

Further, in *Ane Example for His Lady*, he uses the sixteen-line stave in *rime couée*, aaab, aaab, aaab, aaab ; in *Address to the Sun*, the common six-line stave in *rime couée*, aab, ccb; in *Remember Rightly*, the six-line stave, aab, aab, with an additional couplet; and in *Regrate of his Unhappy Luve*, a variation of the six-line stave of *The Address to the Deil* (see *ante*, p. 244), the first head-lines being of five accents, and the second, third, and fourth of four only, while the two tail lines are of only one, the last, 'Bot I' forming a refrain :—

tedious;
learning
Overcome;
sighing

every fellow

'Irkit I am with langsum luvis lair
Oursett with inwart siching sair;
For in the presone of dispair
  I ly,
Seeing ilk wicht gettis sum weilfair
  Bot I.'

In *Sen Fortun* we have an example of the bobwheel attached to a six-line stave rhyming alternately— ab, ab, ab,—the bob of one accent being followed by a line rhyming with the sixth line, the final line which rhymes with the bob, constituting a refrain. In *To his Maistres* he uses a five-line stave with internal rhyme, followed by the old bobwheel of the alliterative romances.

Other staves with bob-wheel.

Montgomerie had also recourse to old English measures, of which no examples are to be found in the Scottish 'makaris,' and he clearly got some of his staves from the new lyric school of England, as the six-line stave ab, ab, cc, named by Gascoigne the 'ballade,' and used by Wyatt, as well as afterwards by Spenser and Shakespeare. This stave Montgomerie also, like Scott (see *ante*, p. 244), used with a refrain.

English stave.

Of the various forms of 'cuttit and broken verse' which Montgomerie affected, it is impossible here to give a minute analysis.   In his more elaborate staves he combined interlacing rhyme with couplets, with *rime couée*, and with various forms of the bobwheel.   Some were written to music, as that long complex stave into which, in *The Mindes Melodie,* he translated 'certayne *Psalmes* of the Kinglie Prophete Dauid, applyed to a new pleasant tune, verie comfortable to everie one that is rightlie acquainted therewith.'

'Cuttit and broken verse.'

But the ingenuity and skill of Montgomerie as a metrist sometimes proved more a snare to him than an advantage.   The mere length and complexity of several of his more elaborate staves tended to dissipate metrical as well as poetic unity, and some of them cannot be regarded as anything more than ingenious metrical exercises.

Metrist rather that poet.

Montgomerie's poetic fame rests traditionally on *The Cherrie and the Slae,* which, containing some spirited description, especially in the introductory stanzas, as well as much shrewd proverbial philosophy, fails of effectiveness not only from the unsuitability of the stave for consecutive narrative, but from the obscurity of the poet's intention.   Perhaps its merits—in description and philosophy—are nowhere better represented than in the two following stanzas :—

'The Cherrie and the Slae.'

> 'The dew as diamondis did hing,
>   Vpon the tender twistis and zing,
>   Ouir-twinkling all the treis ;

hang
boughs;
young

And ay quhair flowris flourischit faire
Thair suddainly I saw repaire
   In swarmes the sounding beis.
Sum sweitly hes the hony socht,
   Quhil they war cloggit soir ;
Sum willingly the waxe hes wrocht,
   To heip it vp in stoir ;
      So heiping, with keiping,
         Into thair hyuis they hyde it,
      Precyselie and wyselie
         For winter they prouyde it.

To pen the pleasures of that park,
How euery blossome, branche, and bark
   Agaynst the sun did schyne,
I leif to poetis to compyle
In stately verse and lofty style :
   It passes my ingyne.
Bot as I muisit myne allane
   I saw ane river rin
Out ouir ane craggie rok of stane,
   Syne lichtit in ane lin
      With tumbling and rumbling
         Amang the rochis round,
      Dewailing and falling
         Into that pit profound.’

Until (margin, left of lines 5–6)

ability (margin, left of "It passes my ingyne.")

a (margin, left of "Out ouir ane craggie rok of stane,")

Then (margin, left of "Syne lichtit in ane lin")

But on the whole the *Bankis of Helicon* is the better poem, for even its aureate language and its classical allusions add to the quaint effect of the stave, and to the old-world courtesy of the ceremonial love-song. At the same time, much of it is mere prose, as indeed is the bulk of Montgomerie’s verse. Yet in *The Night is Neir Gone* we have one of the classics of the sixteenth century. What it may owe to the old song to which the tune was first set it is impossible to tell, but the

‘The Night is Neir Gone.’ (margin, left of third body line)

whole picture of the approach of day is a true poetic
conception presented with much vivid fidelity.   Here
are the three first stanzas:—

> 'Hay ! nou the day dauis ;   dawns
> The jolie Cok crauis ;
> Nou shroudis the shauis   woods
>   Throu Natur anone.
> The thissell-cok cryis
> On louers vha lyis.
> Nou skaillis the skyis :   clears
>   The night is neir gone.
>
> The feildis ouerflouis
> With gouans that grouis,   daisies
> Quhair lilies lyk louis,   flames
>   Als rid as the rone.   rowanberry
> The turtill that treu is,
> With nots that reneuis,
> Her pairtie perseuis :   mate
>   The night is neir gone.
>
> Nou Hairtis with Hyndis,
> Conforme to thair kyndis,
> Hie tussis thair tyndis,   tosses;
>   On grund vhair they grone.   antlers
> Nou Hurchonis, with Hairis,   hedgehogs;
> Aye passis in pairis ;   hares
> Quhilk deuly declaris   Which
>   The night is neir gone.'

Occasional stanzas of some poetic merit may also
be found embedded amongst much that is chiefly
trivial or commonplace.   But trivial or
commonplace very much of his poetry   His defects.
is, and it also suffers from his too frequent peevish-
ness.   *The Flyting* [1] is occasionally clever, but its fun

[1] Montgomerie's opponent in *The Flyting* was Sir Patrick Hume
of Polwarth, one of the gentlemen of the Bedchamber.

is for the most part mere grossness, the grossness in which James VI. delighted to revel. Montgomerie possessed little of the aphoristic wit, or the light and easy gaiety, of Scott, and, notwithstanding his ingenious cleverness, he very rarely attains to Scott's delicate grace. As for his devotional pieces, they are merely rhyming expressions of Reformation theology, written, most of them for special tunes, and some of them to tunes associated with secular songs.

After Scott and Montgomerie, the only 'makar' of this later period who deserves particular mention is the old Scots judge, Sir Richard Maitland, Lord Lethington, who, born as early as 1496, survived to 1586—politically, religiously, and poetically very much a relic of the first half of the century. Descended from an old Anglo-Norman family who had possessed the old keep of Thirlestane from the time that Sir Richard de Mateland held it (if he did hold it) 'heil and feir' against the army of Edward I., the 'auld laird of Lethington' was essentially feudal in all his opinions, political, social, and religious. Patriot rather than partisan, he regarded political and religious questions mainly from the standpoint of an administrator of the law. Throughout the political and religious commotions of his time, and notwithstanding the political entanglements of his brilliant son, William the Secretary, he kept so aloof from party disputes that he continued in his office of judge whichever party was in power; and having, in the words of

Sir Richard Maitland (1496-1586). Feudal Baron and Judge.

James VI., served the king's 'grandsire, goodsire, goodame, mother, and himself,' was permitted, when he resigned his judgeship in July 1584, to enjoy, by special favour, its emoluments during the remainder of his life.

When overtaken by blindness sometime before the arrival of Queen Mary from France in 1561, Maitland resolved to devote his leisure to study—in order, as he stated, to 'occupy himself as in time past,' and because he thought it 'dangerous to "mell" in matters of great importance'—dividing his attention between genealogy and poetry.[1] Though not strictly poetical, his pieces are, several of them, terse, pointed, and witty, and all, while displaying that shrewd practical wisdom and lofty patriotism by which he guided his own conduct, are of more or less historic interest from their references to the customs and events of the time. His imprecatory poem *On the New Zeir*, written in the lifetime of the Queen-Regent, gives a sort of bird's-eye view of his ideal of a well-governed and

Historical interest of his poetry.

[1] Maitland wrote *A Chronicle and Historie of the House and Surname of Seaton*, which was printed by the Maitland Club in 1829 from a MS. in the Advocates' Library ; and the same work, under a slightly different title and from a different MS., was published in Edinburgh, 1830. But his chief service to literature was the collection of old MSS., including his own poetry. This collection, only second in importance to the Bannatyne MS., is now in the Pepysian Library, Magdalen College, Cambridge. It has never been fully printed—the largest selection from it being that in Pinkerton's *Ancient Scotish Poems*, 1786. Maitland's own *Poems* are, most of them, in the Collections of Pinkerton, 1786, and Sibbald, 1807. They were published separately by the Maitland Club, 1830.

prosperous community. *On the Quenis Maryage,*
1558, shows strong French leanings, as does also
Of the Wynning of Calice, 1558 :—

> 'Thairfoir ye all that ar of Scottis blude,
>   Be blyth, rejois for the recovering
> Of that strang toun : and of the fortoun gude
>   Of your maist tendir freynd that nobil king.'

In *Of the Assemblie of the Congregatioun,* 1559,
and *On the New Zeir,* 1560, he indicates, however,
that his chief concern is for the reconciliation of the
parties whose disputes had plunged the nation in the
horrors of civil war :—

> 'I cannot sing for the vexatioun
>   Of Frenchmen, and the Congregatioun,
> That hes maid troubil in the natioun,
>   And monye bair bigging.'

quilding

In his *Satire on the Age* he discourses with much
point on the pride and selfishness of the old ecclesiastics, on the decay of 'mirrieness' through
the poverty of the people, on the oppres-
sion of tenants by spendthrift landlords, and on the
feeble influence of law and justice. The amusing
Satire on the Toun Ladyes touches on a lighter theme,
and supplies us with a picturesque and minute sketch
of the vagaries of female fashion in the Edinburgh of
the 'Evangel' :—

'Satire on the
Age.'

under-petti-
coats must
stripes of
lace

inquire into
husbands

such raiment

> 'Thair wylecots man weill be hewit,
>   Broudirit richt braid, with pasmentis sewit :
> I trow, quha wald the matter speir,
>   That thair guidmen had caus to rew it
> That evir thair wyfis weir sic geir.

Thair wovin hois of silk ar schawin, *striped above;*
Barrit abone with tasteis drawin ; *tassels*
   With garteris of ane new maneir,
To gar thair courtlines be knawin ; *make*
   And all for newfangilnes of geir. *newfashion-edness*

Sumtyme they will beir up thair gown
To schaw thair wylecot hingeand down, *hanging*
   And sumtyme bayth thai will upbeir
To schaw thair hois of blak or broun,
   And all for newfangilnes of geir.

Thair collars, carcats, and hals beidis ! *necklaces ; throat beads*
With velvet hats heicht on thair heidis, *high*
   Coirdit with gold lyik ane younkeir, *young swell*
Broudit about with goldin threidis ;
   And all for newfangilnes of geir.

Thair schone of velvet and thair muillis ! *embroidered slippers*
In kirk thai ar not content of stuillis,
   The sermon quhen thai sit to heir,
But caryis cuschingis, lyik vaine fuillis,
   And all for newfangilnes of geir.'

He is equally effective when he takes up his parable against *The Folye of ane Auld Manis Maryand ane Young Woman,* or illustrates that there is now *Na Kyndes* [recognition of **Other Satires.** kinship] *Without Siller* [money], or tells us of his *Solace in Age,*—

   ' Quhan young men cumis fra the grene
   (Playand at the fute-ball had bene),
     With brokin spald ; *collar-bone*
   I thank my God I want my ene, *eyes*
     And am sa ald,'—

or declaims in the bobwheel stanza of Dunbar's *Donald Owre, Aganis the Theivis of Liddisdaill* :—

' They leif not spendill, spone, nor speit,
Bed, boster, blanket, sark, nor scheit :
" Johne of the Parke,"
Rypis kist and ark ;
For all sic wark
He is richt meit.

searches ;
chest
such work

He is weill kend, " John of the Syide,"
A gretar theif did never ryde :
He never tyris
For to brek byris ;
Our muir and myris
Our gude ane gyide.

known

cowhouses
mosses
Too ; a

Thair is ane, callit " Clement's Hob,"
Fra ilk puir wyfe reiffis the wob,
And all the laif—
Quhatever thay haif :
The deuil resave
Thairfoir his gob ! '

every ; steals
the web
everything
else

mouth

Two sons of Maitland, John of Thirlestane, ancestor of the Dukes of Lauderdale, and Thomas, wrote poetry, but the verses of neither are of much account.

Towards the close of the century vernacular poetry of a secular kind was cultivated only by James VI. and those under his immediate influence.[1]

James VI. Besides his *Essayes of a Prentise*, 1584, containing pieces written before he had passed his eighteenth year, James published in 1591 *Poetical Exercises at Vacant Hours,* also, he states, the work of his ' verie young and tender years.' For so young a man his verses display considerable technical

[1] Rolland's *Court of Venus*, imprinted at Edinburgh by John Ros, 1577, and republished by the Scottish Text Society, 1884, is of no interest except philologically. An edition of the same author's *Seven Sages* is also promised by the Scottish Text Society.

accomplishment, but are deformed, the most of them, by the same absurd mixture of familiarity and pomposity which characterised his own address. Yet he does occasionally attain to a certain semblance of dignity and grace, as in this sonnet prefixed to *The Lepanto* :—

> ' The azur'd vaulte, the crystall circles bright,
>> The gleaming fyrie torches powdred there,
> The changing round, the shyning beamie light,
>> The sad and bearded fyres, the monsters faire,
>> The prodiges appearing in the aire,
> The rearding thunders and the blustering winds,
>> The foules, in hew, in shape, in nature raire
> The prettie notes that wing'd musiciens finds ;
> In earth the sau'rie floures, the metall'd minds,
>> The wholesome hearbes, the hautie pleasant trees,
> The syluer streames, the beasts of sundrie kinds,
>> The bounded roares, and fishes of the seas :
> All these for teaching man the Lord did frame,
> To do his will whose glorie shines in thame.'

But the close is mean and tame; nor has the poem anything of the character of a sonnet. It will also be observed that it is practically in English. Two Englishmen also, Robert and Thomas Hudson, violers to the king, wrote English poetry spelt after a somewhat Scottish fashion. As for William Fowler, who translated *The Triumphs of Petrarch*,[1] and Stewart of Baldiness, who presented to the king *Ane Abbregement of Roland Fvrious translatit ovt of Aroist*,[2] such specimens of their verse as have been printed do not tend to beget any curiosity as to the bulk of it still only in MS.; and

The Court Poets.

---

[1] MS. in the Edinburgh University Library.
[2] MS. in the Advocates' Library, Edinburgh.

the only other name that need be mentioned is John Burel—most probably the John Burel who was master of the king's mint,—who in 1590 wrote *The Descriptioun of the Quenis Maiestis maist honorable Entry into the Toon of Edinburgh,* only of antiquarian interest, and *The Passage of the Pilgrim,* a dull allegorical piece in the stave of *The Cherrie and the Slae.*[1]

During the sixteenth century Latin poetry was cultivated by a number of Scotsmen, and the influence of George Buchanan in this regard was felt down to a much later period.   With this artificial phase of literature we have here no concern; but the idea may be hazarded that its cultivation was aided by the current notion of the frivolity of the merely vernacular Muse.   Except for devotion or religious or politico-religious controversy, vernacular verse was unauthorised by the Kirk.   Alexander Arbuthnot,[2] the Presbyterian Principal of Aberdeen University, who did in secret venture to cultivate the vernacular Muse merely for pleasure or solace, did so in fear and trembling :—

Latin poetry.

'In poetrie I preis to pas the tyme
   When cairfull thochts with sorrow sailyes me ;
Bot gif I mell with meter or with ryme,
   With rascal rymours I sall raknit be ;
They sal me bourdin als with mony lie,
   In charging me with that quhilk never I ment :
Quhat marvel is thocht I murne and lament.'

like
assails
if; meddle

jeer at
which
though

---

[1] Both poems are printed in Watson's *Collection*, Part II., 1710, and the 'Description' is included in Sibbald's *Collection*, 1807.

[2] Three poems of Arbuthnot are included in Pinkerton's *Ancient Scotish Poems*, 1786.

In addition to the verses of Dunbar, Henryson, and other 'makaris' already mentioned, the Bannatyne MS. contains several innominate specimens of Catholic religious poetry, which, if lacking in emotional fervour and simplicity, are at least melodious, eloquent, and imposing. Scott and Montgomerie also, Catholics by early training, wrote in accordance with the spirit of Protestant theology several religious pieces, mainly of interest as metrical exercises; but the chief representatives of the early religious Muse of the Reformation were the brothers Wedderburn and their coadjutors, whose translation of Lutheran hymns and the Psalms of David, but especially parodies of old secular songs, were perhaps more effective in spreading the Reformation *furore* than even the preaching of Knox. At what time these religious pieces were collected into a volume is uncertain. The earliest dated copy is one of 1578, but there is an undated earlier one, and in all likelihood copies were printed and circulated in secret before the 'Evangel' was established. The full title of the book is '*Ane Compendious Buik of Godlie Psalms and Spirituall Sangs*, collectit furthe of sundrie partis of the Scripture, with vtheris Ballates changeit out of prophane Sangis in Godlie sangis, for avoyding of sin and harlotrie.'[1] The book, which was frequently reprinted, was long known as *The Dundee*

The Wedder-burns.

---

[1] A reprint of the 1578 edition was published at Edinburgh by David Laing in 1868; and an edition based on the earlier text by the Scottish Text Society, ed. Professor Mitchell, 1897.

Psalms. Its authorship is assigned by Calderwood to Robert Wedderburn—the youngest of three poetic brothers, sons of James Wedderburn, merchant in Dundee—who, Calderwood states, 'turned the tunes and tenor of many profane ballads into Godlie songs and hymnes which wer called the Psalmes of Dundie.'[1] Of John, the second brother, Calderwood also says: 'He translated many of Luther's dytements into Scottish meeter and the Psalmes of David. He turned manie bawdie songs and rymes in Godlie rymes.'[2] The eldest brother James was, as we have already seen (p. 217), the author of some plays against the Papists. All three brothers were educated at St. Andrews University. James became a merchant, and John and Robert were priests. James finally took refuge in Dieppe. John, who had taken refuge in Germany, returned to Scotland after the death of James v. in 1542, but had finally to flee to England, where he died in 1556. Robert was vicar of Dundee as late as 13th January 1552-3, when letters of legitimation passed under the Great Seal in favour of his two bastard sons. In the Bannatyne MS. are four poems —one a long historical *Ballat of the Prayis of Women*—by one of the Wedderburns, but which of them there is nothing to show.

The Gude and Godlie Ballates were probably, many of them, used at the earlier services of the Reformers; and it can't well have been with other than selections from them that Queen Mary was

---

[1] *History*, viii. 147.　　　　[2] *Ibid.*, i. 143.

serenaded on her first night at Holyrood Palace—
'tant mal chantez,' says Brantôme, 'et si mal accordez
que rien plus.' They possess the actuality   'The Gude
and earnestness which belong to this   and Godlie
  Ballates' and
period of stern religious conflict, but   the old songs.
the main literary interest of the book now lies in
its parodies of the old songs, some of them of
English origin. If these parodies are merely ridiculous caricatures both of the supposed religious
truths they profess to set forth, and of the
original sentiments they seek to appropriate for a
sacred purpose, they contain at least faint echoes of
the old popular lyrics, many of which have wholly
perished — perished because of these *Gude and
Godlie Ballates*. *Richt soirly musing in my
mynde*, in the *rime couée* of Burns's *Address to the
Deil*, is mentioned in *The Complaynt of Scotland* as
a song sung by the shepherds. *Allace that same sweet
Face*, also mentioned in *The Complaynt*, is found in *The
Buik*; but the 'sweit face,' 'onlie to be our remedie,'
is that which 'deit vpon ane tree.' 'To die therefore'
is the refrain of a song beginning, 'Of mercy zit he
passis all.' *For lufe of One I mak my mone* begins a
spiritual lament. *Quho is at my Windo?*—a song of
which the air is in Queen Elizabeth's *Virginal Book*,
and echoes of which are found in many lyrics down
to the time of Burns, is represented by its chorus:—

> 'Quho is at my windo? quho, quho?
> Go from my windo, go, go!
> Quho callis thair, sa lyke a strangair?
> Go from my windo, go!'

but the occupant of the apartment is no less a person than God Almighty. 'In till ane mirthfull Maij morning,' the poet 'is thinkand' not on his mistress but on 'Christ so free,'

Who suffered; pained

'Quhilk meiklie for mankynde
    Tholit to be pynde
       On croce cruellie. La, La.'

He soliloquises—

'My Lufe murnis for me, for me ;
    My Lufe that murnis for me ;
I am vnkynde, hes nocht in mynde,
    My Lufe that murnis for me' ;

not

but 'Who is' his 'Lufe bot God abufe ?' With the shepherds in *The Complaynt* he sings, 'All my hart, ay this is my sang,' but it is Christ who has his 'hart ay.' If again with the shepherds he weep alone 'in great distress,' it is because he is exiled from, not his mistress, but God's word. In *Grievous is my sorrow,* he appropriates *The Dying Maiden's Complaint*—an old English song—for a wholly spiritual purpose. He supplies the beginning of a very old amatory invitation :—

'Johne, cum kis me now,
    Johne, cum kis me now,
Johne, cum kis me by and by
    And mak no moir adow' ;

but adds—

'The Lord thy God I am
    That John dois the call ;
John represented man,
    Be grace celestiall.'

By

The refrain 'Downe sall cum, downe ay, downe ay,' he attaches to a lugubrious ditty on human frailty. In *With Huntis Vp*—a song known to Robert Henryson long before the English song written in honour of Henry VIII.—'The Pope is the fox,' 'Rome is the rox,' the hunter is 'Jesu our King,' and 'the hundis are Peter and Paull.' *The Wind blawis cauld* is represented by the chorus:—

> 'The wind blawis cauld, furious and bauld,
>   This lang and mony day;
> But Christis mercy we man all die   Without;
>   Or keip the cauld wind away.'   must

That very old song, *Ha now the Day dawis*, which the minstrels sang before Dunbar was born, is not forgotten, but its spirit as well as form is no doubt immeasurably better preserved in Montgomerie's masterpiece (p. 261). The 'gude-man' of a traditional song appears in the old chorus:—

> 'Till our gude-man, till our gude-man
>   Keep faith and lufe till our gude-man';   To

but 'our gude-man' of the ballad 'in hevin dois ring' (reign). The chorus,

> 'Hay trix, tryme go trix
>   Vnder the grene wod-tree,'

is attached to a ditty beginning

> 'The Paip, that pagane full of pryde,   Pope
>   He hes vs blindit lang,'

and celebrating the destruction of the monasteries in 1559, after a fashion which retains much of the free

S

allusion of the original song. Finally, we have more than the outline of a popular song in the ballad beginning

> ' All my Lufe, leif me not,
> Leif me not, leif me not,
> All my Lufe, leif me not
>   Thus myne alone :
> With ane burding on my bak,
> I may not beir it I am sa waik :
> Lufe, this burden from me tak
>   Or ellis I am gone.'

The Gude and Godlie Ballates are the chief poetic monument of the Scottish Reformation. In Scotland

Alexander Hume. the Reformation—essentially logical and Calvinistic in its teaching—inspired no original religious poetry corresponding to the Lutheran hymns. Alexander Hume, second son of Patrick, fifth Lord Hume, and minister of Logie, Stirlingshire, published in 1599 ' *Hymnes or Sacred Songs*,[1] wherein the right vse of Poësie may be spied,' but it can scarce be affirmed that he attains to ' poesie ' of any sort, although *The Day Estivall*, if absurdly prosaic, is occasionally picturesque.

Lady Colville of Culross—a daughter of Sir James Melville of Halhill—to whom Hume dedicated his

Lady Colville of Culross. *Hymnes*, wrote, shortly before the end of the century, *Ane Godly Dream*,[2] which may perhaps be best defined as a sort of emotional representation of the extreme Calvinism of the Kirk.

---

[1] Reprinted by the Bannatyne Club, 1832.
[2] First published in 1603, and frequently in the seventeenth century. Included in Laing's *Metrical Tales*, 1826.

But the Protestant verse-writers devoted themselves chiefly to political or ecclesiastical diatribes, such as those reprobated by Sir Richard Maitland in *On the Malice of Poets* :—

'Sum of the poyets, and makars, that are now,
 Of grit despyte, and malice, ar sa fow
 That all lesingis, that can be inventit,
 Thay put in writ, and garris thame be prentit.'

The Reformation Satirists.

full
lies
makes

They were issued chiefly as broadsides from the press of Lekprevick, and nearly all the surviving examples have been published by the Scottish Text Society.[1] The chief laureate of this broadside school was Robert Sempill,[2] who is mentioned in a sonnet by Montgomerie as still alive in 1584. Nothing is known of his parentage or personal history, the attempts to identify him with members of the noble family of Sempill in the legitimate line being quite unsuccessful. Before he turned political or religious satirist he was known as the author of three ballads, entirely secular, and witty after the coarse fashion of that age : on *Margret Fleming*, on *Grissel Sandelandis*, and on *Jonet Reid, Ane Violet and Ane Quhyt, being slicht Wemen of Lyf and Conversatioun and Taverneris*. Sempill was a skilful metrist, and his command of virulent abuse was remarkable even for his time, his masterpiece in that line being *The Legend and Discourse of the Life of the Tulchene Bischope of Sanctandrois*. The other poets whose

---

[1] *Satiric Poems of the Time of the Reformation*, 1889-93.
[2] *The Sempill Ballates* have been published separately, ed. Stevenson, Edinburgh, 1872.

productions are included in the Scottish Text Society's
volume are Sir William Kirkcaldy of Grange, the
supposed author of *Ane Ballat of ye Captane of the
Castell*, in the stanza of *The Cherrie and the Slae*;
Sir John Maitland, Lord Thirlestane, whose political
verses can scarce be termed partisan; John Davidson,
Presbyterian minister, whose uncompromising and
bitter opposition to the King's ecclesiastical policy
got him into serious trouble; and Nicol Burne, who
at one time was Professor of Philosophy at St.
Andrews, but becoming 'be ane special grace of God
ane member of the halie Catholic Church,' published
at Paris in 1581 *The Dispvtation concerning the
Controversit Headdis of Religion*, to a few copies
of which was appended *Ane Admonition to the Antichristian Ministers of the Reformed Kirk of Scotland*, only remarkable for its weak extravagance.   A
satirical piece—not included in the Scottish Text
Society's volume,—the Earl of Glencairn's *Ane Epistle
direct fra the Holye Armit of Allarit to his Brethe-
ren the Gray Freiris*,[1] has some ironical vigour; but
the main interest in this controversial poetry is
historical—the style, the wit, the thought and argument being, almost without exception, hopelessly
mediocre.

[1] Knox's *Works*, ed. Laing, vol. i. p. 72.

IX

ANONYMOUS POETRY OF THE FIFTEENTH AND SIXTEENTH CENTURIES

'THE FREIRIS OF BERWICK'—'THE THRIE PRIESTIS OF PEBLIS'—'SYMMIE AND HIS BRUDER'—'THE WYFE OF AUCHTIRMWCHTY'—'THE WOWING OF JOK AND JYNNY'—'IN SOMER'—'QUHY SOWLD NOCHT ALLANE HONORIT BE?'—'THE MURNING MAIDEN'—'TAYIS BANK'—'IN MAY IN A MORNING'—'O LUSTY MAY'— 'WELCUM TO MAY'—'MY HART IS QUHYT'—'ANE WELCUM TO EILD'—'THUS I PROPONE IN MY CARPING.'

THE present chapter deals with such anonymous poetry of authenticated early date as has not been already noticed in Chapter IV. Two of the best-known poems of a semi-ecclesiastical sort are *The Freiris of Berwick*[1] and *The Thrie Priestis of Peblis*. From a certain similarity in subject and treatment some are disposed

'The Freiris of Berwick.' Was it written by Dunbar?

---

[1] Bannatyne and Maitland MSS. At the end of an edition of *The Thrie Priestis*, 1603, it was advertised as printed by Robert Charteris, but no copy of this edition is known to exist. A copy of an edition by Raban, Aberdeen, has, however, been preserved. The piece was included—from the Maitland MS.—in Pinkerton's *Ancient Scotish Poems*, 1786; and a collated text is in Sibbald's Collection, 1802, and in Laing's and the Scottish Text Society's editions of the *Works* of Dunbar.

to ascribe them to the same author, and *The Freiris
of Berwick* has usually been ascribed to Dunbar.
The similarity is, however, very partial; and whether
or not Dunbar be the author of *The Freiris of Berwick*, he could scarce have been the author of the
more didactic *Priestis of Peblis*. Moreover, excellent
though in some respects *The Freiris of Berwick* is,
it does not seem to be stamped with the impress of
Dunbar's peculiar genius. It is too purely and lightly
comic, too genial, and even too merely superficial,
to be his. The irony possesses little of his subtlety,
corrosiveness, or depth. The style, easy, simple, and
apt though it be, lacks his peculiar strength and
incisiveness. Yet from start to finish the tale is
admirably told; the scenes are full of vivacity and
movement; the characters of the small comedy—the
frail and passive friar Allan, the vigorous, alert, and
sportive friar Robert, the luxurious Abbot (friar
John), the 'dink' and 'dangerous' gudewife, the
open and jolly landlord—are set before us to the
life; the situations are cleverly developed, without
exaggeration, yet with much humorous discernment;
and the *dénouement*—mere piece of horseplay though
it is—is narrated with a gusto that is quite contagious.

The story—a landlady's intrigue with an abbot,
and its amusing discovery, to the private confusion of
both parties, while the husband is none
Its theme.   the wiser—is no doubt partly borrowed,
as most of the old tales were. A similar theme forms
the subject of a French *fabliau* of the twelfth or

thirteenth century,[1] and even the pretended conjuration of the supper has its counterpart in the French story of the *Soldat Magicien*,[2] of uncertain date. There is in truth nothing remarkable about the plot; the literary value of the poem derives from the art of the narrator, and to recognise its excellence we have but to turn to Ramsay's vulgarisation of the tale in *The Monk and the Miller's Wife*.

The poem opens with a description of the noble town of Berwick-on-Tweed, with its walls and ditches, its embattled castle with 'stately tower and turrets high,' its hospital, and its convents, the whole

The silly friars and the landlady.

> 'Moist fair, most gudly, most plesand to be sene ;
> The tovne, the wall, the castell and the land.'

Towards this fair town two friars, who had spent the day among the country people, are returning in the evening :—

> 'Freir Allane, and Freir Robert the vder,
> Thir silly Freiris with wyffis weill cowld gluder ;
> Rycht wondir weill plesit thai all wyffis,
> And tawld thame tailis of haly sanctis lyffis.'

talk scandalously

They were hastening to get home before the convent gates were shut; but Friar Allan could walk but slowly, and though Friar Robert

> 'bure both clothes and hude
> And all thair geir, for he was strong and wicht,
> Be that it drew neir towart the nicht,
> As thai wer cumand towart the tovne full neir.'

baggage; vigorous By

---

[1] Le Grand, *Fabliaux ou Contes du XIIe et du XIIIe Siècle*, 1781, vol. ii. part i.

[2] Quoted by Le Grand.

Being tired and thirsty, they entered 'ane wonder good hostellar' without the town, where, having sat down to their ale, they, as friars were wont, called for more; but just as they began to be 'blythe'

> 'thai hard the prayer bell
> Off thair awin abbay, and than thai wer agast
> Becauss thai knew the zettis wer closit fast.'

On their asking 'herbery' at the inn, the gudewife gave answer 'with grit hicht':—

If
such

> 'Quhat wald Symon say, Ha, Benedicite!
> Bot in his absence I abusit his place?
> Our deir Lady Mary keip fra sic cace,
> And keip me owt of perrell and of schame.'

But at last she consented to give them lodging, provided they were content with a loft at the end of the hall, 'made for corne and hay.'

Her extreme scrupulosity was due to her expectation of an important visitor, none other than Friar John, Abbot of the Black Friars; and no sooner had she got the two 'silly freiris' safe in the loft than she hastened to prepare for his reception. Thrusting fat fowls 'to the speit,' and rabbits to the fire, she gives orders to her maid

Enter the
Abbot.

> 'To flawme and turne and rost thame tenderly';

and going to her chamber

kerchief

> 'Scho cleithis hir in a kirtill of fyne reid,
> Ane fair quhyt curch scho puttis vpoun hir heid;
> Her kirtill wes of silk and silwer fyne
> Hir vthir garmentis as the reid gold did schyne.'

And just as she had covered the board with 'clath of

costly greyne,' the abbot, who brings with him wine, white bread, and a pair of partridges, knocks, and is admitted with warm welcome.

Meanwhile, the inquisitive Friar Robert, discerning symptoms of wakefulness and bustle in the hostelry, becomes suspicious, and cuts a small hole in the board with his knife, whereby he both hears and sees all that is going on between the gudewife and her guest :—

> 'Quhen scho wes prowd, richt woundir fresche and gay,
>   Scho callit him baith hert, lemmane and luve ;
>   Lord God, gif than his curage wes aboif,   *if then ; up*
> So prelat lyk sat he in to the chyre !
> Scho rownis than ane pistill in his eir ;   *whispers ; story*
> Thus sportand thame and makand melody :
> And quhen scho saw the supper wes reddy,
> Scho gois belyfe and cuveris the burde annon,   *presently*
> And syne the pair of bossis hes scho tone,   *then ; bottles ; taken*
> And sett thame doun ⁊poun the burde hir by.
> And evin with that thai hard the gudman cry,
> And knokand at the zett he cryit fast :
> Quhen thai him hard then wer thai both agast.'

But the gudewife is equal to the occasion. The abbot is hid in the meal-chest, the dainties disappear into the cupboard, the fire is put out, the *The landlord comes home.* house is swept clean, and mistress and maid go to bed, allowing the gudeman to knock and shout in vain. At last, however, she pretends to awake from sleep, and having with difficulty been persuaded that it is her husband who calls, she lets him in. Also, she sets before him for supper none of the hidden dainties, but cold meat, cow-heel and sheep's-head. To this he sits down well content, swearing,

'be All hallow,
I fair richt weill, and I had ane gud fallow.'

Now, Friar Robert, who had witnessed the whole comedy from the loft, had no mind to let slip an opportunity for a jovial night, and therefore intimated his presence by a cough. Apprised that the friars were in the loft, the landlord sent them an invitation to join him, which they readily accepted. He politely expressed regret that he had no better fare to set before them; but Friar Robert made known that when in Paris he had been instructed in certain magical arts, which, if he would keep his counsel, he was willing to practise for the good of the company :—

'I tak on hand, and ze will counsale keip,
That I sall gar zow se, or ever I sleip,
Of the best meit that is in this cuntre ;
Off Gascone wyne, gif ony in it be ;
Or, be thair ony within ane hundreth myle,
It salbe heir within a bony quhyle.'

The landlord was more than willing to take him at his word; and Friar Robert, after diverse mysterious antics, directed the gudewife to go to the cupboard, where, without doubt, she found all that she had put there :—

'Scho stert abak, as scho wer in a fray
And san 't hir, and smyland cowd scho say,
"Ha, Banedicitie, quhat may this bene ?
Quha ever afoir hes sic a fairly sene ?
Sa grit a mervell as now hes apnit heir
Quhat sall I say ? He is ane haly Freir."'

Marginal glosses (left column):
- by
- if; a
- The magic supper.
- if
- make
- if
- little
- started
- crossed herself
- before ;
- such ;
- strange thing

All spent a merry night except the misfared gudewife :—

> ' And than annone thai drank evin round abowt
> Of Gascone wyne ; the Freiris playit cop owt.   cup
> Thai sportit thame, and makis mirry cheir
> With sangis lowd, baith Symone and the Freir ;
> And on thir wyiss the lang nicht thai ourdraif[1] ;   this
> No thing thai want that thai desyrd to haif.'

The gudewife's feelings may further be imagined when the jocular Friar Robert proceeded to conjure his familiar, who had supplied the dainties, to rise from the meal-chest in the form of a Black Friar. He was mercifully told to pull his cowl over his face and begone to his abode, but he did not escape quite scot free. Simon, the gude-man—who knew nothing of all this by-play,—was directed to put himself behind the door with a stick, and as the abbot passed him Friar Robert called out, 'Strike, strike hardily.' This Simon did to such pur-pose that he himself fell and cut his head on the mortar-stone, while the abbot in his panic fell over the stair into the mire-hole below, whence, however, he got over the wall ; and the tale concludes :—

Exit the Abbot.

> 'Thus Symonis heid vpoun the stane wes brokin,
> And our the Freir in myre hes loppin,
> And tap our taill he fyld wes woundir ill ;   top over; dirtied
> And Alesone on na wayiss gat hir will ;
> This is the story that hapnit of that Freir,
> No moir thair is, bot Chryst ws help most deir.'

---

[1] Compare Burns's *Tam o' Shanter* :—
  ' The night drave on wi' sangs and clatter.'

The thrie Tailes of the thrie Priestis of Peblis [1] is a more serious performance than *The Freiris*. There is no

'The thrie Priestis of Peblis.'

reason whatever for assigning the work, as seems to be done by Pinkerton, to Dean Steil, and the supposition of Sibbald that it was written by John Rolland, equally unauthorised by evidence, is disposed of by the fact that it was included in the Asloan MS. Although it to some extent anticipates the political zeal of Sir David Lyndsay, it is, like *The Freiris*, the production of a period undisturbed by the faintest foreshadowing of Protestantism. The sketch of the three priests breathes nothing of Puritanic censoriousness. Their joviality, their appreciation of 'good cheir,' their aloofness from 'company,' their love of each other's society and talk,

Now;
tattle

'Umquhyle sadlie ; umquhyle jangle and jak,'

are described with a truly Chaucerian breadth of appreciation. But these priests who thus sat

'full easily and soft,
With monie lowd lauchter upon loft,'

were serious and thoughtful withal, and the tales they recite to each other over their wine deal

Friar John's tale. The answer of the burgess. The diligent trader and his spendthrift son.

with high matters of Church and State.

The first tale, that of the travelled Friar John, relates how a certain king put three questions to the wisest men of his three estates—the burgesses, the nobles, and

---

[1] Published by Robert Charteris, 1603; and reprinted in Pinkerton's *Scotish Poems from Scarce Editions*, 1792, and Laing's *Early Metrical Tales*, 1826.

the clergy—and how it was answered by each. That
put to the burgesses was—

> 'Quhy Burges bairns thryves not to the third air?'   heir

and the answer gives occasion for describing the
progress of a successful Scottish merchant of the
fifteenth century from the time that he began

> 'With hap, and halfpenny, and a lamb's skin ;   chance
>   And purelie ran fra toun to toun on feit   poorly
>   And than richt oft wetshod, werie, and weit,'

until he had a ship of his own—

> 'He sailit our the sey sa oft and oft
>   Quhil at the last ane semelie ship he coft,   Until;
>   bought
>   And waxe sa ful of warldis welth and win ;
>   His hands he wish in ane silver basin.
>   Foroutin gold or silver into hurde,   Beside.
>   hoard
>   Wirth thrie thousand pund was his copburde.
>   Riche wes his gounis with uther garmentis gay :
>   For Sonday silk, for ilk day grene and gray.   every
>   His wyfe was cumlie cled in scarlet reid,
>   Scho had no doubt of derth of ail nor breid.'   fear

But the son who 'entered in the wealth' his father
had won, had nothing of his father's severe apprentice-
ship, and was expert only in spending. The story
of his ruin is simply that of the modern 'pigeon.'
Pampered from infancy by his mother, who 'tholit'
not 'the reik (smoke) on him to blaw'; taught, quite
after the modern manner, to despise the trade to
which he owed his wealth, and refusing to hear,

> 'for very shame and sin,
> That ever his father sold ane sheipis skin,'

he spent his time wholly at the court in the company of the young lords,

Until
    'Quhil drink and dyce have pourit him to the pin.'

The answer of the wise lords as to the decay of hardiness among their order reveals the fact that, then as now, many of the nobility from considerations of lucre intermarried with the children of those who, apart from their wealth, were mere churls; and that of the wise clergy as to the cessation of miracles is that bishops were frequently chosen who had no real vocation for the office.

The answers of the wise lords and the clergy.

Following Friar John, Friar Archibald relates in most humorous fashion how a king, who loved too well the counsel of his young nobles, and despised that of wise and experienced statesmen, was very wisely instructed by a learned clerk, who for this purpose assumed the guise of a fool; and the allegorical tale of Friar William is meant to show that neither wealth, nor wife and children, nor 'other frendis all,' but only almsdeeds and charity, can avail us at the Judgment.

Tales of Friar Archibald and Friar William.

Another semi-ecclesiastical story—probably of at least as early date as *The Freiris* or *The Thrie Priestis*, and written in the stanza of *Christis Kirk*—is that of *Symmie and his Bruder*,[1] two St. Andrews worthies, who assumed the character of begging friars:—

'Symmie and his Bruder.'

---

[1] Bannatyne MS. Published in Laing's *Select Remains*, 1822 and 1885.

'Peipand peurly with piteous granis
Like fenzeit Symmie and his bruder,'

says the author of *Peder Coffeis*.   Piteous they might
be in their professional capacity, but in private they
lived merrily enough :—

'I screw thame that ay leiss   Beshrew
        But lauchter,   lives
Quod Sym to his bruder.'   Without

Finding also that his income could afford it, the
nameless brother laudably resolved to marry :—

'Quhen thai wer welthful in thair wynning,
    Thai puft thame vp in pryd,
Bot quhair that Symy levit in synning,
    His bruder wald haif ane bryd.
Hir wedoheid fra the begynning
    Wes neir ane moneth tyd ;   a
Gif scho was spedy ay in spynning,   month old
    Tak witness of thame besyd   If
        Ilk ane,
    Baith Sym and his bruder.'   Every

And the remainder of the piece—which ends with
an abruptness suggesting that a great portion is
awanting—is occupied with the narrative of some
rude proceedings on the marriage-day, which are
rather beyond modern comprehension.

Two tales more in ballad form—*The Wyfe of
Auchtirmwchty*,[1] and *The Wowing of Jok and Jynny*
—are of special value for their realistic presentments

---

[1] Bannatyne MS., and the Skene MS. in the Advocates' Library.
Published, with many alterations, by Allan Ramsay in *The Ever-
green*, 1724, and correctly with various readings in Laing's *Select
Remains*, 1822 and 1885.

of rustic life in the olden time.   In the Bannatyne MS.
The Wyfe is attributed to Sir John Moffat, but not
by Bannatyne; and without further corroboration
it must be regarded as anonymous.
'The Wyfe of
Auchtirmwchty.' Ritson pointed out that a similar story
is found in the *Silva Sermonum jucundissimorum*
(Basil, 1568), and the passage is printed by Laing in
the Appendix to his *Select Remains*.   But while the
theme is one which might occur to any one, the stories
differ greatly in detail; and even were *The Wyfe*
suggested by the Latin story, it is to all intents and
purposes an original composition.   It relates the
mishaps which befell a lazy and effeminate farmer,
who, envying the supposed comfortable ease of his
wife at home, while he in cold and wet trudged all
day behind the plough, proposed an exchange of
occupations.   Here is a glimpse of the gudeman as
housewife :—

churn; stir	'Than to the kyrn that he did stoure,
until	And jwmlit at it quhill he swatt ;
	Quhen he had jwmlit a full lang houre
	The sorrow crap of butter he gatt.
	Albeit na butter he cowld gett,
vexed	Zit he wes cummerit with the kyrne,
heated ; too hot	And syne he het the milk our hett,
curdle	And sorrow spark of it wald zyrne.
into the house	Than ben thair come ane gredy sow,
could	I trow he cund her littill thank,
big mouth	And in scho schot hir mekle mow,
	And ay scho winkit and scho drank.
caught	He cleikit vp ane crukit club
a heavy blow	And thocht to hitt the sow ane rowt,
	The twa gaislingis the gled had left
stroke; brains	That straik dang baith thair harnis owt.'

The piece is only farce, but of its kind the farce is first-rate—inevitably true to nature, graphically concise, and unfailingly witty, even if the wit be obvious and uproarious, rather than delicate or subtle. The story is emasculated in Allan Cunningham's *John Grumlie*.

The Wowing of Jok and Jynny [1] is a somewhat unique relic of ancient rustic marriage diplomacy. The original of many Anglo-Scottish songs on Jock and Jenny in the black-letter broadsides, it also supplied the opening stanza of the old improper song on *Duncan Gray* which Burns modified. The ballad, in the French octave, begins in this quaintly simple style :—

'The Wowing of Jok and Jynny.'

> 'Robeyns Jok [2] come to wow our Jynny,
>   On our feist evin quhen we wer fow ;
> Scho brankit fast and maid hir bony,
>   And said, "Jok, come ze for to wow ?"
> Scho birneist her, baith breist and brow,
> And maid hir cleir as ony clok ;
>   Than spak her deme, and said, "I trow
> Ze come to wow our Jynny, Jok."
>
> Jok said, "Forsuth I zern full fane
> To luk my heid, [3] and sit doun by zow."
>   Then spak hir modir and said agane,
> "My bairne hes tocher gud anuwch to ge zow."
> "Te he," quod Jynny, "keik, keik, I se zow ;
>   Muder, zone man makis zow a mok."
> "I schrow thé, lyar, full leis me zow,
>   I come to wow your Jynny," quod Jok.'

fow — drunk
brankit — hurried
birneist — burnished
clok — beetle
deme — mother
zern full fane — fondly
anuwch to ge — enough; give
keik — look
schrow thé ... leis me zow — Beshrew thee !; I love you heartily

---

[1] Bannatyne MS. Published in Ramsay's *Evergreen*, 1724, and most subsequent *Collections*, but generally with more or less incorrectness.

[2] Jok, the son of Robert. In old village communities the surname was frequently dropped.

[3] Probably to enter the house by bending his head, though some interpret it as looking his head to see that it is clear of vermin.

T

The 'tocher-gude' (dowry) was, in Jok's view, the
most momentous part of the question; and after the
mother's honest, if alluring, recital of her daughter's
belongings,

by
a
up in the
country

> 'Jok tuk Jynny be the hand
>   And cryd ane feist, and slew ane cok,
>   And maid a brydell vp alland :
>   "Now haif I gottin your Jynny," quod Jok.'

But though conscious that he had had a good
bargain, Jok was also honestly convinced that his
bride had been as lucky as himself :—

know
known ;
enough

> 'I lat zow wit schois not miskareit,
>   It is weill kend I haif anuwch' ;

and he proceeds to give a recital of his personalty, of
which this sample may suffice :—

halter ;
manger
basket
heaps ;
doublet
pommel ;
load saddle
bag; pedlar's
wallet
spinning-
wheel; notch

> 'I haif ane helter, and eik ane hek,
>   Ane cord, ane creill, and als ane cradill,
>   Fyve fidder of raggis to stuff ane jak,
>   Ane auld pannell of ane laid sadill,
>   Ane pepper polk maid of a padill,
>   Ane spounge, ane spindill wantand ane nok,
>   Twa lusty lippis to lik ane laiddill.'

Some humorous tales have already been referred to
under Chapter III. ; others, such as *The Dumb Wyff*,[1]

Other
humorous
tales. 'In
Somer.'

and *The Nyne Ordour of Knavis*,[2] are
merely vulgar or commonplace; while
large portions of several are too frank
for quotation. Here, however, from *In Somer quhen*

[1] Maitland MS. Published in Laing's *Select Remains*, 1822 and
1885.
[2] Bannatyne MS. Published in Jamieson's *Popular Ballads*, 1806,
and Laing's *Select Remains*.

Flouris will smell,[1] is an interesting sketch of the dress of a rustic maid:—

> ' Scho had ane hatt vpoun hir heid
> Off claver cleir bayth quhyt and reid
> With catclukis strynklit in that steid
>   And synkill grene ;
> Wit ze, weill to weir that weid
>   Wald weill hir seme.
>
> Ane pair of beedis abowt hir thrott,
> Ane Agnus Day with nobill nott
> Jyngland weill with mony joitt,
>   War singand doun ;
> It was full ill to fynd ane moit
>   Vpoun hir goun.'

beautiful
trefoil; place
hemlock
know
beseem

Agnus Dei
shake

difficult;
mote

The ballad *Quhy sowld nocht Allane honorit be?*[1]— in a five-line stanza, aaa, bb, with refrain—a modification of the kyrielle (see *ante*, p. 157)—deserves mention, not merely as the earliest authenticated, but much the best, of the ballads on Allan-a-Maut, *alias* John Barleycorn. It is initialled 'Quod Allane Matsonis Suddartis,' and under the same signature is a curious invective against dishonest or incompetent ale-wives, *Quha hes Gud Malt and makes ill Drink.*[1] The author of both may well have been Dunbar. In the following stanzas of *Allane* we seem to hear the voice of the author of *Sanct Saluator* (p. 177):—

Drinking ballads.

> ' My Maister Allane I may sair curss :
> He levis no mony in my purss,
> At his command I mon deburss
>   Moir nor the twa pairt of my fe :
>   Quhy sowld nocht Allane honorit be ?

severely

must
salary
not

---

[1] Bannatyne MS.

And last of Allane to conclude ;
He is bening, courtuss, and gude,
And servis ws of our daly fude,
 And that with liberalitie :
 Quhy sowld nocht Allane honorit be ?'

Similar jovial sentiments are expressed in a clever
ballad, *I mak it kend he that will spend,* signed
'John Blyth,' which somewhat resembles *Back and
Side go Bare* in *Gammer Gurtin's Needle* ; but
'women' rather than 'wine' was the chief theme of
the old Scots balladists or lyrists.

Among the oldest of the love-ballads that have
been preserved is *The Murning Maiden,*[1] mentioned
in *The Complaynt of Scotland.* Written
in a nine-line stave—ab, ab, cc, bbc, the
last five lines forming a bobwheel,—and plainly, like
Henryson's *Robene and Makyn,* the work of an
accomplished 'makar,' it has much of the naïve
simplicity of the old minstrel ballad. A slight
allegorical suggestiveness may be suspected in the
lady's possession of bows and arrows, but the aureate
terms and the imagery of the conventional love
allegory are wholly absent. The sentiment also,
so far from being affected or overstrained, is really
primitive and pagan, though in no proper sense
indelicate : nonconventional not unbecoming. It
merely records how a forlorn damsel, forsaken by her
lover, and living in a forest in hunting dress with bow

'The Murning Maiden.'

---

[1] Maitland MS. Published in Pinkerton's *Ancient Scotish Poems,*
1786, and in various subsequent *Collections.*

and arrows, was persuaded by the owner of the forest
to accept his addresses :—

> ' Than knelit I befoir that cleir ;
> And meikle could hir mercie craif
> That semelie than, with sobir cheir,
> Me of hir gudlines forgaif :
> It wes no neid, I wys
> To bid us uther kys ;
> Thair mycht no hairts mair joy resaif
> Nor uther culd of uther haif :
> Thus brocht wer we to blys.'

maid
much
then ; mien

guess

The ballad *Quhen Tayis Bank* [1]—which may have
some connection with the old tune, *Twysbank,*
mentioned in *Colkelbie's Sow*—is more
artificial than *The Murning Maiden*   'Tayis Bank.'
alike in language, imagery, and sentiment. It is in
the rollicking metre of the old ballads, and the device
of alliteration is also employed to excess. There is
further a profusion of aureate terms and all the
conventional adjuncts of allegorical love poetry : the
precious stones, the flowers and foliage of the
brightest colours, and the lark, the merle, the
nightingale and mavis all in full song. Also the
fair damsel is beheld under a tree, and although
the poet might have accosted her had she stayed,
he was in no wise grieved, because

> ' Sone within a wane scho went
> Most hevinly to behold.'

dwelling

Sufficient for him to know that so fair a creature
lived on Tayside :—

---

[1] Bannatyne MS. Published in *The British Bibliographer*, vol. iv.,
and in Laing's *Select Remains*, 1822 and 1885.

'The reuer throw the ryce cowth rowt
And roseris raissis on raw ;
The schene birdis full schill cowth schowt
Into that semly schaw :
Joy wes within and joy without,
Vnder that vlonkest waw,
Quhair Tay ran down with stremis stout
Full strecht vndir Stobschaw.'

(margin: under-growth; tinkle arbours beautiful wood)

(margin: fairest bank)

(margin: straight)

There is every reason to suppose that the poem celebrates Margaret Drummond, daughter of John, first Lord Drummond, and the favourite mistress of James IV., who, with her two sisters, died suddenly of poison in 1501. The lady of the poem is described as the 'myld, meik, mansuete Mergrit,' and though 'Mergrit' means pearl, the poet may have intended a play on the lady's name; besides which, Stobschaw cannot well refer to aught else than the woods of Stobhall, the seat of the Drummonds.

(margin: The heroine of the poem.)

In the Bannatyne MS. are a number of other anonymous love-ballads, showing considerable expertness after the old artificial manner. *In May in a Morning* deserves mention, if only for its peculiar bobwheel, and the use of the device of iteration as exampled in *The Awntyrs of Arthur* (p. 36):—

(margin: 'In May in a Morning.')

'In May in a morning, I movit me one,
Throw a grene garding, with gravis begone,
As leid without lyking, but langour allone,
For misheiss and mourning, makand my mone,
Bot mo.
With hairt als heavy as a stone,
Of covir confoirt had I none,
As wy that wist of na wone,
Bot wandreth in wo.'

(margin: on overgrown with groves lead misery more)

(margin: heart)

(margin: one; no shelter)

The last line of the stanza is repeated in the first line
of the next, thus:—

> ' For wo and wandreth I waik, I weip and I wring.' keep awake

A few anonymous lyrics of great excellence also
survive. *Quhen Flora had ourfret the Firth*,[1]—in
the French ballade form, except that 'Quhen Flora
the Envoy is awanting, and the con- had ourfret
sonance throughout the three stanzas of the Firth.'
the first rhymes—if too deliberate and artificial, is,
at least, a highly polished production:—

> ' Strang ar the panis I daylie prufe,
>   Bot yit with pacience I sustene,
> I am so fetterit with the lufe
>   Onlie of my lady schene, bright
>   Quhilk for hir bewty mycht be quene, Who
> Natour sa craftely alwey
>   Hes done depaint that sweit serene :
> Quhome I luf I dar nocht assay.' prove

Yet in no wise can it compare with the old song,
O Lusty May, with Flora Quene,[2] every 'O Lusty May.'
line of which is vocal with the joy of
the merry month:—

> ' O Lusty May, with Flora quene,
>   The balmy dropis frome Phebus schene, bright
>   Preluciand bemes befoir the day,
>   Be that Diana growis grene By which
>   Throwch glaidness of this lusty May.'

---

[1] Bannatyne MS. Published in Ramsay's *Evergreen*, and in Mr.
W. E. Henley's *English Lyrics*.
[2] Bannatyne MS. Printed by Chepman and Myllar, 1508, and
modernised in Forbes's Aberdeen Cantus. Wrongly included by
David Laing in Alexander Scott's *Poems*.

Another excellent, though also artificial, lyric is
Welcum to May,[1] beginning :—

> ' Be glaid all ze that luvaris bene,
> For now hes May depaynt with grene
> The hillis, valis and the medis ;
> And flouris lustely vpspreidis.'

One or two other amorous pieces, as *Quhen I think
on my Lady Deir*,[2] *O Mistress Myn*,[2] *Baith Gud and
Fair and Womanlie*,[2] *O Mistress myld,
haif mind on Me*,[2] display some individuality in sentiment or method; and a *Song of
Absence*,[3] which Pinkerton attributes to James I., but
which is plainly of much later date, is an elaborate

Other amorous
pieces.

---

[1] Bannatyne MS. Published in Laing's *Select Remains*, 1822 and
1885.

[2] Bannatyne MS.

[3] Maitland MS. and Pinkerton's *Ancient Scotish Poems*, 1786.
The dove, from the time of the Romans, at least, has been regarded by poets as the representative of constancy. Nevertheless,
a similarity in the use of the simile in a stanza of this poem and in
Letter IV. of the *Casket Letters* is worth noting. Thus writes Mary
Stuart or another : ' Car J'enseray en pein et faites bon guet si
l'oseau sortira de sa cagé ou sens son per comme la tourtre
demeurera suelle a se lamenter de l'absence pour court quelle
soit. Ce que Je ne puis faire ma lettre de bon coeur si ce nestoit
que je ay peur que soyes endormy.' And here is the stanza :—

> ' Evin as men may the turtil trew persaif,
>   Once having lost hir feir,
> On the dry brainche, ay faithful to the graif,
>   Bewayling perseveir ;
>   So my desyre,
>   Kindlit in fyre,
>   Dois soir lament
>   My luif absent.
>   O God, gif amour be ane pane to beir ! '

mate

This stanza also resembles the last one in Montgomerie's *Adieu
to His Maistres*.

and skilful production; but the great bulk of the anonymous love lyrics are monotonously doleful.

Although most of the humorous love-songs have perished — except so far as some of them survive in the parodies of the *Gude and Godlie Ballates* — a few are preserved in the **Humorous love-songs.** Bannatyne or Maitland MSS., as *Thair is nocht ane Winche that I se,*[1] *Sang Againis the Ladeis,*[2] *Sang upon a Maist Melancolie Aventure,*[2] *God gif I wer Wedo now,*[2] and *My Hart is quhyt,*[1] which last is very much in the manner of Scott, and begins :—

'My hart is quhyt, and no delyte I haif of ladeis fair,   *blame;*
I wyte, I flyte, all in dispyte, that evir I leird that lair,   *learned that knowledge without*
Yit but respyte, I clene thé quyte, for now and evirmair,
Thairfoir I dyte this writt perfyte.—Fairweill, now feildis fair ;   *indite*
The suth is so, be God, my jo, I will fenye na mair ;   *truth*
Thocht vmquhile grit wes appetite, thair is wan tyme of wair.'   *formerly; spending*

Among the more seriously humorous is *Ane Welcum to Eild,*[2] which is graphic and picturesque. Here is the last stanza :—   **'Ane Welcum to Eild.'**

'My curland hair, my cristel ene,
    Ar beld and bleird, as all may se ;   *eyes*
My bak, that sumtyme brent has bene,   *bald; dim*
    Now cruikis lyk ane camok tre.   *straight*
    Be me your sampill ye may se ;
For so said wourthy Salomon   *By*
    Elding is end of erthlie glie :
Welcum eild, for youth is gone !'

---

[1] Bannatyne MS.
[2] Maitland MS. Published in Pinkerton's *Ancient Scotish Poems,* 1786.

In a similar vein is *Thus I propone in my Carping,*[1] in the stave of the common rondeau (see *ante*, p. 155):—

'Thus I propone.'

'Eis or diseis
Quhilk God sall send,
   Allyk sall pleis,
   Eiss or diseiss ;
   Aye till obeyiss
Till life mak end,
   Eis or diseis
Quilk God will send.'

Whichever

This chapter concludes our survey of what now re-mains of the poetry of the old Scots 'makaris' except that imperfectly preserved by tradition. Its development was irregular, chequered and complex. The old northern romance school left, at least metrical, traces on nearly all the subsequent poetry, modifying in a great variety of ways the Anglo - Norman staves. But it perished otherwise as an important literary influence with the rise of the sun of the new Scot-tish nationality. For a time patriotic poetry was in the ascendant; and though the original patriotic minstrelsy is now silent and forgotten, much of the patriotic afflatus is still preserved in Barbour's *Bruce* and Blind Harry's *Wallace*. Then, with probably the return of James I. to Scotland, came the great wave of Chaucerianism, which almost promised (or should it be threatened ?) to anticipate Flodden in

Rise and decline of Scots Vernacular Poetry.

[1] Bannatyne MS., and less complete in Maitland MS., from which it was published in Pinkerton's *Ancient Scotish Poems*.

revenging Bannockburn by subjecting the national intellect to the dominance of the great English 'makar.' But salutary and stimulating though Chaucerianism was, the traditional influences in many ways asserted their supremacy—asserted it by absorbing and assimilating Chaucerianism. Then towards the close of the fifteenth century there arose in Scotland a poetic school which not only eclipsed the degenerate Chaucerian school of England, but which, distinguished in itself, was more than remarkable as the product of a country so rude and insignificant, and is only to be explained as the result of the engrafting of Chaucerian and French influences on a vigorous native stem. Of this old original poetry—which has all but perished—echoes are to be found in Henryson and the older humorous tales, and it specially triumphs in *Christis Kirk* and *Peblis.* It is only so far as it again became dominant —dominant in a higher, stronger, and more artistic form—that Scotland again attained to an individual national literature. It is specially dominant in Dunbar, admiring disciple of Chaucer though he was; in Douglas, it only manifests its influence brokenly in the *Prologues*; it inspires all that is worth reading in Sir David Lyndsay; it reasserts itself decidedly in Scott, and even in Montgomerie, notwithstanding that its life-blood was then being sucked by Puritanic Calvinism—which had already superseded its popular lyrics by *The Gude and Godlie Ballates,*—and that it was presently to be reduced to such a state of inanition that its existence became suspended on the fiat of James VI., with whose succession to the English throne it passed out of existence and for a time out of memory.

X

VERNACULAR PROSE

THE Scottish literature in vernacular prose is of a character so fragmental, intermittent, and merely casual, that it is impossible to trace in it any law of development. The close connection of Scottish scholars with the Continent from the time of the astrologer Michael Scott—their almost constant practice to complete their studies abroad, where many of them remained as lecturers or professors—led both to a more general and prolonged use of Latin prose literature by Scots than by English writers. Vernacular prose received a certain impulse in Scotland from the movement that produced the Reformation, but the impulse was partial and fitful, and became even reactive. Though the mere introduction of printing tended to the substitution of prose for verse, old habit for some time preserved the supremacy of

General and prolonged use of Latin in Scotland for prose literature.

verse for popular purposes; and as for the more
learned or intellectual Scot, he continued long after
the Reformation to eschew the vernacular and practise
mainly Latin.

In his *Exclamatioun to the Redar, twycheyng the
Wrytting of Vulgare and Maternall Language*,
prefixed to *The Dialog*, Sir David Lyndsay
deemed it advisable to explain why he
ventured to write on 'so heych mater' in
'vulgair toung':—

Sir David
Lyndsay's
preference for
the vernacular.

> 'Quhowbeit that divers devote cunnyng clerkis
>   In Latyne toung hes wryttin syndrie bukis,
> Our unlernit knawis lytill of thare werkis,
>   More than thay do the ravyng of the rukis.
>   Quharefore to colyearis, cairtaris, and to cukis,
> To Jok and Thome, my rhyme shall be directit,
> With cunnyng men quhowbeit it wylbe lackit.'

It was not that he deprecated the study of Latin,
Greek, and 'Auld Hebrew.' So far from doing so, he
greatly 'rewed' his own ignorance of the ancient
languages. But he was specially desirous of the spread
of intelligence among the people, and he further recognised that a truly national literature was impossible
in a foreign tongue. None of the great writers of the
olden time, he pertinently points out, used any other
than their native language. Still, he had no wish
to interfere with the preferences and tastes of the
learned—those preferences and tastes which concerned only themselves,—and he puts his case thus:—

> 'Lat Doctores wrytt thare curious questionis
>   And argumentis sawin full of sophistrye,

Thare Logick, and thare heych opinionis.
  Thare dirk jugementis of Astronomye,
  Thare Medecyne and thare Philosophye :
Latt Poetis schaw thare glorious ingyne,
  As ever thay pleis, in Greik or in Latyne ;
Bot lat us haif the Bukis necessare
  To Common weill and our Salvatioun
Justlye translatit in our toung Vulgare.'

high
dark

genius

But Lyndsay himself wrote only in verse, and verse as of old remained for a considerable time the main literature of the people. The dissemination of the Scriptures in prose, and the spread of education by means of the parish schools, tended to beget a love of prose literature among the people; but (1) that literature was mainly theological, and (2) it became more and more assimilated to English. Nor if the learned Scot had particularly desired to have recourse to the vernacular could he have found in Scotland a fit or sufficient audience. George Buchanan, though an adherent of the Protestant and popular party, disdained, as scholar, historian, or man of culture, to cast his pearls before the mere vernacular Scot. Even his controversial and political writings were mostly addressed rather to Europe than to Scotland; for Scottish politics when he wrote had, through the meteoric career of Mary Stuart, become of European consequence. For a similar reason, his great controversial opponent Bishop Leslie had recourse mainly to Latin; and though he composed a history of Scotland in the Scots vernacular for Mary Stuart's perusal, wrote

Preferences of the learned Scot for Latin. The vernacular also gradually superseded by English.

little else in Scots, and in some cases got his tractates
Englished for circulation south of the Tweed. The
renewed intercourse between Scotland and England
after the Reformation tended also more and more to
enforce the desirability of a common language, which
common language was bound to be English. John
Knox, for example, wrote for England as much as for
Scotland. Though as good a Latinist as the older
Scottish historians, he did not, like Buchanan, cultivate Latin for its own sake, and was probably
conscious that its use would check rather than
promote the flow of his eloquence and invective, and
dull rather than brighten the scintillations of his wit.
Above all, he was, like Lyndsay, specially devoted
to the interests of 'Jok and Thome.' Even his
History of the Reformation was therefore written in
the vernacular, but the vernacular he chose was a
sort of compromise between Scots and English.

For the reasons now summarised, the bulk of
Scottish vernacular prose can scarce be termed
literature. Much of it is merely con-
Bellenden's troversial or merely theological; and a
translation
of Boece. still larger portion consists of *Diaries* or
Memoirs, not even written for publication, but jotted
down for the writer's own private edification or
pleasure. The earliest vernacular prose work of any
importance is John Bellenden's (see *ante,* p. 232) translation of Hector Boece's Latin *History of Scotland.*[1]

---

[1] Editions were published at Edinburgh, printed by 'Thomas
Dauidson, printer to the Kyngis noble grace' in 1536, 1541, and in

It was done at the request of James v. for the more immediate delectation of the nobles, and presented to the king in 1533. Boece's lively and interesting, if somewhat imaginative, narrative was modelled, as was his Latin style, on Livy, which probably was the reason why Bellenden was commanded by the king to follow his translation of Boece with a translation of the Roman historian.[1] Bellenden's version of Boece is accurate, but rather free. The language is less artificial than that of *The Complaynt of Scotland*, and the style, of remarkable excellence for the period, is clear, flowing, and vigorous.

But Scottish vernacular prose literature may be said to begin with that curious political manifesto, ' *The Complaynt of Scotlande* [2] vyth ane Exortatione to the Thre Estaits to be vigilante in the Deffens of their Public veil.' Its authorship, so far as we can now judge, is mainly a matter of speculation.

' The Complaynt of Scotland.' Its author. Claims of Sir James Inglis.

Dr. George Mackenzie, in his *Lives of Scottish Writers*, attributed it to Sir James Inglis (see *ante,* p. 233), Abbot of Culross, but it is impossible to tell whether he had any reason for doing so other than vague rumour or his own opinion. Anyhow the Abbot, who Mackenzie

another unknown year. It was also reprinted at Edinburgh in 1821, edited by Thomas Maitland, Lord Dundrennan.

[1] First published in 1822 at Edinburgh, edited by Thomas Maitland, Lord Dundrennan.

[2] Four of the original copies of *The Complaynt* are known to exist, but all want the title-page. Two are in the Library of the British Museum, and one in the Advocates' Library, Edinburgh. It was elaborately edited by Dr. Leyden in 1821, and for the English Text Society by Dr. J. A. H. Murray, 1872.

states died in 1554, was assassinated as early as 1st March 1531, whereas *The Complaynt* was at least not completed till 1549. It so happens, however, that another Sir James Inglis was chaplain to the Abbot of Cambuskenneth from 1508 until 1550, and Mackenzie may have merely confounded the two; but while the Culross Inglis was of literary repute, nothing is known of the other except that he was officially in the habit of singing masses for the souls of James III. and Queen Margaret, who were buried at Cambuskenneth.

In the Harleian Catalogue in the British Museum the work is ascribed to Wedderburn, but this again may have been merely the opinion of James Anderson, author of *Diplomatica et Numismata Scotiæ*, who sold his library to Harley, Earl of Oxford. The Wedderburn to whom David Laing was disposed to ascribe it was Robert, vicar of Dundee; but he did so on the supposition that the work was printed at St. Andrews, whereas it was undoubtedly, as Dr. J. A. H. Murray has shown, printed at Paris. For the Wedderburn authorship much stress has been laid on the author's comprehensive knowledge of old ballads and songs; but while the Wedderburns parodied the old songs for godly purposes, the author of *The Complaynt* displays a wholly unregenerate interest in them as well as in music and dancing.

Claims of Robert Wedderburn.

For Sir David Lyndsay's claims a strong superficial case was made out by Leyden from similarities of method, style, and subject-matter. There is no distinct evidence as to Lyndsay's attitude towards the English invasion, and if in this crisis he indicated strong sympathy with the Queen-Regent in her efforts on be- half of the country's independence, this would go far to explain his freedom from persecution for his pungent attacks on the abuses of the Church. But the work is far too indirect and desultory to have been written by Lyndsay, and not quite incisive enough in its exposure of ecclesiastical abuses.

Claims of Sir David Lyndsay.

Dr. J. A. H. Murray argued from the dialect that the writer must have been a native of southern Scotland, which would, of course, dispose of the claims of both Wedderburn and Lyndsay. On the whole, the most pro- bable supposition is that the author was some one more strongly attached to the French interest than either Lyndsay or the Wedderburns; and this theory finds additional support from the fact—unknown to Laing or to Dr. J. A. H. Murray— that the later and allegorical portion of the work was merely an adaptation to the Scottish crisis of Alain Chartier's *Le Quadrilogue Invectif* of more than a century earlier date.

Partly founded on 'Le Quadrilogue Invectif' of Alain Chartier.

The work was probably begun while Scotland, before the arrival of French help in July 1548, was very much at the mercy of Protector Somerset, and when many of the nation—from their Protestant leanings, from

The aim of the work. Introductory chapters.

interested motives, or from sheer despair—were
disposed substantially to agree to the English matrimonial alliance on very much the old conditions
proposed by Henry VIII.; and it is mainly against
this policy of surrender that the writer takes up his
pen. The work opens with a high-flown 'Epistle to
the Qvenis Grace' (the Queen-Regent), in which the
patriotic deeds of her illustrious ancestors are celebrated, and she is declared to have inherited more
than their virtues, and in her noble defence of the
country against the 'cruel woffis of ingland,' to have
even surpassed the achievements of all the ancient
heroines commemorated by Plutarch or Boccaccio.
This is followed by a 'Prolog to the Reader' consisting of a philosophical disquisition on work and
idleness, illustrated by various classical anecdotes—
all this to show that, in taking up his pen in behalf
of his country, the author was not acting the part of
a mere idler, but using his own special talent with
exemplary diligence. Succeeding these preliminaries,
we have still a few more introductory chapters dealing
with the misfortunes of Scotland in their relation to
the judgments of God, and winding up with the
exposition and adoption of the views of John Caron
as to the near approach of the end of the world.

Having by these 'solist and attentive labouris'
caused his body to become 'imbecille
and verye' (weary) and his spirit to be
'sopit' (steeped) 'in sadness,' the author,
before proceeding further with his task, deemed

The Monolog
Recreative. A
night in the
country.

it advisable to recruit him in the country, and was thus led to pen a 'Monolog Recreative,' which to us is the most interesting feature of his strange medley. So great was his delight in rural life and scenes, after his close immersion in study, that on the first day of his arrival he remained out of doors, walking in the woods until the dawn. At this point he of course introduces the conventional classical imagery, and for the description of the approach of day and of the different birds and animals with their cries, he has recourse also to alliteration and consonance, essaying a sort of poetic prose, of which this short specimen may serve as a sufficient illustration :—

'The grene feildis, for grite drought, drank vp the drops of the fresche dew, quilk[1] of before hed maid dikis[2] & dailis verray donc.[3] There eftir i herd the rumour of rammasche[4] foulis and of beystis that maid grite beir,[5] quhilk past besyde burnis[6] and boggis[7] on grene bankis to seik ther sustentatione. Their brutal sound did redound to the hie skyis, quhil[8] the depe hou[9] cauernis of cleuchis[10] and rotche[11] craggis ansuerit vith ane hie not, of that samyn sound as the beystis had blauen.'

Thereafter he hies him to the sea-shore, where he beholds a galasse accoutred for war and preparing for action. Then follows a minute relation of the handling of a ship, and of the various rhymes and cries of the sailors, and a realistic picture of the two ships in action is also attempted. But so little is he interested in the

A sea-fight. The shepherds' entertainment.

---

[1] which. [3] damp. [5] noise. [7] mosses. [9] hollow. [11] rocky.
[2] ditches. [4] in flocks. [6] streams. [8] until. [10] dells.

fight that he stays not to witness the result; and
returns to the green fields just as the shepherds,
having taken out their flocks for pasturage, are
sitting down to breakfast. After a meal of all kinds of
milk and curds, whey, butter, cream, and cheese, with
rye cakes and scones, there follows recreation. The
entertainment opens with an oration of the principal
shepherd on the 'hie stait and dignitie' of the
pastoral life, with of course citation of all the more
illustrious men of antiquity who had elected to follow
the calling, which is further extolled for its beneficial
effects, morally and physically, and the opportunity
it affords for the study of natural science; the
oration concluding with an exhaustive disquisition
on astronomy and physical geography. This most
erudite address his spouse, concerned mainly for the
amusement of the younger portion of the company,
pronounces to be a 'tideous, melancolie oration,' and
proposes that they should now recreate themselves
with 'joyous comonyng.' The list of the old traditional
tales they then told, of the songs and glees they
sung, and the tunes to which they danced, though
declared by the author to be only a selection, would
imply that the entertainment not only lasted, as he
states, until evening, but was prolonged for a month
or more. But it may be that he here only followed
a conventional custom of the old writers, of which
we have an example in *Colkelbie's Sow*; and for the
list we owe him at least more thanks than blame, for
it is invaluable as a record of old literature and

music, regarding which there is in many cases no earlier evidence.

After the rejoicements were over, the author entered a meadow full of all sorts of flowers, grasses, and herbs, of which he gives a list, with a curious account of their special medicinal virtues. Contented, as he well might be, with his period of recreation, he proposed to set off for town that he might proceed with his book, but was immediately overtaken, as he also well might be, by 'Morpheus, that slepy gode'; and reclining on the 'cald eard' with 'ane cod (pillow) of ane gray stane,' he was in the accustomed manner favoured with a vision, which virtually supplied him with all that was required to complete his volume.

The Vision.

As matter of fact, however, the source from which he got the design and much of the method and thought of this latter portion of the book, *The Complaynt* proper, was *Le Quadrilogue Invectif* of Alain Chartier.[1] For Dame France, the Scottish writer substitutes Dame Scotia, and for her 'enfants'—Le Peuple, Le Chevalier, and Clergie—we are presented with Scotia's three sons—Labour, the Nobles, and Spiritualitie. Many passages are merely taken from the French work, but the clergy play a less prominent and dominant part in the conference, and Dame

Dame Scotia and her three sons. Comparison with 'Le Quadrilogue Invectif.'

---

[1] See *Les Oevvres de Maister Alain Chartier*, ed. Tovrangeav, Paris, 1617, pp. 402-455; and for an extended summary, *Alain Chartier*, par Gabriel Joret-Desclosières, Paris, 1897, pp. 30-55.

Scotia indulges in rather more plain-speaking. It is occupied with (1) Dame Scotia's 'Exhortatione to the thrie Estaitis,' mainly in denunciation of England; (2) the 'Complaynt of Labour,' or the Commons, against the nobles and the clergy—his French brother does not venture a word against the Church—who he declares are more cruel to him than even the English, and by their lack of courage and patriotism leave him no choice but meanwhile to feign allegiance with England; (3) Dame Scotia's reply to this, her younger son, in which the faults of the people—their gullibility, fickleness, intemperance, lust, unruliness—are dilated on in very plain terms, and after a citation of *The Thrie Priestis of Peblis* to show that their elevation only develops their faults, she denies the possibility of any one being truly virtuous who has never had 'educatione, eruditione, nor civilitie'; (4) the address of Dame Scotia to the 'nobles and gentlemen,' which discusses the question of the origin and uses of an aristocracy in a fashion that displays the ecclesiastical jealousy of the period against that order, and concludes with a denunciation of their extravagance, in which it is asserted that the horses and dogs of the nobles are virtually as much engaged in eating the 'pure pepill,' as if they were devouring their bodies; (5) Dame Scotia's address to the Spiritualitie, who are rather more mildly dealt with, and while told that schism will be healed only by reform, not by persecution, are reminded that they have nothing to hope for from England, and such of them as are able-bodied are therefore exhorted to exchange their cowls and frocks for 'steil jakkis' and 'coites of mailze,' and take the field against the inveterate enemies of their country; and (6) the exhortation of Dame Scotia to her three sons to cease their intestine strife and combine against the common enemy.

The Chronicle of Scotland,[1] by Robert Lyndsay of Pitscottie, is avowedly a continuation of Boece's Latin history, which John Bellenden translated. The author was related to the noble family of Lyndsay, but nothing certain is known of his parentage and practically nothing of his life. The only editions of Lyndsay's portion of the *Chronicle* yet published do not reach later than 1565, but it was continued by another than Lyndsay until August 1604. Lyndsay's own portion must also have been modernised and partly assimilated to English, either by the continuator, or by later copyists, for we cannot believe that as we now have it, it represents the vernacular of Lyndsay's time.

Lyndsay's
'Chronicle.'
Its scope.

Lyndsay's work is properly neither chronicle nor history. His chronology is vague and frequently erroneous. Many important events are either passed over or treated with the utmost conciseness, and his grasp of his subject is slight and superficial; but he excels as a

A master of
picturesque
detail.

---

[1] Published 1728, 1749, 1778, and 1814, the last edition in two volumes edited by John Graham Dalyell; and a properly edited text is promised by the Scottish Text Society.

story-teller, and may perhaps be best described as
a sort of prose minstrel. A master of picturesque
detail, he has a keen eye for the exceptional, the
striking, the marvellous, and for all kinds of interesting minutiæ. He notes, for example, that James II.,
'more curious than became a king,' stood too close to
his artillery at Roxburgh Castle, and not merely tells
you that he was mortally injured, but that by 'ane
piece of ane misframed gune, his thigh bone was dung
in two'; he is careful to inform you of Cochrane's
attempt to foster James III.'s suspicions against his
brother by aid of the pretended revelations of a witch;
the state kept by Cochrane, his gorgeous apparel and
proud bearing, his rude knocking at the kirk door
(accompanied by armed attendants in white livery)
where the nobles were assembled, his sudden seizure,
his contumelious treatment and unceremonious execution by suspension over the bridge at Lauder, are
detailed with graphic particularity; the account
of Albany's escape from Edinburgh Castle — the
intoxicating of the captain, the sudden attack on
him and the guard, the escape over the wall of the
Duke and his 'chamber-child' by a 'tow' which was
too short for the servant, who fell and broke his thigh
bone, and had to be lengthened for the Duke by
tearing the 'scheittis aff his bed'—is a masterpiece
of minutely vivid narrative; and the hard case of
Johnie Armstrang before James V. is a finely dramatic
episode, of which the climax is the reiver's speech: 'I
am bot ane foole to seik grace at ane graceless face,

but had I known,' etc.; the curious hunting palace
built by the Earl of Atholl for the entertainment of
James V. is described with a mastery of detail which
suggests the modern journalist, who also might well
have compiled the record of the items of the banquet,
and the results of the day's sport; and in the account
of Pinkie Cleugh we have the especially characteristic
information that the dust generated by the character
of the soil, mostly 'red earth,' so 'great that nevir ane
of them might see ane other,' completed the panic
among the Highlanders which was aroused by the
novel sound of the artillery. These are not exceptional instances, but merely average specimens of
his usual method. Curiously enough, his *Chronicle*
becomes less detailed and interesting when it deals
with the later occurrences of his own time, from
which we may infer that, though a Protestant, and
writing on behalf of Protestantism, the events of the
past were of more interest to him than the politics
of the present.

Quite after the modern manner, Lyndsay gives a
list of those to whom he was indebted for information.
They are Patrick, Lord Lindsay of the His authori-
Byres—the brother-in-law of Moray, who ties.
acquired an unenviable reputation for his stern treatment of Mary Stuart in Lochleven; Sir William Scott
of Balwearie; Sir Andrew Wood of Largo, Knight,
grandson of Admiral Wood; John Major, whose
History of Greater Britain was published in 1521,
but who survived till 1550, and, being resident at

St. Andrews, must have frequently been in Lyndsay's company; Sir David Lyndsay of the Mount, his relative and near neighbour; Andrew Wood of Largo, son of Admiral Wood, and 'principall and familiar servant' to King James v.; Andrew Fernie of that ilk, 'ane noble man of recent memory'; and Sir William Bruce of Earlshall, Knight, who was one of his Fife neighbours, and who, he says, 'hath written very justly all the deeds since Floudon Field.'

This list is valuable as showing that for many of his quaint and picturesque details he must have had authentic information; and the inference usually drawn from his inaccuracy as to dates and his loose treatment of some important events, that he is untrustworthy in his more interesting portions, seems to require qualification. We cannot doubt, for example, that the presentation by David Lord Lindsay to James III. of the 'gray courser' on which he made his escape from Sauchie would be vouched for by Lord Lindsay's descendants, and the details of the king's death—the shying of the horse at the woman's water-can, and the heavy fall of the king when the horse leapt the burn, etc.—bear on the face of them the stamp of truth. Nor can we go far wrong in assuming that for the particulars of the capture of Stephen Bull's ship by Admiral Wood in the Firth of Forth he was indebted either to the admiral's son or grandson. Similarly, for his capital version of the Linlithgow ghost story he had the voucher of Sir

For many of his details he had authentic information.

David Lyndsay, and for his account of the death of
James v. at Falkland—his melancholy reception of
the tidings of the birth of his daughter, 'It came with
ane lass, and it will go with ane lass,' with the story
of the manner of the subscription of the will at the
instance of Cardinal Beaton—he must have been
indebted to Andrew Wood, 'the familiar servant' to
the king, and one of the few gentlemen present at his
deathbed. Again, he had clearly special facilities for
obtaining information in regard to all the events
which happened at St. Andrews; and the nameless
outrage of 'ane callit Guthrie' on the dead cardinal
must have been a notorious fact. These instances may
even suggest that the anecdotical and picturesque
portions of Lyndsay's *Chronicle* may be on the whole
the most correct; and if they be, his blunders in
mere dates may well be forgiven him. In gauging
his general trustworthiness it must also be borne in
mind that, Protestant though he was, his partisanship
was not so bitter as that of either Buchanan or
Knox.

The bulk of Buchanan's works, including his
History in Latin, do not come within the scope of
our consideration; and of his *History*   George
it may suffice to state that its Latin   Buchanan
style secured for it a reputation beyond   (1506-1582).
                                            His career.
its historical deserts. Since also his writings in the
vernacular were limited to two political tracts, his
career calls here for but the briefest notice. Born in
February 1506, the son of a small laird in the parish

of Killearn, Stirlingshire, he was educated at the Universities of Paris and St. Andrews, and became the most brilliant Latinist of his time. After holding (1529-61) various scholastic appointments in France, Portugal, and Italy, he returned to Scotland, when he became linguistic tutor to Mary Stuart, and was also employed as translator to the Queen and Council; and in 1566 he obtained the principalship of St. Leonard's College, St. Andrews. The following year he accompanied Moray to the York conference regarding Mary Stuart, where he was employed in putting into writing the charges against her which were afterwards embodied in the Latin *Detectio* published in 1572. In 1570 he was named tutor to the young prince James VI., an appointment he held until his death in Edinburgh, 24th September 1582.

The only tractates in Scots known to be Buchanan's are '*Ane Admonitioun direct to the True Lordis main-tenaris of Justice, and obedience to the Kingis Grace*. Imprentit at Striviling be Robert Lekprevik, 1571'; and the *Chamœleon*, completed probably early in 1571, but not published in Buchanan's lifetime, owing to interference with Lekprevik's printing-office while it was passing through the press. Besides this, two of his letters[1] in the vernacular, and his *Opinion anent the Reformatioun of the Universitie of St. Andrews*,[1] also

His works in the Vernacular.

---

[1] These with the two tractates are included in *The Vernacular Writings of George Buchanan*, edited for the Scottish Text Society by P. Hume Brown, 1892.

survive; but internal evidence shows that the Scots version of the *Detectio*, 1572, sometimes attributed to him, was done by another.

The *Admonitioun* is in substance both a general and specific denunciation of the Hamiltons. Being by descent a feudal dependant of Lennox, The 'Admoni-
tioun.' Buchanan shared in the hereditary enmity between that house and the rival claimants to the next heirship of the Scottish throne. By Mary Stuart's marriage to Darnley, the heirship to the throne had been assured to the Stewarts of Lennox; and it was the queen's alliance with Bothwell against Darnley that aroused against her Buchanan's quenchless antipathy. With the murder of Darnley the Hamiltons were closely associated; they also instigated the plot for the murder of the Regent Moray—the assassin, a Hamilton, being probably the mere tool of the forfeited John, Marquis of Hamilton; and Buchanan was convinced that they would not rest until they had removed the young king, now the only obstacle to the realisation of their highest ambition: 'not content wt ane king's blude, they gaip for his sonnis murthour.' Buchanan has been dubbed 'the pen of Moray,' but there is no evidence that he turned against the queen from motives of self-interest. If he adopted wrong or extreme opinions, they seem to have been the opinions of an honest feudal partisan. The too merely denunciatory tone of the *Admonitioun* detracts, however, from its literary merit, though much of it is cogent, and much of what is not cogent is undoubtedly forcible and clever. Here, for example, is an amusing hit both at the Hamiltons and his old pupil :—

'Thay wer in hoip yat scho sould mary Johnne Hamiltoun ye Dukis sone quhome wt mery lukis and gentill contenance (as scho could weill do) scho enterit in ye gayme of ye glaiks,[1] and causit ye rest of ye Hamiltonis to fon for faynnes.'[2]

The Chamæleon, a satire on the Secretary, William Maitland of Lethington, may be regarded as expres-

'The Chamæleon.'

sive equally of Buchanan's own private antipathies and of the dead Regent Moray's inner sentiments towards his old political associate. No one knew better than Buchanan how the policy of Moray had been baffled by the intrigues of Maitland during the York and Westminster conferences, or the depth of Moray's chagrin at the insubordination of his former lieutenant. It is a more elaborate and effective production than the *Admonitioun*; but it is effective mainly because Maitland's conduct was quite beyond the comprehension of a mere partisan like Buchanan, as it was beyond the comprehension of an age in which mere partisanship was so rampant. Buchanan's satire, merciless though it be, is in no sense feigned. A sincere indignation and hatred, blended with a sort of contemptuous amazement, animates his pen as he proceeds to 'set furth schortlie ye descriptioun of

---

[1] Coquetry.   [2] Play the fool for eagerness.

JOHN KNOX 321

sic ane[1] monsture not lang ago engendrit in Scotland
in ye cuntre of Lowthiane not far from Hadingtoun,
to yat effect yat ye forme knawin, the moist pestiferus
nature of ye said monsture may be moir easelie
evitit.'[2]

As to Buchanan's vernacular style, it is something
too artificial and rhetorical, both the structure of the
sentences and the general manner being
affected by his constant addiction to
His style.
Latin, but withal it is clear and precise, and frequently full of force and fire. Here is an example
in the effective conclusion of *The Chamæleon* :—

'Now I pray zow espy out quhat proffeit ye quene, our
kingis moder, sall gadder of him yat hes bene (as scho knawis) sa
oftentymes traitour to hir moder, to hir selfe, to hir sone, to hir
brother, and to hir cuntre. Scho will be exemplis[3] considder yat
how mony colouris yat euir yis Chamæleon change, yat it can neuir
aganis ye nature of it, turne perfytelie quhyte.'

As partisan Knox has much in common with
Buchanan, both in the virulence of his partisanship
and its special direction, but it was of
different origin and of much wider scope.
Not feudal, nor even political, but
John Knox
(1505-1572).
Sketch of his
life.
wholly religious and rooted in his deepest convictions, it coloured his whole life and became interwoven with the future history of his country. Born
in 1505, in Haddington or its near neighbourhood, of
peasant parents who were feudal dependants of the
Earl of Bothwell, he was educated at Haddington

---

[1] such a.   [2] evaded.   [3] by examples.

Grammar School and Glasgow (and probably St. Andrews) University, but owing, it may be, to poverty did not, as was then very customary, continue his studies abroad. About his earlier life, after he left the University, we have little information. Though at some unknown date he took priest's orders, he never held a cure, and supported himself partly as notary, partly as tutor. While acting as tutor to the sons of Douglas of Longniddry, and Cockburn of Ormistone, he came in contact with the Protestant evangelist George Wishart, whom he accompanied in his preaching tour in Lothian, characteristically acting as his guard with the two-handed sword which it was customary to carry beside him. His public life from the time that in 1547 he made 'his first publict sermon' to the assassinators of Cardinal Beaton and their friends in the parish church of St. Andrews, until, worn out with the labours which established the Reformed Kirk in Scotland, he, with the words 'Now it is come,' quietly breathed his last in his own house in the Netherbow, Edinburgh, 24th November 1572, was, whether at home or in exile, one continuous conflict against a religious system which in his view was not so much erroneous and corrupt, as antichristian and devilish.

His *History of the Reformation* [1] is the record of

---

[1] The only complete edition of the *Works* of Knox is that of the Wodrow Society, edited by David Laing, six vols. 1846-64. The *History* occupies vols. i. and ii. A shortened edition of the *History*, edited by C. J. Guthrie, appeared in 1898.

that conflict, a record so sincere, thorough, and complete, that it is one of the most interesting human documents in literature. Knox was not an accomplished scholar like Buchanan, nor a 'fell' theologian like Calvin, nor, if a more eloquent and a cleverer, a more satisfactory religious controversialist than the Tyries, the Winzets, the Kennedys of that age, none of whose tractates are now of any interest except to the philologist or the religious antiquary. He had much of the intellectual narrowness and rough simplicity of the peasant; he shared in some, though not in all, of the superstitions of the mediæval ecclesiastic, and if he had escaped from the mere formal professionalism of the clerics of his time, he substituted for this an intense conviction of his own personal infallibility as a divinely illuminated prophet of the Most High. Like all the Reformers, he was steeped in the supernaturalism of the Scriptures, particularly of the Old Testament, and, endowed with strong emotional susceptibility, great moral sincerity, an overmastering will, and a lofty ideality (in no degree impaired by his practical common-sense), he bent his energies towards the establishment in Scotland of a sort of Christianised Jewish theocracy. The Church, as reorganised by him, was, as of old, only more so, to be palpably and directly the supreme power in the state and in society. His ideal, no doubt, differed somewhat from the reality which was so soon to become an intolerable tyranny; but even his ideal was but a one-sided solution of the great problem of human life and conduct, for, man of genius though he was, he was by intellectual training the mere product of mediævalism. He was successful mainly as iconoclast; his courage, enthusiasm, eloquence, wit, satire, and dynamic energy were irresistible, not so much in reforming abuses and removing corruptions as in annihilating root and branch the imposing ceremonial and the potent organisation of the Scottish Catholic Church. From many directions, and from a variety of causes, a tempest of wrath had been gathering against its ambition, greed, tyranny, and corruption, but it was Knox who rode 'on the whirlwind directing the storm,' and it was because of his conduct of it that the storm proved so destructive.

In *The History of the Reformation* Knox details the events of this stirring period mainly in their relation to his own personality, and to the work to which he had devoted his life. His laudation or condemnation of his contemporaries is determined very much by their attitude towards his own aims. He hardly even pretends to impartiality, but says as much evil and as little good of his opponents as he possibly can, while he overlooks many patent faults, and even wickednesses, in those who, from whatever motive, have the saving grace to co-operate with him in his great crusade. This, of course, means that he was a bitter partisan; but, in excuse, it must be remembered that in that age the lines of antagonism were

His 'History of the Reformation.' His partisanship.

much more sharply drawn than in this age of compromise. Knox was absolutely convinced that his
cause was wholly the cause of God, and that his
opponents were merely the allies of the Devil. His
instinct for character was also so remarkably keen,
and his intentions so sincere, that, if due allowance
be made for his standpoint, it is comparatively easy
for one, otherwise acquainted with the persons and
events of the period, to read between the lines of
his approval or disapproval. But, agree or dis-
agree with him as we may, he rarely fails to
interest. The narrative part of the book is alive
from beginning to end. The stir and movement
and excitement of the times, as mirrored in his
own strong personality, are transferred to his pages ;
and his literary art, if less elaborately rhetorical
than that of Buchanan, is more direct, graphic, and
irresistible.

The work includes an account of the early Scottish
Reformers—their labours, persecutions, and martyr-
doms, from the death of Paul Craw in
1431,—and a narrative of the events of
his own time down to September 1564,
the remainder of the *History*, down to
1567, being in all likelihood partly derived from his
papers. The narrative, abounding in ' merrie bourds '
and graphic anecdotes, is coloured by a strain of
bitter and contemptuous vituperation against the
opponents of the Reformation. Much of the vituperation is mere gross, though picturesque and

Scope of the work. Its strong and weak points, and its literary excellence.

effective, abuse;[1] but it is redolent of a hatred
that, at least, proved contagious. His effectiveness
both as reformer and historian is, in truth, largely
due to his personalities. In discussing the abstractions and subtleties of theology he is a mere school-
man: he displays his genius only when he deals with
events and facts and concrete human nature. Like
the much less ardent Lyndsay of Pitscottie, he has a
keen eye for graphic details, and he is often vividly
dramatic. The incidents, conversations, anecdotes,
and personal allusions of which his *History* is brim-
ful, lend to it a never-failing animation, and in some
of his stories and narratives the wit, the humour,
or the satire is elaborated with much careful art,
among his masterpieces being—in addition, of course,
to the immortal interviews with Queen Mary—the
Cardinal's assassination, the struggle for precedency
between the followers of the two rival archbishops at
the door of Glasgow Cathedral, and the destruction of
the image of St. Gile by the Edinburgh mob.

When the mob seized and threw down the image
of St. Gile, 'the Preastis and Freiris,' he tells us,
'fled faster than thei did at Pynckey Clewcht';[2]
the ridiculous figure cut by the retreating fathers

---

[1] The monastery of the Grey Friars is, for example, described as
the 'den of those murtharis the Grey Friaris'; and the same Grey
Friars, we are told, 'routed as thai had been ravens, yea rather
they yelled and rored, as devills in hell, "Heresy, heresy,"' etc.

[2] The battle of Pinkie, 10th September 1547, at which a regiment
of priests and monks fought—or rather fled—for Scotland and the
Church, under a sacred white banner.

is also exactly realised to us—'the Gray Freiris gapped, the Blak Frearis blew, the Preastis panted and fled'; and the finishing touch to the picture of this comical street scene is given by the introduction of 'a meary Englissman,' who 'by chance lay upoun a stare,' and 'seing the discomfiture to be without blood, thought he wold add some mearynes to the mater, and so cryed he ower a stayr, and said, "Fy upoun yow, hoorsones, why have ye brockin ordour! Doun the streat ye passed in array and with great myrth. Why flie ye, vilanes, now, without ordour? Turne and stryk everie one a strok for the honour of his god. Fy, cowardes, fy, ye shall never be judged worthy of your wages agane."' As a *raconteur* Knox must have been unsurpassed among his contemporaries; and various allusions also show that his literary art owed something to his acquainceship with the works of the old 'makaris.'

The destruction of the image of St. Gile.

Of the numerous tractates of Knox—in the various forms of Admonitions, Answers, Apologies, Blasts, Declarations, Epistles, Exhortations, Expositions, Letters, Narratives, Sermons, Summaries, and Vindications—the most noted, and the only one that need here be referred to, is *The First Blast of the Trumpet against the Monstrvovs Regiment* [Sovereignty] *of Women*, published anonymously in 1558, and (being intended for England) written virtually in English, or, perhaps, rather Englished by Knox's colleague at Geneva,

Tractates, etc., of Knox. 'The First Blast.'

Goodman, who also himself blew a similar blast in *How Supreme Powers ovght to be obey'd by their Subjects*, Geneva, 1558. In 1557 Knox had asked Calvin his opinion about the 'Regiment' of women, who gravely replied: 'That as it was a deviation from the original and proper order of nature, it was to be ranked, no less than slavery, among the punishments consequent upon the fall of man'; but admitted that occasionally good female sovereigns 'were raised up by Divine authority.' Now, Knox was, of course, convinced that neither Mary of England, nor Mary of Guise, the Queen-Regent of Scotland, belonged to the latter class of sovereigns, and recognising that there was no hope for the Reformation so long as they remained in power, he resolved, as was his custom, to 'strike at the root.' It is customary to regard the pamphlet as violent and imprudent, but it became only imprudent when Elizabeth ascended the throne and resolved to support Protestantism. Had she not supported Protestantism, Knox would have been at liberty to proceed with further blasts against female sovereignty, whose effectiveness against the Queen-Dowager of Scotland and Mary Stuart might have greatly added to, instead of detracting from, his reputation as a practical politician. The pamphlet is a characteristic example of the scholastic methods of the period; and the solemn citations of classical and scriptural authorities in support of Knox's strong and graphic verdicts render it—from the peculiarly unscholastic nature of the theme—very piquant reading.

Bishop John Leslie, the chief Catholic historian of Scotland, was the illegitimate son of Gavin Leslie, rector of Kingussie, Inverness-shire. After completing his education at King's College, Aberdeen, he studied civil law on the Continent; and he was regarded as the most able and learned of the Scottish Catholic ecclesiastics of his time. His residence in the Catholic regions of the North, as pastor of Oyne, Aberdeenshire, also led to his becoming the chief political adviser of the Catholic nobles. In 1562 he was made Professor of Canon Law in Aberdeen, and, after the Darnley marriage, he was appointed in 1566 to the bishopric of Ross. Continuing devoted to the Queen of Scots throughout all her difficulties and disasters, he became her legal adviser and representative at the York and Westminster conferences, and from October 1569 until November 1573 was detained a prisoner in England for his connection with the Norfolk intrigues. On obtaining his liberty he went to the Continent, where he devoted himself, as before, to the cause of the imprisoned queen, being her chief political confidant and agent, and the inspirer of most of the plots on her behalf. About 1580 he was appointed suffragan and vicar-general of the diocese of Rouen, and in 1591 he obtained the bishopric of Coutances in Normandy, but was unable, on account of the distracted state of the country, to take up his residence in his diocese. He died in the Augustinian

Bishop Leslie (1527-1596). His career.

monastery of Geertruidenberg, near Brussels, 30th
May 1596.

Leslie wrote his latest *History of Scotland* in Latin,[1]
and the most interesting portion of this *History*
—the description of the counties and
As historian.
islands, containing much varied information on the social condition of Scotland not to be
found elsewhere—is not included in the vernacular
History, written in 1568-70[2] for the perusal of Mary
Stuart while in prison. This *History* includes the
period from the death of James I. to 1561. A very
careful and judicious historian, Leslie is minute in
his chronology, and must have been well supplied
with original material; but his record is little more
than a mere chronicle, and is wholly lacking in the
vivid picturesqueness of Lyndsay's or Knox's narratives, its manner being very much that of a formal
state document.

Such registers as *The Diurnal of Occurrents,*[3] the
Diary of Robert Birrel,[3] and even *The Historie of
James Sext,*[3] can scarce be ranked as
**Other historical
works in the
Vernacular.**
literature; and the one other prominent
historical work that need here be men-
tioned is *The History of the Kirk of Scotland* (1514-
1625)[4] by the Scottish clergyman, David Calderwood

---

[1] An old Scots translation of the Latin *History,* by Father James
Dalrymple, has been published by the Scottish Text Society, ed.
Cody, 1884-1889.

[2] Printed by the Bannatyne Club, 1830.

[3] Printed by the Bannatyne Club.

[4] Published by the Wodrow Society, 8 vols., 1842-49.

(1575-1650), which, though mainly a mere compilation from Knox's *History*, the *Diary* of James Melville, *The Historie of James Sext*, and other works, and rather a collection of rough materials for history than a properly condensed and continuous narrative, is of interest as an example of the later Anglo-Scots on the eve of the complete extrusion of the vernacular from the prose literature of Scottish authors. John Spottiswoode (1566-1639), Archbishop of St. Andrews, the contemporary of Calderwood, wrote in English his *History of the Church and State in Scotland*, undertaken at the instance of James VI. to represent the Episcopal standpoint; and although a mild form of the vernacular lingered long in private diaries and letters, the educated classes, including the clergy, from the time of the Union of the Crowns aspired in formal compositions to express themselves in English.

Among the many *Diaries, Journals, Memoirs*, and *Memorials* which have been printed by Scottish clubs and other learned societies, only two are of such literary merit as to demand a passing reference—*The Autobiography* 'Diary' of James Melville (1556-1614). *and Diary* of Mr. James Melville, minister of Kilrenny; and *The Memoirs of His Own Life*, by Sir James Melville of Halhill. The *Diary* of the Kilrenny minister, nephew of the better-known ecclesiastic Andrew Melville, is a valuable example of the earlier Anglo-Scots—not Scots intentionally Anglified, as was Knox's *History*, but a curious inartificial mixture of Scots and English. Its main literary

merit is its graphic garrulosity.   The author is a sort
of old Presbyterian Pepys, or rather, perhaps, Boswell,
the facts of his own life and the events of his own
time being his Johnson; and his phrases and comparisons have frequently much naïve vividness and
force.   His portrait of Knox in the pulpit about the
time when Knox, as Knox himself expressed it, had
' one foot in the grave,' is almost startlingly graphic :—
  Bot or he had done with his sermont, he was sae
active and vigorous that he was lyk to ding that
pulpit in blads and fly out of it.' Companion pictures
are those of the young King James VI. in 1574, when
only eight years of age, ' walking up and down in the
auld Lady Marr's hand,' and ' discoursing of knowledge and ignorance '; and that of George Buchanan,
after sending his *History* to press, ' sitting in his chair
and teatching his young man that servit him in his
chalmer to spell a-b, ab, e-b, eb,' etc.; but indeed it
is difficult to open a page of the narrative portion of
the *Diary* without chancing on some anecdote, or
reminiscence, or description that illuminates the past
as with a flash of sunlight.

  The *Memoirs* of Sir James Melville, the great
Scottish diplomat of Mary Stuart, are by no means
so minute and confidential as the *Diary*
of his inimitable namesake, the reserve
and propriety of the courtier having become engrained in his nature, and affecting, we may
well believe, even his private thoughts; but he had seen

'Memoirs' of Sir
James Melville
(1535-1617).

                    ' cities of men,
      And manners, climates, councils, governments,'

and few had been more behind the scenes of his eventful times. His interviews with Queen Elizabeth are as diverting as they are instructive; and his comments on the characters and motives of his contemporaries, and on the incidents and events of this complicated period of Scottish history, are, though qualified by much diplomatic caution, shrewd and honest, and frequently racy and picturesque.

Apart from *History* and *Memoirs*, etc., Scottish vernacular prose literature, during the short half-century or so that filled up its allotted span, is mainly confined to controversial theology, but nothing of any literary value is to be gained by embarking on this troubled and tempestuous ocean. *Theological literature.*

Scottish vernacular prose, as well as poetry, virtually terminates with James VI. That versatile and all-wise monarch also intermeddled with theology, publishing in Scots *Ane Frvitful Meditatiovn* (founded on some verses of the 20th chapter of the Revelation), at Edinburgh, 1588; and another *Meditatiovn* (founded on certain verses of the 15th chapter of 1st Chronicles), at Edinburgh in 1589. But his main works in prose before he ascended the English throne are his *Ane Schort Treatise conteining some Revlis and Cautelis to be obseruit and eschewit in Scottis Poesie*,[1] 1584, and *Demonologie*, 1587. The former is very much the work of a mere schoolboy, and though of some interest from its subject, is remarkably trite in its *James VI. (1566-1625).*

---

[1] Included in the Arber Reprints.

treatment of it. Here, for example, is his Majesty's recipe for originality :—

'Ze man[1] also bewarre with composing onything in the same manner as hes been ower oft vsit of before. As in speciall, gif[2] ze speik of loue, be warre ze descryue your Loues makdome[3] or her fairness. And siclyke[4] that ze descryue not the morning, and rysing of the Sunne in the Preface of zour verse ; for thir thingis are sa oft, and dyuerslie writtin vpoun be Poetis already, that gif ze do the lyke, it will appeare, ze bot imitate, and that it cummis not of zour awin *Inventioun*, quhilk is ane of the chief properteis of ane Poete. Thairfore gif zour subject be to prayse zour *Loue*, ze sall rather praise hir vther qualiteis nor her fairnes, or her shaip ; or ellis ze sall speik some lytill thing of it and syne[5] say, that zour wittis are sa smal, and zour vtterance sa barren, that ze can not discryue any part of hir worthelie : remitting alwayis to the Reider, to judge of hir in respect sho matches, or rather excellis Venus, or any woman, quhome to it sall please zow to compaire hir. Bot gif zour subject be sic, as ze man[6] speik something of the morning or sunne rysing, tak heid, that quhat name ze giue to the sunne, the mone, or vther starris, the ane tyme, gif ze happin to wryte thairof another tyme, to change thair names. As gife ze calle the sunne Titan, at a tyme, to call him Phœbus or Apollo the vther tyme, and siclyke the mone, and vther Planettis.'

A good idea of the change effected on the monarch's language, after his accession to the English throne, may be got by comparing the above passage with a short extract from *The Counterblast to Tobacco*, 1604 :—

'That the manifold abuses of this vile custome of Tobacco taking may the better be espied it is fit that first you enter into consideration both of the first original thereof, and likewise of the reasons of the first entry thereof into this countrey.'

---

[1] must. [2] if. [3] shape.
[4] such like. [5] then. [6] must.

TRADITIONAL BALLADS AND SONGS

THE subject of Scottish traditional ballads and songs is so comprehensive and complicated, and in some respects so shadowy, that it is possible here to touch on only its more general features; and since also the various details of the subject have, up to the present, been dealt with in a compara- tively fragmentary and tentative fashion, one is inclined to indulge rather in queries than in positive assertions. It is hardly necessary to premise that this traditional poetry is not an isolated literature, that it has intimate relations with other forms of literature, some of which have now perished, and that the older popular poetry of Scotland has also a very close connection with that of England. The labours, for example, of the late Mr. Chappell, and of Dr. Furnivall, and Mr. Ebsworth, mainly directed to the critical examination of the old English ballads and songs, have incidentally shed a good deal of light, or have supplied the means of shedding light, on the ballads and songs of Scotland; and in the vast accumulation of MS. poetry and of old song-book,

Complexity of the subject. Labours of Chappell, Dr. Furnivall, Mr. Ebsworth, and Professor Child.

broadside, and chapbook literature, most of which is now of comparatively easy access, there is the possibility of greater illumination than has yet been made manifest. It would also be merely superfluous to insist on the invaluable character of the work performed by the late Professor Child, whose *English and Scottish Popular Ballads*[1] is a sort of library of the different versions—good, indifferent, bad, and worse than bad—of English and Scottish traditional poetry of, or allied to, the ballad form, with very full references to similarities, whether accidental or not, in the older literature of the Continental nations. But this critical attitude towards the traditional ballads and songs is of comparatively recent origin, and thus falsehood, fallacy, and delusion have had an exceptionally long start. Professor Child's great work supplies in an accessible form much raw material for a critical history of popular poetry, but a good deal of the material it supplies is inevitably, and from no fault of the editor, in a sense worse than useless. The chaff is out of all proportion to the wheat; and, alas! chaff and wheat have in many instances become almost inseparably welded together.

The attitude of the earlier collectors and editors of traditional poetry was frequently merely credulous, and when it was not absolutely so, it hardly occurred to them that not merely an exact statement of sources, but a careful inquiry into their trustworthi-

[1] Five volumes, Boston, 1882-1898.

ness, was their first and not their last obligation. Allan Ramsay's faults of omission and commission— excusable because he knew no better, but none the less, many of them, ir- remediable—are too notorious to require more than this mere allusion.   But what seem now sadly careless things have been done also in the green tree as well as in the dry.   The modern inquirer can, for example, regard with only amazement the passive content with which Bishop Percy accepted from Lord Hailes most of the Scottish ballads included in his *Ancient Reliques*,[1] as well as 'the many curious and elegant remarks with which they are illustrated,' when, seemingly, not one of these remarks conveyed the smallest tittle of real information regarding Lord Hailes' sources.   Among the ballads which thus first saw the light were, to name only two of the most notable, *Sir Patrick Spens* and *Edward*.   Editors from the time of Scott have been accustomed to regard *Sir Patrick Spens* (see *post*, p. 350) as the oldest specimen of the historical ballad now existing : but the Bishop tells you nothing more of his autho- rity for it than that it is given from two MS. copies 'transmitted from Scotland.'   Sir Walter Scott was also content to remark that he got his version from 'two MSS. collated with several verses recited by the

Margin notes: Credulity and carelessness of the earlier editors. Ramsay and Bishop Percy 'Sir Patrick Spens' and 'Edward.'

---

[1] This remark does not, of course, touch the unquestioned authen- ticity of the Percy folio MS. of the seventeenth century, which has been published by the Ballad Society.

editor's friend, Robert Hamilton, Esq.'—recited long years after the ballad had been published by Percy. As for *Edward*, which Professor Child affirms is 'not only unimpeachable, but has ever been regarded as one of the noblest and most sterling specimens of the popular ballad,' we are left utterly in the dark as to how Lord Hailes came to be possessed of it, and virtually it is unknown apart from Lord Hailes. True, Motherwell, who recognised that the 'unimpeachable' ballad had, at least to some extent, been doctored, came forward with another version got 'from the recitation of an old woman,' and on this old woman's solitary authority calmly asserted that it might be looked upon as the 'genuine traditionary version,' as if there could be a one and only 'genuine traditionary version'! But this supposed 'genuine traditionary version' may, for anything we know to the contrary, simply derive from the version in the *Reliques*, which, though shamly archaic in spelling, may not have been vouched for as a Scottish traditional ballad, and may even have been derived directly from foreign sources.

One of the most trustworthy of the old collectors was David Herd, and this because (1) he was himself almost incapable not merely of writing but of altering or amending verse; (2) he loved collecting for its own, not for vanity's, sake; and (3) a large number of his versions were got before they could have been suggested by published copies. His *Ancient and Modern Scottish Songs*

David Herd.

appeared anonymously in 1769, and an enlarged edition, with his name attached, in two volumes, 1776. His MS. collections, now in the British Museum, contain also a good number of songs and fragments yet unpublished. But while Herd stated that many of his ballads had 'been recovered from tradition, or old MSS., and never before printed,' he, like Bishop Percy, neglected to give a circumstantial account of how he obtained them.

Other collections published towards the close of the eighteenth century are—Pinkerton's *Select Scotish Ballads*, 1783, which deserves a passing reference, mainly from the attempt of the editor to palm off as old certain productions of his own[1]; Johnson's *Scots Musical Museum*, 1787-1803, which was in great part edited by Burns, and contains, with a few versions obtained by Burns, a miscellaneous assortment of songs, many of which preserve ancient fragments more or less metamorphosed; and Ritson's *Ancient Songs*, 1790, and *Scottish Songs*, 1794, edited with a scrupulous conscientiousness and learning, which, had they been more generally in evidence amongst his predecessors and successors, would have done much to prevent the accumulation of dubiety with which the subject is now enveloped.

Pinkerton, Johnson, and Ritson.

It would be hard to exaggerate the services

---

[1] Pinkerton is sometimes credited with being the first to publish the ballad of Sir John the Ross, but it first appeared in Herd's *Ancient and Modern Scottish Songs*, 1776.

rendered to Scottish ballad literature by Sir Walter Scott, whose *Border Minstrelsy*, which appeared first

Sir Walter Scott.

in 1802, and was afterwards enlarged, aroused a more general interest in the subject than any previous publication; but Sir Walter's attitude towards the older minstrelsy was a good deal that of enthusiastic and unsuspecting admiration; and since also in many instances (see *post,* pp. 362, 366) his own published copies were cooked from different recited versions, they occasionally owe more than a little of their vividness and magic to the great magician himself.

Next in importance to Sir Walter's *Minstrelsy* must be placed *Popular Ballads and Songs from Tradition,* 'with Translations of similar

Robert Jamieson.

Pieces from the ancient Danish Language and a few originals by the editor, Robert Jamieson, A.M. and F.A.S.' (1806), which seemed to mark an epoch in the study of the subject, because, to use the words of Sir Walter, 'Mr. Jamieson's extensive acquaintance with Scandinavian literature enabled him to detect not only a general similarity betwixt these and the Danish ballads preserved in the "Kiempe Viser," an early collection of heroic ballads in that language, but to demonstrate that, in many cases, the stories and songs were distinctly the same, a circumstance which no antiquary had hitherto so much as suspected.' Jamieson's discovery was further emphasised by the publication in 1814 of *Illustrations of Northern Antiquities,* under the joint-editorship

of Jamieson, Henry Weber, and Sir Walter Scott;
but while the discovery was no doubt important, its
importance was not of the peculiar and supreme
character which many vaguely suppose. In view
also of the peculiar importance that has been attached
to it, it is to be regretted that every Scottish version
of a ballad supplied by Jamieson himself, which
manifested this connection, should not have been
authenticated beyond the possibility of suspicion.
Yet, so far from taking this precaution, it was Jamieson's habit to construct versions of his own from
those got from recitation; and while, for example,
his version of *Clerk Saunders* is the only one which
connects it with a Scandinavian ballad, he withheld
the originals on which his version is founded. 'We
may suppose,' says Professor Child, 'that all the
three versions combined contain the passage which
formed the link; but it would be much more satisfactory if Jamieson had given us all three as he
received them'; and to this verdict one can only
add an unavailing Amen.

Among other partly original ballad collections it
may suffice to mention Finlay's *Scottish Historical
and Romantic Ballads, chiefly Ancient,* Other ballad
1808; Cromek's *Remains of Nithsdale* collections.
and Galloway Song, 1810 (mainly the manufacture
of Allan Cunningham); C. K. Sharpe's *Ballad Book,*
1824 (containing various interesting scraps); Allan
Cunningham's *Songs of Scotland, Ancient and
Modern,* 4 vols., 1825 (hopelessly unreliable); Robert

Chambers's *Popular Rhymes of Scotland*, 1826;
Motherwell's *Minstrelsy, Ancient and Modern*, 1827
(prefaced by an interesting, and, in some respects,
valuable introduction); Kinloch's *Ancient Scottish
Ballads*, 1827; Peter Buchan's *Ancient Ballads and
Songs of the North of Scotland*, 1828 (much of it
a mere farrago of unauthentic doggerel[1]); Robert
Chambers's *Scottish Ballads and Songs*, 1829 (containing several songs—some old, some partly fabricated—published for the first time from sources
which Chambers, for publisher's reasons, failed even to
indicate in such a fashion as to guarantee sufficiently
either their genuine antiquity or the purity of his
text); and Maidment's *Scottish Ballads and Songs*,
1859, and *Scottish Pasquils*, 1868.   In all these later
collections the ballads and songs obtained from
tradition necessarily suffer more from corruption
than those in the earlier collections, and some of
the new versions are mere corruptions of versions
previously published.[2]

[1] Many of the numbers were supplied by James Rankine, a blind
beggar, whom Buchan in his MS. states he kept, 'at great expense,'
travelling in Scotland collecting ballads for him.   Professor Child
remarks that many of Buchan's ballads bear this minstrel's 'mint
mark,' and places 'no confidence' in any of his readings.   But as
little confidence can be placed in Buchan, who, it is evident, was
quite inclined to become the dupe of any ballad impostor.   In the
'extreme simplicity' of Buchan's ballads, Scott found 'the most
distinct assurance that he has delivered the latter to the public in
the shape in which he found them.'   But Scott was ignorant that
the 'extreme simplicity' was conferred on them by this 'wight of
Homer's craft.'

[2] A very full bibliography of ballad literature will be found in
Child's *Ballads*, vol. v., 1898.   That work is the only standard

One result of Jamieson's discovery of certain similarities between British and Danish ballads was to deepen the impression (1) that many ballads were of immemorial antiquity, and (2) that this form of literature was in some peculiar sense the special literature of the people. This twofold impression more or less influenced—if only in a vague fashion—the methods of subsequent collectors and editors, and it appeared to gain confirmation and solidity from the isolated results — results in many other ways very valuable and interesting—of the study of folklore. Such supremacy, such decisiveness, was claimed by Mr. Andrew Lang for these results in determining the character and origin of ballad literature, that, in the article 'Ballad' contributed to the ninth edition of *The Encyclopædia Britannica*, he categorically denied, from the very nature of the case, that ballad—and more particularly Scottish ballad—literature could be the product of a special literary class, and more particularly of a class of professional minstrels. 'These minstrels,' he wrote, 'are a stumbling-block in the way of the growth of ballads. The domestic annals of Scotland show that her kings used to keep court bards, and also that strollers, jongleurs as they were called, went about

Influence of Jamieson's theory. The theory of Mr. Andrew Lang.

Collection of British ballads. Ayton's *Ballads of Scotland*, 2 vols., 1858 (and frequently republished), gives a sort of eclectic text of the best standard ballads ; and in Mr. Eyre-Todd's *Scottish Ballad Poetry*, 1893 (in the Abbotsford Series), will be found a selection of original versions of some sixty Scottish ballads.

singing at the doors of farm-houses and the streets of towns. Here were two sets of minstrels, who had apparently left no poetry; and on the other side, there were a number of ballads that claimed no author. It was the easiest and most satisfactory inference that the courtly minstrels made the verses, which the wandering crowders imitated or corrupted.' This account of the old minstrels must have been meant as jocular rather than precise; for, being antecedently convinced that, like Topsy, ballads merely 'growed,' it was needless for Mr. Lang to devote particular attention to a perfectly super-fluous fraternity. Without entering greatly into details, he deemed it sufficient to affirm that the minstrel theory—or any theory of individual author-ship—'failed to account for the universal sameness of tone, of incident, of legend, of primitive poetical formulæ, which the Scottish ballad possesses in common with the ballads of Greece, of France, of Provence, of Portugal, of Denmark, and of Italy.' 'Ballads,' he finally declared, 'spring from the very heart of the people, and flit from age to age, from life to life, of shepherds, peasants, nurses, of all the class that continues nearest to the natural state of man'; and they 'make music with the flash of the fisherman's oar, with the hum of the spinning-wheel, and keep time with the step of the ploughman as he drives his team,' etc. It is not with Mr. Lang, be it observed, a mere question of transmission, but of authorship, and on this point he does his utmost to

be clear and decided. No hint is given of any possible
modification of his theory in particular cases, nor
does he indicate that he so much as dreams of any
possible exception to the general rule. Moreover, all
classes of ballads, historical as well as romantic, are
included in his dictum; and as for the Border ballads,
he finds their parallel in those of Greece: the ballads
of 'Klephtic exploits in Greece match,' he affirms, 'the
exploits of Dick of the Law and Kinmont Willie'—all
alike 'springing,' not from the heart of any particular
individual, but from 'the heart of the people.'

Within the last twenty years Mr. Lang's views
may have undergone some modification, but hardly
any essential change, for in a paper on
'The Mystery of the Queen's Marie,' published as recently as 1895,[1] he mentions
that he would 'fain break a lance with
Mr. Courthope on his general doctrine of the popular
ballad and its indebtedness to literary poetry and
romance.'[2] A writer in *The Quarterly Review* for
July 1898 also finds support in the authority of Mr.
Lang as well as Professor Gummere,[3] for inclining

*'The Quarterly
Review'
(July 1898).
Professor
Gummere.*

[1] *Blackwood's Magazine*, vol. clviii. pp. 381-90.
[2] Must not the lance be broken first with Sir Walter? In *The Minstrelsy* (Introduction to *Lord Thomas and Fair Annie*) he wrote: 'The tale is much the same with the Breton romance called *Lay le Frain* (*sic*), or *The Song of the Ash*. Indeed, the Editor is convinced that the further our researches are extended, the more we shall see ground to believe that the romantic ballads of later times are, for the most part, abridgments of the ancient metrical romances, narrated in a smoother stanza and a more modern language.'
[3] *Old English Ballads*, Boston, 1894.

strongly to the conclusion that 'the ballad belonged
to the people, and was the exclusive property of the
minstrel as little in the making as in the singing.'
He ascribes them to 'an age when poetry was a
common possession,' and he explains that probably
'solitary composition would have been as difficult for
primitive man to understand as communal authorship
is hard for us'; or, in other terms, the ballad—the
ballad as it has actually descended to us—is the
communal literature of primitive man, or, as Mr.
Lang expresses it, of 'the classes nearest to the
natural state of man.'

Besides this extreme theory of Mr. Lang, Professor
Gummere, and (tentatively) of the Quarterly Reviewer, we have, of course, only the choice
of some form of the minstrel theory or
some modification of it. And, as regards
the minstrel theory, pure and simple, we
have the choice of two forms: (1) that of Motherwell,
and (vaguely) of most editors from the time of
Jamieson, that many at least of the ballads which
now survive derive from a period anterior to the
romance of chivalry; and (2) that of Professor
Courthope,[1] and (incidentally) of Sir Walter Scott,
that they are solely the production of minstrels who
were the degenerate successors of the ancient bards,
and who, when they did not select a traditionary
feat of arms, or an historic legend, for their theme,
adapted it from some older form of literature—

The Minstrel theory. Motherwell and Professor Courthope.

---

[1] *History of English Poetry*, vol. i. pp. 445-468.

'the romance, lay, or fabliau.' While, for example, Motherwell, and (vaguely) most editors would assume that *Fair Annie* and the Danish *Skiœn Anna* were originally the work of the same old bard, Professor Courthope would hold that they were fabricated at some later period by two separate degenerate minstrels, who made use of the same or a similar original—some romance or story.

If the theory of a communal authorship is in itself, as the Quarterly Reviewer admits, hard to understand, it must be specially difficult of comprehension in the case of such excellent specimens of literature as are many of the ballads; but the explanation of Mr. Lang and the Quarterly Reviewer is that it was done during the excitement of saltation. Ballads, in the Quarterly Reviewer's opinion, were probably the production of a 'chorus at a village festival,' each, or a number, of the singers and dancers adding his or her contribution; and after 'the ballads' had been 'evolved rather than composed' by the combined genius of the village communities, the minstrel calmly appropriated them as his own, and chanted them to the great delight and edification of the same community who were their real authors. Mr. Lang, on the other hand, ignores the minstrel altogether as a 'mere stumbling-block in the way of the student of the growth of ballads'; but apart from this his position is identical with that of the Quarterly Reviewer, for he holds that they are

The theory of communal authorship as expounded by Mr. Andrew Lang and the Quarterly Reviewer.

all 'popular and primitive in the same sense as märchen,' and that they 'all spring from the same primitive custom of dance, accompanied by improvised song, which still exists in Greece and Russia, and even the valley of the Pyrenees.' Again, it is necessary to emphasise the fact that Mr. Lang does not allude—as Ten Brink and others do—to the evolution of poetry in remote or prehistoric times, but to the authorship of actually existing ballads, Scots or English—*Chevy Chace, Sir Patrick Spens, Child Waters, Kinmont Willie,* or, in short, any other standard ballad you like to name. The only historical evidence adduced for this sweeping conclusion is (1) that in a few instances—there are four in all, viz. *Robene hude, Thom of lyn, Lewis grene* (*The Murning Maiden*), and *Ihonne ermistrangis dance*—the names of the dances in *The Complaynt of Scotland* are identical with the names of certain surviving ballads, and (2) that the song after the victory of Bannockburn was 'sungyn in dances, in carolles of ye maidens and mynstrellys of Scotland.' But (1) in the same *Complaynt of Scotland* the names of many more ballads occur as merely tales and songs; (2) there is no evidence that these dances—even if they were ballad dances, dances accompanied by song—were improvised by the dancers; (3) even the dance song of Bannockburn may have been, and probably was, the work of professional dancers and minstrels (for whom Mr. Lang can find no use), and the work of the chief minstrel, but in any case it is very rude and simple; and (4) it is beyond belief that any of those four ballads whose names occur in *The Complaynt* as dances could have been essentially created either by such artistes as those who celebrated Bannockburn, or even by the most primitive of village communities. Further, whatever connection the ballad may, in primitive times, have had with the dance, something called 'balat-making' was, as we learn from Dunbar's *Lament*—to name merely this solitary evidence—accomplished before Dunbar's day by individual 'makaris.' Thus the theory of absolute communal authorship—whatever it may have to commend it as an explanation of the origin of poetry—is, as regards the ballad poetry we actually possess, founded rather on general *a priori* considerations than on minute inquiry into facts; and the more one seeks to have recourse to it for an explanation of individual examples of the literature for which it professes to account, the more unmistakably does it approve itself a mere 'broken reed.'

We come, then, to the minstrel theory of Motherwell and others, derived from the notion that some of the ballads transmitted to us are of immemorial antiquity, and that we still have historical ballads closely related to very remote historical events. The theory of the very great age of certain historical ballads has been accepted unquestioningly by certain editors owing to the notion that other non-historical ballads are of immemorial antiquity; while the supposition that

Are there any ballads of immemorial antiquity?

we possess certain ballads relating to very remote historical events tends, of course, to foster the belief in the immemorial antiquity of the other classes of ballads.

The few simple and rude rhymes relating to the death of Alexander III. (1285), the siege of Berwick (1296), the battle of Bannockburn (1314),
Historical ballads. 'Sir Patrick Spens' —general belief in its great antiquity. Views of Sir Walter Scott. and the character of the English (1328), are the earliest extant specimens of Scottish popular historic poetry, the authenticity of which may be said to be fairly well established; but an antiquity as remote as the earliest of these has been claimed for what Coleridge has termed the 'grand old ballad of Sir Patrick Spens.' In publishing it for the first time, Bishop Percy remarked that he had not been able to ascertain when the 'fatal expedition happened which proved so destructive'; but Sir Walter Scott, while observing that 'the introduction of the king into the ballad seems a deviation from history,' affirmed that the cause of Sir Patrick Spens's voyage, which 'is pointed out distinctly,' shows that 'the song has claims to high antiquity, as referring to a very remote period in Scottish history,' and broached the theory that it referred to an unrecorded and disastrous expedition of Sir Patrick Spens to bring Margaret, the Maid of Norway, to Scotland after the death of her grandfather Alexander III.

It so happened, however, that—as Fordun records —the ambassadors who in 1281 conveyed Margaret, the daughter of Alexander, to be married to Eric of Norway were wrecked on their return, and although none of the names of the ambassadors resembled in the remotest degree that of Sir Patrick Spens, Motherwell, after fortifying himself by calculating that the 12th of August,[1] on which, according to Wyntoun, the ambassadors set sail for Norway, fell in 1281 on, as stated in the ballad, a Monday, proposed, in contradiction to this same ballad (which was so accurate in regard to the day of the week, but so inaccurate as to the 'time of the year'), to make the ballad refer to this later event—the sending away, not the bringing home, of a king's daughter. Hardly had he promulgated his theory when, of course, Peter Buchan, with the aid of his 'wight of Homer's craft,' discovered the following doggerel stanza which editor after editor has been accustomed gravely to appeal to in corroboration of the Motherwell conclusion :—

Theory of Motherwell. Its final corroboration.

> 'But I man sail the seas the morn,
>   And likewise sae man you,
> To Norroway wi' our King's daughter,
>   A chosen Queen she's now.'

must
so

And since the Buchan corroboration, the Motherwell theory has practically held the field. Robert Chambers ventured to include *Sir Patrick Spens* in the list of ballads which he attributed to the fabrication of Lady Wardlaw, but outwardly did not per-

---

[1] It was really in summer, not in winter, be it observed, that, according to Wyntoun, the ship set sail for Norway.

severe in maintaining his theory against the adverse criticism to which it was subjected; and the final stage in the corroboration of the Motherwell-Buchan theory was the discovery by Maidment in Papa, Orkney, of a tumulus reputed by the natives—instructed it may be by Buchan, or some Buchan enthusiast—to be the grave of Sir Patrick Spens. True, the ballad states that Sir Patrick and his followers lie 'fifty fathom deep' in the ocean, but, as has been pointed out, Papa is about 'half way' between Norway and Aberdour—not, be it observed, the merely Fife Aberdour on the Firth of Forth, but the vastly more probable Aberdour on the Aberdeenshire coast!

Down, therefore, to the publication of Professor Child's second volume (1886), the Motherwell theory was that generally accepted; and it is so still,[1] though it was not accepted by Professor Child. Mr. Lang, who in the *Blackwood* paper refers to the ballad as perhaps the 'most antique ballad of all,' states that the 'historical event which may have suggested it is "plausibly" fixed, says Mr. Child, in 1281'; but though Professor Child did politely refer to the 'plausibility' of the Motherwell theory, and, with his usual anxiety to tell all that was to be known, even informed his readers that Mr. MacMath of Edinburgh

Mr. Lang and Professor Child.

---

[1] Thus Professor Walker, in *Three Centuries of Scottish Literature*, 1893, vol. i. p. 167, writes: 'It seems as fully established as it could well be on any but ancient documentary evidence, that *Sir Patrick Spens* carries us back to the year 1281.'

had found the name Spens in 'five charters of David II. between 1329 and 1370,' his own exact position was that 'this ballad may be historical or it may not,' and he even speculated that Sir Patrick might be 'only a shipmaster of purely local fame who was lost off Aberdeen a couple of hundred years ago.' This, it may be said, is a very improbable hypothesis, but so much the more does it indicate the puzzlement of Professor Child as to the origin of the ballad, and how slight was his faith in the theory of its unique antiquity. Nor is such lack of faith surprising. For, apart from insuperable difficulties of metre and even language, there is the important obstacle not only that no name resembling that of Sir Patrick Spens is known to have been associated with the early embassies to Norway, but that neither the disastrous occurrence to which the ballad professes to refer, nor the remarkable ballad itself, is mentioned by any of the old writers, and that the earliest known publication of the ballad was that in Percy's *Reliques*, 1765.

But for the fact, however, of a preconceived notion of the ballad's great antiquity, a solution of the problem would probably have been looked for in connection with the voyage of James VI. in 1589 to bring home his bride from Denmark. The bride, expected in Scotland in September, had not arrived on the day fixed for the marriage, and all sorts of rumour of disaster

'Sir Patrick Spens' and Sir Patrick Vans.

were in circulation, until a message arrived that having twice been driven back by contrary winds, she had taken refuge on the coasts of Norway, and that the Scots and Danes were in disagreement as to whether she should be brought over at once, or the voyage be deferred till the spring. Then it was that the king resolved, as narrated in the ballad, to send out a ship to fetch her 'at this time of the year,' 'be it wind, be it weet, be it hail, be it sleet'; and among the 'new commissioners directed to the Queen' was, not indeed Sir Patrick Spens, but Sir Patrick Vans of Barnbarroch, a name which might easily, in the popular mind, get changed into the more Scottish name Spens. Further, the same Sir Patrick Vans was also the original ambassador chosen to negotiate the marriage in 1587; and when the king, after appointing the 'new commission' in October 1589, finally resolved secretly to embark himself, Sir Patrick Vans was chosen to accompany him, and remained in Denmark until the marriage, when he returned in December to Scotland to report the king's safe arrival and the conclusion of the cere-mony. The resolve of the king to fetch the queen 'at this time of the year' greatly perturbed the nation, the more especially that the weather continued very tempestuous. A great storm delayed the ships from sailing, and when they at last ventured on their voyage, and got beyond the Forth and out of sight of land, they were driven back twenty or thirty miles by a renewal of the blast, and rode for a time opposite

St. Monans.[1]   May not the ballad, therefore, have been suggested by a rumour of disaster to this adventurous expedition?   And is it not as likely, at least, that Sir Patrick Vans was its hero, as a quite unknown Sir Patrick Spens of the thirteenth century, or an equally unknown skipper of some two hundred years ago?   That is, supposing the ballad is not a mere forgery, which is less likely than the supposition that, as we now have it, it is an improvement by some one—Lady Wardlaw or another—of a minstrel ballad of the late sixteenth century.

Next to *Sir Patrick Spens*, the historical ballad which claims the greatest antiquity is a long recitation, *Auld Maitland*, first published by   'Auld Maitland.' Scott in 1802, who got it from Hogg as recited by his mother, and the date of which Scott placed 'about the reign of David II. or his successor.'   But though Sir Richard and his 'auld

---

[1] 'His Majestie with the rest sould maid saille vpone Sonday at efternoune, the xix day of October instant, at quhilk tyme theare come on sick a deadlie storme, that the schipis lyand all in Leith read were schakin loose, and driven all vp to St. Margarets houpe, and sua the jorney stayed for that nicht. Vpone the xxij day of October, about tuelff houris at evin, his Majestie maid saile to Norroway with fyve schippis in company : his Majestie wes driven back xx or xxx myles with great storme, and read foranent St. Monanis' (Moysie's *Memoirs*, p. 80).   Two women burned for sorcery at Edinburgh in 1590-91 asserted that Bothwell had bribed them to make storms during the king's voyage.   See also, in connection with the Bass, a reference in R. L. Stevenson's *Catriona*. It is worth noting that the earliest version of the ballad represents the disaster as occurring on the outward voyage.

grey beard' are referred to in Gavin Douglas's *Palice of Honour*, and we also learn from a poem in the Maitland MS. that his exploits had been the subject of song and story, it is impossible to resist the conclusion of Ayton and Maidment that the ballad is a modern composition; and it has not been included in Professor Child's volumes.[1]

If, then, we reject *Sir Patrick Spens* and *Auld Maitland* as thirteenth or fourteenth century pro-

The 'Lord of Liddesdale.'

ductions, the most ancient Scottish incident known to have been commemorated in a ballad, of which any fragment remains, is the murder of the Lord of Liddesdale by the Earl of Douglas in the forest of Ettrick, in 1353, as narrated by Hume of Godscroft (1560-1630), who gives the beginning of the old song:—

> ' The Countesse of Douglass, out of her bower she came
> > And loudly there that she did call,
> " It is for the Lord of Liddesdale
> > That I let all these tears doune fall." '

But the ballad itself has not been preserved.

The murder of the Lord of Liddesdale took place thirty-five years before the battle of Otterburn, celebrated in the ballad of which the earliest Scottish

---

[1] On the line, ' And fired the Merse and Teviotdale,' the late Professor Veitch commented : ' That word *fired*, not burned, speaks of the glow of the flame as present to the very eye of the minstrel' (*Poetry of the Scottish Border*, 1893, vol. ii. p. 130). But this use of 'fire' is not peculiar to the minstrel, nor uniquely Scottish, nor in any sense exceptional, but quite common and modern, and it may even have been an emendation of Scott.

version is that preserved by Herd (1776). It contains the line, 'The Percy and Montgomerie met,' quoted in *The Complaynt of Scotland* as the name of a song, but it is impossible to tell whether or not the stanza has 'Chevy Chace, and the 'Battle of Otterbourne.' been interpolated at a later date, especially as it is but a repetition—with the substitution of Montgomerie for Douglas—of a stanza common to both the Scots and English versions of the ballad. The oldest extant version is the English one (*c.* 1550) in the Cottonian MSS., but this, of course, is no proof that the Scottish version was borrowed from the English one; and something may even be said for Professor Veitch's theory, that both versions, as well as the ballad of *Chevy Chace*, which so much moved the heart of Sir Philip Sidney when he heard it sung by 'some blind crowder,' and which is also mentioned in *The Complaynt*, may derive from some 'original ballad of Otterbourne which we have lost.'

After Otterburn, the next earliest event commemorated in a ballad, which has been claimed as ancient, is that of Harlaw, 1411. The *battel of harylaw* is the title of one of the songs in *The Complaynt*; and a copy of a ballad of that name, dated 1688, was at one time in the library of Robert Milne. No doubt it was from some such broadside that Allan Ramsay got the *Evergreen* version of the ballad; and though we can scarce believe that he refrained from altering it, it may be substantially the song referred to in *The Complaynt*.

Since, however, it is written in the French octave, it was most likely composed long after the battle, for there is no evidence that the Chaucerian influence reached Scotland until the reign of James I.

None of the surviving examples of the historical ballad thus date earlier than about the beginning of the fifteenth century, and in view of the fact that nearly all even of the rudest examples of minstrelsy referring to earlier events have perished, is it possible to accept the theory that, in the case of the other ballads, we actually possess examples of the older minstrelsy anterior to the romance of chivalry? As matter of fact, the oldest authenticated specimen of the romantic ballad we possess is that forming part of the romance detailing the confabulations of Thomas of Erceldoune with the Elf Queen, but, as has been already stated (*ante,* p. 23), that romance itself is founded on the older one of *Ogier le Danois.* Thus a conclusion of Professor Walker,[1] that 'the earliest assignable date for the ballads of superstition does lead us into a remoter past than the historical ballads,' wholly loses the significance he attaches to it.[2]

Thomas of Erceldoune.

[1] *Three Centuries of Scottish Literature,* vol. i. p. 171.

[2] A traditional copy of this ballad was obtained by Jamieson from Mrs. Brown of Falkland. Its close resemblance to the old MS. copy has been cited as a proof of the remarkable fidelity with which old ballads may be preserved by tradition from even the time of the Rhymer. But is it not, as Dr. J. A. H. Murray opined, rather an indication that the traditional copy has a comparatively recent connection with the MS.? Similarly can we now believe, with Sir Walter Scott, that any special virtue attaches to a copy 'obtained from a lady residing not far from Erceldoune'?

Antecedent probability, therefore, favours some form of the theory of Professor Courthope: that the traditional ballad is the work of later minstrels than the ancient bard, and that those ballads which do not form a later variety of the *chanson de geste* are adapted from older forms of literature—the romance, the lay, or the fabliau. Moreover, the theory—as even a cursory examination of Professor Child's volume might at least suggest, and a detailed study cannot but confirm—is very strongly countenanced by apparent facts; and any modification of it can be justified, it would seem, only (1) by the discovery of a few apparent exceptions in the case of individual ballads; or (2) by proof that later minstrels were not, as Professor Courthope predicates, 'degenerate';[1] or (3) by the consideration that some of the Scots traditional ballads were originally the work of poets other than minstrels.

Professor Courthope's theory favoured by antecedent probability. How far should it be modified?

Professor Courthope's general theory that the ballads were the work of later minstrels does not, of course, depend on the justness of his verdict that the later minstrels were universally an inferior class of poets to the ancient bards;[2] but is not the question

[1] This question is closely associated with that of how far individual ballads are either corrupted or cooked.

[2] Mr. Lang had no difficulty (*Blackwood*, vol. clviii. pp. 381-90) in exposing the mistaken character of Professor Courthope's theory of degeneracy as applied to the ballad of *Mary Hamilton*, but that exposure left the question as to whether ballads are the work of minstrels exactly where it was.

as to their inferiority a more comprehensive and complex one—especially as regards the Scottish ballads
—than he seems to realise? He compares
Otterbourne and *The Hunting of the
Cheviot* with the Anglo-Saxon *Death of
Byrhtnoth*, much to their disadvantage as
regards especially circumstantiality and
truthfulness; but the fact that *The Hunting of the Cheviot* was in great part fiction had
been noticed by Hume of Godscroft, who makes
mention of a *Scots song made of Otterbourne*, which
'telleth the time, about Lammas; and also the
occasion to take frays out of England; also the
dividing armies betwixt the Earls of Fife and
Douglas, and their several journeys almost as in
authentic history.'[1] But even this ballad, as known
to Hume, probably differed greatly from the original
one. We must make allowance for the deterioration
effected by possibly some centuries of mangling
by reciters; for tradition, contact with the natural
man, contagion from the 'heart of the people'—
which heart, however sincere and strong in its
emotions, is now, and probably ever was, wholly un-
trained in the art of poetic expression—does not
tend as some, not including Professor Courthope,
assume, towards the elaboration of the consummate
qualities of the ballad, but rather, as hundreds of
instances could be adduced to prove, towards their

*Complexity
of the
question.
Deteriorating
influence of
tradition.
'Chevy Chace'
and 'Otter-
bourne.'*

---

[1] *House of Douglas,* vol. i. p. 195.

obscuration, defilement, and final effacement.[1] Many of the traditional ballads are strangely unequal, and at a later period they tended to become a kind of patchwork in which stanzas of startling poetic beauty are occasionally to be found side by side with mere tawdry vulgarity or hopeless bathos; but we may surely believe that the qualities of *Chevy Chace,* which stirred the heart of Sir Philip Sidney as with 'the sound of a trumpet,' were echoes from the heart of a true minstrel, who, like the author of the *Death of Byrhtnoth,* must have felt the reality of the conflict of which he sang. Much of the original beauty and accuracy of the alliteration and rhythm of *Chevy Chace* has plainly been lost, and it may therefore be inferred that both in it and in the English and

---

[1] Assonance, for example, is frequently assumed to be a distinctive and original characteristic of the ballad. Mr. Lang lays much stress on ' the use of assonance in place of rhyme,' as an indication of the ballad's absolute folkness; and the Quarterly Reviewer, though he states that ' rhyme is the basis of the whole musical scheme of the ballad,' affirms that ' alliteration and assonance have their place in it.' But though assonance—that is, mere vowel rhyme—had its place in the poetry of the Romance and other dialects, where it was governed by strict laws, it is not a general characteristic of old poetry. It has no proper place in English verse, and its furtive and haphazard presence in the ballad is evidence only of a dulled and defective ear, or an imperfect command of the resources of common rhyme. Again, while ballads deteriorate by tradition, they also deteriorate still more vilely by being passed through the crucible of the hack balladist, whence they are issued as broadsides, or in chap-books; but by all in town or country, nearest to ' the natural state of man,' these mere abortions of the old ballad were and are received with acclamation. So much for the ' natural man' as the vein in which is to be found the pure deposit of the primæval ballad !

Scottish versions of *Otterbourne* alteration and inter-
polation have wrought sad havoc on the unity and
force of the original recital.[1]

[1] Could we accept Scott's version of *Otterbourne* in *The Minstrelsy*
as bearing throughout anything like a close resemblance to the
original ballad, it would be impossible to regard it as the work of
a minstrel in any sense degenerate; but the original material at
Abbotsford shows that the ballad owes much of its special excellence
to Scott himself.   Indeed, the most vivid and touching stanzas in
the whole ballad—those describing the death of Douglas—stanzas
'which,' in the opinion of Professor Veitch, 'for power and simple
pathos are unsurpassed in ballad literature,' are little more than
Scott's improvement of what was very much the mere concoction
of Hogg.   Here are the four, it is to be feared, guilty stanzas :—

> ' " My nephew good," the Douglas said,
>   " What recks the death of ane?
>   Last night I dream'd a dreary dream,
>   And I ken the day's thy ain.
>
>   My wound is deep; I fain would sleep;
>   Take thou the vanguard of the three,
>   And hide me by the braken bush,
>   That grows on yonder lilye lea.
>
>   O bury me by the braken bush,
>   Beneath the blooming brier,
>   Let never living mortal ken
>   That ere a kindly Scot lies here."
>
>   He lifted up that noble lord,
>   Wi' the saut tear in his e'e,
>   He hid him in the braken bush,
>   That his merrie men might not see.'

matters (margin, beside line 2)
know (margin, beside line 4)
fern (margin, beside line 7)

Now here is all that we have in Herd for the above stanzas :—

> ' The boy's taen out his little penknife,
>   That hanget low down by his gare,
>   And he gae Earl Douglas a deadly wound,
>   Alack! a deep wound and a sare.
>
>   Earl Douglas said to Sir Hugh Montgomery,
>   "Tak' thou the vanguard o' the three,
>   And bury me at yon braken bush
>   That stands upon yon lilly lee." ' '

gave (margin, beside line 3)

Again, Professor Courthope observes, justly enough as regards England, that towards the close of the

---

The stanzas in the Sharpe MS., though they agree with the Herd MS. in attributing the death of Douglas to the boy, more nearly resemble the stanzas in *The Minstrelsy*, but it is merely as moonlight resembles sunlight :—

> ' "Sir Hugh Montgomery, my sister's son,
>   I give you the vanguard over all ;
> Let it ne'er be said unto Old England,
>   That so little made a true Scot fall.
>
> O lay me dowen by yon brecken bush
>   That grows upon yon lilly lea ;
> Let it ne'er be said unto Old England
>   That so little made a true Scot die." '

Now here is what Hogg sent to Scott :—

> ' "My wound is deep, I fain would sleep,
>   Nae mair I 'll fighting see.
> Gae lay me in the bracken bush   , Go
>   That grows on yonder lee.
>
> But tell na ane of my brave men   not one
>   That I lye bleeding wan,
> But let the name of Douglas still
>   Be shouted in the van.
>
> And bury me here on this lee,
>   Beneath the blooming brier,
> And never let a mortal ken   know
>   A kindly Scot lyes here."
>
> He liftet up that noble lord,
>   Wi' the saut tear in his e'e,
> And hid him in the bracken bush
>   On yonder lily lee.'

But where did Hogg get this version, which is, besides, much inferior to the Scott? The whole of the ballad, he told Scott, he got from 'a crazy old man, and a woman deranged in her mind'; but he candidly admitted that for this, the 'most interesting' portion of it, they had both failed him, and he had been obliged to 'take much of it in plain prose.' This 'plain prose' Hogg put into verse, and Scott improving on it, created the 'unsurpassed' stanzas !

fourteenth century the attention of the better classes
was 'occupied either with prose romances, or with
allegorical and other purely literary
forms of poetry, while the lower classes,
who chiefly cared for minstrelsy, had
long been accustomed to the forms of
settled government'; but this by no
means holds true of Border England or of Scotland
generally, as regards either (1) its absorption in
other forms of literature, or (2) its accustomedness
to settled forms of government.

Does Professor Courthope's statement of the causes of degeneracy apply to Scotland?

As for Scotland's absorption in prose romances or
in allegory, there was, so far as is known, no such
absorption. The Chaucerian influence
probably did not reach Scotland until
the return of James I.; and before this
there was, as the whole after-develop-
ment of Scots poetry bears witness, a
vigorous poetic school of native growth.[1] Henryson's
Robene and Makyne owes nothing to Chaucer, and
Henryson's use of the common ballad measure in
other pieces is clear evidence of the cultivation of
the ballad, not merely by inferior minstrels, but by
a class of poets worthy to be designated 'makaris.'
Similarly, *Christis Kirk* or *Peblis* did not inaugurate
a vernacular poetry called into sudden existence by

Scotland not absorbed in prose romances or allegory. The traditional Scottish School.

---

[1] No doubt there was a decay in minstrelsy before the time of
Blind Harry. He himself refers to a time—

reigned

'Quhen gud makaris rang weill in to Scotland,'

but that was subsequent to Wallace.

the poetic sceptre of a merely Chaucerian James I., but bear upon even their structure and metre the impress of connection with a poetry having an unbroken national tradition. In *The Murning Maiden* (see *ante*, p. 292) we have also an example of the primitive pagan simplicity of sentiment characteristic of the old ballads, expressed with a poetic art which is far, indeed, from being 'degenerate'; and it is further scarcely necessary to mention that the use, even by the later Scottish 'makaris,' of the rhymed alliterative measures, and the general predominance of the bobwheel in Scottish verse, are a clear proof of the survival of the old traditional influences down to the very last.

It is not improbable, therefore, that a good deal of the best traditional poetry in the special ballad form, which now survives, was originally the work of 'makaris' other than the wandering minstrels who may have appropriated it to their own use. Moreover, many numbers included in Professor Child's and other collections, as *The Gaberlunzie Man, Hame cam our Gude Man, Lizie Baillie*, etc., are not in the ballad form, and have little or no connection with minstrels or old romance. Nor can we believe that such remarkable sets of verses as *The Twa Corbies*, or *O Waly, Waly*,[1] derive either from degenerate minstrels or

Some of the surviving ballads probably by other 'makaris' than wandering minstrels. Other so-called 'ballads' not in the ballad form.

---

[1] There can scarce be any doubt that *O Waly, Waly* is related to *Willow, Willow, Willow*, the song which is introduced into

the 'natural man,' though the former and its English analogue, *The Two Ravens*, may be founded on an incident in some forgotten romance.

Then, as to accustomedness to settled forms of government, was not Scotland in a state of chronic The Border ballads. Are they genuine transcripts? anarchy until even after the manhood of James VI.? And, more specially, did there not exist in southern Scotland, until the first half of the sixteenth century, a condition of society which fostered a variety of the *chanson de geste* quite as circumstantial and faithful to fact as the Anglo-Saxon *Death of Byrhtnoth*? The very spirit of the reiver breathes in the rudest version of these old ballads, and how much more might be said in their praise could we be certain that such ballads in *The Minstrelsy* as *Kinmont Willie* or *Jamie Telfer* were nearly genuine transcripts of the versions obtained by Scott! 'Rude and raploch' in measure though they be, their swiftness and fire, and passion and imaginative truth create for us again the whole moral atmosphere of those feats of wild adventure; but, alas! as in *Otterbourne* (see *ante*, p. 362), the magic touch, it is to be feared, is mainly that of Scott, or Scott and Hogg.

Shakespeare's *Othello*, Act iv. Sc. 3, which is also included in Percy's *Reliques*, and of which there are black-letter copies in the Pepys and Roxburghe collections. Stenhouse (*Notes to Johnson's Museum*, p. 147) gives a parody of *O Waly* from a humorous Yule medley in 'Mr. Blackwood's MSS., which were transcribed by Thomas Wode in 1566'; but David Laing states that the medley was inserted in the volume by a later possessor, 'evidently not earlier than 1620.'

Here, for example, is the wonderful picture of the fight in *Jamie Telfer* :—

'Jamie Telfer.'
Scott's version.

> ' " Set on them, lads ! " quo Willie than ;
>   " Fye, lads, set on them cruellie !
> For ere they win to the Ritterford
>   Mony a toom saddle there sall be."
>
> Then til't they gaed, wi' heart and hand,
>   The blows fell thick as bickering hail ;
> And mony a horse ran masterless,
>   And mony a comely cheek was pale.
>
> But Willie was stricken ower the head,
>   And thro' the knapscap the sword has gane ;
> And Harden grat for very rage,
>   Whan Willie on the grund lay slain.
>
> But he 's ta'en aff his gude steel cap
>   And thrice he 's waved it in the air.
> The Dinlay snaw was ne'er mair white
>   Nor the lyart locks of Harden's hair.
>
> " Revenge ! revenge ! " auld Wat gan cry ;
>   " Fye, lads, lay on them cruellie !
> We 'll ne'er see Teviotside again,
>   Or Willie's death revenged sall be." '

then

empty

to it they went

faded

Scott, who is the only authority for this version, mentions that there is another ballad under the same title, 'in which nearly the same incidents are narrated with little difference, except that the honour of rescuing the cattle is attributed to the Liddesdale Elliots, headed by a chief, there called Martin Elliot of the Preakin Tower, whose son, Simon, is said to have fallen in

The Sharpe version.

the action.' But here is how the fight reads in the latter version :[1]—

Fall

' "Fa' on them, lads !" can Simmy say,
"Fy, fa' on them cruelly !
For or they win to the Ritterford

empty
Mony toom saddle there shall be."

But Simmy was stricken o'er the head,
And thro' the napskape it is gane.
And Moscrop made a dolefull rage
When Simmy on the ground lay slain.

"Fy, lay on them !" co Martin Elliot
"Fy, lay on them cruelly !
For ere they win to the Kerthop ford
Mony toom saddle there shall be." '

And yet Scott never gives the slightest hint that this version is in any way inferior to that in *The Minstrelsy*!

But those examples from *The Minstrelsy*, since they indicate that many old Border ballads have been

How far are the old ballads cooked? 'Edom o' Gordon.' partly transformed, necessarily give additional point to the doubts that were cast by Chambers on the genuine antiquity

of many ballads which he attributed to Lady Wardlaw. That Lady Wardlaw, as Chambers surmised, was the sole fabricator of those ballads, is hardly possible; but she or another may have improved the old versions, just as Scott improved the Border ballads. And if she did even this, she must

---

[1] Recovered from the Sharpe papers by Mr. MacMath, Edinburgh, and printed for the first time in Child's *Ballads*, 1898, vol. v. pp. 249-251.

have possessed poetic gifts of rare delicacy. The
version of *Edom o' Gordon*, for instance, published in
1755 from a copy furnished by Lord Hailes, is no
whit inferior (to say the least) to either *Kinmont
Willie* or *Jamie Telfer*. The scene of the maiden's
death, whoever — man or woman — conceived or
realised it, is a primitive and pagan masterpiece.
She is beheld as these savage clansmen beheld her :
the pitiless simplicity and truthfulness and reserve
of the balladist are, after their own fashion, matchless :—

'They row'd her in a pair of sheets   wrapped
    And tow'd her owre the wa',   wall
But on the point of Edom's spear
    She gat a deadly fa'.

O, bonnie, bonnie was her mouth,
    And cherry were her cheeks !
And clear, clear was her yellow hair,
    Whereon the red bluid dreeps !

Then wi' his spear he turned her ower,
    O, gin her face was wan !
He said, "You are the first that e'er
    I wished alive again."

He turned her ower and ower again,
    O, gin her skin was white !
He said, "I might hae spared thy life
    To hae been some man's delight.

Busk and boun, my merrymen all !   Ready and
    For ill dooms I do guess :   away !
I canna look on that bonnie face   bad luck
    As it lies on the grass."'

2 A

This, certainly, was not altogether the work of a 'degenerate minstrel.' And as we now have them,

The old ballads as revelations of the past.

and however acquired, many of those ballads possess a fascination which is not to be found in more elaborate verse. Though solemnly serious and devoid of wit and humour, they are utterly true, so far as they go, to human nature, and quite stripped of false sentiment and affectation. In many ways—which there is no space here further to illustrate—they bring us into immediate contact with the antique, pagan, savage, superstitious, elemental characteristics of our race. They have to some extent embalmed for us the essence of old forgotten romances, and the essence of what the old romances embalmed—the sentiments, passions, beliefs, forms of thought, and imaginative wonder and dread of our pagan ancestors. Now little more than a merely imperfect echo of perished literatures, of extinct superstitions, of generations whose codes of honour and conduct were perhaps both better and worse than our own, or of feats and adventures which were, many of them, of merely tribal or local interest; mangled also in form, and distorted as to fact though they often are—the voice of the past speaks in them more authentically than it often does in the most elaborate of histories.

The late Mr. Chappell, in his *Popular Music of the Olden Time*, has successfully enough demonstrated the close connection between English and Scottish popular music from the fifteenth century, but the inference that the connection was mainly of a one-sided character is not such an absolute certainty as he very much takes for granted; for it rests mainly on negative evidence, on the scarcity, namely, of early music preserved in old Scottish MSS. and attached to Scottish words; and this negative

Reciprocal connection of England and Scotland as regards music and song.

evidence is vitiated by the fact that such MSS. must at one time have existed. There is abundant proof of the cultivation of music, both secular and sacred, in Scotland down until towards the close of the sixteenth century. Moreover, a large number of the tunes mentioned in *Colkelbie's Sow*, in *The Complaynt of Scotland*, and in various poems of the old Scottish 'makaris,' as well as of the songs parodied in *The Gude and Godlie Ballates*, are not, as matter of fact, known to be of English origin; and there is in reality no proof that in early times the influence of the two countries, as regards music and song, was not entirely reciprocal.

The Huntis Up, for example, is mentioned in *The Complaynt of Scotland*; and on this fact Dr. Furnivall[1] comments: 'This is a lively English tune well fitted for dancers, printed in Mr. Chappell's *Popular Music*, i. 60,' and he

'The Huntis Up.' Is it Scots or English?

further states that the first mention of the tune is in 1537. Chappell also, on the authority of Puttenham (1587)—who mentioned that one Gray made such a

---

[1] Notes to the *Complaynt of Scotland* (Early English Text Society's ed.), p. lxxxvii, and in *Captain Cox* (Ballad Society), p. clxiii.

ballad in the time of Henry VIII.—supposes that Gray is the original author of the song parodied by John Thorne, and in *The Gude and Godlie Ballates*; but the mere statement of Puttenham is in itself very flimsy evidence, especially when the much earlier existence of the song in Scotland is clearly proved by a line in Robert Henryson's fable of *The Wolf, the Foxe, and the Cadzear*:—

'The Cadzear sang Hunts up, up on hie.'

These *Fables* were probably all written before 1480, by which date, therefore, *The Huntis Up* was already in Scotland what would now be called a folk-song! Since, moreover, it was known as a dance tune among the country people of Scotland before 1549, and is parodied in *The Gude and Godlie Ballates*, which were, many of them, of as early a date as this, is it not as likely to have been of Scottish as of English origin, and all the more that, as we learn from *Habbie Simson*, *Hunts Up* was a favourite tune of the Scottish pipers? The truth is, that of the popular songs and music of the earlier centuries our knowledge is so fragmentary that definite and decided conclusions as to origin are very apt to be delusive.

Dealing with a later period, Chappell also (very justly) regretted the confusion between English and Scottish popular tunes and songs, caused by the methods of Ramsay in *The Tea Table Miscellany*, 1724, etc., of Thomson in *Orpheus Caledonius*, 1725, and Oswald in *Scots Airs*, 1740, and other musical publications—a confusion which was further aggravated by the comments and assertions of many subsequent editors, including especially Stenhouse,[1] whose many sins of omission and commission were only partly rectified by David Laing;[2] but did English broadside and chapbook literature owe practically nothing, as Chappell asserted, to old Scottish tunes and songs? Chappell scouted the very notion that any Anglo-Scottish ballad or song could derive in any way from a Scots original. He referred to them as 'that numerous class of songs and ballads which before the Union of the Crowns had been called "Northern"—a polite substitute for "rustic"—and which under Scottish kings were gradually denominated "Scotch."' 'The change,' he further added, 'may be said to have commenced after Charles II. had been crowned King of Scots.'[3] Of course it was only by such a theory that he could eliminate Scottish songs and tunes from Anglo-Scottish broadsides. Still, though dictated by antecedent conviction rather than derived from an exhaustive preliminary study of the facts, the explanation may be partly true; but (1) a tune may be termed 'Northern' from mere carelessness; (2) tunes are generally termed 'Northern' when the subject of the ballad is not merely 'rustic,' but 'Northern'; (3) 'Northern' is the

The Anglo-Scottish ballad. Its origin. Chappell's theory.

---

[1] *Notes to Johnson's Musical Museum*, 1853.

[2] *Supplementary Notes.*

[3] *Roxburghe Ballads*, iii. 433.

proper designation of tunes common to the North of England and the Lowlands of Scotland;[1] (4) there is no evidence of any change in the method of naming the tunes of individual ballads; and (5) broadsides printed at a much earlier date than the Restoration were written to 'pleasant Scotch tunes,' as *The Northern Lasse*, of which a copy in the Euing Collection was printed before 1629.

This very ballad set to a pleasant Scotch tune called *The Broom of Cowden Knowes*, was, with strange maladroitness, selected by Chappell[2] to illustrate his theory that so-called 'Scotch tunes' are merely English rustic tunes. 'The evidence that the tune is "Scotch" rests,' he said, on this ballad, 'for in other ballads to the same air it is not so described; and Burton, in his *Anatomy of Melancholy*, quotes "O the broom, the bony, bony broom" as a country tune' [as no doubt it was, whether Scotch or English]. And Chappell further adds: '*The Broom of Cowden Knowes* is in the metre of, and evidently suggested by, the older ballad of *New Broom on Hill*.[3] A copy of the original *Broom on Hill* may even yet be discovered, or at least an earlier copy of the tune,

'The Broom of Cowden Knowes.'

---

[1] Chappell, in *Popular Music* (p. 613), objected to the possibility of *Brome on Hill* being Scots for the reason that it is 'not on the incomplete scale which is commonly called Scotch'; but only a small percentage of Scots tunes are on this scale, and indeed tunes common to the North of England and Scotland have no peculiarities to distinguish them from Southern tunes.

[2] *Popular Music*, p. 613.

[3] Black-letter in the Pepys Collection.

and thus set the question at rest.' But (1) though *Broom, broom on hill*, is mentioned by Laneham [1] (1575) as an ancient song in the possession of Captain Cox, it is also mentioned in *The Complaynt of Scotland* (1549) as a well-known Scottish dance; and it is therefore by no means evident that the discovery of an ancient copy of the tune—which may have been long common to both countries—would set the question at rest; (2) even were the tune originally English, it plainly was well known long before 1549 in Scotland, and most likely had been set to Scots words, which, though not known to Ramsay [2]—who allowed a vamp of *The Northern Lasse* to appear in *The Tea Table Miscellany*,—may have been brought to England shortly after the Union of the Crowns; (3) the title 'Northern Lasse,' cannot mean merely 'Rustic Lasse,' any more than the phrase 'north countrie' can mean 'rustic countrie'; (4) not only is the ballad set 'to a pleasant Scotch tune called *The Broome of Cowden Knowes,*' but it introduces 'Cowden Knowes,' of the 'North Countrie,' into the chorus:—

'With O, the broome, the bony broome,
The broome of Cowden Knowes,
Fain would I be in the North Countrie,
To milk my dady's ewes';

---

[1] See *Captain Cox*, ed. Furnivall (Ballad Society), pp. cxxviii-ix.
[2] There is a traditional ballad *The Broom o' the Cowden Knowes*, but its origin is involved in dubiety, the earliest printed fragments —*Bonny May*, in Herd's Collection, 1769—making no reference to Cowden Knowes.

and (5) the ballad actually begins,

> ' Through Liddersdale as lately I went.'

Yet Chappell—who apparently had never heard of the Homes ' who dwelt on " Leader side," ' nor of ' Leader haughs and Yarrow,' nor of Colden Knowes, the old keep of the Homes on the broom-covered braes (or ' knowes,' that is, knolls) of the Leader— had little difficulty in concluding that both Liddersdale and Cowden Knowes—about the meaning of which he showed no curiosity—were somehow the invention solely of the balladist, and that the ballad —tune, chorus, first line and everything—was wholly English !

Similarly, it is a mere assumption that the black-letter *Jockey's Escape from Bony Dundee*,[1] is wholly

---

[1] The tune *Adew Dundee* is in the Skene MS., which does not of course prove it to be Scottish, though the Scottish title is all in favour of this conclusion. As to the lateness of the Skene MS., Chappell failed to prove that the fifth and sixth parts of the Skene MS. are later than D'Urfey. That the tune *Adew Dundee* did not appear in *The Dancing Master* until 1688 proves nothing, and that *The Three Sheep-Skins*, ' an English Country Dance,' did not appear in the same work until 1697 proves as little, for it might take some time to be known if of Northern origin. But Chappell brought forward, in addition, an objection which he regarded as absolutely fatal : that the Skene MS. contained *Peggy is over the Sea with the Soldier*, which ' derives its name,' he said, ' from a common Aldermary Churchyard ballad, to which no earlier date than 1710 can reasonably be assigned.' Certainly this would have been fatal—only it was not true, and this Chappell himself proved, though he failed to note its bearing on the antiquity of the Skene MS.—by discovering the unique and much earlier black-letter *Constant, Faire, and Fine Betty*, ' to the tune of *Peggy went over Sea with a Soldiour* ' (*Roxburghe Ballads*, i. 207), and a little later he edited the ballad of ' *The Soldiour and Peggy* to a new Northern

the creation of D'Urfey, who never elsewhere did anything like the chorus 'Come fill up my cup,' etc., which Scott borrowed. Nor though the only known Scottish version of *'Twas within a mile o' Edinburgh Toon* [1] is modern, can we believe that D'Urfey had no original Scots model for *'Twas within a Furlong of Edinburgh Town*, any more than we can believe that the tune of *The Liggan Waters*, to which the black-letter ballad of *The Bonny Scottish* (not 'Scotch'!) *Lad and the Yielding Lass* is set, has somehow, as Chappell [2] deemed it necessary for his theory's sake to suggest, reference to the Irish not to the Scottish Logan Water; or that D'Urfey's *Scotch Wedding* is the original of *The Blythesome Bridal*; or that

Other Anglo-Scottish ballads founded on Scottish tavern ditties.

---

tune,' which ballad, he said, 'may be dated as within the first half of the seventeenth century' (*Roxburghe Ballads*, ii. 475). Further, he mentioned in his introduction to this last ballad that 'the only known copy of the tune is in the form of an arrangement for the lute ; it is included among the Skene manuscripts.' So that the only copy of this English tune is that preserved in a Scots MS. !

[1] Chappell, to prove that the 'Scotch tunes,' that 'were popular in England, were mostly spurious,' and the words 'invariably so,' quotes from *A Second Tale of a Tub*: 'Each party call for particular tunes . . . the blue bonnets' [*i.e.* Scotch], 'had very good voices, but, being at the further end of the room, were not distinctly heard. Yet they split their throats in hollowing out *Bonny Dundee, Valiant Jockey, Sawny was a dawdy Lad*, and *'Twas within a furlong of Edinburgh town*'; but can we believe that the Scots would 'hollow out' the Anglo-Scots rubbish of the broadsidists in ridicule of themselves? And does the quotation not rather prove that the Scots tunes and songs became known in London by the custom of the Scots to 'hollow' them out in taverns and elsewhere?

[2] *Roxburghe Ballads*, iii. 475.

the various versions of the *Jock and Jenny* broadsides have no connection with the old Scots song in
the Bannatyne MS.[1] The truth, on the contrary, is
that the broadsidists, being by no means inventive in
their themes, were glad to borrow whenever they had
opportunity; while it is also very plain that they
were much amused, not merely by certain specimens
of the Scot they met in taverns, but by the peculiar
ditties which those 'bluecaps' were accustomed to
' hollow out.'

Of the transformation of a Scottish song into an
Anglo-Scottish one, Mr. Ebsworth has unwittingly

Mr. Ebsworth's inadvertent example of an Anglicised Scottish song. supplied a very striking example—an
example which sheds a flood of light on
the subject. In *The Roxburghe Ballads*[2]
he printed from Monmouth's *Manu-
script Note Book*[3] what he termed 'A Scotch Song,
1679,' remarking that it was 'probably a distinct
Scotch song, learned orally in 1679 and written down
then or afterwards; not yet found elsewhere, or in
print.'[4] But in the course of editing the Roxburghe

[1] See *ante*, p. 289.   [2] Vol. iv. p. 544.

[3] Now No. 1527 of the Egerton MS. in the British Museum.

[4] Part of it was, however, in print, the last stanza forming the
first of a version of *Wallifou fa' the Cat*, in Herd's *Songs*, ii. 139:—

> ' There was a bonnie wi' laddie
>   Was keeping a bonny whine sheep ;
> There was a bonnie wee lassie
>   Was wading the water sae deep.
> Was wading the water sae deep,
>   And a little above her knee ;
> The laddie cries unto the lassie,
>   Come down Tweedside to me.'

ballads, Mr. Ebsworth discovered the Anglo-Scots
transmogrification of the ditty in *A New Song of
Moggie's Jealousie or Jockie's Vindication*,[1] and in
the introduction to it he remarked: 'We have
shown that the Duke of Monmouth had been impressed with this song either in 1679, when he was
in Scotland, or at least early in 1685, when he was in
Holland, thus he jotted down several of the stanzas
from memory.   Compare the true text now given with
the memoranda of vol. iv. p. 544.'   Now (1) the black-
letter song *Moggie* was only registered 1st June
1684, so that Monmouth could certainly not have
jotted it down in 1679, nor, probably, even in Holland
in 1685; (2) the song jotted down by Monmouth—
three stanzas only in all—contains two stanzas not to be
found in *Moggie*, and Mr. Ebsworth's second thoughts,[2]
when first confronted with the Anglo - Scottish
Moggie, that the Monmouth piece is 'three verses of
two Scottish songs intermixed,' cannot be regarded
as 'happy,' not only because all three stanzas are in
the same measure, but because the first stanza—
which, with the second stanza, he now regards as
belonging to a different song from the third, and
having nothing whatever to do with *Moggie*—begins
'Wilt thou be wilful still?' which is actually the
alternative designation of the tune appended to
Moggie! (3) the third stanza, which he finally regards as an 'imperfect copy' from *Moggie*, could not

[1] *Roxburghe Ballads*, vi. 170.
[2] *Ibid.*, v. 393.

have been copied from that Anglo-Scottish version, for the very sufficient reason that *Moggie* contains no reference to the Tweed as in the Monmouth stanza; a fact which further shows that the Herd version could not have been got from *Moggie*, but that, on the contrary, the Herd and Monmouth stanzas derive from a common Scottish original; (4) notwithstanding imperfections in spelling, and mistakes in regard to words, the Monmouth song is clearly not an Anglo-Scottish, but a purely Scottish version; and (5) it is impossible to believe that the ballad hack could have written *Moggie*, such as it is, without the aid of some Scots original.

It would therefore seem that their startling discoveries of the methods of Ramsay and his successors, and of the unfounded nature of many of Stenhouse's statements, tended to produce in the minds of Chappell, Mr. Ebsworth, and Dr. Furnivall, a reaction towards the other extreme. They have thus committed themselves to opinions which are confuted by their own subsequent researches; and Mr. Ebsworth's inadvertent illustration of the fallacious character of their general inferences renders great caution necessary in accepting conclusions against the Scottish origin of songs and tunes, even when such evidence as we possess may seem to render their spuriousness almost certain. It is, for example, more than likely, on the evidence, that *My Jo Janet* in *The Orpheus Caledonius* and *The Tea Table Mis-*

Great caution necessary in accepting conclusions against the Scottish origin of songs on mere negative evidence.

cellany was vamped from the black-letter broadside *Jenny, Jenny*,[1] but even if it was, the black-letter was in all likelihood itself vamped from a Scots original, for not only has the chorus a very Scottish jingle, but the tune to which it is set in *The Orpheus* is found in the Straloch MS. (1627-29). Moreover, the Scots word 'Keek'—'Keek in the well'—is actually printed 'Kit,' which raises the suspicion that the broadside hack himself, the author of the ballad, did not understand the meaning of the word.[2]

The significance of these illustrations—which might easily be multiplied—from the black-letter broadsides is that they indicate (1) the existence in Scotland, in the seventeenth century or earlier, of a great variety of now forgotten native lyrics, most of them coloured with the ingenuous indelicacy which, more or less, tinges all our early literature, and some of them very much akin to the ditties collected by Burns, and partly preserved in the volume known as *The Merry Muses*; and (2) that while Ramsay,

Anglo-Scottish ballads in the broadsides, evidence of the existence at one time of many Scottish lyrics now forgotten. But later Scottish song greatly influenced by broadside literature.

Thomson, Oswald, and others borrowed much from English sources, it is (*a*) by no means certain that they always borrow when they seem to borrow, and

---

[1] Printed in *The Roxburghe Ballads*, ed. Ebsworth, vol. vii. p. 350.

[2] Similarly, in *Moggie* we have 'a win sheep,' for 'a wheen [*i.e.* a number of] sheep,' showing that the balladist did not understand the meaning of the words he borrowed—borrowed, undoubtedly, from a Scottish ditty.

(*b*) it is perfectly certain that they often merely borrowed what had previously been pilfered. That they did borrow a great deal is, however, beyond doubt; and, indeed, from the time of Ramsay down to and including Burns, the stream of Scottish popular song—whether as regards words or music—ceased to be of purely Scottish origin, and in many ways—ways that are as yet but imperfectly and confusedly disclosed—is intermingled with the stream of broadside and chapbook literature which reached its highest water-mark in the eighteenth century.

This is especially true of the Jacobite songs—even of those of Burns, Hogg, and others, whose interest in Jacobitism was distant and mainly sentimental. As for the contemporary Jacobite songs, they owe the most of what excellence they possess—and poetically it is very little—to other lyrics. Of that marvellous patchwork, Hogg's *Jacobite Relics*, Chappell remarked that half of the songs in the first volume were derived from 'English printed collections,'[1] and that 'if the modern were taken away, and only the old suffered to remain, the proportion would be much greater.' Many Jacobite songs, also, which Hogg got from MSS. and greatly improved, as well as many Jacobite songs still in MS., were originally, of course, of English origin. But whether the product of Englishman or Scot, the bulk of contemporary Jacobite minstrelsy is merely parody—parody sometimes of older political or

Jacobite songs chiefly parodies.

[1] *Popular Music*, p. 611.

cavalier songs which themselves were parodies, parody even of older Jacobite songs, and parody of very old improper lyrics, Scottish or English;[1] and in their turn these Jacobite parodies, only a few of them in the Scots vernacular, have had no inconsiderable influence on the non-Jacobite vernacular songs of Scotland.

Of the older lyrics of Scotland only a few survive in their entirety. Several have been referred to under ANONYMOUS POETRY (see *ante,* pp. 289-98), and in connection with *The Gude and Godlie Ballates* (see *ante,* pp. 270-74). Others are included in *The Tea Table Miscellany* and Thomson's *Orpheus Caledonius,* very much, perhaps, as they existed before the days of Ramsay and Thomson. Regarding the date of the older lyrics in those publications it would be rash to hazard an opinion, though the humorous *Cock Laird*—which Ramsay slightly altered,—the still more amusing *Maggie's Tocher,* the picturesque *Muirland Willie, My Jocky Blyth, The Fumbler's Rant, What Jocky said to Jenny, John Ochiltree, Andro and his Cutty Gun, The Auld Goodman, The Auld Wife beyond the Fire, Auld Rob Morris,* and that inimitable lay of the sodden tippler, *Toddlin But and Toddlin Ben*—to name the more notable only,—were probably written long before the days of

[margin: The older lyrics.]

---

[1] Such, for example, was undoubtedly *O'er the Water to Charlie,* an old blackguard London song being probably its ultimate source. Jacobite versions of it, and other interesting examples of unimproved Jacobite songs, will be found in *Loyal Songs,* 1750, and *The True Loyalist* (rare), 1779.

Ramsay.   Again, the delightful *On Ettrick Banks*,
since it assumes some amount of prosperity at the ports
of Leith and the 'Broomielaw,' was probably written
after the Union; while that most animated of lyrics,
Maggie Lauder, can scarce be earlier than the first half
of the eighteenth century.   As for *The Gaberlunzie
Man* and *The Jolly Beggar*, the former from its rhythm
cannot be so old as the days of James v., while the
latter, first printed in Herd's *Songs* (1769), seems to
have been unknown as a Scottish song to Ramsay,
and has some connection with an English broadside
in the Pepys Collection :[1]—

> 'There was a jovial beggar man,
>   A-begging he was bound,
> And he did seek his living
>   In country and in town,' etc.

Several of the older Scottish lyrics were also amended,
and in various ways utilised, by Ramsay (see under
RAMSAY, *post*, p. 405), but many, very many, of the
older lyrics have either wholly perished, or survive
only as catchwords, or first lines, or isolated stanzas,
or choruses, or refrains.[2]

Yet notwithstanding this seeming break in the tradition of the older songs, they, rather than either the
national lyrics of England or the broadside literature
of the English taverns, have been the formative in-

---

[1] This fact was first pointed out by Mr. Ebsworth in *Bagford
Ballads*, i. 216.

[2] See especially 'Fragments of Comic and Humorous Songs,' in
Herd's *Songs*, vol. ii. pp. 200-239 ; and also for unpublished ones,
the Herd MS. in the British Museum.

fluence of not all, but decidedly all that is best, in
later Scottish song. Compared with the many waters
of English lyrism, Scottish vernacular *The excellency*
song is the mere tinkling of a mountain *of Scottish*
rivulet; but as popular song it is in *popular song*
—its causes.
a manner unrivalled—unrivalled partly, it is true,
because of Burns, but by no means on this account
alone, for Burns himself stole

> 'fire
> From the fountains of the past
> To glorify the present.'

The old 'makaris' of the fifteenth and sixteenth
centuries, and bards and minstrels whose very names
have perished: these were its original creators and
fashioners, and it was dowered with much of its rare
excellency by inheritance from a poetry which was
not popular in the merely vulgar sense, but the work
of artists of special training and accomplishment.
For many generations the influence of the old
poetic school seemed to be dormant, but its very
suppression, and the denial by the Kirk of the liberty
of new poetic utterance, tended to preserve the old
poetic tradition as it was when the voices of those
old 'makaris' became silent. Thus Scottish vernacular song is more closely linked to the past than
the popular 'minstrelsie' of England; and while it
represents more fully the national sentiments, associa-
tions, and memories, it includes many numbers which,
homely, simple, and popular though they be, bear the
hall-mark of an ancient and noble descent.

XII

BEFORE RAMSAY

'POLEMO-MIDDINIA'—THE SEMPILLS—'TWEEDSIDE'—
LADY GRIZEL BAILLIE—LADY WARDLAW—WILLIAM
HAMILTON OF GILBERTFIELD—WATSON'S 'CHOICE
COLLECTION.'

DURING the seventeenth century the fortunes of
Scottish vernacular literature had reached their
lowest ebb. It was primarily an age of
religious conflict, the old contest between
Kirk and King for supremacy cul-
minating, after the Cromwellian episode
and the Stuart restoration, in the
Covenanting persecution, which was again followed,
after the Revolution, by what, though ostensibly a
victory for the Kirk, was in reality a compromise—a
compromise which inflicted a mortal wound on the
Kirk's pretensions, and inaugurated an era marked
by its gradually decaying authority in the sphere of
general politics, and its diminishing interference with
the intellectual and moral independence of the individual. Up to and even beyond the Revolution,
the Kirk—whether struggling desperately to make

Vernacular literature of the seventeenth century. Repressive influences of the Kirk.

386

the Scottish Solomon its mere tool, or triumphant at
last over Charles I., or subdued and then patronised
by Cromwell, or harried and afflicted by Charles II.
and James II., or nominally restored to power at the
Revolution—remained the supreme social and intellectual guide of almost the whole community, and
its influence was inimical to every form of secular
literature. As regards the vernacular literature, its
repressive tendencies were also accidentally aided by
the accession of James VI. to the English throne in
1603. In the later years of the sixteenth century
vernacular poetry owed its production mainly to
the fostering care of the king; but even before his
departure for England James had himself almost
escaped from his Scottish chrysalis. The old Scottish
vernacular poetry was not eclipsed by the Elizabethan
poetry of England simply because (1) in Scotland
the succession of vernacular poets and interest in
vernacular poetry had all but ceased, and (2) English
poetry was not generally read in Scotland.

The chief Scottish poets of the early seventeenth
century were Sir Robert Ayton, Sir William Alexander,
Earl of Stirling, Sir David Murray of   The chief Scot-
Gorthie, Sir Robert Kerr, Earl of Ancrum,   tish poets of
the early
and William Drummond of Hawthornden.   seventeenth
They all wrote in English; and since,   century wrote
in English.
with the exception of Drummond, they   'Polemo-
Middinia.'
had all gone south with James I., their aim, like that
of their royal master, was to be as English as possible.
Of them only Ayton and Drummond rise above a

very verbose mediocrity; but Ayton certainly does, if he wrote *I do confess thou'rt smooth and fair*, and Drummond (1585-1649) was one of the most accomplished, if not one of the most inspired, poets of his time.   He is, however, outside our present consideration, except as the possible author[1] of the macaronic poem, *Polemo-Middinia* [Midden-Fight] *inter Vitarvam* [Scot of Scotstarvet and his followers] *et Nibernam*[2] [Cunningham of Newbarns].   It describes how the Scotstarvet people, who claimed a right-of-way past the mansion-house of Newbarns, endeavoured to assert it by setting out with a procession of dung-carts, headed by a piper and banners, and how they were dispersed and routed by the valiancy of the Newbarns women.   The rustic battle is described in a dog-Latin—the dog being cross-bred, that is, half Scots and half English —which partly obscures the occasionally very plain language of the piece.   The defiance of Niberna (the

---

[1] It might—only he is not known to have had connection with Fife—have been written by Sir William Scott of Thirlestane (1670?-1725), who specially practised macaronic verse.   Some of those pieces are still in MS., but one is included in his *Selecta Poemata*, published with some Latin poems by Dr. Archibald Pitcairne in 1727.   It is entitled *Ad E—M E—M Equitem, M.D., Villadelphinus Frater*, and begins—

> 'Qualis in terris fabulatur Orpheus
> Natus Irlandis, ubi nulla wivat
> Spidera telam, neque foeda spouttat
>   Toedda venenum.'

Scott has also been credited with the authorship both of *Maggie Lauder* and *The Blythesome Bridal*.

[2] Printed at Edinburgh, 1684, and reprinted along with *Christis Kirk*, ed. Gibson, 1691.   Usually included in Drummond's *Works*.

mistress of Newbarns) is, however, though pithy, quite quotable :—

> ' Ite ait, uglaei felloes ; si quis modo post hac
> Muckifer has nostras tentet crossare fenestras,
> Juro ego quod ejus longum extrahabo thropellum,
> Et totum rivabo faciem luggasque gulaeo hoc,
> Ex capite cuttabo, ferox, totumque videbo
> Heartbloodum fluere in terram.'

From the mere fact that the Scottish vernacular is now the language of the common people, a vague impression prevails that the vernacular poetry has some special connection with the mere peasantry; but though latterly this was partly the case, the old poetry, on which the later vernacular poetry is almost entirely modelled, was rather the creation of the aristocracy and the clergy. Barbour was archdeacon of Aberdeen; Henryson, a learned educationist, was probably in holy orders; Dunbar was a secular priest, and Douglas a bishop, and both they and Kennedy were of noble descent; Sir David Lyndsay was a Fife laird; Montgomerie was a cadet of the Eglinton family; and Scott, whose descent is unknown, was a town gallant and courtier. Most or all of these poets were specially patronised by royalty, and they wrote for the delectation of the better classes. So must have done the innominate authors of many of the older songs. Most of those preserved in *The Tea Table Miscellany*, such as *Maggie's Tocher, The Cock Laird, Jocky said to Jenny, Toddlin But and Toddlin Ben*, and *The Blythesome*

[margin note:] Vernacular poetry not specially connected with the peasantry until after Ramsay.

Bridal, depict the humours of rustic life from the standpoint of the upper and educated classes, not of the peasant. The simplicity and realism of the old vernacular poetry belonged to the olden time; it is in no sense a vulgarised literature, but merely a literature which, by its antique sincerity and lack of convention, can be appreciated even by the peasants of later generations.

But the old race of poet-ecclesiastics having become extinct at the Reformation, it was mainly

The poetry of the revival, before Ramsay, owes its existence to the gentry.

among the aristocracy and gentry that the traditions of the old vernacular poetry could linger; and although, as we have seen, with the accession of James VI. to the English throne there was a tendency among the Scottish courtier poets to cultivate exclusively English poetry, many of the gentry retained an acquaintanceship with the poetry of the older 'makaris.' They were not so much as the other classes under the domination of Puritanism; and thus the poetry of the vernacular revival, up to the time of Ramsay, owes its existence mainly to them.

Whether, during the first half of the seventeenth century, the vernacular muse was wholly silent or

Robert Sempill (1595?-1660?) author of 'Habbie Simson.'

not, there is no authentic record of its voice until we hear it in *The Life and Death of Habbie Simson, the Piper of Kilbarchan.* The poet who thus broke the long silence was Robert Sempill, son of Sir James Sempill of Beltrees, author of *The Packman's Pater-*

noster (not in the vernacular, and therefore outside our consideration), and grandson of 'John Sempill [son of the great Lord Sempill] the dancer' of Knox's *History*, who married Marie Livingstone, one of the Queen's Maries, and, according to Knox, 'surnamed the Lusty.' Born about 1595, he was educated at the University of Glasgow, where he matriculated in 1613. As *Habbie* might suggest, he sided with Charles I. against the Kirk, serving as a cavalier officer, and he was afterwards active in promoting the Restoration. *Habbie* is supposed to date about 1640, and its author died between 1660 and 1669.

That Sempill was well read in the old vernacular poetry—of which he must have possessed specimens in MS.—is very evident from the stanza he selected for *Habbie*, a stanza of which so few examples in the older vernacular *'Habbie Simson.' Its influence on later verse.* are now preserved (see *ante*, p. 244), that, not perhaps Ramsay (who knew the Bannatyne MS.), though he named the poem 'Standard *Habbie*,' but most other editors, until quite recently, have been in the habit of crediting Sempill with its invention. The poem, as poetry, is in no way remarkable, but it affords us a curious glimpse of old village amusements and customs; and the description of Habbie and his doings is in a way quite admirable, genial appreciation being finely tempered with pawky humour. Here in three stanzas are three separate glimpses of the piper in his pride :—

'At fairs he play'd before the spear-men,
  All gaily graithed in their gear man :
  Steel bonnets, jacks, and swords so clear then
     Like ony bead :
  Now wha will play before such weir-men,
     Sen Habbie's dead.

At clark-plays when he wont to come,
  His pipe played trimly to the drum ;
  Like bikes of bees he gart it hum,
     And tun'd his reed :
  Now all our pipers may sing dumb,
     Sen Habbie's dead.

And at Horse Races many a day,
  Before the black, the brown, the gray,
  He gart his pipe, when he did play,
     Baith skirl and skreed :
  Now all such pastime's quite away,
     Sen Habbie's dead.'

(marginal glosses: clad; accoutrements; war-since; made)

The *Epitaph on Sanny Briggs*, who was Habbie's nephew, and butler to the Sempills, is usually attributed to the same author, and was, no doubt, either his or his son's. *Habbie* became the model for humorous elegy in the vernacular : being widely circulated in broadsides towards the close of the century, it was imitated by many poetasters, as well as by Hamilton of Bangour, Ramsay, Fergusson, and Burns ; and since, in addition, it reintroduced the most characteristic stanza of later vernacular poetry, the stanza which was the vehicle for much of the best verse of the three latter poets, it has some claims to rank as one of the 'epoch-making' productions of poetic literature.

The poetic tradition of the Sempills was continued by Sir Robert's son Francis, whose longest poem is *The Banishment of Povertie,* narrating his hard shifts as debtor until relieved by the Duke of Albany shortly after he had taken refuge in the debtors' retreat at Holyrood. Written in the French octave, it is correct in rhythm and rhyme, but its wit is not very sprightly; and one can scarce credit that the same author wrote either *The Blythesome Bridal* (which may, however, have been written by the father), or the very much cleverer *Maggie Lauder.* His claims to the authorship of *She rose and let me in,* published by D'Urfey, will not bear examination; and if he has any connection with the oldest known version of *Auld Lang Syne,* it was probably merely as the refurbisher of an older song, for the original broadside bears the title 'An excellent proper ballad, entitled *Old Long Syne.* Newly corrected and amended, with a large and new addition of several excellent love lines.'[1]

Francis
Sempill
(d. 1685).

Before Ramsay we have various other indications either of a revived interest in vernacular poetry, or that it had all along been cultivated and appreciated by many in private, but the principal names associated with it previous to him are Lady Grizel Baillie, Lady Wardlaw, and William

'Tweedside.'

[1] This broadside, published anonymously, contains what was, no doubt, the burden of the old song ; and this burden, together with the first line of the broadside, is the main germ of Burns's song.

Hamilton of Gilbertfield. The song *Tweedside*, Burns mentions, is 'said to have been written by Lord Yester,' and Robert Chambers[1] affirms that this must have 'been John, eventually second Marquis of Tweeddale' (1615-1713), because Scott of Satchells, in his *History of the House of Scott*, compliments the Marquis on 'his poetical abilities'; but Herd, who first published the song, and is the only authority for the text, knew apparently nothing of its author, and merely termed it *The Original Tweedside*. But whoever wrote it seems almost to smirk while expressing doleful despair, and, where he is not inapt, he is wofully commonplace.

This certainly cannot be said of *Werena my Heart Licht I wad Dee*[2] by Lady Grizel Baillie. Lady

Ladie Grizel Baillie (1746).

Grizel, born in 1665, was the eldest daughter of Patrick Hume, afterwards Earl of Marchmont; and when her father had, in 1684, to go into hiding under the family vault in Polwarth Church on account of his suspected connection with the Rye-House Plot, she secretly supplied him with food. From 1686 until the Revolution the family were in exile in Holland. After her return she married, in 1692, George Baillie of Jerviswood, son of Robert Baillie, who, being suspected like her father of conspiring against the Government, was, in 1684, caught and executed. Lady Grizel died in 1746. Lady Murray

---

[1] *Scottish Songs*, iii. 311.

[2] First published in *The Tea Table Miscellany*.

of Stanhope, Lady Grizel's daughter, in her *Memoirs* [1]
stated that she possessed a MS. volume of her
mother's containing various of her songs and poetic
fragments; but the volume has not been recovered,
and she is known only as the authoress of *Werena
my Heart Licht*, and a fragment, *The Ewe-Buchtin's
Bonnie*. [2] The mournful romance and inimitable
simplicity of the former song indicate the inspiration and art of true genius; and *The Ewe-Buchtin's
Bonnie* is very much in the same manner, and possesses the same delicate charm :—

> ' The Ewe-buchtin 's bonnie, baith e'enin' and morn,
>   When our blithe shepherds play on the bag-reed and horn ;
>   While we 're milking, they 're lilting, baith pleasant and clear,
>   But my heart 's like to break when I think on my dear.'

Lady Elizabeth Halkett, daughter of Sir Charles
Halkett of Pitferran, and married, in 1696, to Henry
Wardlaw of Pitreavie, is now regarded as
the author of the ballad *Hardyknute*.
First published by James Watson, in 1719,
Lady Wardlaw (1677-1727).
as a genuine old ballad, it was included in Percy's
Reliques, 1767. The story circulated by her brother-
in-law, Sir John Hope Bruce of Kinross, was that it
had been got from an old manuscript in a vault in
Dunfermline ; but its antiquity being questioned
after its appearance in the *Reliques*, Lord Hailes

[1] Published in 1822.
[2] First published on a broadsheet by C. K. Sharpe. The original
consists of only two stanzas, the others being additions by another
author

informed Percy that Lady Wardlaw had confessed to being the authoress of it. The ballad is certainly a very clever imitation of the older minstrelsy. It is plain that Lady Wardlaw had a wide acquaintance with the old ballads, and it is thus not improbable that she improved a good many of them. That *Hardyknute* is not by any means equal to many of those with which she may have tampered may be explained by the fact that it was wholly invention, and also by the probability that she endeavoured, in this case, to imitate the old simplicity, while in other cases her main endeavour may have been to improve the poetical defects of the versions she got from recitation. Here, for example, is a quatrain from *Hardyknute*:—

> 'On Norway's coast the widowed dame
>   May wash the rocks with tears—
> May lang look o'er the shipless seas
>   Before her mate appears.'

It cannot compare with the following stanza from *Sir Patrick Spens*:—

> 'O lang, lang may the ladies stand
>   Wi' their gold kems in their hair,
> Waiting for their ain deir lords,
>   For they'll se thame na mair';

but then we cannot tell what original suggestion Lady Wardlaw—if she improved *Sir Patrick Spens*—may have had for the stanza.

But the main link in the succession between the Sempills and Ramsay is William Hamilton of Gil-

bertfield, whose *Last Dying Words of Bonnie Heck*
(a famous Fife greyhound) first appeared in Watson's
Choice Collection, 1706. This piece (whose William
chief merit is its sportsmanly sympathy Hamilton
of Gilbertfield
with the greyhound), a variation on (1665 ?-1751).
Sempill's *Habbie*, became, in turn, the special model
of Burns's *Death and Dying Words of Poor Mailie*,
as before Burns it had been of Ramsay's *Last Speech
of a Dying Miser* and *Luckie Spence's Last Advice.*
Hamilton, a retired lieutenant in the army, afterwards made the acquaintance of Ramsay, with whom
he corresponded in that series of rather clever
rhyming epistles (included in Ramsay's *Works*) in the
same stanza which Burns, in his 'emulating' fashion,
also adopted for his poetic epistles, even parodying,
occasionally, Hamilton's phrases and sentiments.[1]

In his first epistle Hamilton signed himself 'Wanton

---

[1] Compare the first stanza of Hamilton's *Epistle II.* :—

> 'When I received thy kind epistle
> It made me dance, and sing, and whistle ;
> O sic a fike and sic a fistle
> I had about it !
> That e'er was knight of the Scots thistle
> Sae fain I doubted '—

compare the above with the last stanza of Burns's *First Epistle to
Lapraik* :—

> 'And to conclude my lang epistle,
> As my auld pen's worn to the grissle,
> Twa lines frae you wad gar me fissle,
> Who am most fervent,
> While I can either sing or whistle,
> Your humble servant.'

And many similar comparisons might be made.

Willy,' and under the signature ' W. W.' he contributed
to *The Tea Table Miscellany* the song *Willy was a*
Wanton Wag, suggested and more by the

'Wanton Willy.'

English *O Willy was so blythe a Lad* (in
Playford's *Choice Ayres*, 1650), but full of humorous
abandon, as for instance :—

gold

'And was not Willy well worth gowd ?
  He wan the love of great and sma' ;
For after he the bride had kiss'd

whole

  He kiss'd the lasses hale-sale a'.

rolled

Sae merrily round the ring they row'd,

by

  When be the hand he led them a',
And smack on smack on them bestow'd
  By virtue of a standing law.'

But the greatest, if not the best, achievement of
Hamilton was his abridgment and paraphrase or

Abridgment of 'Wallace.'

Blind Harry's *Wallace*, which, however
lacking in poetic qualities, commended
itself by its subject to the patriotic Scot, and achieved
an instant and lasting popularity. It was in it that
Burns read the ' story of Wallace ' which poured the
' tide of Scottish prejudice ' into his veins ; and it is
largely responsible for Burns's *Scots Wha Hae*, and
for many much less admirable manifestations of
patriotic fervour.

Hamilton's paraphrase of *Wallace* appeared in

Watson's 'Choice Collection.'

1722, but a good many years before this
symptoms of awakening interest in
Scottish vernacular verse had begun to
manifest themselves — the most remarkable and
decided being the publication of Watson's *Choice
Collection of Scottish Poems*, 1706-1711. The mere

issue of such a work in Scotland was a certain
sign that narrow Biblicalism was no longer the
power in the land it had been, and that the icy
winter, which so long had frozen the springs of
natural human feeling, was gradually breaking up.
Watson's *Collection* is rather miscellaneous : old
and new pieces, and of the new some in the vernacular, others 'quite English,' jostle one another in
admired disorder. Some of those in the modern
vernacular had already appeared in broadsides,
and the broadside was really the chief means of
reawakening the love of vernacular poetry and
song among the people.   The modern vernacular
pieces include *The Blythesome Bridal*, *The Banishment of Povertie*, *The Speech of a Fife Laird*, *Habbie
Simson*, a clever piece, *The Mare of Collingtoun*, in
rime couée—aaab, cccb,—*Bonnie Heck*, and an epitaph
in the *Habbie* form on *William Lithgow*. Among
the English specimens are Drummond's *Forth Feast-
ing*, *Linton's Address to the Prince of Orange*,
by Alexander Pennecuick, *Coelia's Country House
and Closet*, by Sir George Mackenzie, *Poems on the
King and Queen of Fairy*, by Archibald Pitcairne, and
In Praise of Women, by Montrose. Lastly, the old
vernacular pieces include *Christis Kirk*, *The Cherry
and the Slae*, Burel's *Passage of a Pilgrim*, and
Montgomerie's *Flyting*. A rather various, and not
particularly happy or representative selection, but
sufficiently noteworthy as the first important symptoms of the dawn of a great vernacular revival.

XIII

RAMSAY TO BURNS

RAMSAY—ALEXANDER BANNATYNE—ALEXANDER ROSS
—THE SONG-WRITERS—FERGUSSON.

THE main agent in the vernacular revival was Allan
Ramsay. Descended from the Ramsays of Cockpen,
a younger branch of the Ramsays of
Dalhousie, he was the son of Robert
Ramsay, superintendent of Lord Hope-
toun's lead-mines at Leadhills, Lanarkshire, by Alice
Bower, a native of Derbyshire. He was born in the
village of Leadhills, 15th October 1686, and received
all his education at the parish school. Having had
the misfortune, while still in infancy, to lose his
father, he was, after the death in 1700 of his
mother, who had married a small neighbouring pro-
prietor, sent to Edinburgh to be apprenticed to a
wigmaker. In 1707 he opened a wigmaker's shop
of his own in the Grassmarket, which he conducted
successfully until 1719, when his special tastes and
his literary success induced him to adopt the business
of bookseller opposite Niddry's Wind.

Though keenly intent on his business, Ramsay found time for both conviviality and study. From an early period he developed a strong love of poetry, and besides perusing the older English classics, including Chaucer, Spenser, Shakespeare, Ben Jonson, the Fletchers, Drummond, Milton, Cowley, and Dryden, he was well read in the verse of the day from Pope down to his friend Tom D'Urfey, with the latter of whom he had much in common. In the clubs and taverns he also got to know many of the old racy vernacular ditties; but few of the older vernacular classics, with the exception of the works of Sir David Lyndsay, being in circulation, he had already himself acquired some fame as a verse-writer before he accidentally got access to them in the Bannatyne MS. A Jacobite in politics, and of genial and epicurean habit, he represents the commencement of the literary reaction among the middle and lower classes against the repressive tendencies of the Kirk. He was especially the poet of the jovial burgher, and of the taverns and clubs which were the centre of this reaction; and much of his verse reeks of their peculiar atmosphere. Among his earlier pieces was his *Elegy on Maggy Johnstone*, the ale-wife of Bruntsfield Links, who died in 1711, modelled on 'Standard *Habbie*.' Its success when issued as a penny broadside induced him to venture similar essays in verse, including elegies on *Lucky Wood*, *John Cowper*, and *Pat Birnie*, *Lucky Simson's Last Advice*, and various others, some of them

2 c

now lost, in a still grosser comic vein. For some years he was the recognised laureate of the streets, his satires on street incidents, as *The Flytin' of Lucky Duff and Lucky Brown*, or mock elegies, or sketches of well-known city characters, or rhymes on passing events, being, it is said, the favourite reading of the common gossips over their teacups. His admission to the Easy Club also stimulated him to the production of English verse, which, mediocre and wholly artificial though it was, secured him much approbation from the members, some of whom—such as Hepburn of Keith, Dr. Pitcairne, Dr. Patrick Abercrombie, and Dr. Thomas Ruddiman—were amongst the most intellectually emancipated of the Edinburgh citizens. His reputation was still further enhanced by the publication in 1716 of *Christis Kirk*, with an additional canto of his own composition ; and in 1718 appeared a second edition of the poem with an additional canto. The same year he brought out an edition of *Scots Songs*; and in 1721 he published by subscription a volume of his own poems. Then followed in 1724 the first volume of ' *The Tea Table Miscellany*, a collection of choice songs Scots and English,' a good many of them partly or wholly his own; and in the same year, *The Evergreen*, a selection of old Scots poetry obtained chiefly from the Bannatyne MS. A second volume of *The Tea Table Miscellany* appeared in 1725, a third in 1727, and a fourth in 1732. In 1725 he also published the most popular of all his pieces, *The Gentle Shepherd*, part of it in the form of an eclogue, under the title *Patie and Roger*, having appeared in 1721, with a sequel in 1723, entitled *Jynny and Maggie*. Prosperous in business and famed as a poet, he in 1726 removed to the Luckenbooths, where he adopted as his sign the heads of Ben Jonson and Drummond of Hawthornden. From his new shop he issued in 1728 a new edition of his poems, and in 1730 *Thirty Fables* in verse. In 1731 he was honoured by the publication of an edition of his poems in London, Dublin following suit in 1733. In 1736 he brought out a volume of *Scots Proverbs*; but from this time he wholly ceased to intermeddle with literature, except as bookseller, the only remaining incident in his life that calls for notice being a spirited though vain contest with the bigotry of the period, in an attempt to establish a theatre in Edinburgh, which at the instance of the clergy was closed by order of the Magistrates. He died, 7th January 1758, in the picturesque mansion which he had erected for himself on the Castle Hill, Edinburgh, and was buried in Greyfriars Churchyard.[1]

If not the victim of the contradictory poetic models, English and Scots, which he sought combinedly to imitate, Ramsay, except in the case of *The Gentle Shepherd*, was nothing advantaged, either as Scots or English versi-

His popularity.

---

[1] The best edition of Ramsay's *Works* is that ed. Chalmers, with essay by Lord Woodhouselee (frequently reprinted), but a critical edition is still a desideratum.

fier, by any compensating result of the twofold influence. His familiarity with the vernacular song and some of the verse of the old Scots 'makaris,' in no wise tended to modify the pompous commonplace of his more ambitious essays in English verse, while his acquaintance with the English classics exercised little truly educative influence on his vernacular method. But this twofold acquaintanceship assisted him to construct a species of Scoto-English song which was rampantly popular both in Scotland and England. While his vernacular pieces won him universal fame among the lower classes of his native land, and his English verse was read with something resembling admiration by the more enlightened classes of both countries, his songs—as is abundantly testified by the song-books and sheet music of the period—were warbled, to rapturous applause, by the favourite vocalists at the London 'gardens,' and other places of popular resort. Familiar with the old popular songs of both countries, he utilised them for his own purposes with much superficial cleverness. His manner was exactly that which the masses could thoroughly appreciate, and the Scottish flavour, comparatively mild as it was, conferred on them a piquancy which in England greatly aided their popularity.

Some of them—as *Nany, O, Bony Jean, I'll never leave Thee, Clout the Caldron,* and *Through the Wood, Laddie*—were reminiscent of old English broadsides. A great many more, usually

Character of his songs.

published as his own, are founded on older Scottish songs, some of them poetically much superior, and all of them at least equal to Ramsay's versions. They include *Bessy Bell and Mary Gray, Auld Lang Syne, The Bob of Dunblane, The Collier's Bonnie Lassie, For the Sake of Somebody, The Highland Laddie, My Daddy Forbad, O Mither Dear I Gin to Fear, Jenny Nettles, Steer her Up and Haud her Gaun,* and *This is no my Ain House,* in addition to many old songs which he merely amended. Indeed, Ramsay can claim comparatively few songs as wholly his own. Among his best are *The Lass of Patie's Mill*—which some assert is not wholly his—and *Lochaber No More,* and both are marred by solecisms. Yet he has written one admirable lyric, perfectly faultless in its simplicity, *My Peggy is a Young Thing.* His worst defect is his *penchant* for the grovelling, and when not grovelling, he is too apt to be stalely commonplace.

The Soger Laddie, for example, which used to create a *furore* at Mary'bone Gardens, and other popular London resorts of the eighteenth century, but expresses the unadorned sentiments of Mary Jane, in language even more prosaic and banal than many a Mary Jane would employ:— 'The Sodger Laddie.'

> 'My soger laddie is over the sea
> And he will bring gold and money to me ;
> And when he comes hame, he'll make me a lady ;
> My blessing gang with my soger laddie.

go

> My doughty laddie is handsome and brave,
> And can as a soger and lover behave ;
> True to his country, to love he is steady,
> There 's few to compare with my soger laddie.
>
> Shield him, ye angels, frae death in alarms,
> Return him with laurels to my langing arms ;
> Syne frae all my care he 'll pleasantly free me,
> When back to my wishes my soger ye gie me.
>
> O soon may his honours bloom fair on his brow,
> As quickly they must, if he get his due :
> For in noble actions his courage is ready,
> Which makes me delight in my soger laddie.'

longing
Then

Nor even in the best of his convivial songs does he embody the true rapture of good fellowship. *Up in the Air* begins fairly well, and stanza ii. contains a rather picturesque allusion to a snowy night; but the piece is wholly lacking in poetic glamour, while the last stanza is but stiffly wooden :—

Convivial songs. 'Up in the Air.'

> 'Steek the doors, keep out the frost ;
> Come, Willy, gie 's about ye'r toast,
> Fill it lads, and lilt it out,
> And let us hae a blithsome bout.
>   Up wi 't there, there,
>   Dinna cheat, but drink fair ;
> Huza, huza, and huza, lads, yet,
>   Up wi 't there.'

Shut
give us

have
with it
Do not

But as the comic satirist of low life Ramsay evidenced the possession of a strong vein of clever clownish humour. The *Elegy on John Cowper* and *Lucky Spence's Last Advice*, are caustic and graphic enough after their own rancid fashion ; and the elegies on *Maggy Johnstone*

As comic satirist.

and *Lucky Wood* supply us with a curious photo-
graphic picture of the tavern life of Old Edinburgh.
The portrait of Lucky Wood, the pattern ale-wife of
the Canongate, is indeed quite admirable:—

> ' She ne'er gae in a lawin fause,
>   Nor stoups a' froath aboon the hause,
>   Nor kept dow'd tip within her waws
>   But reaming swats ;
> She ne'er ran sour jute, because
>   It gees the batts.
>
> She had the gate sae well to please,
> With gratis beef, dry fish, or cheese,
> Which kept our purses ay at ease,
>   And health in tift ;
> And lent her fresh nine gallon trees
>   A hearty lift.
>
> She gae us oft hail legs o' lamb,
> And did nae hain her mutton-ham ;
> Then aye at Yule whene'er we cam,
>   A braw goose-pye ;
> And was na that good belly-baum ?
>   Nane dare deny.
>
> The writer-lads fow well may mind her ;
> Fruthy was she, her luck design'd her
> Their common mither ; sure nane kinder
>   Ever brake bread !
> She has na left her mak behind her,
>   But now she 's dead.'

gave ;
reckoning
neck
stale tipple ;
walls
new ale

gives ; colic

method

order

whole
spare

fine

full
Pleasant

peer

But the most elaborate effort of Ramsay's in ex-
pounding the humours of common life is his two
additional cantos to *Christis Kirk*, which,   'Christis
while lacking the vivid conciseness of the   Kirk.'
earlier piece, and indeed little better than a mere
vulgar parody of its method, depict realistically

enough the more sordid aspects of Scottish mirth.
The first canto of Ramsay describes a wedding-feast,
ending with the bedding ceremony; and in the second
the rejoicings are renewed on the morrow until all
the men reach the becoming condition of brutal in-
toxication. It is all true to nature and all most
grotesquely comic, but not all quite quotable. Here,
however, are some quaint stanzas depicting the arrival
of the gossips on the morning after the marriage :—

'Be that time it was fair foor days,
  As fou's the house could pang,
To see the young fouk ere they raise,
  Gossips came in ding-dang.
And wi a sos aboon the claiths
  Ilk ane their gifts down flang :
Twa toop-horn-spoons down Maggy lays,
  Baith muckle-mow'd and lang
        For kale or whey.

Her aunt a pair of tangs fush in,
  Right bauld she spake and spruce :
"Gin your goodman shall make a din,
  And gabble like a goose,
Shorin whan fou to skelp ye're skin,
  Thir tangs may be of use ;
Lay them enlang his pow or shin,
  Wha wins syn may make roose
        Between you twa."

Auld Bessie, in her red coat braw,
  Came wi her ain oe Nanny,
An odd-like wife, they said, that saw
  A moupin' runckled granny ;
She fley'd the kimmers ane and a',
  Word gae'd she was na kanny ;
Nor wad they let Lucky awa,
  'Till she was fou wi' branny,
        Like mony mae.'

Marginal glosses (left column):

- By ; daylight
- full ; pack
- higgledy-piggledy clothes
- Each
- ram-
- big-mouthed
- broth
- fetched
- If ; husband
- Threatening ; drunk
- Those
- head
- then ; boast
- fine
- grandchild
- mumping
- wrinkled
- frightened the young women
- went ; was a witch
- drunk ; brandy
- many more

Ramsay's *Tales and Fables* call for little comment. A good many are in English or in Scoto-English, and the majority in the octo-syllabic couplet. Some, he states, were 'taken from Messieurs la Fontaine and la Motte,' and those which are his 'own invention with respect to the plot as well as the numbers' he leaves the reader 'to find out,' or if any one thought 'it worth his while to ask' him, he professed his willingness to tell him. Ramsay is now beyond interrogation; but one may venture to affirm that *The Monk and the Miller's Wife*, which was long credited to him, was neither his own invention nor 'taken from Messieurs la Fontaine and la Motte,' but is merely a modernised and vulgarised reading of *The Freiris of Berwick*; and that his most elaborate tale, *The Three Bonnets*, a long-winded, complicated, and occasionally gross satire on the Union, is most probably all his own.

'Tales and Fables.'

Ramsay's satires entitle him to rank as at least a cleverly comic vernacular Zola, but for the author of *The Gentle Shepherd* something more than this may be claimed. If not quite poetry, it is at least admirable 'kailyaird.' A most pleasing because a quite unaffectedly homely and simple sketch of rustic courtship—somewhat idealised—it almost by mere accident reveals a literary talent which had been partly smothered by his imperfect training and untoward circumstances. Here his twofold course of poetic study stood him in much better stead than usual. The English pastorals,

'The Gentle Shepherd.'

which he so far made his model, exercised a certain
restraining influence on his rather too realistic Scottish
method, while by electing to write in the vernacular
he avoided the worst pitfalls of artificiality. It has
given him a certain acknowledged position in literature, and not undeservedly; but though also as a
vernacular satirist his strenuity and wit—often too
much tinged with squalidity—are undeniable, and
though he contrived one excellent and one or two
passably good lyrics, it is rather as editor than author
that he occupies his peculiar place in the

As Editor.
vernacular revival. The results of his
editorial enterprise were twofold: (1) *The Tea Table
Miscellany*—dedicated gallantly (and pawkily)

> 'To ilka lovely British lass,
>   Frae Ladies Charlotte, Anne, and Jean,
>   Down to ilk bony singing Bess,
>   Wha dances barefoot on the green'—

in conjunction with Thomson's *Orpheus* aroused—
curious patchwork of old and new, of Scots, English,
Scoto-English, and Anglo-Scots, though it be—in a
new fashion the old interest in popular song among
the bulk of the Scottish people; and (2) by *The
Evergreen*—which he described as 'a Collection of
Scots Poems wrote by the Ingenious before 1600,'
and which included, besides a few ballads such as
Hardyknute, Johnie Armstrang, and *The Battle of
Harlaw*, and *The Vision* (which may be wholly or
partly his own), and one or two of *The Gude and
Godlie Ballates*, a large number of the best productions (often very freely altered) of the old 'makaris'

preserved in the Bannatyne MS.—he was the first to rescue from oblivion the old vernacular poetry of the fifteenth and sixteenth centuries, which, thus resurgent after a trance of some century and a half, was found to have lost comparatively little of its ancient vitality, and by its vivifying effects partly rekindled in the eighteenth century the old vernacular poetic flame.

A sort of double of Ramsay was Alexander Pennecuick (d. 1730), an obscure Edinburgh citizen of whom scarce anything is known except that, having died in extreme destitution, he was buried in Greyfriars Churchyard, 30th November 1730, but who is sometimes confounded with Dr. Alexander Pennecuick (1652-1722), author of a *Description of Tweeddale*, which, with various poems in English, appeared at Leith in 1815. Some of his poems had previously appeared in a *Collection of Curious Scots Poems*, Edinburgh, 1762. They include *Truth's Travels*, a long, semi-vernacular piece written in the French octave. The more vernacular Pennecuick published *Streams from Helicon*, 1720, and *Flowers from Parnassus*, 1726; but many of his effusions were also issued as penny broadsides, and in 1756 there appeared at Edinburgh '*A Collection of Scots Poems on Several Occasions*, by the late Alexander Pennecuick and others,' the others including Ramsay. He was very partial to Ramsay's themes. Like Ramsay he commemorated the dowager Anne, Duchess of Hamilton, in an ode; while Ramsay wrote a masque on the marriage of

Alexander Pennecuick (d. 1730).

the fifth duke to Lady Anne Cochrane in 1723, Pennecuick celebrated the same event in a pastoral; he also constituted himself a sort of laureate of the Royal Archers, and he disputed the laurels of Ramsay as the bard of the streets, as he certainly rivalled him in the indelicacy of his squalid humour: his *Elegy on Robert Forbes*, Kirk Treasurer's man, and also his *Presbyterian Pope*—in which he presents us with a dialogue between the Kirk Treasurer's man and one of his female informants—being quite as unvarnished in their allusions as the *Elegy on John Cowper*. He is also credited with *The Elegy on William Lithgow*, published in Watson's *Choice Collection*, 1706, but his longest piece, if not his *chef d'œuvre*—interesting as an accurate presentment of the sentiments, ideas, and vernacular of the lower-class women of that peroid —is *The Mery Wives of Musleburgh, at their meeting together to welcome Meg Dickson after her Loup from the Ladder*, 1724, of which there is an anonymous broadside in the British Museum, and which is included in Pennecuick's *Collection*, 1756. Meg was a fishwife who by an accident escaped death by hanging; and in the poem she details her experiences to the assembled gossips. It begins:—

> 'That day, when Meg fair taste got
>   Wi' Hangie's beeds about her throat,
>   Three clavering carlings o'er the pot,
>   A' spewing fou,
>   Whinge'd when they thought on Maggie's trot
>   Doon the West-bow.'[1]

gossips
All; drunk
Wept

---

[1] From the prison to the place of execution.

Among contemporaries and friends of Ramsay were—in addition to William Hamilton of Gilbertfield — Sir John Clerk of Penicuik (1684-1755), the accomplished lawyer and antiquary, who erected at his country seat an obelisk to Ramsay's memory, and is the reputed author of *O merry may the Maid be that Marries the Miller*, published in *The Charmer*, 1751, and founded on an old improper song,[1] partly preserved in the first stanza; Robert Crawford (d. 1730), son of the laird of Drumsoy, Renfrewshire, whose pleasant, if slightly artificial, lyrics *Tweedside*, *Leader Haughs and Yarrow*, *The Bush Aboon Traquair*, etc., mostly contributed to *The Tea Table Miscellany*, are almost wholly English in manner, and only faintly Scots in language; William Hamilton of Bangour (1704-1754), an accomplished versifier in English, and the author of the archaic and finely symphonious ballad, *The Braes of Yarrow*; and David Mallet or Malloch (1700?-1765), who, though he indicated his desire for Anglification to the extent of changing his surname, and, in the words of Samuel Johnson, 'cleared his tongue from his native pronunciation so as to be no longer distinguishable as a Scot,' perhaps deserves mention here for his somewhat frigidly tragic ballad of *William and Margaret*. Mallet has also rival claims

Ramsay's contemporaries and friends.

---

[1] Maids and millers were a favourite theme of the old vernacular bards, and they also figure prominently in the black-letter broadsides.

with James Thomson to the authorship of *Rule
Britannia*, which appeared in 1740 in their joint
masque of *Alfred*.

The most prominent of Ramsay's early disciples
was Alexander Ross, who, the son of an Aberdeenshire farmer, after graduating M.A. at
Marischal College, Aberdeen, became a
teacher, and finally settled as parish
schoolmaster at Lochlea, Forfarshire. In 1768 Ross,
who was then in his seventieth year, published a pastoral entitled *Helonore the Fortunate Shepherdess.*
Written in the quaint and pithy Aberdeenshire
dialect, it achieved some popularity in the north of
Scotland, but notwithstanding some happy descriptions of natural scenery, and the help of a raid of
Highland caterans, it is on the whole a rather dull,
and even dreary, performance. This, however, cannot
be said of his songs, their witty expositions of the
humours of domestic life being, indeed, almost over-
whelmingly vivacious. Among the best known are
*The Rock and the Wee Pickle Tow, Wooed and
Married and A', and The Bridal O't.* Here is the
first stanza of *The Rock*:—

(margin note: Alexander Ross (1699-1784).)

very little   'There was an auld wife had a wee pickle tow,

go   And she wad gae try the spinning o't;

bent;
distaff;
caught fire
wept;
scolded

become
frantic

'There was an auld wife had a wee pickle tow,
      And she wad gae try the spinning o't;
She louted her down, and her rock took a low,
      And that was a bad beginning o't.
She sat and she grat, and she flet and she flang,
      And she flew and she blew, and she wriggled and wrang,
And she choked and boaked and cried like to mang,
      Alas for the dreary spinning o't.'

With the exception of Fergusson, most of the
vernacular bards before Burns are each mainly
associated with only one or two songs. John Skinner
The *Tullochgorum* of John Skinner, (1721-1807).
Episcopal minister of Longside, Aberdeenshire,
written to the old tune of that name, and in a form
of *rime couée*—twelve lines divided into three equal
sections, three head lines and one tail line each, with
a curious iterative refrain in the middle section,—was
pronounced by Burns, in his enthusiastic way, to ' be
the best Scots song Scotland ever saw,' and is at least
a most jovial, genial, and inspiriting production.
Somewhat similar in style but less individual in
character is *Tune your Fiddles*, while *The Ewie wi'
the Crookit Horn* possesses much of the quaintly
pathetic humour of Burns's own *Poor Mailie*. But
Skinner's *Christmas Ba'ing*, in the stanza of *Christis
Kirk*, must be classed with the less successful imitations of that original.

Alexander Geddes, an accomplished and learned
Catholic priest, and the author of a great variety of
works in prose and verse including two Alexander
clever macaronic pieces, is credited with Geddes (1737-
the capital Jacobite song, *O Send Lewie* 1802).
Gordon Hame*, and also with *The Wee Wifukie*,
which, however, has also been claimed for Alexander
Watson, Lord Byron's Aberdeen tailor (who is said
also to be the author of the much inferior *Kail Brose
o' Scotland*), and may have been written by neither.
Written by Geddes or Watson or another, it is a

masterpiece of its kind: the bewildered case of the
'wifukie' (who, having got 'a wee bit drapukie,' had,
while taking a nap on the roadside 'coming frae the
fair,' been by a packman not merely robbed of her
money and purse, but shorn of her golden locks),
being set forth with a droll verisimilitude that could
scarce be outdone :—

not
killing

> '"This is nae me," quo' she, "this is nae me,
> Somebody has been felling me, and this is nae me."'

To three ladies—Mrs. Cockburn, a relative of Sir
Walter Scott's, and one of the sprightliest and most
charming of Edinburgh hostesses; Jane
Elliot, third daughter of Sir Gilbert
Elliot, Baronet, of Minto, and sister of Sir
Gilbert, the author of the pastoral song
Amynta; and Lady Anne Barnard, of the Balcarres
Lindsays—we are indebted for three lyrics, each after
its own fashion mournfully beautiful, and all suggested by older originals. If Mrs. Cockburn's and
Miss Elliot's versions of the *Flowers of the Forest*
were written independently of each other, they must
have been founded on the same original, for both
have the refrain ' The flowers of the forest are a' wede
away.' Mrs. Cockburn's version appeared in *The
Lark*, 1765; and Stenhouse avers that Miss Elliot's
ballad was published anonymously about 1755, but
he states not where. It was known to Herd, who
included it in what he termed 'a version made
up from various copies of the old ballad collated';
but Scott got for *The Minstrelsy* an authorised copy

Mrs. Cockburn
(1712-1794), Jane
Elliot (1727-
1805), and Lady
Anne Barnard
(1750-1825).

from Dr. Somerville, who told him that the first and last lines of the first stanza were

> 'I've heard them lilting at the ewes milking,'

and

> 'The flowers of the forest are a' wede away.'

It is to be regretted that Scott either displayed no further curiosity about the old ballad, or was unable to obtain further information about it. As for Lady Anne Barnard's song, *Auld Robin Gray*, she told Scott that it was suggested by an older Scottish melody, *The Bridegroom Greets when the Sun gae's doon*, sung at Balcarres by an old lady—'who lived before your day'—who 'did not object to its having improper words,' though Lady Anne [1] did.

Other bards whose vernacular fame rests mainly on a single song are William Julius Mickle (1734-1788), a miscellaneous verse-writer of some note, who translated Camoen's *Lusiad*, was the author of the rather stately *Cumnor Hall*, and may possibly have written (as Jean Adams, the piously metaphysical Greenock poetess, certainly did not) *There's nae Luck aboot the Hoose*, which as matter of fact was claimed by neither, and which Burns (who, less flatteringly than usual, declared it to be 'one of the most beautiful songs in the Scots or any other language') states 'came first on the streets as a ballad,' about 1771 or 1772; [2] Dougal Graham (1724-

Other song-writers.

---

[1] See Lockhart's *Life of Scott*, and also Lady Anne Barnard's revised version of the ballad, with continuation, edited by Sir Walter Scott for the Bannatyne Club, 1824.

[2] The song may be a relic of Jacobitism.

1779), the Glasgow bellman, whose *Metrical History of the Rebellion* and numerous penny vernacular chap-books, which he both wrote and printed, are now forgotten except by collectors, but whose *Turnimspike* (Turnpike) is a most realistically witty sketch of the language and thoughts of the unsophisticated Gael, when he first beheld the roads of General Wade, and was actually asked to pay toll in the neighbourhood of his native heath :—

> ' But I'll awa' to the Hielan' hills,
>   Where te'il a ane dare turn her,
> And no come near to your Turnimspike
>   Unless it pe to purn her ' ;

John Ewen (1741-1821), an Aberdeen merchant, to whom Burns attributed *O weel may the Boatie Row*, which is no doubt founded on an older song; George Halket (d. 1756), on whom Peter Buchan fathered *Logie o' Buchan*, and *Whirry Whigs awa'*, the former of which he could not have written if the evidence of his own published *Poems* is to be credited, and the latter of which is a traditionary Jacobite ballad whose current version is an amalgam by Hogg; the Rev. Murdoch M'Lennan (1701-1783), minister of Crathie, Aberdeenshire, who celebrated the battle of Sheriffmuir in the rather clever *Race of Sheriffmuir*, with the refrain :—

> ' And we ran and they ran,
>   And they ran and we ran,
> And we ran and they ran awa', man ' ;

Rev. John Barclay (1734-1798), Berean minister of

Edinburgh, who wrote the picturesque *Dialogue betwixt William Lickladle and Thomas Cleancogue,* modelled after the older ballad of *Killycrankie* (1689), and altered by Burns for Johnson's *Musical Museum*; and Adam Skirving (1719-1803), a gentleman farmer of Haddington, to whom is attributed the ballad of *Tranent Muir* (Prestonpans), made on the same models, and also the much wittier *Johnie Cope.*

Thus for some half-century after Ramsay the vernacular revival was evidenced mainly in the production of occasional songs, many of them suggested by, and others mere adaptations of, older ditties. Apart from songs, the main link between Ramsay and Burns is Robert Fergusson. The second son of William Fergusson, who came from Aberdeen to be accountant in the British Linen Company's Bank, Edinburgh, and of Elizabeth Forbes, also of Aberdeenshire descent, he was born, 5th September 1750, in the Cap-and-Feather Close, a lane the site of which is now partly occupied by the present North Bridge Street. By the aid of a Fergusson bursary he was able to prosecute his studies at the University of St. Andrews, where he matriculated in February 1765 with the view—according to the parental ambition—of studying for the Kirk. At the University he manifested a certain scientific bent, but distinguished himself chiefly by his frolics and his poetry. Among the few pieces of his University days which survive

Robert Fergusson (1750-1774). His student days.

is his rather irreverent elegy—modelled inevitably after 'Standard *Habbie*'—on Professor David Gregory, who died 13th August 1765 :—

> 'He could, by Euclid, prove lang syne
>   A ganging point composed a line ;
> By numbers, too, he could divine,
>   Whan he did read,
> That three times three just made up nine,
>   But now he's dead !'

long ago
moving

Reminiscent of these years is also his *Elegy on John Hogg, late Porter to the University of St. Andrews* :—

> 'Ah, Johnie !   Often did I grumble
> Frae cozie bed, fu' ear' to tumble,
> When art and part I'd been in some ill
>   Troth I was sweer :
> His word then brodit like a wumel
>   Frae ear to ear.'

comfortable ;
full early

loth
penetrated ;
gimlet

The truth was that his mercurial and frolicsome temper and extreme sociability were a surer passport to popularity with his fellows than to professorial approval, although Professor Wilkie of the absurd *Epigoniad* seems to have recognised his mental attractiveness, and to have treated him very much as a personal friend.

The death of Fergusson's father in 1767 deprived him—nothing to his regret—of the wherewithal to persevere in his studies for the Kirk, and after an unsuccessful attempt by the aid of his maternal uncle to secure a better start in life, he was fain to content himself with the situation of copying clerk in the office of the commissary clerk of Edinburgh. For one of his temperament and

In 'Auld Reekie.'

talents the occupation was one of mere drudgery. From the beginning it exercised a depressing influence, from which he vainly sought relief in the convivial clubs which were then a social feature of 'Auld Reekie.'[1] Some fleeting glimpses of satisfaction he no doubt gained through his increasing local fame as versifier, but his poetic repute also widened the circle of his convivial companions, and introduced him more fully to the alluring attractions of pleasure. His contributions to Ruddiman's *Weekly Magazine* began, in February 1771, with pastorals and various other stilted pieces in English; and in the following year he commenced, with *The Daft Days*, the series of contributions to vernacular verse which, to use the words of R. L. Stevenson, were to be 'the models of great things to come'[2]—to 'come,' however, by Burns, not by Fergusson. A small volume of verse which appeared in 1773 added to his fame, and supplied him with some much-needed ready money; but it did little to remove the cloud of depression that had begun to settle on him. With his high-strung nervous system and lack of physical stamina, he could not, living as he did, long escape the inevitable tragedy. By the close of the year his health had become palpably wrecked, and he began to exhibit symptoms of mental instability — the

[1] 'Auld Reekie' (*i.e.* Old Smoky) was Fergusson's pet name for 'Edina, Scotia's darling seat.'

[2] Letter in Dr. A. B. Grosart's *Robert Fergusson* (Famous Scots Series).

malady, by virtue of what R. L. Stevenson has termed his 'damnatory creed,' assuming the form of religious mania. The shock of a fall down a stair, when returning from a convivial party, completed the catastrophe, and he died in the city madhouse, 16th October 1774.

In comparing the poetic achievement of Fergusson [1] with that of Ramsay or Burns, it is but fair to consider that he died, as Stevenson puts it, in his 'acute painful youth'—before he had 'outlived his green sickness,' and when he had merely begun to 'imp his wing' for greater flights. At the age when Fergusson had ceased to write verse, Ramsay was known only as a rising wigmaker, and Burns had done nothing of merit except *Poor Mailie*, and one or two songs. Fergusson's English verses do not here concern us, but they may be left out of account even in a general estimation of his position as poet, for the reason that, though equal in bulk to his vernacular pieces, they display little or no indication of emancipation from the stilted methods of the time. That emancipation might have come to him through his vernacular verse, but he did not live to realise it; and even in the vernacular his work was scarce more than tentative and experimental.

His work mainly tentative and experimental.

As to form, Fergusson's favourite staves were those

---

[1] The earlier editions of Fergusson's *Poems* were superseded by that edited by A. B. G., 1851, and frequently republished. A shilling edition of his *Poems* appeared in 1898.

of *Habbie Simson* ('Standard *Habbie*') and *Christis Kirk*, although he made frequent and clever use both of the octo-syllabic and heroic couplets. **His staves.** In *The Farmer's Ingle*, also, he adopted the nine-line stave formed by adding a line to the old alternately rhyming octave—the arrangement being ab, ab, cd, cdd; while *Hallow Fair* (not *The Hallow Fair*), modelled on *The Blythesome Bridal*, is in the old ballad stave. In the 'Standard *Habbie*' stave we have, of course, various Elegies, as well as Epistles, modelled after those of Ramsay and Hamilton of Gilbertfield; but Fergusson showed also a much more comprehensive partiality for the stave than Ramsay—a partiality which was to infect Burns,—and demonstrated something of its capabilities for picturesque narrative and description, for which it had certain aptitudes that were awanting in the less flexible and more mannered stave of *Christis Kirk*.

Though the verse of Fergusson is apt to manifest imperfect fusion of thought and emotion, as well as a lack of 'body' and fulness, its quality **Characteristics.** is much finer than that of Ramsay, and it is plainly the product of a much more highly disciplined intelligence. He rarely or never lapses into the utterly vulgar or squalid, nor does he display any of Ramsay's partiality for time-hallowed commonplace. His humour is seldom broad or boisterous, but like that of Stevenson—who recognised a mental kinship with him—quiet, dry, and

insinuative, and part and parcel of himself. Moreover, like Stevenson, he had a cunning sense of style,[1]
and here his influence is very manifest on Burns,
who time and again echoes not merely his sentiments
but his phraseology. A characteristic example of his
insinuative humour, and his terse and picturesque
vernacular, is the following extract from the 'Bill of
Fare,' which, had he been master of the ceremonies,
he would have prepared for the regalement of Dr.
Samuel Johnson when banqueted by the St. Andrews
professors :—

'Imprimis, then, a haggis fat,
Weel tottled in a seything pat,
Wi' spice and ingans weel ca'd thro'
Had help'd to gust the stirrah's mow,
And plac'd itsel in truncher clean
Before the gilpy's glowrin een.
Secundo, then, a gude sheep's head
Whase hide was singit, never flead,
And four black trotters cled wi' girsle,
Bedown his throat had learn'd to hirsle.
What think ye, neist, o' gude fat brose
To clag his ribs ? a dainty dose !
And white and bloody puddins routh
To gar the Doctor skirl o' drouth ;
Whan he cou'd never houp to merit
A cordial glass o' reaming claret,
But thraw his nose, and brize and pegh
O'er the contents o' sma' ale quegh :
Then let his wisdom girn and snarl
O'er a weel-tostit girdle farl,
An' learn, that, maugre o' his wame,
Ill bairns are aye best heard at hame.'

Marginal glosses:
boiled
onions;
mixed
taste ; man's
mouth
fellow's
staring eyes

singed ;
flayed

move down
with
difficulty

in abundance
cry out for
thirst

gripe ; pant
cup

oatcake
belly

---

[1] Fergusson had a subtler knowledge of vernacular Scots than
Burns—or rather his Scots was the Scots not of the rustic but of
the educated classes, who made daily use of it in Edinburgh at even
a later date.

But Fergusson was more than a clever wit or humourist. None but a true poet could have written the first stanzas of *Daft Days*— More than a clever humourist.

> ' Now mirk December's dowie face   dark; drooping
> Glowrs owre the rigs wi' sour grimace,   over the ridges
> While, thro' his *minimum* of space,
>   The bleer-ey'd sun,
> Wi' blinkin' light and stealing pace,   glimmering
>   His race doth run,' etc.;

or the eerie Old Greyfriars Kirkyard scene in *The Ghaists*, or *The Lea Rig*, or the opening stanzas of *The Farmer's Ingle*, or the opening stanzas of *Leith Races*.

And granted that his work is fuller of promise than performance, the promise for one of his years is remarkably full, and the actual achievement is so considerable as at least to render his individuality recognisable, and to furnish a living record of himself and his Edinburgh environment. The The bard of 'Auld Reekie.'

> ' Auld Reekie ! wale o' ilka town   best of all towns
> That Scotland kens beneath the moon ;
> Whare couthy chiels at e'ening meet   social fellows
> Their bizzing craigs and mou's to weet :   buzzing throats
> And blythly gar auld Care gae bye   make ; go smiling;
> Wi' blinkin' and wi' bleering eye,'   blearing

or Auld Reekie in the oyster-shops of Musselburgh or Newhaven, or assembling or assembled at Leith Races, or

> ' At Hallowfair, where browsters rare
> Keep gude ale on the gantries,'   barrel stands

or deafened—in the person of the poet—by the

jangling *Tron Kirk Bell*, or expounded in the midnight dialogue of *Planestanes and Causey* 'in their mither tongue,' or simmering in the bustle and revelry of an *Election*,—all this very human, if not highly proper, aspect of the old burghal life is delineated with a sprightly wit and discernment which perhaps have never met with due recognition, especially from the generations of Fergusson's own fellow-citizens.

XIV

BURNS AND AFTERWARDS

ROBERT BURNS — JOHN MAYNE — JAMES TYTLER —
HECTOR MACNEILL — SUSANNA BLAMIRE — ELIZA-
BETH HAMILTON — MRS. GRANT OF CARRON — MRS.
GRANT OF LAGGAN — JOANNA BAILLIE — BARONESS
NAIRNE — JAMES HOGG — SIR WALTER SCOTT — SIR
ALEXANDER BOSWELL — ROBERT TANNAHILL —
ALEXANDER CUNNINGHAM.

ROBERT BURNS has, especially in Scotland, been the
theme of such universal and perpetual allusion, and
his qualities, real or imaginary, both as
man and poet, have been expounded in
such a variety of methods, from the blind

Robert Burns
(1759-1796)
and Scotland.

encomium by the village enthusiast, up to the critical
and splendid eulogy by Mr. Henley,[1] that even in an
account of Scottish Vernacular Literature there is
scarce occasion for more than a mere indication of
his unique place in the succession of Scottish bards.

His birth on the windy morning of 25th January
1759, in the 'auld clay biggin'' at Alloway, Ayrshire;

[1] *Burns—Life, Genius, and Achievement*, by W. E. Henley, reprinted from *The Centenary Burns*, Edinburgh, 1898.

the noble and intelligent efforts of his struggling peasant father to procure him a good education; his own high enthusiasm for learning, and for such limited literature as was within his reach; the not wholly scatheless triumph of his ardent genius and splendid physique over circumstances that would have overwhelmed or suppressed all but the strongest; his early initiation into the 'sublime notions and high mysteries' of love and poetry; the turbulent years of his early manhood; his adventurous quests and chequered fortunes as an amorist; his complex encounters with desperate circumstances and Calvinistic Puritanism, and the Kirk and himself; the sudden gleam of success and hope that followed the appearance of the Kilmarnock volume in 1786; the animating episode of Edinburgh, intermingled with its varied experiences and the Clarinda sensibilities and raptures; his practical farewell to brilliant hopes, and new half-formed ambitions, and the great world—to the spell of whose influence he was by no means insensitive,—and his return, impelled less by free choice than by what he deemed stern necessity, to his own people and his old mode of life; the final absorption of his great gifts mainly in the routine duties of exciseman, which duties, it has been triumphantly demonstrated, he performed 'pretty well'; the half-unconscious but utter revolt of his nature against his lot; the insufficient, or rather fatally perilous, character of his safety-valves, and the solution of a problem—which was ever becoming other-

Burns's career.

wise more difficult of explication—by his premature death, 21st July 1796;—all this, it may be taken for granted, the reader is already pretty well acquainted with.

In his career—his endeavour, achievement, and tragedy—the attribute which seems to have been determinative both for good and evil was his exuberant vitality. Physically he *His exuberant vitality.* was gifted, as only the elect favourites of Nature are, with strength and beauty, and his physical endowments were but the reflex of a rarely dowered intelligence. As to the dominance of his personal charm, testimony is unanimous. Thus the Duchess of Gordon confesses that he was the only man who 'carried her off her feet'; his friend Syme compares his eyes to 'coals of living fire'; Maria Riddell expresses the conviction that Poetry was 'actually not his forte,' that none ever outshone him 'in the charms—the sorcery I might almost call it—of fascinating conversation,' and 'that no man was ever gifted with a larger portion of the *vivida vis animi*'; and such was his magnetism over even the average stolid Scot, that 'if he entered an inn at midnight, after all the inmates were in bed, the news of his arrival circulated from cellar to garret, and ere ten minutes had elapsed the landlord and all his guests had assembled.' But this noble faculty, this exuberant physical and mental vitality, was to spend itself very largely in beating against the walls of its prison-house. At the outset it was to be all but fatally injured by the iron drudgery of Mount Oliphant—a drudgery which, as he said, combined the 'cheerless gloom of a hermit with the ceaseless toil of a galley slave'; and which left behind debilities and tendencies that were bound to evince themselves in some form, and do much to explain his restless craving for excitement, and for those 'violent delights' which

> 'have violent ends,
> And in their triumph die.'

Nor, apart from its undue straining in his earlier years, was he ever in circumstances where it did not suffer, more or less, from the tedium and harm of repression; and thus it acted too much as a mere fever in the blood, and never became the fully beneficent influence either to himself or the world that it might have been amid more congenial surroundings, and with free scope for its employment and full expansion.

But our concern, here and now, is less with what Burns might have been than with what he was, and less with that aspect of his life which was mistaken, ineffective, and calamitous, than with that which, after all, was its right aspect—the aspect which was fortunate and successful as it is given to few lives to be; for in his case, more than that of most, the maxim of Mark Antony has been reversed—the good that he has done has lived after him, and the evil has been interred with his bones. One beneficent result that

Burns and Calvinistic Puritanism.

has accrued specially to many of Burns's own country-men from Burns's exuberant vitality was deliverance from the nightmare of Calvinistic Puritanism, that bastard form of scholastic monasticism under whose spell the bulk of the Scottish community had been tossing in 'unquiet slumbers' from the time of the Reformation. With Burns came the glimmerings of dawn and the dispersal of many clouds and shadows. No one ever asserted more convincingly man's inherent right to the fulness of his humanity, or more vehemently denied the innate accursedness of present happiness and joy. Not only did he war directly with the results of Calvinistic Puritanism in numerous incidental skirmishes and in such satirical attacks as *The Unco Guid, The Holy Fair, The Epistle to MacMath,* and the matchless *Holy Willie's Prayer,* but by the consummate utterance of natural human feeling throughout the whole gamut of emotion—love, passion, desire, sympathy, humour, joy, sorrow, and regret—he charmed from the nation —as David by his playing did from Saul—the 'evil spirit' that so long had 'vexed' it, and it was 're-freshed and was well.'

For his exuberant vitality Burns found one of his main outlets in poetry. As Maria Riddell conjectured, poetry may actually not have been his forte. He was perhaps more especially gifted for practical ascendancy over his fellows. With his strong and broad human sympathy, his piercing intelligence, his eloquent speech, his magnetic

Becomes a poet.

personality, he possessed most of the qualities which
go to fashion a great statesman, a statesman who is
able so to identify his personality with the personality
of a nation that he dominates, or seems to dominate,
its will, and at least interprets, if he does not in a
measure shape, its destiny. But poetry it was destined
to be; and this, for one thing, because whether by
natural endowment, or as the result of repression or
of overstrain, he felt within him the workings of a
strong artistic impulse, the need of fit expression for
emotion; and for another, because it was difficult, if
not impossible for him, situated as he was, to find
otherwise an outlet for his mental vitality; and lastly,
and perhaps chiefly, because he discovered in the
poetry with which in his youth he was mainly
charmed—the vernacular poetry of Ramsay and
Fergusson, and the song-books which he pored over
driving his cart or going to labour, and of such of
the old 'makaris' as he knew—the needed antithesis
to, and counteractive of, Calvinistic Puritanism: what
represented in the language of his daily life (1) the
old primitive non-conventional aspect of things which
appealed directly to the peasant, and (2) the repressed
poetry and the repressed life of himself and of the
nation—the poetry which the Kirk had forbidden, and
which the nation in its blindness had departed from,
and the life of unrestrained intelligence and natural
human joy, and art and music and the beautiful,
which was, as yet, all but denied to Scotland, but for
which he felt 'immortal longings.'

The early poetic models of Burns were thus primarily the old 'makaris' and the modern vernacular bards, represented by Sempill, Ramsay, and Fergusson. The old 'makaris' he knew mainly as they were to be studied in *The Evergreen,* and possibly in Lord Hailes' *Ancient Scottish Poems,* 1770. No doubt he was also well read in 'Davie Lyndsay,' and he knew Blind Harry's *Wallace,* as represented in the version of Hamilton of Gilbertfield. Before he wrote *Tam o' Shanter,* he must, at least, have glanced at Gavin Douglas; and he further got to be acquainted with Barbour's *Bruce,* as he no doubt did with Pinkerton's *Ancient Scotish Poems,* 1786, and with various later collections edited by Pinkerton and others. Of still more importance was the fact that he had conceived a very special affection for the old songs, and that, besides minutely conning over those in the collections verse by verse, and 'carefully noting the tender and sublime from affectation and fustian,' he latterly came to possess—through opportunities afforded him during his wanderings as exciseman, as well as by means of correspondence—a very varied knowledge of the old traditional songs, and indeed a quite unique assortment of the old vernacular lyrics which, except surreptitiously, have never appeared in print.

At school he had read Gray's *Elegy,* and various scraps from other English poets, especially those of the eighteenth century, and by and by he began to study more systematically, and to admire and

2 E

intermittently to copy and imitate, Gray and
Thomson, and that 'celebrated poet' Shenstone,
whose 'divine Elegies do honour to our

His English
models.
language, our nation, and our species.'
At a very early period he had also chanced on the
Works of Pope, from whom his style may have gained
something in point and polish; but towards Milton his
attitude was if anything equivocal, and while he was
also accustomed to peruse the plays of Shakespeare,
he was, like all the strange English generation of his
time—indeed, the English generations from the time
of Shakespeare's dethronement by the Puritan reaction, for even after the Restoration Shakespeare
lay partly *perdu* as a literary influence until the
nineteenth century—almost insensate to the spell of
Shakespeare's enchantment, and, it may be, did not
rate him quite so highly as 'the celebrated poet'
above mentioned. His English models were thus
mainly the later eighteenth - century poets; and
partly from the unaffected modesty which was one of
his most engaging traits, partly from the conscious-
ness of his own hap-hazard and unsystematic mental
training, he was disposed to adopt towards them too
much the attitude of mere admiration. Neither with
Thomson, nor Gray, nor the 'celebrated' Shenstone,
had he almost anything in common, and so far as
he attempted to tutor himself to the assumption of
their particular modes of 'sensibility'—to indulge
in the contemplative raptures of Thomson, or the
cloistered enthusiasm of Gray or the refined

sentimentalism of Shenstone—he was merely forg-
ing chains to curb and fetter his own strong
vitality. No doubt they were his masters in the
technique of English verse, but only for the reason
that in the higher and more elaborate forms of
English verse he never advanced beyond the stage
of pupilage.

Carlyle has asserted that had Burns been 'a regular,
well-trained, intellectual workman,' he might 'have
changed the whole course of British His poetic
literature'; but this of course Burns was possibilities.
very far from being. Time, opportunity, and environment were alike wanting for it; his poetry was the
product of moments of leisure snatched from hours
of grinding toil amid the companionship of simple
rustics. Moreover, at a very early period he had got
mentally habituated to the old Scots vernacular
staves, especially those which had been revived by
Ramsay and Fergusson; and this early bias was not
helpful, but the opposite, to success in English verse.
These metrical forms had become effete in England—
effete because of changes in the idiosyncracy of the
language, and advancement in the art of poetical
expression since the days of the old vernacular
'makaris.' For Scottish vernacular they were still
the most suitable, if not the only possible, forms; but
the constant practice of them tended, if anything, to
dull the ear for the appreciation of the fuller and
richer and more subtle and varied melody of modern
English verse, or at least introduced a disturbing

influence which embarrassed endeavours after accomplishment in its special achievements.

Moreover—it may be deemed rank blasphemy and worse, indeed has already been so deemed, to put the question, but—was Burns specially gifted to excel in the higher and purer forms of poetic expression? Carlyle—who, however, was not partial to poetry for its own sake—plainly doubted if he was, at least he expresses the opinion that the bulk of Burns's verse was merely rhymed eloquence rather than poetry, and under the shadow of this great Scottish rock one feels a certain security against the charge of presumption for daring to have at least an open mind on the question. But at any rate, circumstanced as he was—toiling as an Ayrshire peasant-farmer, or perambulating as a Dumfries exciseman—it would have been the miracle of miracles, which it isn't, had he become the equal of Shakespeare, or Milton, or Shelley, or Tennyson, as a master of English verse.

We are thus left a good deal in the dark as to the actual possibilities of Burns as a poet—the only outstanding fact being that they were never fully manifested. Clearly he had much in common with Byron, both being endowed with the same exuberant vitality, the vitality which made Byron the great European personality of his time, while Burns, if less passionate and petulant in his sincerity, had the same uncompromising regard for reality which underlay all Byron's masquerading, and while naturally the finer artist of the two, had a much

Burns and Byron.

greater capacity for taking pains.   But then the stage
of Byron was primarily Europe, and the stage of
Burns was primarily only Mauchline and Dumfries;
and the great things that were possible for Burns on
the wider stage are, after all, a matter of conjecture.

Some of these great things were perhaps possible
for him even so late as Edinburgh—possible had he
not been fatally entangled with the past,   His partial re-
both by circumstances and habit; but   nouncement of
knowing himself—his needs, obligations,   a poetic career.
and capacities—better than we can know them, he
decided to renounce the rose-coloured future that
may for a brief period have pictured itself on the
horizon of his hopes, and to return to his old, narrow,
rustic environment as peasant-farmer.   Had he even
succeeded as farmer, some of the poetic ambitions
which he still continued to cherish might have been
realised; but misfortunes and monotonous toil and
care, and latterly the exacting duties of exciseman,
more and more lowered 'the pitch of his resolution.'
He made various desultory efforts to perfect his
poetic training by wider reading in French as well as
English, and momentarily entertained strong hopes
of inaugurating a new form of Scottish drama; but
even so much as an attempt to realise them was
meanwhile an impossibility, and the very burden of
his poetic impossibility drove him more and more to
seek his chief consolation in conviviality.   Thus, apart
from songs—his addiction to which in his later years
meant that if he had not been 'made weak by time

and fate,' he had meanwhile ceased either to 'seek' or
'find' a fuller poetic utterance—his career as poet, which
had really extended over little more than a short two
years, virtually terminated with the publication of the
first Edinburgh Edition in 1787, the only great poem
of the last nine years of his life being *Tam o' Shanter*,
which he was led to undertake very much by accident.

The vernacular staves of Burns were mainly those
which had already been revived by his predecessors
of the eighteenth century — Sempill,
Hamilton of Gilbertfield, Ramsay, and
Fergusson.   The 'Standard *Habbie*'
stave of Sempill (see *ante*, p. 391) suggested the Elegies
on *Poor Mailie*, *Tam Samson*, and *Captain Matthew
Henderson*, but besides adopting it, after Hamilton
of Gilbertfield, Ramsay, and Fergusson, for his episto-
lary verse, he made it the vehicle for such a variety
of sentiments and emotions that it virtually became
part and parcel of his poetic individuality.

Its only rival is the *Christis Kirk* stave, which in
The Dream and *The Ordination* he wrote in the
exact Ramsay form, building the octave
—derived from the original ballad stave
—on two rhymes, as in the original
Christis Kirk and in Ramsay's cantos, and, like
Ramsay, contracting the old bobwheel of two lines
into a refrain of one line ending with 'day.'   In
The Holy Fair and *Halloween* and *The Mauchline
Wedding*,[1] he, however, adopted the modification of

[1] Published for the first time in *The Centenary Burns*, ii. 42-44.

the ballad octave used by Fergusson in *Leith Races*
and *The Hallow Fair*, building it usually on four
and occasionally on three rhymes. In *Halloween*
he also, of course, substituted 'night' for 'day' in
the refrain. Further, occasionally, and especially in
Halloween, he introduced internal rhymes, thus
virtually transforming either the first quatrain of the
stave into the six-line stave in *rime couée*, fashioned
on the imperfect iambic tetrameter (see *ante*, p. 164),
or the whole into one of twelve lines :—

> 'Upon that night,
>   When fairies light
> On Cassilis Downans dance ;
>   Or o'er the lays,
>   In splendid blaze,
> On sprightly coursers prance,' etc.

This ballad stave, in its four-rhyme form, he also
employed without the refrain in the *Address to
the Unco Guid* and *Epistle to a Young
Friend*, but modified it throughout by
the use of double rhymes in the second, fourth, sixth,
and eighth lines :—

Ballad Stave.

> 'O ye, wha are sae guid yoursel,
>   Sae pious and sae holy,
> Ye've nought to do but mark and tell
>   Your neebours' fauts and folly.
> Whase life is like a weel-gaun mill,   well-going
>   Supplied wi' store o' water ;
> The heapet happer's ebbing still,   hopper
>   An' still the clap plays clatter.'   clapper

Further, in *Guildford Good* he adopted the modified
form of the ballad stave—which, on account of the
use of internal rhymes throughout, virtually assumes

the *rime couée* form—derived from the old ballad *Killychrankie*, the last word of the double rhyme, 'man,' forming practically a kind of refrain.

The next most characteristic stave of Burns is that of *The Cherry and the Slae*. This piece as well as *The Vision*—usually attributed to Ramsay himself, who, at any rate, made use of the stave in other pieces, as *The Petition to the Whinbush Club* and *The Address to the Town Council*—Burns had read in *The Evergreen,* and he also got to know *The Bankis of Helicon,* which was published in Pinkerton's *Ancient Scotish Poems,* 1786. In *The Epistle to Davie,* and one or two other pieces, the stave is employed in a somewhat mechanical fashion, without any realisation even of the picturesque effects attained by Montgomerie; but this cannot be said of the recitativos in *The Jolly Beggars,* where its capabilities are first fully mad manifest :—

Stave of 'The Cherry and the Slae.'

'First, niest the fire, in auld red rags, *(next)*
 Ane sat, weel brac'd wi' mealy bags,
  And knapsack a' in order ;
 His doxy lay within his arm,
 Wi' usquebae an' blankets warm, *(whisky)*
  She blinket on her sodger. *(leered / flushed with drink)*
 An' aye he gies the tozie drab *(other / sounding)*
  The tither skelpin kiss, *(mouth)*
 While she held up her greedy gab
 Just like an aumous dish : *(alms)*
  Ilk smack still, did crack still, *(each)*
   Like onie cadger's whup ; *(hawker's)*
  Then swaggering and staggering,
   He roar'd this ditty up.'

Other poetic forms of the old 'makaris' used by Burns, under sanction of Ramsay and Fergusson, were the octo-syllabic and heroic couplets, and, like them, he used those forms chiefly for tales or narratives; but those simplest of rhyme-forms had, of course, also survived in English verse. *The octo-syllabic and heroic couplets.*

But a stave which neither Ramsay nor Fergusson had ventured to attempt, and which Burns got from *The Evergreen*, was the French octave. Obtaining it directly from the old 'makaris,' he wrote it with much more punctilious correctness, as regards both rhythm and rhyme, than was his custom, and while using it with discretion for such 'heich and grave subjects' as *The Lament* and *The Address to Edinburgh*, he applied it to a subject that was neither 'heich' nor 'grave' in one of the recitativos of *The Jolly Beggars*, where its ancient gravity is at least admirably burlesqued :— *The French octave.*

> 'Poor Merry-Andrew in the neuk
>   Sat guzzling wi' a tinkler-hizzie ;
> They mind't na wha the chorus teuk,
>   Between themselves they were sae busy.
>   At length, wi' drink an' courting dizzy,
> He stoiter'd up an' made a face ;
>   Then turn'd an' laid a smack on Grizzie,
> Syne tun'd his pipes wi' grave grimace.'

corner
tinker-wench
cared not

struggled

then

The only other stave in *rime couée*, in addition to Standard *Habbie*,' used by Burns is—in *Epistle to Lord Daer* and *Fintry My Stay*—the six-line stave divided into two equal *'Sir Thopas' staves.*

sections, of which the simplest form is that of Chaucer's *Sir Thopas* (see *ante*, p. 162), which is built on two rhymes. There are no examples in *The Evergreen*, though it is common in later English verse, and Burns, who employs the form built on three rhymes, probably got it from Ramsay's *Address of Thanks*.

Examples of various other staves of the old 'makaris' Burns, of course, saw in *The Evergreen*,

Limited range of Burns's accomplishment in the old vernacular staves, and in English verse.

but he made no attempt to utilise them, and, it may be, wisely, so far at least as his popularity with the masses was concerned, for the eighteenth-century Scot had already become thoroughly enamoured of the two main verse-forms which Burns elected to make his own. Nor must we forget that *The Evergreen* did not bring home to him the poetic individualities of Henryson, or Dunbar, or Scott, or even Montgomerie, as it is now possible to recognise them.[1] But whatever variety of reasons may account for it, the fact remains that, compared with the old 'makaris,' the range of his accomplishment in the old vernacular metres was extremely limited; nor within his limited range is he the equal of any of those four 'makaris' in faultlessness of art, much of his work, especially as regards rhyme, being lawless and irregular. It is in the very simple stave of 'Standard *Habbie*' (a stave which almost writes

---

[1] Burns never seems to have recognised the strong individuality of Dunbar, which is the more remarkable that he had so much in common with him; but then to him, as to Ramsay, Dunbar was a mere name.

itself), that he is most effective; and when he attempts
the more complex, or more nobly and variedly musical,
forms of English verse, he is merely a blind Samson
'grinding in fetters,' with his 'heaven-gifted strength.'
As a vernacular lyrist he is often altogether magical
and irresistible, but the strain of his enchantment is
simple in the extreme, none of the more exquisite
rhymal and rhythmical effects of English lyrism being
so much as attempted.

We thus reach the inevitable conclusion that
Burns triumphs neither by virtue nor by aid of
supreme technical accomplishment, but
in spite of an almost merely elementary
knowledge of the metrical art. It is the
marvellous success achieved by simple
means that renders him, within his own sphere, the
rare and peerless poetic artist that he is. Take for
example *The Jolly Beggars*. Metrically it is a mere
disordered and incongruous medley of scraps from the
old vernacular 'makaris' and the innominate rhymers
of tradition, and the broadsides and the penny chap-
books. It is resonant of the echoes and refrains and
sentiments of a miscellaneous crowd of preceding
bards, celebrated and obscure. It is wholly lacking
not merely in artistic originality, but almost in individuality of metrical achievement, and never was
a literary victory so renowned gained by methods so
wholly unauthorised by the higher conventions, and
in fact so unpretentious almost to contemptibility.
But the victory is none the less complete and none

His successes
achieved by
simple means.
'The Jolly
Beggars.'

the less intrinsically great. Out of what seems poetic chaos he creates a nobly harmonious poetic unity, and in the realisation of his purpose he is so brilliantly, even radiantly, successful that this blackguard carousal in the squalid Ayrshire dosshouse becomes instinct with a human interest so genuine and alluring that only the very dullest or morosest can resist its spell.

But what, then, is the outstanding quality of this

Exuberant vitality in the form of humorous sympathy. singularly anomalous classic? Is it not its exuberant vitality? the *verve*, the *élan*, the abounding and 'unremitting energy,' which

'pervades,
Adjusts, sustains, and agitates the whole'?

The vitality is as all-pervading as it is ardent, being rooted in his own deep and full humanity, and expressing itself in the only form in which it could, in the circumstances, be adequately effective — the form of humorous sympathy. Had he been merely witty he would have ceased to be in any sense sympathetic: the humanism of the scene would have vanished, or become merely secondary, and we should have been treated to a merely cleverer repetition of the Zolaesque squalidity of Ramsay's *Christis Kirk*. Nor, except in the form chiefly of humour, could he have denoted his sympathy without revolting the finer susceptibilities—without, that is, degrading himself entirely to the level of his company, and thus practically ceasing to be poetical.

It is the abundance and depth of his humorous sympathy which is Burns's most idiomatic characteristic, as it is certainly the secret of his unique hold over the affections of His responsiveness. the great mass of his countrymen, who are necessarily as blind to his inevitable limitations as they are to the higher beauties and refinements of his art. Few poets, even, have ever been so immediately and fully responsive to external impressions. Thus Gilbert says that in his youth 'he was constantly the victim of some fair enslaver,' and that in this condition 'the agitation of his mind and body exceeded anything I know in real life.' This same exceptional responsiveness may be discovered even in his correspondence, so that merely from his letters it would be rash to assert anything very decisive as to his individual opinions on many important matters of life and conduct. He was 'Hail, fellow! well met!' with almost every son or daughter of Adam or Eve who manifested any smallest tincture of genial humanity, from 'that part of mankind commonly known by the ordinary phrase of "blackguards,"' up to professors of Moral Philosophy like Professor Dugald Stewart, or staid and worthy matrons like Mrs. Dunlop. In any company where he found himself, whether that of the revellers in some village tavern, or that of the wits and beauties of elegant Edinburgh *salons*, he was 'the soul of all the rest,' and this by virtue of the subtle responsiveness by which he adapted himself to its atmosphere, and reflected in a glorified form its special mood. To use his own phrase, he was like the 'Æolian harp passive,' and gave forth music as the chords of his nature were moved by the varying influences of the moment.

With this abundance and depth of humorous sympathy, Burns could scarce have been aught else

His eloquence, his poetic glamour, and his art.

than eloquent, and perhaps, as Carlyle opined, he is rather eloquent than strictly poetical; but after all, poetry is only a higher form of eloquence, and it is difficult to define where the one merges in the other. If Burns was in no degree a poet in the almost disembodied sense that Shelley sometimes was, he was at least a sufficiently poetic realist; and if he never attained to a thorough mastery of the more elaborate technique of poetry, he did succeed in enveloping himself and all that concerned him in a glamour which has been poetical enough to bewitch the mass of his fellow-countrymen, and to fascinate a very large proportion of the educated outside world. His art is at least wholly admirable of its kind and within its own range. If lacking in rhythmical variety and subtlety and in the more refined forms of poetic beauty,[1] no poetry was ever more genuinely and inevitably true to nature, or more exactly and delicately expressive of the poet's intention. 'All my poetry,' he told Mrs. Dunlop, 'is the result of easy composition but of

[1] See especially on this subject a note in Mr. Henley's *Essay* in the *Centenary Burns*, vol. iv. p. 275.

laborious correction,' which is simply to say that it combined genuine inspiration, as all true poetry must, with painstaking art; and by virtue of the results of his laborious correction—that is, as he also expresses it, of his 'finishing polish'—Burns ranks with the greater poetic artists.

Burns has been measured and equalled in all sorts of ways with the great English poets; by one critic or another he has been endowed with what the particular critic deemed the most admirable qualities of Chaucer, or Shakespeare, or Milton, or Thomson, or Wordsworth, or Shelley, while some scarce scruple to affirm that he con- centrates in himself the most shining excellences of the whole galaxy.

Cannot properly be measured with English poets. Mainly fashioned by the old Vernacular tradition.

If in such predicamental cir- cumstances one might venture a comparison at all, it would be in the direction of suggesting that he is a sort of rustic Shakespeare; though there are of course whole regions of thought and emotion and poetic accomplishment in Shakespeare that Burns leaves untouched—untouched because they were out- side his purview, and so wholly outside of it that he scarce even dreamed of their existence. But in the case of Burns comparison with Shakespeare or any other English poet is almost wholly futile, for the reason that among modern British poets he is, at his best, entirely *sui generis*. What connection he had with the modern English school was com- paratively superficial. He obtained from it neither

the inspiration nor discipline correspondent to his
finer issues. His true poetic ancestors were the old
Scots 'makaris,' and in a measure—that is, so far
as they were the interpreters of the old 'makaris'—
Ramsay and Fergusson, and the 'glorious old Bards'
of the 'Ancient Fragments,'—glorious old bards,
whose 'very names are buried amongst the wreck
of things that were.'

More especially was Burns beholden to the 'Ancient
Fragments.' As we have seen, before the coming of
Burns, and through the offices of Ramsay
and others, a modern lyric school had
arisen in Scotland of somewhat miscellaneous nationality, but so far as it
got its inspiration from the old vernacular tradition
representing an art which had its beginnings in the
far past, and bore unmistakable impress of the
varied skill of a considerable succession of poetic
artists. Several successors of Ramsay were more
faithful to the old vernacular tradition than Ramsay,
and manifested in isolated songs a much truer inspiration. Burns, on the whole, was also faithful to
the old tradition, and unmistakably faithful to it
in vernacular song. He did write a variety of
Scoto-English song, but it was not the amorphous
variety of Ramsay; and he also wrote—mainly at
the instance of Thomson of the *Scottish Airs*, and
out of the abundance of his own good nature—a
number of songs in English after the inflatedly
sentimental fashion of his time. Even in these

His indebtedness to the 'Ancient Fragments' and the old tradition.

stray gleams of genius may be discerned, and they nearly all display something of his 'finishing polish,' but he probably set little store by the most of them. And whether or not, it is only so far as he has been faithful to the old vernacular tradition—as he has caught its tone, and adopted, while glorifying, its methods — that he has earned for himself a place amongst the greatest of British lyrists. Indeed, it may even be affirmed that he triumphs more especially when the strain of his song is very much the echo of an 'ancient fragment,' an echo which he merely enriches and prolongs; and that if we subtract from his lyrical achievement the songs not so derived, we rob him of a good deal more than half his claim to be regarded as the supreme lyrist of his country.[1]

Burns, then, owes his peculiar place apart among great poets very much to an exceptional conjuncture of circumstances reaching back to the period when the old school of Scots 'makaris' became not merely extinct, but whelmed in temporary oblivion. He thus, in a sort of vicarious sense, represents the nation's poetic past, and he was enabled to do so very much by virtue of his peasanthood. Had he been the fully equipped intellectual workman of which Carlyle dreamed, and which some suppose him

Advantages of his peasanthood. More than a peasant poet, and exceptionally the national poet of Scotland.

[1] For Burns's relation to the 'Ancient Fragments,' see *The Centenary Burns*, vol. iii., and Mr. Henley's *Essay*, vol. iv. pp. 321-334.

to have been, his poetic achievement would doubtless have been even greater than it is, but it could not have been so peculiarly Scottish.   A great vernacular poet on the old lines—as a fully equipped intellectual work-man, and representing the blossom of the nation's con-temporary culture—was no longer possible in Scotland. He could represent little more than its past, and could sway it mainly by reviving its old forgotten memories; and so to represent and sway it, it was necessary that he should, in a measure, be detached from artificial modern influences, so that nothing should intervene between him and the ancient tradition.   Thus his peasant upbringing and surroundings were almost an essential part of Burns's training; and yet he is much more than a mere peasant poet, and this because he had, by virtue of the enforced silence of the Scottish muse for several generations, fallen heir to the old poetic tradition—a far higher poetic tradition than could derive from even an ideal peasantry, and a much nobler poetic heritage than any other peasantry ever possessed.   Though he came in the guise of a peasant, and as the glorifier of common things, he came therefore as the Scottish national poet in a sense unexampled and unique.   By virtue of his instant and universal responsiveness he was able almost to identify his personality with the person-ality of the nation, and especially to create a form of lyric which, while exactly expressive of his own rare individualism, is diversified and enriched, and, so to say, nationalised, by the combined experience, emotion, and lyric art of many generations of poetic predecessors.[1]

The fame and personality of Burns naturally tend to dwarf those of contemporaries and successors; and while they helped to prolong the old vernacular tradition, with him that tradition necessarily reached the climax of its influence. By the very nature of the case a repetition of his achievements as vernacular poet was impossible, and we need not here follow this decaying tradition beyond the more prominent of his immediate successors.

In Burns the revived vernacular poetry attains its climax.

Among his contemporaries was John Mayne, who, though born in the same year as Burns, won quicker fame as a verse writer. As early as 1775 he had published a portion of his lively and picturesque, if not quite poetic, *Siller Gun*, and to his *Halloween*, which first appeared in *Ruddiman's Magazine* in 1780, Burns was indebted for something more than the mere name of his poem on the same subject; while Mayne's *Logan Braes*—founded on an older ditty—is an admirably simple expression of true love sentiment, and indeed superior to Burns's semi-political and wholly artificial *Logan Water*.

John Mayne (1759-1836).

A collaborateur with Burns on Johnson's *Museum*

[1] Much of the sentiment and emotion expressed in Burns's lyrics lies outside his own personal experience. Nor could any single poetic individuality have invented such varied forms of lyrical expression. Their charm derives largely from their relation to generations long anterior to ours; and it is Burns's chief praise to have embalmed this ancient charm in a modern lyric.

was James Tytler, a gentleman of good education
James Tytler and varied accomplishments, and who,
(1747-1805). besides editing and in great part writing
the second edition of the *Encyclopædia Britannica*,
engaged in numerous literary ventures, but so un-
successfully that Burns describes him as dangling
'about Edinburgh as a common printer, with leaky
shoes, a sky-lighted hat, and knee-buckles, as unlike
George-by-the-Grace-of-God, as Solomon the Son of
David.' Tytler, like Burns, had clearly access to the
Herd MS., and mainly devoted himself to the adaptation of old songs. Burns specially praises his *Bonnie
Brucket Lassie* for its original ending.

Though older in years than Burns, Hector MacNeill
achieved his earliest success as a vernacular poet with
Hector *Scotland's Skaith*, 1795, and *The Woes o'*
MacNeill *War*, 1796, intended to illustrate the
(1746-1818). insidious evils of the drinking customs of
the time, which they do with some pathetic power ;
but he is now mainly remembered for his lyrics, which
are at least perfectly sincere and natural, while their
somewhat commonplace emotion is frequently expressed with much humorous vivacity. Among the
best are *Mary of Castlecary, My Boy Tammie*,[1] *I Lo'ed
ne'er a Laddie but Ane*, and *Come under my Plaidie.*

---

[1] *My Boy Tammie* preserves echoes of an older song, as the
following fragment from the Herd MS. witnesses :—

> ' I am to court a wife,
>   And I 'll love her a' my life ;
>   But she is a young thing,
>   And new come frae her mamie,' etc.

Several ladies, contemporaries of Burns, have been more or less successful in vernacular lyrics. Susanna Blamire (1747-1794), the 'Muse of Cumberland,' achieved in *The Nabob* a not unsuccessful variation on *Auld Lang Syne*, and in *And ye shall Walk in Silk Attire*, and *What Ails this Heart of Mine?* found graceful expression for somewhat hackneyed sentimentalism. A vein of true poetry is, however, revealed in Elizabeth Hamilton's (1758-1816) *My Ain Fireside*, which must ever remain the classic utterance on the subject; while Mrs. Grant of Carron (1745-1814) in *Roy's Wife* expresses with humorous felicity the light-hearted regrets of a jilted swain, and Mrs. Grant of Laggan (1755-1838), in *O Where, tell me Where*, is, after the Jacobite manner, though not on a Jacobite theme, sentimentally martial.

Lady contemporaries of Burns.

The reputation of Joanna Baillie is assured apart from her Scottish lyrics, some of which are very much in the English manner; but *Saw Ye Johnie Comin'?* is so radically vernacular that Burns—who affirmed that 'for genuine humour in the verses and lively originality in the air' it was 'unparalleled'—took it 'to be very old.' Among other successes of Miss Baillie is a version of *Woo'd and Married and A'*; and she was also not unsuccessful in humorous narrative, as in *Tam o' the Lin* and *It was on a Morning*.

Joanna Baillie (1762-1851).

But the laureate among Scottish poetesses is Carolina Oliphant, Baroness Nairne, on whom some have almost ventured to affirm the lyric mantle of Burns has descended, though she is, of course, wholly lack-

Carolina, Baroness Nairne (1766-1845).

ing in Burns's depth and passion. With her and her house Jacobitism was almost a religion, and her Jacobite lyrics are on the whole her best. Nowhere is the pure romantic devotion of Jacobitism more finely and ardently expressed than in *Will ye no Come back again?* or in *He's Ower the Hills that I Lo'e Weel*; and in *The Hundred Pipers* its martial sentiment is conveyed with an admirable blending of humour, pathos, and defiance. Her love lyrics, as *Huntingtower* and *The Lass o' Gowrie*, are in sentiment a little hackneyed and superficial; but pathos, homely yet tender and strong, is manifested in *The Rowan Tree*, *The Auld Hoose*, *The Land o' the Leal*, and even in *Caller Herrin'*; and the old-world episode of *The Laird o' Cockpen* is narrated with delightfully graceful *naïveté* and humour.

The only rival of the Baroness Nairne among the lyric successors of Burns is James Hogg, the Ettrick

James Hogg (1770-1835).

Shepherd, whose *Jacobite Relics* generally owe most of their finest poetic qualities to Hogg himself, and whose own original Jacobite lyrics, as *Rise, rise, Cam' ye by Athol*, and *Maclean's Welcome*, have at least a fine rhythmical ease and swing, and display a truly martial *verve*. But Hogg has little or no connection with the wider Scottish vernacular tradition. The bulk of his verse, and even of his lyrics, is in English, and some only

partially in English might as well have been wholly
so. He did cherish the ambition to become Burns's
successor; and perhaps he possessed a more purely
poetic temperament, but he was essentially a Border
reiver. His tradition was that of the old Border
minstrels; and his poetry represents especially the
old Border spirit of adventure and romance, blended
with a superstitious mysticism closely allied to that
of the Highland Celt. His worst and damning fault
is his diffuseness, and, notwithstanding many fine
poetic touches, his long-drawn sweetness tends to
pall upon the reader. Still, the mystic charm of
Kilmeny is undeniable, and not less the weird
diablerie of *The Witch of Fife*; while in *The Mountain Bard* the wild, adventurous, lawless, superstitious
reiver lives again. Hogg's facility in versification
was apt to prove a snare to him, but he is always
graceful and musical; and nowhere has the charm of
the peaceful aspects of Nature—the charm peculiar
to the haughs and valleys of southern Scotland—
been more delightfully and delicately set forth than in
such lyrics as *The Skylark* and *The Kye comes Hame*.

Hogg as a poet was very much a rustic Sir Walter
Scott,[1] who was, besides, the founder of a vernacular
school of his own, that of the vernacular   Sir Walter
novel—a subject too vast for our present   Scott (1771-1832).
consideration,—but who very seldom in his poetry
drops into the vernacular and makes very chary

---

[1] For Scott's relation to the Traditional Ballad, see *ante,*
pp. 362-3, 366-8.

use of it even in his lyrics, the only almost pure examples being the spirited *Jock o' Hazeldean*—founded
on an old ballad,—the witty character sketch of *Donald
Caird*, and his new version of *Carle, now the King's
Come*; but *March, march, Ettrick and Teviotdale*—
derived from the old *General Leslie's March*—contains
at least one vernacular exclamation; and the vernacular slightly tinges his re-reading of D'Urfey's *Bonnie
Dundee*. Moreover, if neither the wild *Macgregor's
Gathering*, nor the stirring *Pibroch of Donald Dhu*,
nor the wailing *Mackrimmon's Lament* can be strictly
termed Scots, neither are they quite English.

A contemporary of Hogg and Scott was Sir
Alexander Boswell, the eldest son of Johnson's

Sir Alexander
Boswell
(1775-1822).

'Bozzie.' An Ayrshire squire, he was an
ardent admirer of Robert Burns, and
the originator of the movement for the
erection of a monument to him at the Tam o'
Shanter bridge over the Doon. He wrote occasional
verse, both in English and the vernacular, for recital
at county banquets and other functions. His humorous lyrics, *Jenny's Bawbee* and *Jenny Dang the
Weaver*, are, however, much above the 'occasional'
level; and his *East Neuk o' Fife* is a drolly realistic
sketch of a matrimonial duel, which, on the wife's
part, begins in this promising fashion :—

old fellow
yawning
varlets
ugly, stupid

'Auld gudeman, ye're a drucken carle, drucken carle ;
A' the lang day ye're winkin', drinkin', gapin', gauntin' ;
O' sottish loons, ye're the pink and pearl, pink and pearl,
Ill-far'd, doited ne'er-do-weel.'

But the battle in the end remains drawn.

Robert Tannahill (1774-1810), chief of the many Paisley poets, is little more than sweetly sentimental; but his *Jessie, the Flower o' Dunblane,* *The Braes of Balquhither, The Bonnie* *Wood o' Craigie-Lea,* and many more, all in the same gently amorous, or gently musing vein, have found a permanent place in Scottish song-books.

Robert Tannahill (1774-1810).

Among somewhat later bards, Allan Cunningham has the most assured position. He had a knowledge of old traditional song similar to that of Burns, and though Cromek's *Remains of* *Nithsdale and Galloway Song,* 1810, was largely his concoction, it embodies some 'remains' of older lyrics. *Bonie Lady Ann* is a clever amalgam of the homely, the ornamental, and the romantic; and *Hame, Hame, Hame* is prettily, if merely artificially, Jacobite; and if *John Grumlie* echoes only very faintly the admirable humour of *The Wyfe of Auchtirmwchty, My Nanie, O* is quite equal to Burns's song of that title, and *The Wee, Wee German Lairdie* is at least boisterously funny; but his best song, *A Wet Sheet,* is wholly English.

Allan Cunningham (1784-1842).

With Allan Cunningham our record of Scottish Vernacular Literature must close. Various later song-writers have achieved isolated successes, as William Laidlaw (1780-1845) in *Lucy's Flittin'*; William Thom (1789-1848) in *The Mitherless Bairn*; William Watt (1793-1859) in *The Tinkler's Waddin'*, and the

The deepening twilight and the night.

comic masterpiece *Kate Dalrymple*; Robert Gilfillan (1798-1850) in *O, Why Left I my Hame?* and William Nicholson (d. 1849) in the eerie ballad of *Aiken Drum*. The antecedence of Burns may also be discerned in the work of all the more characteristically Scottish writers from Sir Walter Scott to R. L. Stevenson and Mr. J. M. Barrie; but as regards vernacular poetry, his death was really the setting of the sun; the twilight deepened very quickly; and such twinkling lights as from time to time appear only serve to disclose the darkness of the all-encompassing night.

INDEX

459

WORKS ON MEDIÆVAL LITERATURE

PUBLISHED BY

DAVID NUTT IN THE STRAND.

MALORY'S MORTE D'ARTHUR, edited by Dr. H. OSKAR
SOMMER.

The ' Morte D'Arthur ' is not only a monument, unsurpassed in many
ways, of English prose, it must always remain the best means of access to
the Arthurian romance, Britain's greatest contribution to the world of
imaginative fiction. Dr. Sommer's edition is the only one which provides
an accurate text and a full apparatus for the critical and literary study of
Malory's compilation.

Sommer's ' Morte D'Arthur ' is complete in 3 vols. 4to (Vol. I. Text;
Vol. II. Glossary, Index of Names and Places, etc. ; Vol. III. Study on
the Sources), costing together £2, 10s. nett, in stiff wrappers, or £3 in
Roxburghe binding.

**To place this great monument of English Literature within reach
of all Students, Vol. I. (the Text), a magnificent 4to of 800 pages,
may be had in plain wrapper at 7s. 6d. cash (8s. 3d. post free).**

THE LEGENDS OF THE WAGNER DRAMA ('The Niebe-
lungen,' 'Parsifal,' 'Lohengrin,' 'Tristan,' 'Tannhäuser'), by
JESSIE L. WESTON. 6s.

The only work in English in which the relations of Wagner to his
legendary sources are fully set forth and discussed in a scholarly spirit.
Full summaries of the original legends are given, as well as of Wagner's
dramas.

THE PARZIVAL OF WOLFRAM VON ESCHENBACH,
translated for the first time into English verse by JESSIE L. WESTON.
2 vols. 10s. 6d. nett.

Wolfram's ' Parzival,' upon which Wagner founded his music-drama of
' Parsifal,' is the most interesting and individual work of mediæval literature prior to the ' Divina Commedia.' In addition to her rendering Miss
Weston discusses the poet's sources, and artistic and ethical treatment of
his theme, so as to bring out the full importance and significance of this
great work.

Works on Mediæval Literature—*Continued.*

THE LIVES OF THE TROUBADOURS, translated from the original Provençal of the thirteenth century, with specimens of the poems of the Troubadours, translated into English for the first time, and accompanied with Introduction and Notes by IDA FARNELL. 6*s.* nett.

The old Provençal 'Lives of the Troubadours' are the main source alike for the history of Provençal literature, and of information concerning the feeling and manners of the days of chivalry and the courts of love.

THE SONG OF ROLAND. A summary, with verse translation of the leading passages, by FREDERIC SPENCER and ARTHUR S. WAY. 1*s.*

The best introduction in English to the study of the greatest of the *Chansons de Geste,* the masterpiece of French mediæval epic.

THE MIRROR OF PERFECTION. Being an English version of the 'Speculum Perfectionis' of Brother Leo, the favourite disciple of St. Francis of Assisi, by SEBASTIAN EVANS. 16mo, elegantly printed at the Ballantyne Press, and bound in specially designed cloth cover. 2*s.*

SIR GAWAIN AND THE GREEN KNIGHT. Abridged in Prose from the Middle-English Alliterative Poem by JESSIE L. WESTON. With designed title-page and chapter headings by M. M. CRAWFORD. Minuscule 4to, printed on handmade paper, cloth, gilt top. 2*s.* nett.

The poem here translated for the first time, faithfully, save for a certain amount of abridgment, has long been recognised as the masterpiece of English pre-Chaucerian narrative poetry, and as one of the finest Arthurian romances extant. In this story Sir Gawain, the pattern of knighthood and courtesy, has to undergo trials alike of his courage and of his loyalty in the face of amorous temptation, and comes out of both unscathed. The interesting relations between the English romance and some of the oldest Irish heroic legends are briefly glanced at in the Editor's Introduction.

'Sir Gawain and the Green Knight' is the first of a series of Arthurian romances unrepresented in Malory's 'Morte D'Arthur,' and derived for the most part from an earlier and more mythic stage of the legend than that found in Malory. A list of the series will be sent on application.